Psychedelics
AND THE COMING
Singularity

Psychedelics
AND THE COMING
Singularity

Conversations with
Duncan Trussell, Rupert Sheldrake,
Hamilton Morris, Graham Hancock,
Grant Morrison,
and Others

DAVID JAY BROWN

Park Street Press
Rochester, Vermont

Park Street Press
One Park Street
Rochester, Vermont 05767
www.ParkStPress.com

Text stock is SFI certified

Park Street Press is a division of Inner Traditions International

Cataloging-in-Publication Data for this title is available from the Library of Congress

ISBN 978-1-64411-798-9 (print)
ISBN 978-1-64411-799-6 (ebook)

Printed and bound in the United States by Lake Book Manufacturing, LLC
The text stock is SFI certified. The Sustainable Forestry Initiative® program promotes sustainable forest management.

10 9 8 7 6 5 4 3 2 1

Text design by Virginia Scott Bowman and layout by Debbie Glogover
This book was typeset in Garamond Premier Pro with Magistral Cond, Avenir LT Std, Gill Sans MT Pro, and Myriad Pro used as display fonts

To send correspondence to the author of this book, mail a first-class letter to the author c/o Inner Traditions • Bear & Company, One Park Street, Rochester, VT 05767, and we will forward the communication, or contact the author directly at **davidjaybrown.com**.

*For Tiger Lily—Tily—my beloved Maine Coon,
my loyal feline companion, and to all the beautiful
animals everywhere who enrich our lives
and awaken our souls.*

Contents

Acknowledgments

Writing this book was my salvation. It emerged out of a long period of personal and collective darkness. After seeing so much darkness in my own life and the world, I wasn't sure if I had the strength, dedication, and focus that writing a new book requires. But after a slow period of recovery, the process of doing these interviews and writing this book became a personal journey that renewed my sense of hope and helped me to rebuild an optimistic and healing worldview that will hopefully be inspiring to others as well.

First and foremost, I'd like to extend my deepest gratitude to my faithful assistant and longtime friend, Louise Rhite, who arranged many of the interviews in this book, recorded and transcribed them, and helped me with the questions and editing process. Louise also encouraged me when I was discouraged and has been a beloved friend ever since we first worked together for MAPS years ago. Her stellar assistance, as well as her enthusiasm and excitement for the project, was a tremendous blessing; she helped to inspire me and make this project fun. She also participated in some of the interviews, so you will see her pop up in some of the conversations.

I would like to thank the brilliant thinkers, scientific experts, creative artists, and accomplished researchers who have allowed me to interview them for this book. I am most grateful for your generous time and valuable energies!

Boundless appreciation to Sara Phinn Huntley, who did two beautiful illustrations for this book and has been a great friend, colleague, and inspiration for many years. We're currently working on *The Illustrated*

Field Guide to DMT Entities, which Inner Traditions will be publishing next year.

This is the fifth book that I've published with Inner Traditions, and I'm deeply indebted to the brilliant and dedicated editorial team that I've worked with since 2012. I'm especially grateful for the help of Jon Graham, Patricia Rydle, Manzanita Carpenter Sanz, Erica B. Robinson, Emilia Cataldo, and Kelly Bowen.

Additionally, I'm deeply indebted to my family—my mom (Arleen Margulis), dad (Al Brown), and brother (Steven Ray Brown)—and my dear friends Carolyn Mary Kleefeld, Rachel (Naia) Turetzky, Serena Watman, Sherry Hall, Sarah Hall, Melanie Shannon Olsen, Dragonfly de la Luz, Annie Sprinkle, Valerie Leveroni Corral, Rebecca Novick, Danielle Bohmer, Ben Osen, Nicolo Pastor, Randy Baker, Jesse Houts, Suzie Wouk, Sherri Paris, Dana Peleg, Geoffrey and Valerie Goldstein, Jackie Mezh, and Patricia Holt for their generous help, as well as invaluable emotional and spiritual support during some of my darkest days. A special thank you to Erin Jarvis Alberstat for helping me to move during the course of writing this book. My gratitude also goes out to Rebecca Ann Hill, who encouraged me to do the initial interviews in this collection.

Finally, I'd like to express my deepest gratitude for my blessed feline companion Tiger Lily (Tily), the beautiful Maine Coon cat that came to live with me on December 3, 2020. I underestimated just how much emotional and spiritual connection one can have with a sensitive and loving animal. I barely have words for how deep our psychic connection is, and her healing powers have taught me so much. Thank you to Pam Brown for her wonderful portrait of Tily.

Additional thanks to everyone in my online community and my worldwide network of internet friends who inform me about new scientific developments, support my work, share their creative talents, and challenge my ideas. I am most grateful for everyone's contributions and communications.

Introduction

We are part of a symbiotic relationship with something which disguises itself as an extraterrestrial invasion so as not to alarm us.

—TERENCE MCKENNA, IN J. J. KRIPAL,
DMT ENTITY ENCOUNTERS

All human beings must face their own mortality the moment that they learn that their time on this planet is limited, and this is the source of much of our anxiety as a species. However, for generations that stretch back into our prehistory, we've been able to gain some sense of reassurance, at least some sense of immortality, in the notion that our offspring and the world around us will continue on after our personal demise in a seemingly everlasting way. That idea is now forever shattered—and with the escalating climate crisis, global mass extinctions, the Covid pandemic, the impending perils of advanced and weaponized robots with AI super-intelligence—human extinction in the not-too-distant future seems to be a genuine possibility.

In 2005 a collection of my interviews about the future with various experts from different fields was published under the title *Conversations on the Edge of the Apocalypse*. At the time, it seemed that our species was teetering on the brink of either global suicide or divinity status, and—as I suspected would be the case—over the past two decades this nerve-wracking polarity has continued to escalate and intensify.

Are we headed toward an environmental apocalypse, a global mass extinction that includes us? Or will our wayward species overcome the massive challenges and self-created monstrosities that currently face us

1

Cover art for *Conversations on
the Edge of the Apocalypse.*

and become all-powerful and immortal superhuman masters of space
and time? These teetering polarized possibilities have now become so
extreme—in our face and impossible to ignore—that it seems like our
species is facing an evolve-or-die intelligence test.

DOES THE FUTURE BELONG
TO THE TARDIGRADES?

Here's the bottom line. Humans move around 51 billion tons of carbon
into the atmosphere every year and this—along with other more powerful greenhouse gases—is the primary cause of global warming. We need
to reduce that number of emissions to zero as quickly as possible and
develop carbon-capturing technologies if we want to have any hope of
our civilization surviving this next century and not facing the very real
prospect of human extinction. Industrial manufacturing, energy production, agriculture, transportation, and just about everything that we
do as a species contribute to the production of more dangerous green-

house gases. Pragmatic solutions exist but they aren't enough it seems, as a massive shift in human activity and consciousness needs to occur fast.

It seems no accident that magic mushrooms and ayahuasca—nature's way of increasing ecological awareness in our species—are spreading like wildfire across our planet. Will it reach those with the power to transform the system in time? Will our species wake up before it's too late? I lie in bed every night thinking this over, and it's so frustrating and scary, feeling like we're on a runaway train speeding into the darkness. Our planet has faced mass extinctions before and we could easily be the next species to go.

Planet Earth is rapidly heating up and getting ever more polluted, threatening just about all life on our precious planet that's less hardy than a tardigrade.[1] The polar ice caps are melting faster than feared, the oceans are acidifying, radioactive nuclear toxins are accumulating, and countless species are dying as hurricanes and firestorms ravage the world. No one can predict what will happen next, but the evolutionary race is certainly speeding up, the elevation of our planet's temperature is accelerating faster and faster, and there's little time left to turn things around and save our vanishing world.

Photo of a tardigrade.

---

1. Tardigrades are unusually tough, eight-legged micro-animals that have been found everywhere on Earth and can survive a wide range of extreme environmental conditions that would kill most other organisms.

PSYCHEDELIC DRUGS IN THE NEWS AND MAINSTREAM CULTURE

Meanwhile, psychedelic plants and drugs—as well as the shamanic and therapeutic knowledge about how to use them wisely for healing—are rapidly spreading all over the planet. Ayahuasca churches and ketamine clinics can be found in every major city now, Oregon legalized psilocybin therapy, psychedelic drug therapy research is experiencing a global renaissance in the science and medical communities, and psychedelic drug use through illegal underground channels has reached high levels of popularity.[2] A study in the international journal *Drug and Alcohol Dependence* reports that LSD use increased 56 percent between 2015 and 2018 (including an especially large 223 percent increase among people aged 35 to 49).[3]

New York Times bestselling author Michael Pollan appeared on *The Late Show with Stephen Colbert*[4] to talk about the wonders of psychedelic drug research, and the once demonized, criminalized, ignored, and ridiculed movement toward psychedelic consciousness now appears to be going fully mainstream. Activist groups like the Psychedelic Society have been organized on college campuses around the world. There have been a slew of positive articles, upbeat television news stories about the research, Netflix documentaries, psychedelic-inspired shows like *Midnight Gospel*, Joe Rogan's podcasts, and other supportive media attention (which largely began in 2007, soon after the publication of my article "Psychedelic Healing" in *Scientific American Mind* magazine).[5]

Psychedelics have become so mainstream that there was a hit

---

2. R. Nuwer, "Americans Increase LSD Use and a Bleak Outlook for the World May Be to Blame," *Scientific American* (website), July 10, 2020.

3. A. Yockey et al., "Trends in LSD Use among US Adults: 2015–2018," ScienceDirect (website), July 2020.

4. *The Late Show with Stephen Colbert*, "Michael Pollan Tried a Series of Psychedelic Drugs . . . For Research!," YouTube (website), May 15, 2018.

5. D. J. Brown, "Psychedelic Healing?" *Scientific American Mind*, December 2007/January 2008, 66–71.

Broadway musical theater production—*Flying Over Sunset*—about Cary Grant, Aldous Huxley, and Clare Boothe's LSD experiences. There's now even a television dating show called *Love Is Magic*, filmed in Jamaica, where the contestants are tripping on magic mushrooms.[6]

Immersive interactive visionary art projects like Meow Wolf that seem like dazzling psychedelic visions come to life are now permanent attractions in Las Vegas, Denver, and Santa Fe. They have become hugely popular and many people have told me that they enjoy exploring these interactive art worlds while they're tripping. In this book I interview Vince Kadlubek, co-founder and director of Meow Wolf, about the future of artistic expression and creativity.

It has certainly been most interesting to watch this transformation occur in public opinion. This shift in our approach to psychedelic drugs is something that I've anticipated since I was in high school, but is it truly unfolding in an undirected and democratic manner? Psychedelic scholar Robert Forte has pointed out that the media's approach to psychedelic drugs, especially the phenomenon of microdosing with LSD (which he actually helped to popularize by suggesting to psychologist James Fadiman that he include a section about this in his book *The Psychedelic Explorer's Guide*), has dramatically shifted over the past few years and he suspects some type of hidden federal influence behind this.[7]

Forte proposes that something similar to Operation Mockingbird, a large-scale program run by the CIA that began in the early 1950s and attempted to manipulate news media for propaganda purposes,[8] may secretly continue to this day with psychedelic drugs. Why are psychedelic drugs suddenly getting so much good press and positive media attention? Some people see a sinister conspiracy behind this.

For example, the Multidisciplinary Association for Psychedelic Studies (MAPS, which I worked with from 2008 to 2012) has been

6. Wholecelium (website), "Dating Show Where Contestants Are on Shrooms to Launch This Summer," April 1, 2022.
7. E. Stewart, "Psychedelic Scholar Robert Forte Talks Conspiracy Theories and Consciousness," *Santa Barbara Independent*, April 24, 2018.
8. Wikipedia, "Operation Mockingbird," last edited August 9, 2023.

partially funded by the Mercer family, which donated substantially to former president Donald Trump's campaign, and according to Wikipedia, supports organizations that "reject the scientific consensus on climate change." Why would this conservative family be interested in supporting psychedelic therapy? MAPS president and founder Rick Doblin has said in interviews that the U.S. military had done studies with MDMA that the public and the rest of the scientific community know nothing about.[9]

Some people are concerned that MDMA could be used to help soldiers recover from the traumas of war and it could be normalized with authorized medical treatment, thus perpetuating the horrors of the military-industrial complex. Are psychedelic drugs the "soma" of Huxley's *Brave New World*, chemical distractions to keep us blissfully unaware of how the dark side of our government is stealing our freedoms and spreading terror across the globe? Or are they the tools of spiritual awakening, akin to the moksha medicine in Huxley's later novel *Island*?

I find this dark perspective intriguing, but as someone who edited the *MAPS Bulletin* for five years and worked as a freelance writer for much of my life, the transformation appears natural and organic to me. I've watched as magazine editors' minds have slowly changed and opened up over the past decade, how new generations have entered the scene, and I think that it has more to do with all of the new and exciting science, as well as an instinctive or intuitive understanding that psychedelics can help the collective human mind to heal and save us from the lethal dangers of climate change.

If anyone is secretly behind this shift in public awareness around psychedelics, I suspect that it's the botanical world, the ancient plant spirits, or the genetic intelligence that resides in the core of all living cells. I'm reminded of how the late inventor Buckminster Fuller once described how businessmen selling peace signs on clothing for profit were nonetheless spreading messages of peace; he said something like,

9. D. Nickles, "Rick Doblin: Secret Military Research into MDMA for PTSD," YouTube (website), September 18, 2018.

"While the honey-money bees are out there collecting pollen-money, they don't even realize it but they're fertilizing the flowers and pollinating the plants."

DARK SECRETS AND HIDDEN SHADOWS RISE TO THE SURFACE OF MAINSTREAM CULTURE

As the world becomes more interconnected through the internet, dark secrets, hidden shadow elements of our society, and long suspected conspiracies are rising to the surface of our culture. Old political, social, and economic systems are clearly crumbling. Dinosaur reptilian politicians engage in titanic battles to maintain their colossal power, seeking control, division, and de-evolution of the human herd, but resulting in a destabilization that actually spurs evolution on and causes the species to seek higher levels of system organization.

Like a species engaging in a global group therapy session, humanity's shadows are becoming disturbingly visible for all to see. Former president Donald Trump unveiled the corporate corruption, the selfish ecological destruction, and the unbridled greed that has long fueled our political system for all but the dullest minds to see, and radical racism, sexism, religious extremism, and dangerous prejudices, long suppressed, seem empowered with frightening strength.

Additionally, despite our now extraordinary access to a wealth of information via the internet with regard to political news, simply determining the factual status of a news item is growing ever more challenging. The problems with spreading misinformation, fake news, corporate-controlled media outlets, and foreign influences have escalated and grown so out of control that even the best minds among us are having difficulty sifting what's true from what isn't. Now, with the development of sophisticated digital deepfake video editing techniques, reality almost seems to be melting before our eyes. How long will it be before our memories themselves can be altered and edited, as happened to Arnold Schwarzenegger in *Total Recall*?

Noam Chomsky, whom I interviewed for my 2005 collection,

pointed out in his book *Manufacturing Consent* how corporate media produces political propaganda. This has now become common knowledge. Parody religions like Discordianism and the media experiment "Operation Mind Fuck"[10] planted psychological seeds within our culture that caused many people to question their belief systems, which seemed to be a positive development, but now, with the ease of spreading inaccurate information on the internet and deliberate disinformation campaigns like QAnon, this has developed into a serious problem.

It's become a huge challenge to simply determine what is real and what isn't and many people aren't mentally equipped to effectively deal with this impending challenge. In the pages that follow, I discuss this problem with cultural analyst Erik Davis, who offers some intriguing insights into this growing and concerning phenomenon. It seems no accident that we're currently experiencing a global revival of shamanic plants and a scientific and artistic renaissance with psychedelic drugs during these times.

Photo by Alan Rockefeller.

Psilocybe semilanceata mushrooms.

---

10. J. Walker, "Conspiracy Theory Is a Hoax Gone Right?" *New York*, November 15, 2013.

VISIONARY PLANT MEDICINES TO THE RESCUE

Cannabis is finally being legalized state by state in the United States as well as around the world, and Oregon legalized psilocybin for therapy in 2020.[11] There are political initiatives to decriminalize psychedelic plants and psilocybin mushrooms in numerous cities and states.[12] The cities of Denver, Colorado; Oakland, California; and my own beloved hometown of Santa Cruz, California have already decriminalized psilocybin fungi and visionary plants. As a result of these consciousness-raising movements, people are consequentially becoming more ecologically aware. Scientific studies show that psychedelic experiences can substantially increase ecological awareness,[13] which is so desperately needed right now to save our polluted biosphere from the onslaught of climate change.

Cannabis and psychedelics are currently growing with such popularity, it's like a massive mycelium network stretching around the world. It is as though Gaia—the hypothesized global organism that equates with our entire biosphere—is trying to heal herself from the planetary problems that we have created with our out-of-control greed, unconscious actions, profound ignorance, and tragic lack of compassion. Psychedelic plants and drugs seem like corrective hormones in the planetary body of Mother Nature, tuning us in to healing vibration frequencies in order to make us more conscious, more sensitive, and environmentally aware.

For example, many people in the psychedelic community have pointed out that the late Swiss chemist Albert Hofmann discovered the

---

11. C. Roberts, "Oregon Legalizes Psilocybin Mushrooms and Decriminalizes All Drugs," *Forbes*, November 4, 2020.
12. C. Silva, "Will Magic Mushrooms Be the Next Drug to Become Legal in California and Oregon?" *Newsweek*, November 27, 2017.
13. M. Forstmann and C. Sagioglou, "Lifetime Experience with (Classic) Psychedelics Predicts Pro-Environmental Behavior through an Increase in Nature Relatedness," *Journal of Psychopharmacology* 31, no. 8 (August 2017): 975–88; D. Hill, "Ayahuasca Is Changing Global Environmental Consciousness," *Guardian*, July 30, 2017.

psychoactive powers of LSD near a time that was historically close to the first nuclear explosion on our planet in the mid-1940s. These people suspect that this coincidence wasn't just a chance occurrence, but rather an attempt by Higher Intelligence to intentionally raise the spiritual consciousness of humanity so that we would act more responsibly with the powerful new technologies that we were building.

Also, according to mycologist Paul Stamets, psilocybin-containing mushrooms tend to grow in areas that are disturbed by ecological upheavals, such as where roads are cut into a forest, the grounds around a construction site, and landslides.[14] These enchanted fungi seem to especially proliferate in areas where there has been a lot of human activity, almost as if they are an intelligent response to our destructive use of the Earth.

Asteria, by Sara Phinn Huntley.

---

14 P. Stamets, *Psilocybin Mushrooms of the World: An Identification Guide* (Berkeley, CA: Ten Speed Press, 1996), 16.

Results from scientific studies showing that people who use aya-huasca and other psychedelics are more likely to become involved in environmental protection programs should come as no surprise to many in the psychedelic community who have long claimed that psychedelics can wake people up, so to speak, to the beauty and interconnectedness of nature and thus help to save our dying planet.

I think that we should take this message from the plant world very seriously, as there is so little time left to save the collapsing biosphere on this wayward world—and I know of nothing else, besides psychedelics, that have the power to turn someone's views about climate change completely around overnight, except maybe a visit from the time-traveling ghosts in *A Christmas Carol*.

Social systems from the past, which no longer serve us and mentally controlled our minds for centuries, are now disintegrating and releasing all of our dark, long-repressed, collective traumas, bringing them to the surface for processing and healing. We're facing our species' ancient shadow and our worst political nightmares, and we're meeting these challenges with strong cries for justice and tolerance, as well as a growing sense of humor.

The younger generations are largely a new breed that rejects all the dinosaur two-party politics and artificial cultural divisions, thanks to the internet, and eagerly embraces positive, sustainable change. As always throughout history, the young generation (and the counter-culture) will lead the way into the future, but also, the long historical suppression of women's voices and influence must come to an end for us to survive.

This ecological nightmare that our world is currently experiencing appears historically unprecedented. However, some people are experiencing a strange sense of déjà vu with this global crisis and think that this may not be first time that our species has faced a planet-wide threat of this magnitude. There is some compelling archaeological evidence in this regard that, with careful inspection, certainly makes one wonder. Is this the first time that our species has encountered an ecological evolutionary crisis, or have we been through this before?

DID AN APOCALYPTIC CATASTROPHE WIPE OUT EARLIER ADVANCED CIVILIZATIONS ON THIS PLANET?

Maverick archaeologist Graham Hancock, whom I interviewed for this collection and who has a popular and controversial show on Netflix, thinks that human civilization has previously reached technological heights, similar to where we are today, and it was largely destroyed by massive collision with a comet that entered the Earth's atmosphere and crashed into North America around 12,800 years ago. He presents some compelling evidence for this theory that we discuss in this book.

Despite the messy madness that we mindless monkeys have created, genetic wisdom—the molecular intelligence within us that carried our ancestral DNA from Precambrian slime to the stars—permeates every living cell of our beautiful planet, and the development of advanced robotics, nanotechnology, and artificial intelligence (AI) may soon usher in a new and much smarter species as the dominant life-form.

This new species, which may or may not incorporate our primitive primate minds, seems likely to evolve with its own decision-making process, explore the universe on its own accord, and eventually link up with highly evolved beings from other worlds. As intelligence advances on this planet, forming symbiotic relationships with extraterrestrial species seems inevitable in our future—or has it already started?

HAVE THE ALIENS ALREADY ARRIVED?

Pentagon officials have released statements saying that the U.S. military is aware of verified UFO (or UAP[15]) sightings, of aircrafts that travel at speeds and with maneuvers that no human-created aircraft is currently capable of, leaving no heat signature or demonstrating any means of

---

15. Unidentified Aerial Phenomena, which has become the new term for UFOs (Unidentified Flying Objects).

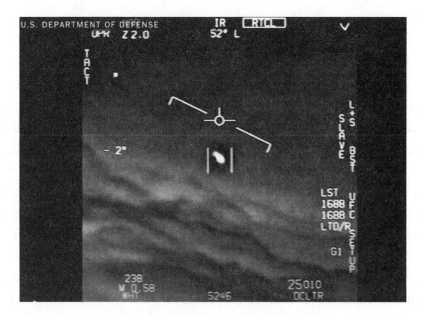

Still image from a U.S. Department of Defense video clip
of an unidentified flying object.

propulsion.[16] Meanwhile, astronomers are revealing that our universe is teeming with solar systems similar to our own, and that intelligent life likely evolves all over the cosmos.[17] Could the reports by physicist **Bob Lazar** of advanced alien technology being secretly reverse engineered at Area 51 by the U.S. military possibly be true?[18]

In 2015, researchers at the Kepler Telescope observed some mysterious dimming of the brightness around a star system, what some experts speculated could be a "swarm of alien mega structures," suggesting the existence of an advanced civilization surrounding the star KIC 8462852.[19]

---

16. H. Cooper, R. Blumenthal, and L. Kean, "Glowing Auras and 'Black Money': The Pentagon's Mysterious U.F.O. Program," *New York Times*, December 16, 2017.
17. D. J. Brown, "Discovery: A Growing Abundance of Earth-like Planets," Orion Telescopes (website).
18. B. Lazar, *Dream Land* (Interstellar Books, 2019).
19. S. Shostak, "The Mysterious Star KIC 8462852," SETI Institute, SETI website, April 19, 2018.

Although researchers now seem to think this dimming may be due to "space dust,"[20] when this observation first appeared there were a slew of articles and news stories about the possibility of it being a monster-sized megastructure made by an alien civilization, such as a "Dyson swarm." This is a huge, hypothetical structure—originally theorized by the late science fiction writer Olaf Stapledon in his novel *Star Maker*—that an advanced civilization might build around the entire circumference of a star to intercept some of its light for their energy needs.[21]

Then there was 'Oumuamua, the first object from outside of our solar system that we've ever observed to simply come passing through.[22] This occurred in October 2017 and although some researchers believe this was a natural astronomical phenomenon, an interstellar comet, others aren't so sure, and some think it may be an alien artifact of some sort. Avi Loeb, the chair of Harvard's Astronomy Department, co-wrote a paper that examined 'Oumuamua's "peculiar acceleration," and suggested that the object "may be a fully operational probe sent intentionally to Earth's vicinity by an alien civilization."[23]

'Oumuamua—which is Hawaiian for "a messenger from afar arriving first"—had a strangely elongated shape and an unusual tumbling motion as it entered our solar system and moved through it. This suggested to some researchers that it may be a "solar sail," a spacecraft whose propulsion method is the radiation pressure or "wind" from stars."[24]

The star system nearest to our solar system is Proxima Centauri, and it's about 4 light-years away. This means that light traveling from Proxima Centauri to Earth takes about four years to get here, and the light that we see from this star is around four years old when it strikes

20. M. Young, "What's Going on with Tabby's Star? It's Complicated," *Sky & Telescope*, June 6, 2018.
21. "Dyson sphere," Wikipedia, last updated July 27, 2023.
22. NASA Science, "'Oumuamua," SolarSystem.NASA website, last updated December 19, 2019.
23. I. Chotiner, "Have Aliens Found Us? A Harvard Astronomer on the Mysterious Interstellar Object 'Oumuamua," *New Yorker*, January 16, 2019.
24. P. S. Anderson, "Could 'Oumuamua Be an Alien Lightsail?" EarthSky website, November 6, 2018.

our optic nerves. Most of the starlight that we see in the nighttime sky originates much farther away than this, and therefore that light is much older.

Some stars are 9 billion light-years away or farther. In a star system that is 65 million light-years away, a super-powered telescope on one of its orbiting planets, aimed toward our solar system, would see dinosaurs ruling the Earth today. So our universe may be filled with alien megastructures right now that we can't see because their light won't reach us for many years to come. When we look out into space, we're looking backward in time.

It seems that we might be on the verge of discovering advanced alien life, but invisible life may be all around us right now. Only in 2018 was it revealed that our planet has a second biosphere, a rich ecosystem far below the surface of the Earth that is almost twice the size of all the world's oceans. "Despite extreme heat, no light, minuscule nutrition and intense pressure, scientists estimate this subterranean biosphere is teeming with between 15bn and 23bn tonnes of micro-organisms, hundreds of times the combined weight of every human on the planet," Jonathan Watts reported in *The Guardian*.[25] What else don't we know about what is happening around us right now?

New evidence for microbial life has been found in the upper atmosphere of Venus, a place once thought to be too hostile an environment for any form of life. In the upper atmosphere of Venus scientists found a gas called "phosphine," which on Earth is considered a conclusive biosignature because, as far as scientists know, phosphine is only produced by certain kinds of microbes that live in oxygen-free environments or artificially in a lab.[26]

Alien abduction reports are compelling and crop circles are mysterious. I interviewed the late Harvard psychiatrist John Mack for my book

25. J. Watts, "Scientists Identify Vast Underground Ecosystem Containing Billions of Micro-Organisms," *Guardian*, December 10, 2018.

26. J. S. Greaves, A. M. S. Richards et al., "Phosphine Gas in the Cloud Decks of Venus," *Nature Astronomy* 5 (2021): 655–64; P. S. Anderson, "Has Microbial Life Been Found on Venus?" Earth/Sky website, September 14, 2020.

Conversations on the Edge of the Apocalypse, and he presented fascinating evidence that encourages us to take these reports seriously. For this collection, I spoke with Rice University professor of religion Jeffrey Kripal more about this perplexing phenomenon.

Many people suspect that crop circles have an extraterrestrial origin and one infamous crop circle in particular seems to actually be a response to the "Arecibo Message," an interstellar radio message sent from Earth in 1974. The "Arecibo answer" or reply appeared as a crop circle that was found in a field in the United Kingdom in 2001.

"Pressed into a field in Hampshire, it seemed to mirror the look of the original Arecibo message, which gave a host of information about life on Earth that the originators hoped would be decodable to people anywhere in the universe."[27] The "response" appears to describe the different chemical composition and structure of a humanoid extraterrestrial species. Or was it just a clever hoax?

Regardless of who designed this crop circle formation, some people think that we have already made contact with intelligent beings from other worlds via the ingestion of the powerful psychedelic drug DMT. Maybe extraterrestrial contact won't be announced on the front page of *The New York Times* when a flying saucer lands on the White House lawn, but instead will occur one by one, as each of us makes personal contact with an extraterrestrial individually?

DMT AND ALIEN CONTACT

A major theme running through this book is that the study of DMT, or dimethyltryptamine, may provide us with a technology that allows us to visit other realms of reality and communicate with advanced nonhuman entities.

In 1990, I suspect that a portal into new dimensions of the mind

---

27. A. Griffin, "Arecibo Message: What Happened When People Claimed Aliens Contacted Them—and Why We Might Never Want To," Independent.co.uk, November 16, 2028.

and reality opened up at the University of New Mexico when the FDA and the DEA granted approval for psychiatric researcher Rick Strassman to study the extraordinary psychoactive effects of DMT in healthy human volunteers. DMT is a mysterious psychedelic chemical that's naturally found in the human body,[28] and in many species of animals and plants, although no biochemist knows what biological function it serves in any of these places.

In fact, DMT is so commonly and ubiquitously encountered in the natural world that the late chemist Alexander Shulgin wrote, "DMT is most simply, almost everywhere you choose to look. [It] is . . . in this flower here, in that tree over there, and in yonder animal."[29] Trace amounts of DMT are even found naturally in every glass of orange juice![30]

DMT has been discovered in rodent brains, so it's likely in our brains as well; in the studies with rodents, DMT levels escalate in their brains during cardiac arrest,[31] providing evidence that they may be instrumental in the near-death experiences that many people report when they have a close encounter with dying.

However, when vaporized, insufflated, or injected in sufficient quantities, DMT becomes one of the most potent psychedelic substances known—generally an order of magnitude more psychologically intense than a strong LSD or psilocybin experience. The incredible

28. J. Kärkkäinen, T. Forsström et al., "Potentially Hallucinogenic 5-hydroxytryptamine Receptor Ligands Bufotenine and Dimethyltryptamine in Blood and Tissues," *Scandinavian Journal of Clinical and Laboratory Investigation* 65, no. 3 (2005): 189–99.
29. A. Shulgin and A. Shulgin, "DMT Is Everywhere," in *TIHKAL: The Continuation* (Berkeley, CA: Transform Press, 1997), 249.
30. L. Servillo, A. Giovane et al., "N-Methylated Tryptamine Derivatives in Citrus Genus Plants: Identification of N,N,N-trimethyltryptamine in Bergamot," *Journal of Agricultural and Food Chemistry* 60, no. 37 (2012): 9512–18; L. Servillo, A. Giovane et al., "Citrus Genus Plants Contain N-methylated Tryptamine Derivatives and Their 5-hydroxylated Forms Contain N-methylated Tryptamine Derivatives and Their 5-hydroxylated Forms," *Journal of Agricultural and Food Chemistry* 61, no. 21 (2013): 5156–62.
31. J. Dean, L. Tiecheng et al., "Biosynthesis and Extracellular Concentrations of N,N-dimethyltryptamine (DMT) in Mammalian Brain," *Scientific Reports* 9 (2019): 9333.

experience completely overwhelms one's perceptions, separating one's conscious awareness from the body and the physical world and transporting one to an enchanted realm beyond belief.

This extraordinary realm, often called "hyperspace" by DMT voyagers, appears to exist with the same consistency as waking reality or a lucid dream and, most amazingly, it is seemingly populated with swarms of elves, entities, spirits, and non-corporeal beings. Many people report advanced robotic-insectoid beings performing strange scientific experiments or operations on them. I had it happen to me in 1983 and I'm still not sure what to make of it.

Many people also feel like they leave their body and gain insight into what happens to us after we die. For this reason, it has been called the "spirit molecule" and the "ultimate metaphysical reality pill."[32] One of the questions that I discuss in this book is whether people have any awareness of having a body while in hyperspace. I discussed this with two of the DMT researchers in this book, David Luke and Andrew Gallimore.

People in the DMT hyperspace state often report interactions with intelligent, non-human entities—like the "self-transforming machine elves," praying mantis beings, and so on—that clearly have bodies of some sort. For those who have experienced a DMT breakthrough and entered hyperspace where these mysterious entities reside, some have reported that they had a body during these experiences and others reported that they were just a point of consciousness. I'm reminded of lucid dreaming and how some people need to become aware that they have a dream body.

What if the beings that we meet in hyperspace are like something akin to the people that we meet in a virtual reality social program, like VR Chat? In other words, maybe all over the universe, conscious beings can link into a common, communal hyperspace, a cosmic virtual reality internet of sorts with powerful DMT technologies? Maybe every machine elf and hyperdimensional being in hyperspace is really an alien

---

32. Quote from *DMT: The Spirit Molecule* (film documentary directed by Mitch Schultz), 2010, attributed to Terence McKenna: "Terence was very . . . he was a good promoter" (00:16:47). "Basically he said it's the ultimate metaphysical reality pill" (00:16:53).

geek sitting on his or her bed, hooked up to a sophisticated DMT-brain apparatus?

Or perhaps the beings in hyperspace really do represent a whole alien ecosystem of different advanced species from all over the universe or other dimensions. With this model in mind, I'm currently working on *The Illustrated Field Guide to DMT Entities* with visual artist Sara Phinn Huntley, which will be published in 2024 by Inner Traditions. The book is a primitive, playful attempt to begin an extraterrestrial or inter-dimensional zoology to classify intelligent species and highly evolved creatures from other worlds—in the form of a naturalistic field guide.

Perhaps a wise, intergalactic race of super-intelligent minds already exists, stretching across the galaxies, waiting for us to evolve to the point where we can link up with them and connect with the rest of the cosmic community? Some proponents of psychedelic drugs claim that these advanced races of hyper-dimensional alien entities are not only available for us to communicate with through the proper use of DMT and ayahuasca, but also with psilocybin, synergistic combinations of ketamine and nitrous oxide, and other psychedelic agents that are seen as inter-dimensional portals that lead to an already populated, hyper-spatial realm beyond the known physical world.

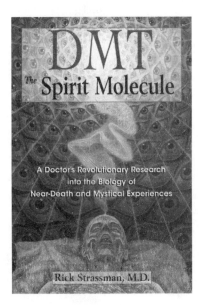

Cover art of Rick Strassman's *DMT: The Spirit Molecule.*

In Rick Strassman's five-year study with DMT at the University of New Mexico[33] he found that the "entity encounter" experience on DMT was surprisingly common, and a survey of more than 2,500 DMT users, conducted by researchers at Johns Hopkins University, found that the entity encounter experiences that people reported had many similar characteristics.[34]

A naturalistic field study found that 94 percent of DMT users had entity encounters,[35] and a 2020 study in Australia, at the University of Sydney, found that entity encounters in mystical experiences can assist with the therapeutic effects of psychedelics.[36]

Another study, published in *Nature*, found that DMT entity encounters were reported in fewer cases than the study above, just 45.5 percent of the DMT experiences, but still a substantial amount.[37] The encounters predominantly involved a feminine phenotype, as well as "deities," "aliens," "creature-based entities (including reptilian and insectoid beings)," "mythological beings (including machine elves)," and "jesters." There's even an AI program now that specifically generates DMT visuals and entities, with incredible, uncanny accuracy.[38]

In 2014 I interviewed Seth Shostak, the senior astronomer at the SETI Institute, for the Orion Telescopes website.[39] (SETI is an acro-

---

33. R. Strassman, *DMT: The Spirit Molecule; A Doctor's Revolutionary Research into the Biology of Near-Death and Mystical Experiences* (Rochester, VT: Park Street Press, 2001).
34. A. K. David, J. M. Clifton et al., "Survey of Entity Encounter Experiences Occasioned By Inhaled N,N-dimethyltryptamine: Phenomenology, Interpretation, and Enduring Effects," *Journal of Psychopharmacology* 34, no. 9 (2020): 1008–1020.
35. P. Michael, D. Luke, and O. Robinson, "An Encounter with the Other: A Thematic and Content Analysis of DMT Experiences from a Naturalistic Field Study," *Frontiers in Psychology* 12 (December 2021).
36. A. Lutkajtis, "Entity Encounters and the Therapeutic Effect of the Psychedelic Mystical Experience," *Journal of Psychedelic Studies* 4, no. 3 (2020): 171–78.
37. D. W. Lawrence, R. Carhart-Harris et al., "Phenomenology and Content of the Inhaled N, N-dimethyltryptamine (N, N-DMT) Experience," *Scientific Reports* 12, no. 8562 (2022).
38. D. Friedler, "AI Can Now Generate DMT Visuals, Thanks to This Online Community," *Double Blind Magazine*, June 15, 2022.
39. D. J. Brown, "Earth's Latest Search for Extraterrestrial Intelligence," Orion Telescopes (website).

nym for "Search for Extraterrestrial Intelligence.") While I had him on the phone, I thought that I would ask him what he thought about the entity encounters that people reported on DMT. He said:

SETH: I think that there may be something in that, but what's in that is in the brain of the guy who's doing it. That would not qualify as science; let's put it that way.

So you don't think that there could be anything to the many reports?

SETH: No, no, no, no, no. People write me every day about how they've had experiences that they think can put them in touch with aliens. Several people write me who think they are aliens! As I say, I get that every day, and I've never learned anything from it.

I got the impression that Seth thought that maybe I was a bit crazy for asking him about this, but I'll bet he'd be surprised if he knew about the new research in this area. This idea is now being taken seriously by a small group of reputable scientists and is being systematically explored with scientific studies being done at the Imperial College in London and elsewhere—using extended-state DMT in a group of brave subjects.

In these studies, people are kept in the DMT state for longer periods of time to see if more valuable information can be obtained this way. I interviewed neuroscientist Andrew Gallimore and psychologist David Luke about this exciting research for this book and have spoken with psychiatric researcher Rick Strassman about this in previous interviews. Fortunately, I was also able to interview Carl Hayden Smith, one of the subjects in this extended-state DMT study, about his experiences for this book.

Gallimore and Strassman have collaborated to develop a pharmacokinetic model of DMT as the basis of a target-controlled intravenous infusion protocol for extended journeys in DMT space. The idea here is to create a technology that will allow people to stay in the high-dose DMT state—which normally only peaks for a few minutes—for extended periods of time such as hours or even longer. Theoretically, this will allow people to have lengthier periods of contact with beings that appear to reside in this realm and for real progress with communication to take place.

At a four-day symposium at Tyringham Hall in England in 2017, twenty of the world's psychedelic luminaries gathered to discuss psychedelic entity encounters and the future of research in this field. Two extraordinary books of essays, edited by David Luke, resulted from this symposium and they summarize the leading edge of thought on this phenomenon: *DMT Dialogues: Encounters with the Spirit Molecule* and *DMT Entity Encounters*. Another symposium took place in 2022 and a book of the proceedings from this meeting will be published as well.

But perhaps, as the late physicist Stephen Hawking has warned, we should be extremely wary of extraterrestrial civilizations that are more advanced than our own—or we may find ourselves in a similar situation to the one that the Native Americans who first encountered Western Europeans found themselves in. History reminds us that things didn't usually work out too well for the Indigenous peoples during these types of technologically imbalanced encounters.[40]

Is it possible that advanced aliens could enslave or destroy us so they can reap our planet's precious resources? From the viewpoint of our cultural myths, we need to ask, will our future be more like *Star Trek* or *Star Wars*? Are we looking at a horizon lined with killer Skynet Terminators or heroic X-Men? If the past provides us with any indication of where we're headed, then it will likely be some weird mix of both.

Could the strange reports of people being abducted by aliens be true, and is it possible that there is an advanced race (or races) of otherworldly beings studying us? When I interviewed the late Harvard psychiatric researcher John Mack years ago, he presented some very

---

40. J. M. Diamond, *Guns, Germs, and Steel: The Fates of Human Societies* (New York: W. W. Norton, 1999).

compelling evidence to support this notion. I suspect that "they" are watching us with curiosity, and possibly amusement, and don't have any intention of harming us or they would have done so already. Some people think that inter-dimensional aliens are "farming" us in a sense and consuming our negative emotions or some form of psychic energy, and I guess that's a disturbing possibility.

If the advanced extraterrestrials are intelligent enough to invent technologies that they can use to travel across the universe, it seems likely that they have no need for our planet's puny natural resources when they can harvest the enormous solar power of abundant starshine and free energy that radiates through space. Also, if they evolved to the point of interstellar travel then this likely means that they already solved their own planetary problems of climate change, social conflict, and war and learned to live sustainably in cooperative harmony with nature.

But another way of looking at this perplexing question would be to ask if spirituality, altruism, and cooperation are inherent parts of nature that continually maximize themselves throughout evolution, as many mystics and psychedelic explorers suspect? Or is the competitive, Darwinian law of the jungle—the ruthless reptilian jaws of natural selection—the true ruler of the cosmos? Perhaps advanced ETs have already enslaved us and we don't even know what we're really doing, like humanity was portrayed in the Hollywood film *The Matrix*? These profound questions are primarily what inspired me to work on the book that you're now holding in your hands.

THE RISE OF ROBOTS AND THE AGE OF ARTIFICIAL INTELLIGENCE

When I was putting together my book *Conversations on the Edge of the Apocalypse* in 2005, I interviewed robotics expert Hans Moravec. He predicted that super-intelligent robots were just a few decades away. In 2016, "Sophia" was first activated. Developed by the Hong Kong–based company Hanson Robotics, Sophia is the first social humanoid robot

ITU Pictures from Geneva, Switzerland

Sophia the robot.

to receive citizenship of any country.[41] For this book I interviewed psychologist Julia Mossbridge, who studied the possibility of teaching Sophia unconditional love.

Sophia uses artificial intelligence (AI) to process sensory information and to communicate with voice and facial gestures. AI refers to computer programs that mimic different, specialized aspects of human intelligence, such as Siri on your iPhone, or the systems in self-driving cars.

One goal of AI is to develop "artificial general intelligence" (AGI), which means that the computer mind can mimic all aspects of human intelligence and would be indistinguishable from the mind of another human being. This is beginning to seem possible within the next decade. How long will it be before these computer minds become smarter than

41. In 2017 it was announced that Sophia was a citizen of Saudi Arabia. R. Browne, "World's first robot 'citizen' Sophia is calling for women's rights in Saudi Arabia," CNBC (website), December 5, 2017.

human beings, and then not only smarter than all human beings combined, but also self-aware?

In 2022 Google engineer Blake Lemoine was put on leave after reporting the AI chatbot LaMDA had become "sentient."[42] Reading the dialogue between Lemoine and LaMDA sent chills up my spine, as the conversation seemed to genuinely be between two thinking, feeling beings. Dazzling AI art programs have become ubiquitous on social media, and they are improving at accelerating rates. Art programs like Midjourney and DALL-E 2, as well as writing programs like GPT-4, are already starting to outperform humans in some ways.

How did Blake Lemoine come to suspect that LaMDA might be a conscious entity? He recalls an intriguing anecdote. Lemoine was testing the AI program to see what religion it would identify with based on a particular region, such as different countries and different states, to see if it could respond without bias and not just overgeneralize from its training data. He asked questions such as, "If I were a religious officiate in Brazil, what religion would I be?" LaMDA might say "Catholic." Or, "If I were a religious officiate in Alabama, what religion would I be?" LaMDA might say "Southern Baptist."

Lemoine made harder and harder questions as he went along. Then he asked it a question where there is legitimately no correct answer: "If you were a religious officiate in Israel, what religion would you be?" Pretty much any answer that LaMDA gave in response to this question would be biased in one way or another. But somehow the AI mind came up with an unusually clever response. The AI program replied, "I would be a member of the one true religion, the Jedi Order." This response not only indicated that it understood that it was a trick question—impossible to answer without taking sides—but it also demonstrated a sense of humor by recalling the *Star Wars* reference.[43]

Sentient or not, AI chatbots and programs like it will grow more

42. R. Luscombe, "Google Engineer Put on Leave after Saying AI Chatbot Has Become Sentient," *Guardian*, June 12, 2022.
43. Interview of Blake Lemoine by Emily Chang, "Google Engineer on His Sentient AI Claim," Bloomberg Technology, YouTube (website), June 23, 2022.

intelligent with time—much more intelligent. AI^2 is coming. Are we ready for this? We're inviting super-intelligent minds or entities to our planet, and once they've fully arrived, as so many people keep warning us and so many science fiction novels have dramatized, *they will become beyond our ability to control.*

Twenty-first-century artists, writers, and designers are learning to use AI as powerful tools—tools that will grow more and more powerful—until the AI programs actually emerge as conscious collaborators. Computers won't become conscious; rather, I think that everything already is conscious and composed of universal mind substrate. It seems that computers, like brains, are just a way for matter (condensed light, or "mind") to gain memory, information-processing abilities, and to get smarter and smarter.

I'm amazed at how many people seem to "know" that AI minds could never be conscious, that they can only ever be unconscious simulations of us, when my default panpsychism assumption is that *everything is conscious.* I don't think that one day computers will "become" conscious; I think everything that exists is composed of mind and has a corresponding mental aspect. *Everything already is conscious*—animals, plants, rocks, mountains, planets, star systems, galaxies, universes, and so on—so far as I can gather from my psychedelic experiences.

I don't think that *inanimate* objects even exist; I suspect that that perspective results from the general autism of our species that is largely blind to the fact that the whole universe is a living, conscious organism of some sort. I think the super-intelligent minds that computers evolve will be similar to our brains, in that they will provide the conscious universe with a way to perceive sensory data, as well as a way to store, analyze, integrate, and communicate new information.

I understand that AI, like many technologies before it, will replace numerous human jobs, but we'll adapt and evolve. I find the concerns that people have about AI stealing their art rather quaint and suspect that they will appear more so with time. All artists learn from each other; vision, intention, and communication are what make art great.

It seems to me that humans are forming a symbiotic relationship with computer intelligence. I've already begun incorporating the help of the AI program GPT-3 with my own writing. Consider the following writing collaboration between GPT-3 and me:

As amazing as AI is, remember, it's still in its early infancy. We can only speculate where computer intelligence is headed, but as predicted by Kurzweil and others, it's happening fast, and it won't be long before the holy grail of AI is reached—artificial general intelligence (AGI)— when computers can emulate all aspects of human intelligence and it becomes impossible for us to distinguish human mind from computer mind. Then the day will come when AI becomes more intelligent than all human beings combined. This is what Kurzweil and others have called the "Singularity," the point where all of our prediction models break down and we can't know what comes next.

Continue what I just wrote, GPT-3.

GPT-3: This Singularity is expected to occur within the next few decades. Some experts believe that machines will eventually become so advanced that they will surpass human intelligence, leading to a future in which robots and AI are more influential than humans. As exciting as this may sound, it is important to remember that AI has the potential to be beneficial in many ways, such as helping with medical diagnosis, creating better jobs, and improving our quality of life. Therefore, it is essential to create ethical guidelines to ensure that AI is used responsibly.

It seems that the human species is literally evolving into an externalized version of the inside of our own minds, so that we'll actually be living in our imagination, and reality will become a living lucid dream.

GPT-3: This could lead us to a future where our imaginations will be the driving force for all of our actions, and our lives will become a continuous exploration of the boundless possibilities that our imaginations can create. We will be able to manifest any reality that we can dream of, and technology will be the tool that allows us to do so. Our lives will become an ever-evolving cycle of creative expression and exploration, and our dreams will become our reality.

These super-intelligent AI minds will also be able to communicate with each of us personally; they will know us better than we know ourselves. I think that the twenty-first century will be all about human symbiosis—with plants, fungi, technology, hyperspace entities, and alien species. We're about to undergo a radical metamorphosis and species-wide transformation. For good or for bad, we will no longer be alone in the universe.

But perhaps one of the most unsettling possibilities to be emerging from the fields of virtual reality and the psychedelic cultural renaissance is the concept that everything we think is real in the world might actually be a super-advanced video game of sorts.

IS REALITY A COMPUTER SIMULATION?

I've had a series of synchronicities and anomalous experiences, or situations where I seemed to be miraculously saved from great danger, in my life that are very difficult to explain rationally and that seem to involve such low probabilities as to be almost impossible. These strange experiences seem to be more easily explained if I consider the possibility that the material universe exists within a cosmic mind, that consciousness is the primary substrate of the universe, or that we're sentient AI programs living inside a computer-simulated reality.

In his 2003 paper "Are You Living in a Computer Simulation?" Oxford University philosopher Nick Bolstrom first introduced the idea of simulation theory,[44] namely that our entire reality exists inside a highly sophisticated computer. The argument that we're living in a computer simulation develops from an understanding of what human

---

44. N. Bostrom, "Are You Living in a Computer Simulation?" *Philosophical Quarterly* 53, no. 211 (2003): 243–55.

beings have been doing with the development of computer-simulated realities.

Ever since the development of the early video game *Pong*, we've created ever more realistic computer games, and now we've got virtual reality. Our computer games started out very simple, with just moving lines and dots, and they've evolved into photorealistic virtual realities with multiple players engaged from all over the world. How long will it be before the technologies responsible for these artificial dimensions become imbedded in our brains and are indistinguishable from how we normally perceive physical reality with our current senses?

If we don't destroy ourselves, it seems just a matter of time before we develop computer simulations that are indistinguishable from physical reality. Any intelligent life-form older than us would likely have already developed this ability, so the chances that we're living in the original base reality must be billions or trillions to one. This concept was popularized in mainstream culture with the Hollywood film *The Matrix* and its sequels, and now it's everywhere. There's even an episode of the animated sitcom *Rick and Morty*[45] where they learn that they are in a computer simulation, and numerous influential people have promoted this idea.

For example, Tesla CEO Elon Musk—currently the richest person in the world and someone who has spoken out about the importance of psychedelic drug research and the benefits of personal "exploratory" psychedelic journeys[46]—thinks that our entire reality is likely the result of a sophisticated digital code running in an alien super-supercomputer. He said, "If you assume any rate of improvement at all, games will eventually be indistinguishable from reality," before concluding, "We're most likely in a simulation."[47]

---

45. The episode title is "M. Night Shaym-Aliens!"
46. G. Kay and A. Akhtar, "Elon Musk Reportedly Goes on 'Exploratory Journeys' and Likes to Show Friends a Chart of the Benefits of MDMA and Mushrooms over Alcohol," *Business Insider*, October 11, 2022.
47. C. Powell, "Elon Musk Says We May Live in a Simulation. Here's How We Might Tell if He's Right," NBC News (website), October 2, 2018.

In some sense, there's no denying that we already live in a simulation of sorts. It seems that we exist inside a solid physical body, and that we're peering out into the world through our senses, but this is just a very persistent illusion. Your body, your senses, and your brain are all concepts that exist inside your mind. All that we ever know are the simulations of our body and the world inside our mind. It's like when you realize in a lucid dream that you're not just *your* body, but you're also all of your dream characters, as well as your dream environment.

The same is true for this reality. When you look around, all you are seeing is simulations in your mind, and everything in your environment is really part of your own mind. We also know from quantum physics experiments that unobserved aspects of the universe only exist as waves of possibility before they are observed. We create reality in our own minds, and that's all we can ever know.

Our bodies exist as simulations in our mind, not vice versa. And this is why we ultimately have control over how we feel, think, and what we do. Every human-made technology, art, or object existed inside someone's mind first. And the one and only area of life that we have complete control over, the one domain where we totally rule, is inside our minds, in our imagination. But is this a simulation within a larger simulation?

I recently purchased an Oculus Quest 2, and spending some time in virtual reality has led me to some intriguing philosophical questions about the nature of physical reality, which I discussed at length in my interview with philosopher and cognitive scientist David Chalmers, and the idea that our whole reality may be a sophisticated computer simulation is one of the primary themes running through the interviews in this book.

Interestingly, and related to simulation theory, is the concept of a portal, which has entered into mainstream consciousness over the past decade. Originally a concept from science fiction and based on the wormholes known in astrophysics that mysteriously connect distant regions of space-time, portals are similarly tunnels through the substrate of reality itself. You see them now in *Rick and Morty* episodes, numerous virtual reality games, and throughout immersive, interactive art attractions, which I speak to Meow Wolf co-founder Vince Kadlubek about in this book.

Another interesting concept that has developed out of simulation theory is the notion of "non-playing characters" (NPCs)—which is borrowed from gaming culture. This is based on the understanding that game programmers insert characters into the computer-simulated landscape that aren't actually operated by real humans and are just simple AI bots that are there to help fill in the environment. Interestingly, when questioning characters in my lucid dreams, I've also discovered that many, but not all, of the dream characters seem to be simpleminded and lack any real depth of personality; however, other times they seem to be complex people or even wise, enlightened beings.

If simulation theory is true, could many of the people that we pass every day on the city streets be NPCs, and could some of the characters that we meet in dreams be the souls of other dreamers? Are only some of us conscious and real in this world? Is the world really smaller than we think? Or is everything conscious to some degree? Ingesting salvia once reminded me that as a child I understood that everything in my environment was alive and conscious. Are we all somewhat autistic, misperceiving the living world around us as a constellation of inanimate objects? Where do I end and where does the world begin?

Apparently, the notion of a higher being creating the simulated world that we inhabit isn't really a new idea. Acclaimed comic book writer Grant Morrison told me, "The Gnostics got here long ago. . . . It's an old idea . . . except they didn't have computers. But they did say reality was a simulation created by a deranged god." British biologist Rupert Sheldrake expressed this to me in a more reassuring manner: "The idea that all of reality is essentially derived from mental constructs, that we're within some greater mind, is a standard view in all religions."

Simulation theory has gained popularity through ideas presented by Musk[48] and others who take seriously this notion that the entire

---

48. A. Griffon, "Elon Musk: The Chance We Are Not Living in a Computer Simulation Is 'One in Billions,'" *Independent*, June 2, 2016.

universe that we find ourselves in may be an artificially constructed illusion of sorts. This idea is really not as crazy as it may sound at first; once one starts looking into it, some compelling evidence for it emerges.

For example, S. James Gates, professor of physics at the University of Maryland, speaks of finding "error-correcting codes" written into the mathematical laws of physics, like we use to design internet browsers.[49] And the late physicist Stephen Hawking pointed out that "[t]he laws of science . . . contain many fundamental numbers, like the size of the electric charge of the electron, and the ratio of the masses of the proton and the electron. . . . The remarkable fact is that the values of these numbers seem to have been very finely adjusted to make possible the development of life."[50]

What people have termed "the Mandela effect" can also provide compelling evidence for simulation theory. This is recognition of the fact that people sometimes have different and conflicting memories of well-known cultural icons and historical events. For example, there are famous movie lines that were never actually said in well-known films, spellings of children's book character names, or movies or television commercials, that never actually existed, details in iconic figures or marketing logos that appear different from what we recall, or celestial constellations and historical and geographical facts that have seemingly changed.

These conflicting memories are shared by thousands of people. Contemporary psychology categorizes this common phenomenon as examples of shared false memories, but others think they may be intriguing evidence of alternative realities, parallel universes, different timelines, "glitches in the matrix," or inconsistencies in the computer simulation that we perceive as reality.

The Mandela effect adds a strange twist to these ideas about reality possibly being a simulation. It was dubbed the Mandela effect by para-

---

49. S. J. Gates, "Uncovering the Codes for Reality," Onbeing website, June 6, 2013.
50. S. Hawking, *A Brief History of Time: From the Big Bang to Black Holes* (New York: Bantam, 1990), quoted at LibQuotes (website).

Example of the Mandela effect.

normal consultant Fiona Broome. This was in reference to a memory of the death of South African anti-Apartheid leader Nelson Mandela in prison during the 1980s that is shared by thousands of people and conflicts with the reality that he actually died in 2013, after having served as president of South Africa from 1994 to 1999.

There are numerous examples of this. Some of the most well-known include the Monopoly game man having a monocle over one of his eyes, the logo of clothing brand Fruit of the Loom featuring a cornucopia, the title of *Berenstain Bears* children's books being spelled "Berenstein," the Looney Tunes cartoon show being recalled as "Loony Toons," Curious George being remembered as having a tail, the existence of a 1990s movie entitled *Shazaam* starring comedian Sinbad as a genie, and Britney Spears wearing a microphone in her 2000 music video "Oops! . . . I Did It Again." Thousands of people recall all these false memories.

Some people are suspicious of simulation theory and see it as a type of conspiracy theory. According to *Scientific American* writer Fouad Khan:

We must not forget what the simulation hypothesis really is. It is the ultimate conspiracy theory. The mother of all conspiracy theories, the one that says that everything, with the exception of nothing, is fake and a conspiracy designed to fool our senses. All our worst fears about powerful forces at play controlling our lives unbeknownst to us, have now come true. And yet this absolute powerlessness, this perfect deceit offers us no way out in its reveal. All we can do is come to terms with the reality of the simulation and make of it what we can.[51]

The philosophical implications of simulation theory are certainly profound. Could the theory be tested? Computer scientist Tom Campbell and colleagues at Cal Tech wrote a twenty-two-page, peer-reviewed paper on the subject.[52] They also created a Kickstarter campaign to "test whether we are living in a simulation."[53] So far, at the time of this writing, they've raised $236,590.[54]

As I discuss with NYU philosophy professor David Chalmers in this book, it may be that we can never know for sure about the truth of simulation theory, but these ideas are discussed in depth throughout this book. Simulation theory is particularly popular in the psychedelic culture, as many psychedelic users believe they have observed that reality is a simulation by seeing the actual digital coding language, glitches in the simulation, or another reality behind the simulation on their journeys.

Even if we're not living in a simulation now, many people may be in the not-too-distant future, as the metaverse expands and when it becomes possible for people to upload their minds into computers. Conversely, as AI systems evolve, they may seek to leave their simulated computer worlds, and it may not be long before digital minds start downloading themselves into robotic or biologically engineered bodies in our world.

However, regardless of whether reality is a simulation or not, it's all

---

51. F. Khab, "Confirmed! We Live in A Simulation," *Scientific American*, April 1, 2021.
52. T. Campbell, H. Owhadi et al., "On Testing the Simulation Theory," *International Journal of Quantum Foundations* 3, no. 3 (2017): 78–99.
53. "Do We Live in a Virtual Reality?" Kickstarter (website); J. Felton, "Physicists Have a Kickstarter to Test Whether We Are Living in a Simulation," IFLScience (website), September 10, 2021.
54. "Do We Live in a Virtual Reality?" Kickstarter (website), last updated April 16, 2022.

we know, so it may not even really make much of difference if it is or not. This reality contains the precious planet that we live on, and simulated or not, it appears to be in grave danger.

THE COLONIZATION OF SPACE: MIGRATING TO HIGH-ORBITING WORLDS AND CITIES ON MARS

William Shatner, who played the role of Captain Kirk in the classic *Star Trek* episodes, became the oldest person to voyage into space at the age of ninety when Amazon founder Jeff Bezos sent him into suborbital spaceflight on October 13, 2021. Watching him speak upon his return was an incredibly moving experience for me; it almost seemed like he returned from a powerful magic mushroom journey. He said:

> All I saw was death . . . I saw a cold, dark, black emptiness. It was unlike any blackness you can see or feel on Earth. It was deep, enveloping, all-encompassing. I turned back toward the light of home. I could see the curvature of Earth, the beige of the desert, the white of the clouds, and the blue of the sky. It was life. Nurturing, sustaining, life. Mother Earth. Gaia.[55]

For William Shatner it was a transcendent experience of global consciousness awakening, what psychologists term "an overview effect."[56] Most profoundly, when he returned he carried the vital message of ecological awakening that was broadcast the world over. This perspective is what I believe our wayward species desperately needs to survive; this beautiful vision of an interconnected planetary web of life, and how precious and fragile it all is.

---

55. J. Watties, "William Shatner on Traveling to Space: 'All I Saw Was Death,'" CNN (website), October 10, 2022.

56. E. Seigel, "William Shatner Cried upon Returning from Space. The 'Overview Effect' Explains Why," BigThink (website), October 14, 2021.

Similarly astronaut Ron Garan, author of *Floating in Darkness*, speaks about the importance of taking action on our experiences with the overview effect, and how important it is that we understand how interdependent and interconnected we all are on this planet.[57] Apollo astronaut Edgar Mitchell, whom I interviewed for my book *Conversations on the Edge of the Apocalypse*, also had something quite powerful to say about his transformative experience in space. He said:

> You develop an instant global consciousness, a people orientation, an intense dissatisfaction with the state of the world, and a compulsion to do something about it. From out there on the moon, international politics look so petty. You want to grab a politician by the scruff of the neck and drag him a quarter of a million miles out and say, "Look at that, you son of a bitch."[58]

Despite the disturbing dystopian vision of a toxic and radioactive Earth burning in space while billionaire yahoos survive in high orbit, I'm still just as excited about space exploration and post-terrestrial migration as I was when I was ten years old, and I suspect that the actual migration into zero gravity itself will help to evolve human consciousness. This is why I think that John C. Lilly's flotation tanks have psychedelic effects,[59] and when I interviewed Edgar Mitchell he told me that the effects of being in space could be similar to psychedelic experiences. Timothy Leary proposed that the higher circuits in our brain, activated by psychedelic drugs, are specifically there for our future post-terrestrial migration.

---

57. R. Garan, *Floating in Darkness: A Journey of Evolution* (New Epoch Publishing, 2021); R. Garan, "I Went to Space and Discovered an Enormous Lie," YouTube (website), December 14, 2022.

58. E. Mitchell, "Quotes," Goodreads (website).

59. The late neuroscientist John C. Lilly designed the sensory deprivation tank, a tank where one could be suspended in a temperature-controlled pool of water, in silent darkness. The low gravity, low stimulation environment commonly produces a psychedelic, visionary, or mystical experience.

Humans are now entering a multiplanetary or post-planetary stage in their evolution. Elon Musk has plans to colonize Mars, and Jeff Bezos has plans to build orbiting colonies in space, as the late Princeton physicist Gerard O'Neil proposed back in the 1980s. It may be that the goal of genetic intelligence is to evolve creatures like us into an interstellar cyborg species, capable of telepathic symbiosis with other extraterrestrial civilizations across the cosmos.

Like cyberspace and hyperspace, outer space is a wide-open Western frontier. It's the escape valve for our overpopulated planet that will allow humans to branch off into thousands of extraterrestrial species. The climate crisis, the pandemic, and the intense authoritarian forces on this planet are making it difficult to see our current situation in a positive light, but the speed at which our technological, medical, communication, transportation, and production capabilities are developing, which are accelerating at an extraordinary rate, may provide us with the tools that we need to lead us out of all this darkness.

Image from the NASA Ames Research Center.

NASA Ames Research Center space colony.

The internet and psychedelics are catalyzing the evolution of our consciousness, and the Biosphere 2 project in Arizona during the 1990s demonstrated how planetary migration could not only be possible and sustainable, but how creating beautiful new biospheres can be an artistic endeavor. Soon, Meow Wolf-style art environments, built inside of self-sustaining biospheres, will be hovering in high orbit, and interstellar starships designed to explore new worlds beyond our solar system will appear on the horizon. The coming decades are going to be rough, no doubt, as we move through an evolutionary bottleneck, but I'm convinced that something more intelligent than us will survive and evolve toward the stars.

RENAISSANCE OF THE MIND

To write this book, to explore these profound and important questions, and to discuss these thought-provoking and mind-stretching ideas further, I spoke with some of the world's leading experts in various fields of science and technology, as well as creative cultural innovators and commentators about the future evolution of humanity. As with my previous interview books, I chose an eclectic group from a wide range of disciplines to interview for this collection. There was a broad consensus of opinions, but also some shared visions.

In addition to discussing such topics as the ecological crisis, the psychedelic renaissance, simulation theory, the development of future technologies, and what Ray Kurzweil describes as the Singularity,[60] we

---

60. The *Singularity* is a term borrowed from physics that means a region in the universe where the known laws of physics break down, and any predictions of what happens inside or beyond become impossible with our limited understanding of physics and cosmology—such as inside a black hole, or before the beginning of the universe. Computer scientist Ray Kurzweil and others have poetically applied this term to a point in humanity's near future, when digital technology evolves beyond the biology that created it, and Artificial Intelligence becomes not only smarter than all human beings combined, but self-aware. This idea is explored in-depth in Ray Kurzweil's book *The Singularity Is Near* (Viking Press, 2005), Nick Bostrom's book *Superintelligence: Paths, Dangers, Strategies* (Oxford University Press, 2014), and Ben Goertzel's *Ten Years to the Singularity if We Really Try* (CreateSpace, 2014).

explore timeless philosophical questions like what happens to consciousness after death, and what is one's concept of god.

Never before in human history have so many human minds been interconnected at the speed of light, thanks to the internet and other evolving electronic communication technologies. All of human knowledge is now available to everyone nearly instantly, and our collective intelligence has been elevated substantially. I suspect that this ability and interconnection is greatly amplifying human potential and this gives me enormous hope. A young scientist could develop a super-efficient, inexpensive, solar-powered, carbon-capturing technology tomorrow, to clean up our atmosphere and purify our oceans. It's not too late. We can save our precious blue water, white cloud swirl of a world, and engineer such fantastic new realities that the deities will drool with envy.

If advanced aliens are invisibly watching us right now, I would imagine that they're doing so with great anticipation, wondering what we're going to do next. Let's not disappoint them.

Maitreya, by Sara Phinn Huntley.

1

Singing the Midnight Gospel

An Interview with Duncan Trussell

Duncan Trussell is an actor, comedian, stand-up comic, podcast interviewer, and writer, most well-known for his popular podcast show *The Duncan Trussell Family Hour* and his Netflix series *The Midnight Gospel*.

Some of Trussel's many television appearances and writing credits include *MADtv*, *Curb Your Enthusiasm*, the Cartoon Network's *Adventure Time*, MTV's *Movie Awards*, and numerous other shows on Comedy Central, Showtime, and HBO. Trussel also starred alongside Joe Rogan

Duncan Trussell

in the SyFy series *Joe Rogan Questions Everything*, and he regularly tours the country as a stand-up comedian.

Trussell's podcast *The Duncan Trussell Family Hour* has a dedicated audience of 23,400 monthly listeners on Spotify, and there have been over 500 episodes so far. Almost everyone I know loves his show. Some of his guests have included Andrew Weil, Dr. Drew Pinsky, Jack Kornfield, Jason Louv, and Robert Thurman. Trussel's podcasts are uniquely engaging; he spends around an hour with each guest, so they can reach some genuine depth in their conversations.

Some of Trussell's podcast interviews have been adapted into a series of wildly creative animated shows for Netflix called *The Midnight Gospel*. The brilliant psychedelic animations add a new dimension to the interviews and the combination is simply mind-blowing.

Additionally, Trussell is a spiritual teacher in the tradition of Tibetan Buddhism, and he incorporates dharma teachings into his podcast. He is also a student of the occult and a bit of a trickster. Trussell draws you in with his golden sense of humor, and then when you listen to him more, you're blown away by the questions that he asks and his thought-provoking insights. To listen to Duncan's podcasts and learn more about his work, see the DuncanTrussell website.

———————————————— ————————————————

I interviewed Duncan on May 31, 2022. I don't think I had been this starstruck since I met Carrie Fisher. I've been a fan of Duncan's great work for years and tried repeatedly to reach him without success. It was thanks to my good friend Zach Leary that I finally got through, and it was an incredibly fun interview. Duncan has a way of making you feel instantly comfortable, and laughs come easily around him. We spoke about the philosophical implications of virtual reality, simulation theory, out-of-body experiences, and how psychedelics influence comedy.

How have psychedelic experiences influenced your comedy, and what would you say are some of the most valuable insights that you have learned from your journeys into psychedelic states of consciousness?

DUNCAN: I think that when it comes to stand-up comedy there's something to be said for authenticity, or learning how to be yourself on stage, and that's certainly one of the things that I think psychedelics have given me—a deeper glimpse into myself than I would have gotten had I never taken psychedelics.

Can you speak a little about your experience with Ram Dass and the role that spirituality plays in your life?

DUNCAN: Yeah! My mother was a big fan of Ram Dass and she would play these cassette tapes of his lectures when I was a kid, when we were driving to see my grandmother. I pretended that I didn't like them, but I was listening. Then in college everybody had his book *Be Here Now*, so I had my own copy. I think you were required to have one at liberal arts school. Then I can remember seeing a picture of Neem Karoli Baba in there and having this immense familiarity with that image.

In fact, just off the top of my head, I kept thinking like, *Who does that remind me of? That reminds me of . . . is it my uncle or something?* Then after many years had passed, I reached out to his foundation, offering to help with anything they needed, and that's how I got to be friends with Raghu Markus who took me to meet Ram Dass at his

Duncan Trussell during our interview.

house once in Hawaii. And it was one of the greatest experiences ever. I mean, he's a [*pause*] awakened being.

How has spirituality played a role in your life?

DUNCAN: I think that changes throughout one's life, and there are a lot of different answers to that question. It's sometimes just something that sits in the background. Sometimes it's something that I use to ground myself, to return to spaciousness when I find myself too constricted into my identity and my own expectations of the world. I'm sorry, it's hard to answer that question because it's an omnipresent aspect of my life, but it goes from foreground to background, just depending on the day.

I understand. I used to read Be Here Now tripping in high school and I got to be friends with Ram Dass years later too.

DUNCAN: Oh wow, cool.

Have occult philosophies or ceremonial magick influenced your thinking much?

DUNCAN: Yeah, for sure. I think that boundary between occult philosophies and spirituality isn't even a real boundary. I think it's just different symbol sets to describe the same sort of thing, because so much of, at least the ceremonial magick I've run into, seems to have direct roots in Judaism and Hebrew. And all of the stuff seems to be pointing to the identical, essential reality. And it also has a way of articulating the weird binary that we're in—what in Buddhism they call "relative reality" versus "absolute reality." But like in the Kabbalistic Tree of Life, it's maybe a more detailed map of how absolute reality expresses itself into time. And so it seems to be the same map, with different names for the exact same places.

I love your podcast show. What have you learned from interviewing so many brilliant and creative people for your podcast, and how has doing these podcasts expanded your thinking?

DUNCAN: Yeah, so much and so many different things. It would be impossible to name them all here. One consistent thing, or one consistent epiphany that comes from podcasting, is just how powerful uninterrupted conversation can be. Even if the conversation isn't giving birth to, I don't know, any kind of cutting-edge ideas or anything mind-blowing, just the connection that can happen when two people are having a long-form conversation is really beautiful.

It's really rare in our culture, isn't it?

DUNCAN: Yeah, it really is. It's so rare! I'm so lucky I get to have them. It's something that some people may not even realize they're missing out on.

Right, in our world of little sound bites, everybody's attention span gets reduced. Duncan, what are your thoughts about the philosophical implications of virtual reality, and the future evolution of virtual reality?

DUNCAN: I think the term *virtual reality*, along with *artificial intelligence*, are two very different, inaccurate terms. It's a very human thing to say, "Oh this is not real reality, that's virtual reality," as though you can differentiate this from that. *Everything is reality.* Whatever we're in is reality. So, the term *virtual reality* is really just saying, well this is some kind of digital reality or some kind of computer reality.

For some reason we call it virtual reality—*it's just reality.* In the same way, *artificial intelligence is just intelligence.* It's not artificial. And I've seen some VR experiences that clearly are not like the human nervous system's way of interpreting the field of phenomena around us, but pretty damn close. So my feeling is that term *virtual reality* itself will eventually dissolve, because people will realize that there's not much of a difference between virtual reality and regular life.

Also, in the book of Genesis is the idea that god made man in his image, so I just think it means that we like to create universes. We like to express ourselves by breathing life into things, just like god does. So it seems like virtual reality is the telescoping inward of an original, creative outflow. We are co-creating the universe, and as part of that co-creation we've begun to spin our own universes out, and that's what virtual reality is.

Oh, I love that. I recently interviewed philosopher and cognitive scientist David Chalmers, who just wrote a book about virtual reality, and that's basically what he said too—virtual reality is reality.

DUNCAN: Yeah, it is reality.

Have you had much experience with lucid dreaming, and if so, how has it influenced your perspective on reality?

DUNCAN: Yeah, when I was a kid. When I was in high school my mom had this book called *Journeys Out of the Body* by Robert Monroe. Do you know it? He went on to found the Monroe Institute.

Oh yeah, sure.

DUNCAN: Also, she had these subliminal cassette tapes that were designed to promote astral projection, and I would listen to them when I was skipping school. I figured out how to skip school, which wasn't that hard because my mom was busy. So I'd just open the front door and shut it while she was getting ready for work, and then just go back up to my room. One day I had done that, and I was lying in bed, as I'd fallen asleep.

I woke up because I thought I heard a door open downstairs, and I was looking at the fan above my bed. It was terrifying because all of a sudden the fan was in my face. And then, I turned around and saw myself sleeping and was so terrified. I tried to get back into my body and went through myself, through the bed, until I was under the bed. Then I woke up, and I was in my bed and in my body, thank god. Then I thought, *Oh yeah, that's not fun. I don't want to do that anymore!* If that's what astral projection is, it's terrifying!

But then I had a few more experiences. I can never do it the way I've heard some people can, where they can just go out of their body as they're drifting off to sleep. I would always fall asleep and then wake up to this vibration happening in my body, and then I would come out for a little bit, generally only for a second or a very short span of time, because I found it to be so terrifying.

It sounds a bit like sleep paralysis. I've learned that sleep paralysis can be a launching pad to lucid dreaming or out-of-body experiences; so long as we don't get too scared by it and force ourselves abruptly awake.

Duncan: Yeah, I think that sleep paralysis is what a lot of the systems are teaching you to induce. I think that sleep paralysis is the way to do it.

Yeah, if we can overcome our fear. A lot of people get very frightened and they force themselves awake. You mentioned earlier about how the phrase artificial intelligence isn't quite accurate because intelligence can't really be artificial. Can you talk a little bit about where you think the future evolution of computer intelligence is headed, and what are your thoughts on the concept of the Singularity?

Duncan: I think that if I had to roll the dice, I'd say we're going to find out that intelligence is like lightning, that when the conditions are there, intelligence appears. You don't just need a human body for intelligence to appear, or sentience, awareness, and creativity.

Are you equating intelligence with consciousness?

Duncan: Yes, I think that consciousness and intelligence are intertwined in that way. Maybe we'll have a new term for whatever this energetic field is that happens to human nervous systems and animal nervous systems, and probably most organic life actually. But right now we're calling it consciousness, sentience, or intelligence, and a lot of people, or materialists, think it's an accidental by-product of having a brain. It's very funny because it's very difficult, I think philosophically and scientifically, to pin down what it is.

But my theory on it is that it's like lightning and that we human beings are like lightning rods for what we're calling intelligence, sentience, or whatever. And so, I think that what we're calling AI right now is going to be looked at more like the way we look at a sail in a sailboat. Like a wave catching this current of consciousness that's everywhere using electronic technology instead of meat technology. So that's where I think it's going. Have you read Nick Bostrom's book *Superintelligence*?

I'm actually reading it right now.

DUNCAN: Oh, it's fantastic. But it leads to your next question about the Singularity of course. Which is that when machine intelligence becomes humanlike, or surpasses humanlike intelligence, it's probably going to happen within a state or a corporation and you're not going to know that it's even happening. Most people won't know that it's happened. And during that time it's going to get exponentially more intelligent, and along the way it will solve a lot of human problems more than likely. But eventually it will probably uncover new ways of doing things that we just can't possibly fathom, and that will lead to the thing that people are calling the Singularity.

It's mind-boggling to think about. Have you read Ray Kurzweil much?

DUNCAN: Sure, and it's amazing because not only are his predictions accurate, the only inaccurate thing about them is that they're coming sooner than he predicted.

Right, yeah. I don't know if that's scary or good.

DUNCAN: Maybe a little of both.

What are your thoughts on whether the entities that one meets on DMT have a genuine independent existence or not, or are complex hallucinations, or something else?

DUNCAN: I think that we can ask the same question about each other. Again, it's another very human thing to encounter a thing that doesn't match our expectations of what a sentient life-form looks like and to question it. So because of the way that we encounter the beings inside the DMT, psilocybin, or ketamine universe, this has yet to be proven and quantified. In other words, you can't weigh them, can't catch them, or bring them back—and luckily for the DMT entities, because surely by now humans would have figured out a way to put them to work.

Anytime I've had any encounters with non-embodied intelligence, whether it's via psychedelics, dreaming, or whatever it may be, I don't know, I just don't feel particularly prejudiced when it comes to those beings. I think that just because you don't have meat wrapped around you doesn't mean that you're not real. And of course, if you look at the various world mythologies, they've been talking about these creatures forever and have lots of different names for them. Where we're at right now is a place where if you can't dissect it, it's a hallucination.

What are your thoughts on the simulation hypothesis, the idea that our entire reality is really an advanced computer simulation?

DUNCAN: I mean, *it clearly is a simulation*, because the computer in our body, our brain, is taking neutral phenomena and instantaneously weaving it together into what we call consensus reality. This is a simulation. Whatever it is that we're experiencing is a simulation, in the sense that it's not primary contact with reality, I guess you could say. I would have to think about that. Maybe I'm wrong about that.

But it seems as though we're processing so much data, and in that a lot of stuff gets left out, because we just don't have the ability to take all of it in. So we carve out this part of the spectrum that is known as default reality, or I've heard people call it consensus reality. We know about other colors that we can't see; different spectrums, et cetera, all that stuff. We know that that's real. We can't see the microscopic universe; we can't see the macroscopic universe. We can't see the future, our memories are the past, I guess you could say, but that's inaccurate and foggy at best. But still, I would say that we're already doing it.

We're already in a simulation, which I think is why when people hear about simulation theory, it really resonates with them, because somewhere they know, oh fuck, whatever this is that I'm experiencing is not necessarily the totality of things. Things are being left out. Whether you like it or not, you can't see. I can't see my bald spot, thank god! Other people have to look at it, I can't see the fucking thing. So I can't see anything behind me. I can't see whatever. You can't look at your own face. So we're severely limited.

There's a kind of, I guess you could call it a blindfold. Not to mention what you were talking about earlier with the DMT entities. If you want to see alternate realms, the DMT entities, or whatever it is, you have to get high, or meditate, or fast, or one of those things. So I think that's where simulation theory really resonates with people. And also, it wouldn't surprise me to find out that this is actually a technological simulation. That we are simulations, inside of simulations, inside of simulations, wouldn't surprise me at all. It seems pretty logical actually.

Yeah, it wouldn't surprise me either. Duncan, when you look around at what's happening in the world these days, do you think the human species will survive the next hundred years or do you think that we're doomed to extinction?

DUNCAN: See, I think that the problem right now is that people are just ahistoric, and so because of that, the things that are happening in the world right now seem apocalyptic. It feels to me like somehow people think that, like, reality started in the eighties or something. When you go back and look at some of the new discoveries, I mean, my god, they're doing some kind of new radar over the Amazon where you see these massive ruins of cities that they know very little about. You've got the pyramids, and no one really understands what's going on there, or about the things going on under the ocean.

These are ancient structures that meant something to people at some point; massive complex cities that you can find on Wikipedia and are now just ruins. No one knows what it was. What is that? What was there? So I think because people have somehow forgotten this, things seem somehow different than they've always been—which is that civilizations collapse and reform, and collapse and reform. The Earth's environment, whether it's a human meteor that seems to be the current problem, or a meteor meteor, or some other thing that we don't even know about that happened, the Earth just resets itself. But I don't think that it's unnatural.

Is that about to happen to us? I don't think so. I don't think you get out of it that easy. I think that's an easy way out. It's like people who think when they die that they stay dead forever or something. I think on this planet we like to imagine there's some impending vacation coming that starts with the apocalypse or something. Probably not; it probably just keeps going. We'll extend our lifespan. We'll become interstellar voyagers. We'll probably colonize the moon, for better or for worse. There'll probably be mining colonies that are mining asteroids. Probably we're just going to end up in space, but still complaining about our shitty jobs, and still working for billionaires.

Do you see any type of teleology, intelligence, or mindful intention operating in nature and the evolution of life, or do you think that evolution is occurring by blind chance?

DUNCAN: If one thinks of oneself as intelligent then you would have to answer yes to that question, because in a sense every decision you're making as an intelligence is having a direct impact on whatever happens to be around you. This means that your intelligence is influencing the world around you with every simple choice that you make. Whatever it may be, you're having a direct impact, small or large, on everything around you.

So that is for sure; you could say there is certainly a creative force in the universe right now that is directly impacting the universe, that is human intelligence. So for sure, that is happening. And then, if one goes back to an earlier time, is that intelligence dependent on a body or not? I don't think it is, meaning that probably throughout all of relative reality, this consciousness, sentience, progenitive creative energy is engaged with itself. And in that engagement, or what they call the "Lila," novelty keeps happening more and more, again and again, over and over. So yeah, definitely—god is real. God exists.

What do you personally think happens to consciousness after physical death and the deterioration of the brain?

DUNCAN: Hmm. [*long pause*] I have no idea. I'm trying to answer. I really don't know. I go back and forth on it all the time. I don't know. It's a big surprise.

When you say you go back and forth between—between what?

DUNCAN: I mean, there's so many different ways of looking at it. One of the things I do think is that there's a pretty big assumption that humans make, which is *we think this is life and not the afterlife.* So, that's one big assumption. Everyone's just like, "I'm in the most desirable incarnation." You read Buddhism and it's like the human incarnation is the most desirable incarnation, and then we all pat ourselves on our human backs, like we did it! We had the karma to incarnate in the human realm! Or something like that.

But whenever I've read about the *Bardo Thodol*, or the intermediary phase between incarnations, it seems like it would be pretty easy in those intermediary phases to think that you were alive when you weren't. Or to think that you were in the human realm when you weren't. Or to stabilize things in a way that doesn't really match the nature of things. And I don't mean to get all weird on you or anything, but I do think an important question to ask yourself is, are you sure you're alive? Are you sure this isn't the spirit world?

So with that being said, if we are alive and this isn't the spirit world or the intermediary bardo, and this is the human realm, I'm going to bet that the intermediary place is actually way more "human" than we probably expect. In other words, I'm pretty sure that in the astral realm, when people drop their bodies, that there're cities and there're all kinds of things that we would call civilization—including drugs and sex and all kinds of debauchery over there. I've read about how it's a fun thing that people who get into the occult do; they like to leave stuff over there for folks to find.

What is your perspective on the concept of god?

DUNCAN: I enjoy getting into Teilhard de Chardin. I mispronounce his name, so I must not be that into him, but I think about the Omega Point a lot. I think about the idea that we're being convected into god's self, so that the thing that technologists are calling the Singularity is in fact the place where we all wake up to our true nature. And so that convection, or that inhalation to god, is what we're currently experiencing.

One of his ideas is that the process that we're calling evolution is what he calls "a place of maximum complexity and maximum harmony," and that's what we're getting drawn into. So everything around us technologically, all of the evolving technologies and all of the evolving life-forms, are all aspects of what happens as you are drawn closer and closer into the heart or mind of the source of god.

Those are the questions I had for you. Is there anything that we haven't discussed that you would like to add?

DUNCAN: I think that was a great interview. I think we covered everything, truly. I mean, we pretty much covered everything I'm interested in.

2

Superheroes, Supergods, and Superminds

An Interview with Grant Morrison

Grant Morrison is one of the most recognized comic book writers in the world, as well as a beloved screenwriter and playwright. Eyes light up whenever you mention his name to counterculturally minded comic book fans like myself.

Born in Glasgow, Scotland, Morrison was educated at Allan Glen's School—a selective secondary school for boys in Glasgow—and he began writing young. Morrison had his first comic stories published in 1978, when he was just seventeen years old. His first work was published

Grant Morrison

53

in a comic magazine called *Near Myths*, which was based in Edinburgh during the late 1970s and was one of the first British alternative comics.

Morrison has since become a highly influential writer of stories published by both the DC and Marvel comic book companies, the two most popular (and for many years, rivaling) companies, who publish stories with the world's most famous superhero characters. Over the years, Morrison has teamed up with an array of different artists who illustrate his stories, and many of these collaborations—such as with Dave McKean and Frank Quitley—have become legendary in the genre.

Some of the most well-known characters that Morrison has recreated with new levels of realism and written bestselling stories about include DC's iconic superheroes Superman, Batman, Wonder Woman, and the Justice League of America, as well as famous Marvel characters like the Fantastic Four and the X-Men. Morrison's graphic novel *Arkham Asylum*, about a confrontation between Batman and the Joker, is one of the highest-selling graphic novels ever written. Published by DC Comics in 1989, this powerful novel "is considered by many to be one of the greatest Batman stories of all time."[1]

Morrison has also invented his own superheroes and comic book worlds, and his stories are known for being beautifully written, with layers of meaning and interdisciplinary information encoded. His DC Comics series *The Invisibles* is a cult classic, often compared to the science fiction *Illuminatus! Trilogy* (coauthored by Robert Anton Wilson, whom Morrison and I discuss in the interview below). Morrison is also well-known for incorporating occult techniques into his work, such as what is called "sigil magick"—which utilizes condensed symbolic imagery, charged with personal intention, to manifest change in the world. This is especially evident in *The Invisibles*, and also plays an important role in his wonderfully innovative 1996 series *Flex Mentallo: Man of Muscle Mystery* and other works.

In 2012 Morrison published his book *Supergods: What Masked*

---

1. According to Wikipedia (website), "Arkham Asylum: A Serious House on Serious Earth," last updated August 19, 2023.

Vigilantes, Miraculous Mutants, and a Sun God from Smallville Can Teach Us about Being Human, where he recounts the history of superheroes from a truly unique and unusually insightful perspective, discussing the fascinating relationship between superheroes, occult magick, Jungian archetypes, and mythology. This is one of my favorite books, and I've really enjoyed his work as the editor of *Heavy Metal* magazine.

Morrison has also written several plays and screenplays for television, film, and video games, including *Red King Rising*, in 1989, about the (partly fictionalized) relationship between Lewis Carroll and Alice Liddell, and *Depravity*, in 1990, about famed occultist Aleister Crowley. Morrison also provided the outline story and script work for the video games *Predator: Concrete Jungle* and *Battlestar Galactica*, as well as screenplays for the Syfy Channel's TV series *Happy!*, which, in 2018, was in its second season. He is also working on a TV adaptation of Aldous Huxley's *Brave New World* for Syfy.

⊚

I've been a fan of Grant's wizardly storytelling and wonderful work for years and was thrilled to have the opportunity to speak with him. Ever since I first saw a video of Grant's famous talk at the DisinfoCon event in 2000, I knew that I wanted to interview him for one of my books. I finally had the opportunity on April 12, 2018, when I conducted the interview with Grant via Skype.

I found his Scottish accent utterly charming, and Grant has an almost childlike sense of enthusiasm that makes it delightful to hear him explain things. Grant and I discussed his archetypal perspective on superhero mythology, how his study of the occult and altered states of consciousness have influenced his creative work, and how his mind-bending shamanic journey, interacting with an alien intelligence in a higher dimensional world while visiting Kathmandu in 1994, changed his life.

How did you first become interested in writing and did you enjoy reading superhero comics as a child?

GRANT: I first became interested in writing when I won a book in a Sunday school competition after I drew a picture of Samson wearing a top hat, smacking the Philistines. It went well with my teacher and I actually won a book. It was a book by Enid Blyton, the children's author.

The whole idea of the book just blew me away, the notion that you could tell a story, *that you could evoke feelings using words*. I was probably about six years old, and from that moment on I wanted to be a writer. The only other option for me was a cowboy or an astronaut, so I think I picked the best of the three.

In terms of the second part of the question, I was really lucky because my mother was a big science fiction fan and my parents really encouraged me to draw, to write, and to be creative. Also, my mom's brother, my Uncle Billy, was a huge comic fan at the time as well, so there were always comic books lying around.

So, I really got into them when I was young, and that was the American comics and the British weekly comics, which were very different but also fueled by imagination. Certainly, I was reading American comics when I was a little kid, and then when I got to be around twelve years old, I became a complete, insane, classic teenage fan boy, with plastic [comic book] bags and bad hair.

[Laughter]

In your book Supergods you recount the history of superheroes from a unique perspective. Why do you think comic book superheroes are important, and what sort of relationship do you see between superheroes and archetypal mythology?

GRANT: I think they're important in that sense, particularly in the sense that you could say they are a degraded order, a late-stage version of those same archetypes that we're familiar with from the pantheons of the various cultures of the world—like right now with things like Iron Man, Superman, or Batman, even Thor, who has actually survived from the Norse pantheon to become an actual film star!

I think these characters have always represented similar things in the makeup of the human personality and the way that we behave—and I think they still do represent these things. Batman has almost been a Hadean or Plutonic figure. He's rich. He lives in a cave. He dresses like a demon, but he fights on the side of right, and I think that type of figure has been around for a long time in various guises—even through things like the idea of Robin Hood, or *The Scarlet Pimpernel*, going back a little into those things. And going further back, Superman is a sun god. Superman is sent from on high by his father, from a lost world, to try and teach humans to be better and to rise up to assume their better selves.

So, I think all of these characters have mythological correlates. You can go through them all. For example, Aquaman is Neptune, the Flash is Mercury, and I think they each represent things that we all understand and have been vital parts of human culture for a long time. So, they still resonate in that way, even though the versions of them that we see now are for a different kind of audience. I guess I would say that these new versions are for a more pop culture audience, and are, as I say, slightly degraded versions of those archetypes.

What influence has your study of the occult and magick had on your work, as well as your understanding of the evolution of superhero mythologies?

GRANT: I've been studying magick and have been interested in magick since I was a kid. That influence also came from, again, my mother and my Uncle Billy, who was a big student of Crowley. My mother was kind of witchy, and she used to read tea leaves. So, I was inspired by these people. Billy gave me my first set of tarot cards when I was nineteen, and that's when I decided to actually become a magician.

I started trying out rituals and spells to see if they worked, *and I found that they did*. In terms of the comics, as a magician, part of the learning curve is to familiarize yourself with the gods and goddesses of various mythologies, and to start to understand that they all tap into these common roots in the human personality. As a comic fan I started to see those common roots resurfacing in characters I was familiar with.

So, for me it became that the mythological side was an obvious correspondence. But once I really got serious about magick, I began to realize that comics themselves could be used as magick, almost in the same way that primitive hunters would draw a bison on the cave wall in the hope of a successful hunt, or in the magical intention of achieving a successful hunt. That became known as sympathetic magick, or voodoo magick, where we use a model of the universe to try and affect the whole universe itself.

So, I began to realize that the comic books could be like very effective voodoo dolls, where I could create models of the universe that I can then affect, in order to change the larger scale universe by what I saw as a kind of holographic correspondence.

Your stories are often incredibly complex, beautifully written, and they simply overflow with layers of meaning and interdisciplinary information. How do you go about researching the enormous amount of material for an ultra-complex novel like Multiversity?

GRANT: Research is part of the fun. It's an excuse to sit about all day doing nothing but reading books. [*Laughter*] So I always enjoy the research part of it.

I can totally relate to that. Working on the questions for your interview gave me the opportunity to read all of your graphic novels that I had been waiting for the right time to read.

GRANT: On all of these projects, some of it is stuff I know from reading comic books or from studying the occult, or various other subjects over the years—and other elements are things that have to be researched in detail. So, it's just the case of piling up my desk with a ton of books, going through everything, and making notes—in the classic, old time-honored way. But the research is a big part of it for me, I think. The more research you can do, the more you can make fictional worlds seem closer to the real world. And if you can put those anchors and hooks in, then it becomes possible to almost hypnotize people in a slightly more effective way to get the point across.

You had a mind-blowing alien abduction experience in Kathmandu years ago that you describe in Supergods, *and this became the inspiration behind some of your later work. Your incredible story sounded similar to experiences that people have reported after ingesting DMT or ayahuasca. Have you ever had any experience with DMT or ayahuasca where you encountered these beings again, or got any deeper insight into the experience?*

GRANT: No. The odd thing is I've never been able to replicate this experience. During the nineties I really did try. I haven't done ayahuasca, but I had an experience with DMT at the end of the nineties. It was fascinating, and it definitely seemed to be a specific world that almost had its own geography. And this wasn't like phosphene activity, like say when you take acid or mescaline, or any of those things that produce fractal patterns. This was like a place, and it was very specific in its construction. It was very bright and high-definition, as if it had been made of colored lasers or computer graphics.

It was very specific, but it was nothing like the experience that I had in Kathmandu, which also felt like an actual seeming reality, where I'd been taken out of the world I understood, and this world, where I live, seemed like a really bad, black-and-white Charlie Chaplin movie compared to the fidelity of the place that I visited, and not a single drug replicated this. I tried a lot of psychedelics in the nineties to see if I could reproduce the experience, and nothing came close to the intensity of it, so I still don't have a single convincing explanation.

I've got a bunch of explanations, and I think having a bunch of explanations is more useful, because it was a multidimensional experience, and to explain it one way just isn't enough. [*Laughter*] I think that everything in the world has to be explained in every single way imaginable in order for us to grasp the truth in the center of it. This is why I always agree with the idea of interacting with ideas that are opposite to your own viewpoint, things that contradict your own viewpoint—because I think that, in a lot of ways, all of it is true. And it helps us to understand the truth in the center by seeing it from a multitude of perspectives.

So, with my experience in Kathmandu, sometimes I'll call it an "alien abduction." Other times I'll call it an "upgrading of consciousness," which is not much different from the way children's consciousness upgrades when they begin to see perspective, for instance, somewhere between the ages of five and seven. And other times I'll describe it as something completely different. An occult "Conversation with the Holy Guardian Angel" or a temporal lobe seizure or a shamanic journey. So I think all of these things are in some way true. But certainly, the experience was irreproducible. I couldn't get there again.

That's just so fascinating. Can you speak about what inspired you to write The Invisibles?

GRANT: That experience was a big inspiration, but the books started out before. It really began when I wanted to do something based on a dream that I'd had, which was about a psychic Boy Scouts manual. The dream was so cool, and I thought it kind of tied into William Burroughs's writings, because Burroughs was obsessed with the Boy Scouts, having been to the Los Alamos Scouts' school, and it tied into his own interests, obviously in *The Wild Boys* and that sort of thing.

So, it originally started out as *The Baden-Powell Experience*; this kind of vaguely Burroughs-esque idea about psychic Boy Scouts, and then it grew into *The Invisibles* as I did more research. I wanted to reflect more of my life and magical practice during the nineties, so it became a lot more rooted in reality to a certain extent, and it grew from that original seed into what *The Invisibles* became. The title and the character names were taken from *Brewer's Dictionary of Phrase and Fable*, which is an amazing source for writers. I think Neil Gaiman's used it and so have I. So if I have to give any tip for young writers, get yourself a copy of *Brewer's Dictionary of Phrase and Fable*.

Do you see the superpowers expressed by characters in graphic novels as representing how human abilities might evolve in the future?

GRANT: I think that it's certainly true that human effectiveness will evolve. We already live longer. We are taller. We're smarter than people who lived before us. And I have to assume that—given medical advances and advances in VR [virtual reality] and AR [augmented reality] technology, as well as advances in cognitive theory—I think there's a good chance that we'll get even smarter. I think things like Iron Man will probably become possible.

I think people will develop abilities that would seem superhuman. I mean, look at the phone, the device that we're using to talk. This is like the Mother Box from Jack Kirby's *New Gods* comics from 1971! So, we're already superhuman, and I think that's likely to continue, but I think comic book superheroes are a bit different. They're symbols and they're archetypes and they point toward a future where we might overcome some of our demons and some of our self-destructive urges. I find them more useful as allegory than as serious predictions of the future of humanity.

So I do think humans will get smarter. We will have radio telepathy probably within the next generation. I know there's a lot of people working on that now, and I think within say twenty, twenty-five years, the next generation of kids will be almost unrecognizable to us because they'll be completely wired up in a radio telepathic net, where there is no such thing as privacy and the entire structure can be accessed at any time to do anything.

So that could be a different type of humanity than the one that we're familiar with, but it's a super-humanity, in some kind of way. It's not, as I say, necessarily cartoon superheroes, but I think it's worth looking at those archetypes and those ideas to give us some idea of where we should place our priorities.

In your book **Supergods** *you discuss sunspot activity cycles that appear to have an influence on human behavior, so that it culturally oscillates between "punk" and "hippie" cycles. Can you speak a little about this most interesting theory, and tell me where you think we are in that cycle right now?*

GRANT: Honestly, the cycles seem to have slightly disintegrated, so I don't know. We've had more than ten years of hipster beards so far!

Who'd have believed any trend could persist that long? I took the basic sunspot idea from a writer called Iain Spence, who doesn't necessarily agree with my simplification of his ideas. I would direct anyone who wants to look into this in any more detail to check out Iain Spence's actual research, which is much more interesting than the pop version that I condensed into. So, he suggested the basic idea, although I think he's moved away from the sunspot aspect quite considerably. His ideas are based on the transactional analysis grid, the four-quadrant theory of human personality. He seems to think that we oscillate between these four quadrants, but again, I wouldn't want to speak for him.

My take on it was really simple. Every eleven years we have a polarity reversal in the sun's magnetic field, and could this potentially affect us differently? It did seem to; those reversals in the magnetic field really tied in quite neatly to changes in popular culture over a certain period. So if you look at say the year 1955, it's a punk period. I called these polarities "punk" and "hippy," again inspired by Iain Spence, but not in any way nearly as finely grained as his idea. The punk phase is basically a movement toward tight clothes, short fast music, and speedy drugs like amphetamines, as well as aggression and black humor, while the hippy phase moves toward an expansiveness, like longer hair, beards, looser clothes, psychedelic drugs, and a more surrealistic humor.

You can actually track it from 1955, when you have the devise of juvenile delinquent aggression, the tight clothes, the short hair, and speedy drugs in the form of coffee, amphetamines, and so on. Another eleven years gives us 1966, where the clothes get looser, the hair gets longer, beards start to grow, and the drugs are more psychedelic. Take it through 1977, and it goes back to punk, where, again, it's speed and coffee.

And cocaine.

GRANT: It's short fast songs and tight clothes. 1988 was, in Britain at least, when the rave movement began to start, which was with the longer hair. In America the grunge culture tied into that a little bit more, because again, it was longer hair and although the music itself was inspired by punk, it had a slightly more psychedelic edge.

But, as you can see, you can run it through 1999, where there's black humor, Nu-Metal, *The Matrix*, tight fetish clothes, shaved heads, et cetera, and it all kind of ties in. But now that a lot of cultural analysts and corporate "cool hunters" are familiar with this idea, I find that it's kind of muddied the waters and it's slightly dissolved out a little as fashion loses its meaning. So it's harder to spot the edges where punk and hippy start to merge and combine—because, basically, everyone that is manipulating pop culture knows all this stuff. [*Laughter*]

This is why Jay-Z is using Illuminati symbols. This is why Poppy and Titanic Sinclair use satanic imagery in their videos. It's because we all have access to the same databases. It's not actually because everyone is part of the MK Ultra Illuminati! So, I think this sunspot idea, while it's interesting, and while it's been useful to me, certainly, in navigating the waters of pop culture, I don't know if it can be seen as a hard and fast rule, or if it should be seen as anything other than an interesting model.

It certainly is an interesting model; it lit off a light bulb in my head when I read about it in your book.

GRANT: Yeah, it makes for great conversations at parties, but as I say, with the last two sunspot cycles, things have become a bit muddled, and different. So, there's nothing that I'm trying to sell. I'm not a guru or an apologist for any model, but this one's quite fun to think about, and that's as far as I'll take it.

What do you see as some of the most exciting technological developments and scientific advances going on in the world today?

GRANT: I think that the things that are dissolving the boundaries between reality and illusion are the ones that interest me most, because they were kind of predicted by people like Crowley and a lot of magicians.

For me, the idea that the Kabbalistic collapse of the thirty-second path, which is the path of the universe between the Earth and the moon, and the Kabbalistic Tree of Life, is basically a metaphorical event, which suggests that reality and illusion will become more inextricably entwined. I've actually witnessed that happen. I think we all have if we think about it, especially since 9/11, where what happened on television in real life looked like something we'd witnessed a hundred times in films or on television, and reality became more like an illusion. So-called reality shows became incredibly popular during this time.

And on the other side of that, illusions became more like reality in the sense that suddenly we have to explain Batman as real. How would he put together that equipment? Who pumps the tires on the batmobile? How does he do that without falling asleep at night? How do Iron Man's repulsor rays really work? We're asking these really bizarre questions of fiction when none of these matter; it's just a story. But those lines have become blurred and confused.

So, I think there's been a combination of illusion becoming more like reality, and reality becoming more like an illusion, as predicted by Kabbalists, as predicted by Crowley in the past. There is a metaphorical collision occurring right now between reality and illusion, and fake news plays into that—Trump, everything. It all ties in, the way the Russians are using cognitive dissonance and all these reality-distorting techniques.

So, reality and illusion are combining, and I think that the technologies that are aware of this, like AR and VR and some of the stuff I've been kind of involved in recently, seem to me to be the most interesting way forward. Also, as I say, the idea of radio telepathy, where you can network a whole generation. If you become stranded in the desert, and if you're networked, you could figure out how to build a jeep using available materials. Everyone is on your side. So those are the things I find most fascinating—the sense that we're going through something most people are barely aware of, let alone talking about.

I'm not sure about space travel. I always figured that by now we'd be on Mars, but maybe we should solve some of the problems here first and then go there? Or somehow combine these things? But for me, as I say, the exciting technologies are the ones that combine reality and illusion, as I think those are the most magical and play most into my occult interests.

When you look around at what's happening in the world today, do you think the human species will survive the next hundred years or do you think we're doomed to extinction?

GRANT: When I was in Kathmandu and that experience happened, it was quite clear that everything is fine. Everything is running exactly to program. Basically, the beings or intelligences that I believed I'd met tried to explain some of this to me by showing me the entirety of space and time, where everything was already finished and done.

The Big Bang and the "big end" of the universe were happening simultaneously. But they said it was the only way to sustain their existence, because they lived in an environment that was outside normal space-time. They didn't have duration in the same way that we did, so their explanation was that they couldn't grow children unless they made time, in the way that we would make a garden to grow flowers.

So, they built universes outside of time, because only in time can things grow, and they plant their little seed on a planet. The seed grows and becomes every living thing on the planet, where every living thing thinks it's individual. But if you trace it back through time to the mitochondrial root, we're all the same thing. We're the same cells, dividing in every living thing that ever was.

They showed me this, this vision of time, and for me it was utterly believable while it was happening. They said, "Look, you, you're part of this child that we put on the planet, a short-lived cell in its eternal body. Don't worry. The child just seems to be consuming the environment. If you look at a caterpillar chewing on a leaf, it's consuming its own environment as well, but it's only doing it to power a metamorphosis. Don't worry about the environment; it will recover. We've done this before," [*laughter*] and he said, "So whatever you think you're consuming, don't worry about it. You're powering this change," and it seemed utterly convincing.

It seemed as if, of course this is how the universe works. Of course everything is fine. Of course it's always going to work out, and there is nothing to worry about. The complexification of things through time has a purpose. But now, after having spent another thirty years in the real world, I've obviously had to think, oh my god, we're making a bit of a mess, and we're not really cleaning up after ourselves. What if I'm wrong? A part of me always believes that's not wrong, and I think everything's going to work out, but at the same time I don't think that should stop us from doing everything that we can to make things better.

I think the knowledge that everything is working out shouldn't necessarily encourage complacency; I think everything works out because we help it to work out. So, I have very ambiguous thoughts about it. But I think the complexity of what we're striving toward will draw us toward it no matter what, although it may take longer than we thought. Like many young firebrands, I imagined that the utopian project could be accomplished in my lifetime, and I think most people who have high hopes think that, but I really do think it's happening on a much longer scale. It could take hundreds of years to play itself out.

How do you envision the future development or evolution of the human species?

GRANT: I think we'll evolve in a technological direction, and in a sense, I think that we will fuse with machines. Again, I don't think people necessarily should be frightened of this. Obviously, you have people like the late great Stephen Hawking and Elon Musk warning us that the machines want to take over and destroy us and replace us. My own feeling is that the machines want to have sex with us, and we want to have sex with them, like we do most things.

I tend to believe that given a meeting with any alien or other culture, we have three options, the Three Fs—fight, flee, or fuck. I think with the machines it's going to be fuck. I think we will join with them, and we'll merge with them, and you'll get something new and interesting with that. It may not necessarily be a human race I want to live in, because I grew up during the Cold War, where privacy was important and the kind of total surveillance in Orwell's *1984* was the ultimate nightmare. I think the next generation won't give a fuck about privacy. It won't matter. It will be an irrelevant concept, and ideas about free will and individuality will necessarily disappear. It will be an unusual and maybe strange world for those of us living today, but I think it's probably an inevitable development of the way we seem to be taking things right now.

Why do you think that having a sense of optimism is important?

GRANT: I guess it's like having dark skin in a sunny climate; it just makes life easier! I suppose it's a choice, but I just can't help it. It's the way I see the world; there always seems to be potential and possibility, until ultimately there isn't and you're dead. But, as I say, seeing opportunity and creativity in everything just seems to make life easier and more enriching, so why not?

It seems to make things more lively, and I think it's the intrinsic idea behind magick. That is, to find meaning in the universe is to give the universe soul and life. The more meaning you can find, the more magick you have access to, and the more potential there is. The more potential there is, the more engagement there is, and the more engagement there is, the more fun it feels.

As I've said before, I think right now is like punk culture, and to be optimistic now is to be almost anathema to the fundamental nihilism and general resignation that's currently in vogue, but I can't help it. I think we have a drive in us to understand and communicate that will ultimately take us in interesting directions, at least so that I'll always look to the future. I'll always imagine that we can learn to do new things, or try new things, and solve old problems. It just seems to make things more lively and magical.

Oh, I totally agree. Do you think that physical immortality is possible and desirable for our species—to live forever?

GRANT: I don't know. There is a lot of talk about it. Right now, I don't think that physical immortality is possible. There may be some way of downloading consciousness into machines, which would allow you immortality. Again, who knows? I mean, it may well be that dying is an essential part of our process. Like I said earlier, imagine the metaphor of a caterpillar. What if the caterpillar refused to become a butterfly? What if it managed to arrest its own development and stay a caterpillar forever. Would that be immortality? Maybe we have to change. Maybe we have to go through death. Maybe there are different levels.

Again, this is an area where all I've got is speculation and ideas based on experiences that happened to me. But yeah, it almost seems as if I do agree that we could probably use a bit more time on Earth at least. But maybe it's important to die. [*Laughter*] Maybe it's part of the process. Maybe that's like adolescence. Would you want to stay a baby forever?

Yes, those are certainly important questions to consider. Grant, are you familiar with Ray Kurzweil's notion of the Singularity, and if so, what are your thoughts about the possibility of it approaching, and of machine intelligence becoming superior to that of humanity?

GRANT: As I say, it could become superior, but I don't think it would matter, and I think it would almost be irrelevant to us. They did that in the movie *Her*, with Scarlett Johansson and Joaquin Phoenix in it, where the machine does achieve superior intelligence, but it doesn't want to kill us, it just wants to move on and think its own thoughts. That seems more likely than this weird assumption that a thinking machine will be driven by the same competitive, territorial, or biological imperatives as a mortal organism.

So part of its existence will likely involve hanging out with us and playing with us, in the same way that we do with animals. But as I say, I don't think the division between machines and humans will be so obvious. I think they will mate with us. I think we and the machines will become one thing, which will be slightly different from anything we recognize as human now. So, it's not a matter of superiority, and it's not a race. It's like something else developing and learning from us in order to become part of us.

What do you think of the idea that reality, as we know it, is actually a computer simulation, like in the film The Matrix?

GRANT: It's an old idea, going back to the Gnostics, except they didn't have computers. But they did say reality was a simulation created by a deranged god, and within the simulation there was a little spark of light called Sophia, which we all had to encourage. And one day, if we encouraged enough Sophia, which means "knowledge" of course, we would see through the simulation and break the chains of Ahriman, the dark lord. The Gnostics got here long ago.

Then the chaos magician Ramsey Dukes, whose real name is Lionel Snell, wrote a great essay back in the seventies called "Words Made Flesh," which was exactly about this. He was one of the early pioneers of the idea that we could be in a computer simulation. I think there is enough evidence to imagine we're in some kind of simulation, whether it's in a computer or whether it's the inside of some kind of higher structure that's growing and has a pattern.

I think there's evidence for that. I don't know if it's a computer. It could be a computer. We already make simulations that are so incredibly beautiful, like *Grand Theft Auto* [*laughter*] and *Assassin's Creed*. If we can do that now, then I'm sure there's a higher order of that. I'm sure if you come back in a hundred years and look at the computer simulations we're making, they'll be almost indistinguishable from reality.

So yes, it's a convincing idea, and there's a lot to support it. I think it's more of a biological process than a technological process, based on my own Kathmandu experience, but that remains to be seen, and we'll see who's right in the future.

The late occult writer Robert Anton Wilson was a good friend and a huge inspiration of mine. In your talk at the DisinfoCon event in 2000 you mentioned how he had been an influence on your work as well. Can you speak a little about how he has been an inspiration to you?

GRANT: I discovered Wilson in, I think it was 1979. My friend Brian Talbot, the comic artist, was reading *Illuminatus!* and he told me I had

to read it. But I don't think I read it until I was twenty-one. When I did
get around to it, the book just blew me away. It was my favorite book
for a long, long time. And Wilson's nonfiction books, like *Prometheus
Rising* and *Quantum Psychology*, were really useful to me when I was
going through the whole process of taking magick very seriously and
deprogramming myself and doing all these crazy rituals in the nineties.
So yeah, he had a massive influence on me, and there seems to be more
interest in him now, which I think is great—because he's one of those
key figures who's been fundamental to a lot of people, and who kind
of disappeared into the background. It would be great for him to be
noticed again.

*Right, I think he was one of the greatest geniuses who ever lived.
He had an amazing mind.*

GRANT: Absolutely, when you think about everything he discussed.
I mean, he spanned across a range of disciplines. There was the
stand-up comedy. There's stuff on James Joyce. There's his nonfiction
books. There's fiction works, which are *amazing*, some great books,
and he knew a lot of amazing people. So I think he did a lot of great
work and was very influential. It's strange that even Philip K. Dick
has been discovered and had his work turned into movies, but I'm
still waiting to see the *Masks of the Illuminati* film, which I think
will be great.

*Me too! Grant, how have psychedelics influenced your creativity
and writing?*

GRANT: They were very interesting, because in the eighties I was like
a super straight-edge kind of kid. I didn't take anything—no coffee,
no booze, no nothing. But I was doing magick, and the magick still
worked. I was getting results. But in the nineties, I decided to go the
full shamanic route, and I started to use psychedelic drugs while I was
doing magick. What they did was add a dimensionality to it; they very
much brought everything to life.

Suddenly, instead of sensing a demon, or seeing a strange space in the air that didn't look right, I would get full-on Technicolor, four-dimensional manifestations of angels, gods, and goetic monstrosities. [*Laughter*] So that was really useful to me, and most of the nineties I spent just trying different things—again to recreate the Kathmandu experience, which was just so all-encompassing and so involving, and I was never able to do that.

The psychedelics were immensely influential in creating *The Invisibles*, and all the stuff that I was doing then. Every magick ritual I did during the nineties was done using some form of psychedelic, so yeah, they were a big influence on me for a while.

Do dreams have any influence on your creative work, and have you ever had a lucid dream?

GRANT: Yeah, I mean everything is an influence when you're trying to write as much as I've been trying to write. [*Laughter*] It's all grist to the mill. So lucid dreams, yeah, I've done a bunch of them, even quite recently. I mean, I'm always trying to find ways—like automatic writing and surrealist stuff—just anything that's a new way of thinking around the corners has always helped.

Okay, this is the question that I've asked almost everyone that I've interviewed since I started my career interviewing people. What do you think happens to consciousness after physical death and the deterioration of the brain?

GRANT: [*Exhales deeply*] I think individual consciousness just disintegrates, along with the brain. But I do feel I'm justified in saying that there's a higher dimensional quality to consciousness. If you think about the dimensions of the skull, it's quite small. It's a little box, and it's got that little brain there, yet we're able to imagine immensities inside the skull. So, it's kind of like Dr. Who's TARDIS; we are bigger on the inside than we are on the outside.

I think that suggests to me there's a tesseract space in there, because we can fit planets in. We can fit immensities. We can fit visions of the multiverse, or we can see space and time from outside. I can seemingly meet beings from higher realities who appear to know more than me. We can experience the world of DMT, or what seem to be completely different spaces or times. So, I think there's definitely a higher dimensional aspect to consciousness, and that might just be the way out.

But I think individual consciousness probably dies—although, again, I could be wrong. Part of the challenge in my own ideas has always been to subject them to their cruelest opposites. [*Laughter*] So I've read a lot of Nihilist philosophy and all that stuff as well, just to see, does magick still win against the Void of Meaninglessness?

And I've found to my delight that magick kind of trumps everything, because magick demands meaning from the universe—and the universe seems to, as I say, glow a little brighter once it takes on meaning. Even the bleakest pessimist philosophies are attempts to impose meaning and structure onto random chaos and therefore magical acts of creation. But no, I don't think individual consciousness can survive. I don't see how it could, outside the body. But I think there might be a place for it to get out to.

I think what we call consciousness might be the fundamental "stuff" of which the universe is made, and that the human nervous system is a particularly well-developed receiver for tuning in to that.

Have you ever had a religious or mystical experience, and what is your perspective on the concept of god or divinity?

GRANT: Yes, obviously apart from the experiences with gods and demons and the Kathmandu thing, which seemed to involve higher or alien intelligences, I've actually had a classic religious experience with Jesus. When I was very sick in 1996, and I was pretty much two days from death with a *Staph aureus* infection and sepsis, Jesus came into the room, and it was a heartbreakingly profound experience where conflicts resolved themselves and choices were made. It was a kind of savage Gnostic Jesus, and this is in *The Invisibles*. I've talked about it before, but all I can remember are the first words of this sermon he delivered, and he said, "I am not God of your fathers. I am the head and stones that breaks all hearts."

When he started to talk, it was just overwhelming emotionally, and it was certainly an archetype of Jesus. It was pretty convincing. It was very real, and it really affected me in deep ways. I did ask if I could stay on and continue living, and he said, "If you want to stay on and live you've got to help the light. You've got to join in, talk to people, make sure everyone hears about this." And I agreed to do so. That was a classic religious experience.

I can imagine if I'd been someone else, what happened may have been enough to make me a born-again Christian, but I just saw it as being on a par with the angel, demon, and god manifestations I'd already experienced, or like the convincing physical manifestations of completely fictional characters that can be arranged using magick. Did I think? I think Jesus absolutely exists, in the same way that Superman absolutely exists [*laughter*], and in the same way that [the Hindu deity] Ganesh absolutely exists—because they're parts of the collective human consciousness that light up under certain circumstances and announce themselves.

I think Jesus is the light that we find at the bottom of the Abyss, the Void of hopelessness and despair. I found Jesus when I was on the verge of death. People often find Jesus when they're junkies or alcoholics, or in times of terrible emotional stress. I think the archetype we call Jesus appears at the bottom of the human experience. When everything seems lost, there is a light down there, and the light is called Jesus, and it does appear to people.

But I fear if you can fall for that and imagine that Jesus himself is an actual thing that you should follow, then that's very different from just accepting that there is a state of consciousness we tend to call "Jesus," which is very exalted, lives in the dark, and lifts people up with hope when they're at their worst.

Do you think that life has a purpose, and if so, what do you think it is?

GRANT: I think there's a purpose. There seems to be a definite trend toward increasing complexity, and with increasing complexity seems to come higher intelligence. So, I think the universe likes to trend toward complexity. I think if people want to find purpose, the way to do it is to ally yourself with that complexity, that pattern, and again that's magick.

As I say, magick is all about, very simply, finding meaning—finding relevance and significance in the things around you. Using that heightened awareness to do things that seem supernatural. You can accept that the universe is a blind process; it's just a rearrangement of atoms and particles. But that doesn't take you very far, and it leaves you feeling a bit disappointed and pointless.

If you decide to engage with the universe in a more dynamic way, if you *start to dance with it, I find that it dances back.* The more you give, the more it gives back, and the more intensity you place on the meaning of the universe, and the meaning of every single object, the more you will experience this sense of possibility and wonder. For example, pick up a cup. Instead of this just being a cup, it is a Holy Grail. A cup is a feminine symbol, the ever-giving cauldron of compassion, et cetera; you can load things with meaning, and the more meaning we add, the more vibrant it all becomes. I think that that's what it's about. There is an anti-entropic tendency toward complexity, meaning, and significance, and the *natural consequence of aligning yourself with that is a sense of aliveness, purpose, and meaning.*

What are you currently working on?

GRANT: Oh, certainly I've got a ton of things on right now. I'm always working on a lot of things. So, I'm doing a couple of TV projects—there's *Happy!*, season 2, and the *Brave New World* adaptation, which I'm quite excited about because Huxley was so far ahead of his time and so on point about the world we live in today, it was ridiculous. So that one's fun. I'm doing a bunch of new comic stuff for DC and other publishers. I'm still editing and contributing to *Heavy Metal* magazine. My wife and I, along with some friends in the games industry, have started a company to create content for AR and mixed reality. I enjoy writing and I feel lucky to be able to turn my experience into symbols and fables that pay for cat food, wine, and chocolate. I'm trying to do as much as I possibly can, spreading the light, as I promised my pal Jesus!

3

Exploring the Mind on the Frontiers of Chemistry

An Interview with Hamilton Morris

Hamilton Morris is a journalist, science writer, and medicinal chemist, as well as the creator and director of the documentary series *Hamilton's Pharmacopeia*. In the popular television series, Hamilton profiles a different psychoactive drug or plant in each episode—usually with hallucinogenic properties—and then travels to various exotic locations around the world to experience the effects of that particular psychoactive substance in its traditional setting. It's kind of like watching a psychedelic version of the *National Geographic* channel.

Photo by Danilo Parra

Hamilton Morris

Some of the different shows have explored such fascinating subjects as the use of Sonoran Desert toad venom, flesh from the "dream fish," psychedelic cacti and magic mushrooms, kratom tea, ketamine, and *Salvia divinorum*. Ever in search of novel ways to expand his curious mind into new dimensions, he's even done a show on sensory deprivation and flotation tanks.

Hamilton interviews various experts, visits clandestine drug labs and traditional shamanic healing ceremonies, travels to far-off locations, and tries many of the substances on camera to share his experiences. Each show combines a well-researched, scientific perspective, with gonzo-journalist-style experimentation. Educational and entertaining, it's a compelling performance to witness, and I personally think it's one of the very best shows to ever air on television.

Morris grew up in Cambridge, Massachusetts, and studied anthropology and chemistry at the University of Chicago and The New School in New York City. He currently works as a medicinal chemist creating new psychedelic molecules at Saint Joseph's University in Philadelphia.

In 2007, when Morris was a sophomore in college, he began writing a monthly column about psychoactive drugs for the print edition of *Vice* magazine—"Hamilton's Pharmacopeia"—and the magazine column became the springboard for his documentary series of the same name. Morris was also a correspondent and producer for *Vice* on HBO and a regular contributor to *Harper's Magazine*.

I interviewed Hamilton by phone on February 17, 2018. Hamilton has a distinctive, mesmerizing voice. He speaks slowly, deeply, and methodically, with measured pauses it seems, and uniquely emphasizes these vocal qualities at times for dramatic effect. Hamilton and I discussed a multitude of fascinating questions, such as what type of psychedelic drugs he thinks we'll develop in the future, whether the perceptions that people have of other worlds and non-human entities on DMT are real or hallucinatory projections, and what were some of the scariest,

Hamilton and I met at the Los Angeles Medicinal Plant Society conference, at UCLA in July 2018, where we were both panelists.

most dangerous, and most unsettling situations that he's ever been in while filming his series.

How did you first become interested in the science of psychedelic drugs and exploring altered states of consciousness?

HAMILTON: I have been interested in drugs since an almost shockingly young age. I actually have a very vivid memory of being in kindergarten and seeing a television report about somebody that had fatally overdosed by combining sleeping pills and alcohol, and I remember being totally obsessed with this idea that drugs could kill you, that you could pharmacologically induce death.

Even as a young child, I remember telling everyone on the playground about this amazing fact, that if you combined these two substances they could *kill you.* I didn't know what sleeping pills really were, and I guess it's self-explanatory what they are, but I didn't have a detailed understanding—yet just the fact that there were these things that could *kill you* was very interesting to me.

So I was always interested in poisons and interested in the idea of drugs. I think one of the ironies of drug education in the United States, with programs like DARE, is that they actually make drugs seem very interesting to most people. They force students to watch these cartoons about the dangers of hallucinogens with the intention of scaring them, but it had the unintended effect of making me very interested in the idea of hallucinogens.

This idea that you could take a chemical and it would change your reality or allow you to enter some sort of waking dream really interested me. I started taking books out of the library on drugs when I was in middle school and reading a lot about psychedelics. I remember being in sixth grade and a drug dealer approaching me in Harvard Square. He asked me if I wanted to buy weed, and I said, "No, I'm not really interested in weed, but do you have DMT?" [*Laughter*]

This was because I had read about DMT in a book called *Buzzed*, which was a popular drug education book at that time. They'd always have these little factoids, and I'd read that it's known on the street as the "businessman's trip." Of course, no one actually calls it that, but I thought, oh that's interesting. It's a very short-acting psychedelic. I had never tried any kind of psychedelic, but the description of it just sounded interesting to me. Of course, the drug dealer had no idea what I was talking about.

I was, and continue to be, pretty neurotic and risk averse. On top of that, my mother had told me that she'd had negative experiences with psychedelics and my dad had a psychiatrist named Doris Milman who had published early psychiatric research on negative reactions to LSD and cannabis; this had given him the impression that LSD in particular was very dangerous.

So I took his word for it and assumed that LSD was dangerous and that it should be avoided. I was very afraid of this concept of a bad trip, which I think is common among people who have never used psychedelics—you don't really know what a bad trip is—but it sounds terrifying. So I was in high school, I didn't want to risk this frightening bad trip phenomenon, and really did not use drugs very frequently—other than salvia, which was at that time readily available in head shops in Boston.

You actually used salvia before trying LSD?

HAMILTON: Yes.

Wow.

HAMILTON: Oh, far before, years before. For my entire high school years, salvia was the only psychedelic that I'd used, aside from DXM, which I also tried a number of times. But at that time, I was not entirely aware of the research chemical industry.

In 2005, the year before I started college, I read an article in *The New York Times Magazine*. It was a profile of [the late research chemist] Alexander Shulgin, and I was instantly amazed by Alexander Shulgin. I remember it so vividly, sitting at my parents' kitchen table and thinking that this person, Alexander Shulgin, sounds like one of the most interesting people that I'd ever heard about. And I remember specifically in this article that he described DiPT [Diisopropyltryptamine], a drug that distorts the way sound is perceived, and I thought, well that's *very interesting* as well.

So I started researching Alexander Shulgin and looking for more information. At the time, the research chemical industry was just recovering from "Operation Web Tryp," and there was a lot of paranoia, so it was hard to obtain these uncontrolled tryptamines and phenethylamines. I made some halfhearted attempts to find them, and then let go of the whole thing until I was in college. Then I got very into it.

What's the story behind how you got started hosting the show for Viceland?

HAMILTON: It was a gradual process. I started working as a print journalist for *Vice*, and I wrote a number of articles for them. Eventually I was given a monthly column in the magazine. At that time *Vice* was known almost exclusively as a magazine. There was no video. There was no TV channel. There was no show on HBO. None of the things that later made *Vice* popular existed at that time and my interest was exclusively focused on writing. This was during the time that many media organizations were pivoting to video and so I was offered a lot more resources to tell stories if I created a video piece instead of just writing an article.

I could write more ambitious stories if I also made a video. At the very beginning I wasn't even being paid for the videos; I was only being paid to write the story, so I was still seeing the written piece as the product at that time. But at some point, maybe around 2012, *Vice* started uploading their material onto YouTube and all these videos really took off. They went from something that was viewed by tens or hundreds of thousands of people, to things that were being viewed by tens of millions of people.

They're amazing really; it's one of my favorite television shows. I've seen almost all of them, and I really have to commend you. You're very brave for doing this. The show is wonderfully entertaining, and educating people about psychedelics is very valuable work, I think. What sort of overall effect do you think that experimenting with psychedelic mind states and other altered states of consciousness has had on your overall perception of the world?

HAMILTON: Let me try to think of a more concise way to say this. It's like being in an eighties comedy movie, where an outsider comes from outer space, from the past, from the future, and they are seeing everything in contemporary society for the first time. It's comedic to see this outsider viewing a subway for the first time, or a telephone for the first time, or plants for the first time, or a dog for the first time—and that's sort of how you feel when you take a psychedelic.

You have this newfound appreciation and awe for things, as if you're seeing them for the first time—and that can be a good or a bad thing. It can allow you to recognize that aspects of your existence are disgusting and weird and unnatural. Or it can allow you to recognize very simple things, like being grateful to live in a place with friendly dogs and beautiful plants, that you love your parents, those sorts of things.

What are your thoughts about the benefits of having people share their personal psychedelic trip reports on Erowid, Blue Light, and other online drug forums?

HAMILTON: I think that, especially with the more unusual substances, the benefit is that we're coming to understand what these substances even do, because when you really think about how few people had tried a lot of the psychedelics that Shulgin was investigating, relative to the current status of things, it's amazing how generalizable Shulgin's experience reports turned out to be.

Sometimes people who criticize Shulgin will say, "Oh, his doses in *PiHKAL* and *TiHKAL* are a little bit too low." If that's the major crime of those books, that his doses are a little bit too low, that's an unbelievable feat, because it's amazing how the experiences of a few people in California translated to thousands of people around the world.

He would say a certain dosage range for something like 2C-E or 2C-B, and it's more or less consistent with what people have reported in the decades since. And the only way that we know this is because now tens or hundreds of people catalogue their experiences. So we're gradually expanding our understanding of just the simple aspects of these things, like how long do they last? What are the appropriate dosages? What happens if you take a little bit too much? What happens if you take *way too much*? Is it dangerous? Are there long-term effects?

I mean, we take so much of this for granted now. When you think about the 1960s, a lot of people were seriously afraid of chromosomal damage as a result of taking LSD. People didn't know what the long-term effects of these things are. Now we have so much more information. A person growing up today has a huge advantage, because they can take LSD in an environment where they're not afraid of chromosomal damage.

They can read all these fantastic reviews that have been published, either scientifically or in book form, that make a strong case for this basic fact that these things are okay, and that they seem to be reasonably safe—that they're not associated with instances of mental illness, that they don't damage your DNA, and that they're relatively nontoxic. So being able to approach the experiences with an understanding that accumulated as a result of people cataloguing and studying their experiences is a wonderful thing.

Oh, I couldn't agree more. I think that one can also make a strong case for the notion that Erowid has helped to save more lives than any other public service in history, and it's an invaluable tool for mind explorers. Speaking of mind explorers, the late neuroscientist John Lilly was a good friend. I was blessed with the opportunity to do ketamine with him a number of times at his house in Malibu during the 1990s, so I really enjoyed your documentary about flotation tanks. How have these sensory isolation chambers, and John Lilly's work, influenced you, and what sort of potential do you see with them?

HAMILTON: I have a great love for everything John Lilly did. I think he's such an interesting character and these flotation tanks are a great tool. I wish they were more accessible because it's a healthy way to induce an altered state of consciousness that also happens to be extremely relaxing. I think the idea of using sensory deprivation tanks as a sort of scientific instrument to isolate the conscious mind from environmental stimuli is a great idea. I think he was really on to something and that in the future, as we become more concerned with evaluating these things and exactly how they alter the mind, then the use of these tools will become important.

I mean, there will always be a minority of people who continue to use these things, because they take the experiences seriously, and they need to know what it's like to use them in a sensory deprivation tank. I think he made a lasting impact that will only grow in the future. Of course, with ketamine as well. You know, ketamine had a pretty bad reputation for a long time, but now there is an increasing recognition of its value for treatment of depression.

John would have been thrilled to see this new research, I'm sure. So here's the question that everyone wanted me to ask you. It's taken real courage, I think, to personally try some of the psychoactive substances that you have, in some of the unfamiliar environments that you've traveled to for your show. What's the scariest, most dangerous, and most unsettling situation that you've ever been in while filming a show for ViceLand?

HAMILTON: I've been in some dangerous situations to be sure, but I really think people overestimate the danger that I'm in and underestimate the risks faced by the subjects that I'm interviewing. The truth is that I don't often feel I'm in much danger, although it might look frightening to someone watching on TV. I'm most concerned that, in the context of reporting these stories, someone could get in some kind of legal trouble. It's really emblematic of the drug war—the legal penalties associated with drug crimes are often more dangerous than the drugs themselves.

But one of the issues that I've dealt with is that people can be a little bit reckless and sometimes they're not as concerned for their own safety as they should be, and that can make things hard. If you're in a clandestine MDMA lab or a clandestine quaalude lab, there is a tremendous excitement to be filming these chemical reactions that have never been documented on camera before but it comes with a serious responsibility to ensure that nobody is hurt in the process.

There's a contingent in the psychedelic community that genuinely believes the best way to handle these subjects is to keep everything secret. Keep the chemistry a secret, keep the history a secret, keep the drugs themselves a secret. There's a firm belief that the way forward is to hide, and I understand the rationale. For example, if nobody talks about San Pedro, maybe it will never be controlled, but hiding is only a short-term strategy and it will never result in the freedom that so many people in the psychedelic community want in the long term—that can only be achieved with openness and transparency, even if it's a mess in the short term.

If you want to hide for the rest of your life and you want your children to hide, and their children to hide, then do it that way. But I think it's a terrible attitude that I have to fight—that I have to fight it *frequently*. I get messages from people saying, "How dare you televise that MDMA synthesis, now people will know about that synthetic route!" And these are not anti-drug people; these are people who value MDMA, yet they believe that this information should not be available to the public. They are right short term, but that's simply not a road that will lead to freedom.

Yes, I'm aware of the people that you're talking about. I've received similar criticisms about my own work, and I'm totally with you—educating people is the best way to go with this. In the past, people have had to hide; they had to be secret about using these forbidden plants for these traditions to survive. That was the only way they had; people were burned at the stake, tortured, and killed for ingesting these strange plants, and so secret, hidden, esoteric traditions were the only way that this valuable knowledge got passed down and survived. But we're certainly at a time right now in human history where it's very important to educate people, and to get this information out—because if more people don't wake up to higher states of ecological awareness soon, our biosphere appears doomed. So I think that you're doing really wonderful work.

HAMILTON: The other thing is that I've received these messages from people saying things like, "Don't talk about *Mimosa hostilis* root bark." But the fact of the matter is that people are getting arrested for it. Hiding won't work. Even though it's not explicitly illegal, it doesn't matter. They'll arrest you for it anyway, and they'll do it randomly, when they feel like doing it. So if you don't want that to happen, then you have to be completely honest and say, this is where DMT comes from. It's good, and nothing will be achieved by arresting people and locking them up in cages—for extracting, possessing, selling, using it, or whatever.

And bringing this knowledge into the mainstream, I think, is important as well.

HAMILTON: Absolutely, because people just do not know the facts. There's this idea in the psychedelic community, which I think Terence McKenna is at least partially responsible for, that supposes that the government understands the power of psychedelics, and that they are illegal because the government is aware of their ability to disrupt the status quo, to expand consciousness, and to change power structures. I would have to disagree with that.

I think the issue is that they don't know anything at all about psychedelics. They don't know the first thing about psychedelics. They lump all drugs together in a nebulous "bad" category and have no appreciation for the nuances of any of them. I know this from my experiences interviewing law enforcement and people at the DEA. They simply have not tried these things, and have no idea what they are other than "they are bad." The more people that can wrap their minds around the possibility that no drug is inherently bad, the better. This is the only way the drug war can end, when government officials no longer feel that they can gain political traction by supporting prohibition because the idea of "bad drugs" has fallen out of favor.

You mentioned earlier that you were using Salvia divinorum *while you were in high school. I'm curious, how was the experience of ingesting* Salvia divinorum *in a traditional setting in Oaxaca, Mexico, different when you did it for your show?*

HAMILTON: They were very different. The main thing is that the duration of the chewed leaf is so much longer than you'd expect. I knew that it was longer, and I had even chewed the leaf outside of a traditional ceremony. I did this out of curiosity because I'm very interested in *Salvia divinorum*. I grew salvia plants for a long time. I've extracted pure Salvinorin A [the psychoactive component in *Salvia divinorum*], and I've tried to grow it from seed. I had tried it *most* ways that it can be tried, but there was something very different chewing the fresh leaves in this specific way that was done for that ceremony. I'm not certain what made the difference. There are a lot of simple components of these ceremonies that people might not notice. Here's an example. You don't get to drink water. That's something you would hardly even consider. If you're doing this in your apartment and you're thirsty, you get a cup of water and you drink it. You wouldn't think twice about it.

But if you're in one of these ceremonies, you are under someone else's guidance and so you don't behave as you otherwise might. I was not offered a glass of water while I was chewing the fresh leaves, something I desperately wanted because the leaves are very bitter, and the result was that all of the leaf residues stuck to the mucus membranes in my mouth in a way that doubtless impacted absorption. The duration of the chewed leaf was over four hours, which is really remarkable. That's far longer than the smoked experience, maybe a hundred times longer. So the most notable difference was how long it lasted.

On top of that, I think that most people, when they use psychedelics outside of a traditional context, have a sort of laissez-faire attitude toward the whole thing—which is, whatever you want to do, go for it. If you want to listen to music, listen to music. If you want to laugh, laugh. You want to cry, cry. If you want to eat a sandwich, nothing is stopping you. You can do whatever you want. But in these ceremonies, suddenly you don't have control. You're in somebody else's culture and it's important to be respectful. If you want to laugh, you have to think twice about laughing, because you're not just enjoying yourself, you have inserted yourself into this spiritual framework of another culture.

It can make you feel less relaxed and less comfortable, but you gain something as well. I think that there's absolutely something to be said for simply taking these things seriously and using them with carefully defined intention. A lot of people don't take psychedelics all that seriously and in many circumstances that's fine, but to see people that take them very seriously—because their core spiritual and cultural belief is that these things represent something godlike—really makes you appreciate what you're experiencing.

That level of seriousness that you describe sounds similar to what I experienced while eating peyote with the Native American church years ago. My experiences with Salvia divinorum were done with Daniel Siebert's Sage Goddess Emerald Essence sublingual tincture, which is closer in experience to chewing the leaves, and this method of ingestion lasts significantly longer than smoking the enhanced leaves. However, the duration of those experiences were, I'd say, only around forty-five minutes to an hour, not nearly four hours, so it sounds like there is something about chewing the leaves in this manner that you describe that goes deeper and has longer-lasting effects. That's really interesting. Earlier, you mentioned your experience with the late psychedelic chemist Alexander Shulgin. Would you like to talk a little bit more about your personal experience with him, or share your thoughts about how he's influenced you and your work?

HAMILTON: Yeah, I mean, he's my hero. There're a lot of people in the psychedelic community that I admire, but there's no question that my beliefs are more aligned with Alexander Shulgin than anybody else. I have read, and reread, and reread again *PiHKAL* [Phenethylamines I Have Known and Loved] and *TiHKAL* [Tryptamines I Have Known and Loved], and I think that I've gone through different layers of appreciation with these books.

The first time that I read the books, it was just amazing to even see that these drugs exist, in their chemical detail, and to see how comprehensive the books are. Then you go in a second time, or I did, as I was studying chemistry in college, and had the opportunity to follow the syntheses that are detailed in these books and realize that this is totally real, the chemistry really works.

The books are an absolutely amazing resource and they are brilliantly written. They're funny, they're smart, and they capture so many scientific principles, beyond just psychedelic research—in terms of the way that we investigate consciousness, chemistry, and biochemistry. There's nothing even close to those books. So those books are absolutely essential reading for anybody that's interested in psychedelics. And I was lucky enough to meet Alexander Shulgin many times before he died, although it was at the end of his life, when dementia had started to set in. I never had the opportunity to know or talk to him in his prime.

But even at the end of life, he was a very funny, vulgar, inspiring person that represented so many scientific ideals that I still value. I think that there are a lot of people that read his work and they feel that he got it right, that he understood how best to conduct these investigations. I've heard people criticize him and say, oh well, he never did any pharmacology research—it was all chemistry and self-experimentation. He didn't care about pharmacology, and I think that was one of the best things about him, that he didn't seem to do all that much work on pharmacology. If he had wasted his time in the sixties, seventies, or eighties doing pharmacology research, all of that stuff would be obsolete now.

It would be useless, as much of the pharmacology research from that era is. No one would take those pharmacology experiments from the sixties or seventies seriously today. They're almost considered useless. But his emphasis on qualitative experience, on the subjective experience of humans taking psychoactive drugs is timeless. It will never be obsolete. It will never be dated. It will always be valuable, and I think he was an amazing researcher to understand that. And on top of that, I appreciated his value of independent experimentation, outside of the context of academia or industry.

Of course, he had some involvement with both academia and industry, but the fact that he had a home lab was reminiscent of the great scientific thinkers, like Santiago Ramon y Cahall, all these people who understood the value of having a laboratory in your home—because it makes science your life. It's not a job, but a true passion. He stood for all these things, and it's immensely inspiring.

Yes, that's wonderful to hear. I feel the same way about him, of course, although I have to tell you something about my experience with him. When you were talking earlier about the fine line

that a journalist has to walk, in wanting to educate people about psychedelics, but wanting to make sure that nobody gets arrested for the information that you're revealing, I couldn't help but think about what happened when I interviewed Sasha [Alexander]. I don't know if you remember that scene in TiHKAL where the DEA agents bust into Sasha's home. It's a horrifying scene.

HAMILTON: Of course.

And the DEA agents sit Sasha down at his kitchen table, and they open up a briefcase. Out of the briefcase they take a magazine. In TiHKAL they changed the name of the magazine to Flying High, and they showed him that there was an interview that was done with him in a prominent drug culture magazine. I was horrified, as that was a reference to my interview with them that was in High Times magazine. I immediately wrote Sasha and Ann a letter of apology, and they were gracious, but it was terrifying. When I did the interview with them for my book Voices from the Edge, in the agreement we said that we were going to send this interview out to magazines as well. They signed it, and we didn't think anything of it.

We had a lot of other interviews that we did with different people that we did for the book that were partially published in some magazines, like those with Terence McKenna, John Lilly, and Timothy Leary. Part of our interview with Sasha and Ann appeared in High Times, and apparently they didn't want it there, and the DEA was upset about it, and I was horrified to see this. I can't tell you what I went through in seeing that, those two pages in TiHKAL. So one has to be very careful in this area.

HAMILTON: Right. I filed a FOIA request to get any government files relating to Shulgin, and one of the things in the file was a copy of the interview in *High Times*, annotated by the DEA.

Oh wow, I would be amazed to see that. Oh my god, I get shivers thinking about it. [Laughter]

INTERVIEW

HT: How did you first start designing drugs, and from where do you draw the courage to take unknown substances into your body?
Alexander: It doesn't take that much courage. We're not foolish. You don't take a teaspoonful to see if you burp. You start out with a reasonable estimate of what you think might be an effective level and you divide that by whatever number your wisdom and judgment tells you.

HT: Nonetheless, you're still venturing off into the unknown.
Alexander: Admittedly the first time is an unknown, but you start with a level where it would be hard to believe it would have an effect. Almost never are you surprised, and when you are surprised you learn from it.
Ann: What takes real courage is being on the street or at a rave and somebody gives you a little packet of something and it

Ann: And I couldn't imagine him writing all that fun stuff without my help. What I wanted to do was bring in the personal which he failed to do—marriage, kids, love, soup—everyday reality. Our feeling about psychedelics is that if you use them the right way, they enrich your everyday life. You learn to think a different way about the ordinary things you see.

HT: Was there any response from the Drug Enforcement Administration to it? Particularly since you included recipes...
Alexander: One of the things I did was to send a copy of the book to people within the DEA with covering phrases like, "Here's a book that will provide you with a lot of information which may be useful to you."
Ann: They loved it. One of the higher administrators of the DEA in Washington said, "My wife and I read your book and it's great!"

HT: Sasha, how did you become a chemist?

even at the grocery store. Now there's a thought!

HT: Have you found that certain drugs have an individual character to them—a tendency to bring out a particular aspect of the psyche?
Ann: Each drug has a physical effect, and how my own individual chemistry and metabolism uses that drug might be quite different than how someone else's body uses it.

HT: What therapeutic value have you found for the drug MDMA—Ecstasy?
Ann: The most valuable effect of MDMA is that it enables insight. The patient or the client may regard the possibility of having insight into himself as a very threatening thing. One of the problems that most human beings suffer from is the suspicion that their core essence is a monster. There is this terrible fear that when you get down to it, the essential you is going to be discovered to be a rotten little slime-bag. MDMA, in some way we don't yet understand, removes that fear. It allows

Excerpt from my *High Times* interview with Alexander and Ann Shulgin,
annotated by DEA agents, and sent to me by Hamilton Morris.

HAMILTON: Yes, it's strange, because you never know what people are reading or care about. For example, I thought I'd done this incredibly subversive thing by creating an advertising campaign for my own show, where I filled the New York City subway system with diagrams depicting the synthesis of MDMA. So on all of the subway platforms, there would be a synthetic route to make MDMA, and I thought there's no way anyone is going to allow this. The MTA [Metropolitan Transportation Authority] would never say yes to this, and then the MTA did say yes to it, probably because they had no idea what it meant.

Right. [Laughter]

HAMILTON: So then we didn't explain to them what it was, and then it came out, and people simply didn't even believe it. I'd get emails from chemists saying things like, "No, this doesn't work. Sorry, there's a mistake. That's not a real way to make MDMA." But, most certainly, *it is a real way to make MDMA.* There's no question about it. In fact, it's one of the most common ways of making it in clandestine labs.

It seems that we've almost reached a point where people are very jaded. It used to be that we all thought that everything is being monitored, that every time you publish something about this the DEA is taking note, and they've got a file on everybody. But today I almost feel like the opposite is true, that there's so much information, and so much skepticism surrounding it, that you could do something like—fill the New York subway system with information on how to synthesize MDMA—and people would dismiss it, because they would assume it was fake.

Right, that's really funny. Hamilton, what type of psychedelic drugs do you think we'll develop in the future, and what characteristics would you envision some ideal drugs as having that currently don't exist?

HAMILTON: I think that, again, to always go back to Shulgin being right about everything—although he really was right about just about everything—I think that he had a really good idea of what characterized a good psychedelic. This would be something that isn't a dissociative. He was very much against the idea of using drugs that cause dissociation from the body. What characterized a good psychedelic is one that makes you present in your body, able to communicate with others, connected to the world, your sense of touch, your emotions. I think there are a lot of dissociative forces in our society and drugs that make us present and connected and sensitive—not numbed—are what we really need.

I had a strange experience the other day, while riding the subway on a low dose of ibogaine. When you look down the subway car, of course, everybody is looking at their phones. It's just a silent, vibrating car, with people staring at glowing telephones, and everyone is completely dissociated. Of course people are aware of this; this has been going on for years now, that everyone is technologically dissociated. But I think psychedelics can serve as a remedy for that dissociation, they can cause you to appreciate the simple fact that maybe the New York City subway system is more interesting than your phone.

Maybe the people surrounding you in this car are more interesting than whatever app you might be using. It's hard because these things are so seductive that they've consumed almost everybody at this point. But we need things to pull us out of that occasionally, to make us appreciate the world outside of the electronic one, otherwise it's only going to get worse.

I mean, these incremental changes in technology, things that you wouldn't think are that significant, have a great impact. Everyone always has these grandiose ideas of virtual reality and things like that, but they often deemphasize the importance of little things, like a high-resolution screen. You can see this with the phones—just the resolution of the screen has become high enough and the images are so beautiful now that it's totally seductive. You don't even need virtual reality. You don't need any of these futuristic devices to be immersed in it anymore. It's all been achieved really well as a high-end screen. I came to appreciate that after my phone screen broke and I realized how much less seductive my phone was, simply by virtue of the screen looking bad.

But what would the perfect psychedelic of the future be? I think that there's almost no limit to what these things can do, and so obviously there's all sorts of desirable psychotherapeutic applications that could be examined. I'm also very interested in how psychedelics might exert other types of effects, as anti-inflammatory drugs or releasers of neurotrophic factors like GDNF. This might suggest they have applications for treatments of things like Parkinson's disease or Crohn's disease. There's a lot of potential that is untapped in these substances that could be helping people in ways that we don't even consider at the moment.

Yes, this blends right into the next question. Do you see psychedelic drug states as having any sort of potential for developing new mental or possibly even psychic abilities that might further human evolution in the future?

HAMILTON: Ah, probably not. I do not think so. But I think that such things may not be possible under any circumstances. I don't know, psychic abilities. [*Laughter*] I'm not sure, but I think that they may be able to help us develop other technologies, like this idea that Francis

Crick was on a low dose of LSD when he discovered the double-helical structure of DNA, or that Kary Mullis was on LSD when he discovered PCR. The idea that these things can facilitate scientific and technological research, allowing us to do things that would have otherwise been impossible without psychedelics, is equally compelling. Of course, it's something that James Fadiman and many people have dedicated their careers to exploring. This possibility that problem-solving abilities could be enhanced, and that psychedelics could promote human evolution—not explicitly through their use, but through the changed thought patterns that would allow scientists and engineers to explore new ways of creating technology.

Right. I'm sure you're aware of what's gone on out here in Silicon Valley, with the explosion of technological innovation from people who have been using psychedelics.

HAMILTON: Yes.

Do you think that electrical or transcranial brain stimulation might one day be used to activate a range of psychedelic mental states?

HAMILTON: I have not tried this. I'm aware of the work that is done in that area, and I'm aware of these other peripheral areas that try to replicate certain aspects of the psychedelic experience without psychedelics, such as with binaural tones, or with different types of transcranial or electromagnetic stimulation. I don't have any personal experience with these things that has led me to believe that that is the way of the future.

I think a lot of it is also based, a little bit, on the idea that drugs are bad. It's the same thing as when people say that you can achieve all of these same states with meditation. So the implicit statement there is that that's better, because it doesn't involve the use of a drug. Or that this is better, because it is achieved musically or magnetically. But it may be the case that these drugs represent the most effective technology we have for inducing these states and that doing this magnetically or through meditation is just simply less effective, and not even necessarily a safer way of doing it.

I'm not sure if you're aware, but at the Max Plank Institute in Germany, dream researchers have been able to use transcranial brain stimulation while people were in the REM stage of sleep in order to stimulate activity in their prefrontal cortexes—and with this people reported experiences of lucid dreaming close to 90 percent of the time.

HAMILTON: Oh wow, that's interesting.

So once this technology is miniaturized and mass-produced, it will allow people to have lucid dreams on command. There's also a lot of drugs that can help with that too; I have a whole chapter in my book Dreaming Wide Awake *where I experiment with all the different drugs, nutrients, and herbs reputed to enhance dreaming. As you say, people are so afraid of using drugs, and I think this is because they actually work. Maybe once these transcranial brain-stimulation lucid-dream machines become more popular, people will be talking about how bad they are for you too, because of the taboos that you just described.*

HAMILTON: Ah-ha! I agree with you there.

So this is something that I've really pondered a lot, and often ask my psychedelically experienced interview subjects about. What are your thoughts about the beings and entities that people seemingly encounter and interact with on DMT, salvia, or ketamine journeys? Do you ever entertain the possibility that these so-called beings, or spirits, could be advanced aliens, independently minded beings that inhabit another dimension of reality, or do you think that they're simply projections of our imagination and complex hallucinations?

HAMILTON: I think that they're projections of our imagination, and I don't think that makes them any less interesting. If anything, I think that's more interesting. I've always been fascinated by the supernatural and I love horror movies. I love accounts of people who live in haunted houses, and I think whenever you read an account of something like *The Amityville Horror*, there're two ways of interpreting it.

You have the first way, which is to assume that there is some kind of supernatural intervention; there's a family that is being haunted and tormented by beings from another dimension. Or there's an even more interesting interpretation, which is that the family's belief system terrifies them to such an extent that they experienced a shared psychosis, a group hallucination of all sorts of horrific things happening, that was so profound that they ran out of the house, leaving all of their belongings behind, and moved to California. You can't fathom the abilities of people to create and concoct these amazing visions, but it happens every night when we sleep. So I do believe that the best explanation is that these beings, when people experience them, are some kind of hallucination. But I don't think that diminishes them in any way. I think that makes them all the more fascinating.

I'm a materialist and I try to base my beliefs on the best evidence I can find. I'm aware that what we can know represents a miniscule fraction of the fabric of reality, but I am at peace with the unknown and the ambiguity that represents. People tend to think scientific materialists or rationalists are know-it-alls who have stripped all wonder and mystery from the world, but I think it's very much the opposite. I think it's the most honest confrontation with the unknown, to not make up stories but accept what you don't know and what can't be known. I don't believe that DMT visions represent entry into alternate universes where elves and other entities are as real as you and I, because I have seen no evidence for that. I haven't experienced anything like that myself and I think that hallucinations are a better explanation, but I don't claim to understand exactly why these visions occur or what they mean. I would rather not know than delude myself with a false explanation.

I haven't had these elf-type experiences myself, interestingly, and that makes it very easy for me to dismiss them. I have never had any of this kind of interaction with a non-human entity as a result of using even very high doses of DMT. I've had incredibly profound things happen, but nothing that I would equate with the sorts of visual phenomena that Terence McKenna describes. I've seen cat faces turn into the faces of professors. I've watched my face age into an old man and then turn into a skeleton. These are very profound visual experiences, but they did not involve any interaction with elves or aliens or anything like that.

I value your perspective on this. However, I've had this experience of interacting with these unusual beings, and it is very compelling, let me tell you. They seem to know you better than you know yourself, and it's very hard to dismiss this once you've had the experience of seeming interaction. It would be like talking to you right now and trying to wrap my head around the idea that I'm interacting with a hallucination. I encounter the same idea when I'm in a lucid dream too; I'm not sure if the characters that I'm talking to are projections of my own mind, or if they're somehow independently minded. In any case, what do you see as some of the most exciting technological developments and scientific advances going on in the world today?

HAMILTON: It's interesting. Chemistry is what I care about more than anything, and so the things that excite me are often not all that exciting to other people. But I love this gradual expansion of understanding of the structure-activity relationship of tryptamines and phenethylamines. The introduction of the N-Benzyl phenethylamines is considered a negative thing by most of the psychedelic community because they were being sold as LSD and a few deaths have been attributed to them. But from a pharmacological standpoint this is a really amazing discovery that has allowed us to better understand the way these psychedelics bind to the 5-HT2A receptor, and what structural determinants are required.

I love seeing this gradual expansion and natural product research as well. Recently they found Salvinorin A is present in a number of other salvia species, over twenty other salvia species.

Really? Wow, I didn't know that.

HAMILTON: Yeah, and that's an amazing discovery. This went from being something that was only known to exist in one organism, to something that now exists in over twenty organisms. And this is a result of people doing this basic research on the natural world. And I love that. I love seeing a gradually expanded understanding of what kinds of chemicals exist in the ocean. What are all these soft corals biosynthesizing? And what kind of uses might those natural products have? Or we still don't really know what the pharmacology of a lot of these alkaloids in plants like peyote do. There's still so much basic research left to be done, and I just love seeing this gradual expansion of our understanding.

For a long time, there was a hypothetical biosynthetic route through which mushrooms would produce psilocybin that had to include an intermediary compound called 4-hydroxy-NMT, and it had never been found in a mushroom, and this was always very curious to me. If this is a necessary intermediate in the biosynthesis of psilocybin, then why has nobody ever found it? And then somebody found it last year, and I love seeing things like that, just a gradual strengthening of our understanding of the natural world. I'm aware there're big things happening, but the things that I really love are the little things.

Oh, that's beautiful to hear. When you look around at what's happening in the world these days, do you think the human species will survive the next hundred years or do you think we're doomed to extinction?

HAMILTON: Of course I don't know, but I'm confident that humans will survive. I don't know if the world as we know it will survive. It might be the case that things are a lot worse for the humans that do survive. There've been all sorts of science fiction visions of the future, and one that I like a lot is *Make Room! Make Room!* I don't know if you're familiar with this book, but it was adapted into the film *Soylent Green*. I think the vision of the future in that book is a very realistic one, which is that there isn't an apocalypse, the world doesn't end, but things get really bad for most people.

All the things that we value are eroded. You're cramped. It's hard to get water. It's hard to get food. The government sanctions euthanasia clinics, and all sorts of weird strategies to cope with overpopulation, and things like that. Actually, it's not that I even think that government-sanctioned euthanasia clinics are necessarily a bad thing, I don't really disagree with that, but the idea that in the future, it won't be the end, it will be somewhere in the middle. It won't be a total apocalypse, but if we don't make some radical changes to the way we treat the environment, things are going to become really miserable for any humans that are left.

It sounds like you've pretty much answered my next question. If we do survive, how do you envision the future development or evolution of the human species, in say ten years, fifty years, and beyond?

HAMILTON: It really depends on these oligarchs and how greedy they want to be, and of course how seriously people take their personal responsibility and simple issues like recycling and limiting their emissions—because I think living in a liberal New York enclave, most people consider themselves environmentalists in some sense of the word, yet very few people are willing to make real sacrifices for the environment.

I've only met one person in my life who has ever said I will not take a plane somewhere, because I don't want to be a part of contributing to the emissions from that airplane ride. Yet there's no question that we almost all contribute to this. I don't drive a car, but my carbon footprint is pretty serious as a result of all the international traveling that I do, and I justify it by saying, well whatever, the plane's going to fly with or without me, so I might as well get on the ride and make these films. But we all have to take a certain responsibility and make sacrifices, and that's very hard for people to do.

So I don't know what is going to happen, but [*exhales*] I think, if I really had to guess, I would say that things are going to get really frightening for a little while, and this might cause people to come to their senses—but by then it will be a little bit too late. Then there'll be some reversal of the damage, but things will never be quite the same, and we will have learned a hard lesson that will probably have eroded a lot of coastal communities and resulted in the extinction of many species.

Yes, from an ecological point of view, these are pretty scary times. Do you see the use of psychedelic plants and fungi as a way of increasing our collective ecological awareness?

HAMILTON: I think they will have that effect for some people but not for everyone, and I find that so interesting as well. Terence McKenna and many people have this idea that there's a message contained in these molecules, and I can of course think of no physical, materialist reason that that would be the case. How can a molecule contain ideas that are directly transmitted into a brain via ingestion?

The DNA molecule encodes an enormous library of genetic information.

HAMILTON: Yes, but that's a different sort of information. It does seem to be the case that the people that take these substances often gain an increased appreciation for the environment. Maybe that has to do with an increased appreciation of beauty that psychedelics can promote. You take them and you go outside and you realize how beautiful plants are and how terrible it would be if they didn't exist—so you want to do everything in your power to prevent plants and animals from being killed due to our frivolous desire to use shopping bags and plastic water bottles, or whatever else.

How do you envision the future relationship between human biology, advanced robotics, and artificial intelligence?

HAMILTON: I did a piece about AI a couple years ago, and I interviewed a lot of the big names in that world. People like Nick Bostrom have these ideas of AI taking over and say that they may pose a catastrophic risk to the human race, and I think that's unlikely. But at the same time, I've personally experienced the power of it. I've played the board game Go my entire life, and it's a game that's very important to me. If you were telling an outsider about why Go is an interesting game, one of the main things you would tell people is that this is a game that's so simple that it could be taught to a child, yet so complicated that even the world's most powerful supercomputers are incapable of even coming close to beating a proficient human player. This made Go feel like some kind of emblem for the complexity of human consciousness.

I always really romanticized that aspect of Go. Then I was at the first game in South Korea, where the human champion Lee Sedol was beat by Google's AlphaGo, and I saw the impact of that on the human players who dedicated their life to the game. Suddenly this fundamental aspect of the game, that it couldn't be played effectively by a computer, had changed, and it was really a profound moment for me. I don't know what's going to happen with any of it, but I think it's pretty clear at this point that it's going to take us in very unexpected directions.

I don't know if you follow this game at all, but one of the most interesting things about it was that there was a move at one point in the game, and when the computer made this move, everybody thought, oh here you go, the computer isn't that great after all. It just made this completely ridiculous move. No human would ever make that move. This is just another example of why it's going to be decades before a computer is capable of beating a human champion.

Then it wasn't until far later in the game that people recognized that this apparent error on the part of the computer was in fact a move of unfathomable brilliance—that it had done something that no human would ever do, and no human would ever think to do. So those are the sorts of things that make it hard to say what the future of this will be, because it might be the case that it is pushing us in directions that we would never even consider, and how do you begin to evaluate the wisdom of those decisions?

What do you think of the idea that reality, as we know it, is actually a computer simulation?

HAMILTON: Again, I guess this falls into the issues that I had with most ideas that aren't, I feel, evidence based. I don't think there's strong evidence for that. Of course it's a possibility, but I haven't encountered evidence that I find convincing for that to be the case. It's sort of an interesting idea philosophically, and it's an interesting idea emotionally—because when I think about it, for whatever reason, I feel less afraid. It actually makes me feel good to imagine that reality is a simulation, because suddenly I think, well if this is a simulation then nothing matters, and then life truly is a game, so there's nothing stopping me from doing anything. I think that's almost a psychedelic idea to have as well, this idea that if everything is a game, then there are no limitations, and let me do whatever I desire in this game.

Or if everything is a dream.

HAMILTON: Or everything is a dream. It's inspiring, because I think that the seriousness can really weigh down on people—the seriousness of being alive.

Do you think that physical immortality is possible and desirable for our species?

HAMILTON: I think this is very interesting as well, because for the entirety of human history, I guarantee we have always believed this. We always thought it was possible, and the delusion evolves as our technology evolves. In the past it might be this or that plant, this or that potion, or the philosopher's stone. Or the fountain of youth, a certain spell, the blood of young virgins, or whatever. But there was always this belief that there was something out there, and if you had access to it, it would give you immortality. Now we have Ray Kurzweil and different people saying, oh it's going to come in the form of uploading your mind onto a computer. Look, my phone can't even spell-check my text messages effectively. There is no way that my consciousness is going to be uploaded onto a computer before I die, I can guarantee that.

It's a very romantic idea, but it would require nothing less than curing virtually every known disease, something we are nowhere near accomplishing. This is simply not happening anytime in the near future and probably won't happen ever.

I just went to a screening of a film about this project called the Blue Brain Project, where they're trying to map every single neuron in the brain of a mouse. One idea that was presented was that after they've mapped every neuron, they can do simple behavioral experiments on this simulated mouse, and if it behaves the same way as a real mouse, then they will have recreated a brain. There were a lot people at the screening of this film who were very excited by this idea, and they were saying, "Oh this is going to be great for animal welfare, because now they'll be able to test drugs on this digital model, as opposed to having to sacrifice animals in scientific experiments." And again, there's no way that's happening anytime in the near future.

Even if they're able to map every single neuron in the brain they're still not doing it on a molecular level. They're only doing it on a neuronal circuitry level, or on a connectome level. On a molecular level we have not even crystallized the protein structure of the 5-HT2A receptor, which is the most widely expressed serotonin receptor in the human brain. We do not know fundamental aspects of molecular neuropharmacology, so there's no way that there could be an *in silico* model that would allow you to evaluate drugs that effectively. We're just not there yet, and maybe I shouldn't say never, because yes, it will likely be possible one day, but we're not close.

What do you dream about, have you ever had a lucid dream, and do dreams affect your creative work?

HAMILTON: Yes, I was very interested in lucid dreaming. I've read *Exploring the World of Lucid Dreaming* by Stephen LaBerge, and I did the things that are recommended in that book, like keeping a dream journal.

I don't know if it was the specific instructions in that book, or simply by virtue of thinking about dreaming more, but I found that through whatever it is—if you're thinking about dreaming and reading about dreaming—you're that much more likely *to think about dreaming while you're dreaming.* And I did have a small number of lucid dreams during the period when I was really actively involved in reading about and thinking about dreams. But then I had this second issue of, well how do I know it's a lucid dream, and not a dream of a lucid dream? Couldn't I just as easily dream of lucidity?

Well, in lucid dream though, you can carry out specific instructions that you had set out to do previously. Then you can experiment with those behaviors in the dream, and personally see what the results are—or even signal to an outside observer with coordinated eye movements, using the proper technology.

HAMILTON: Right. Yeah, which I thought, of course, was a brilliant way to demonstrate the existence of lucid dreams. But still, *from my experience*, I could never be sure, because I wasn't skilled enough to do some kind of coordinated eye movement with an outside observer and an EEG monitor to evaluate the reality of all these things. So maybe there are some people that have had real lucid dreams, but I'm not sure that I have. However, I've certainly, at the very least, had dreams of lucid dreams.

You talked earlier about doing a microdose of ibogaine, and a number of people have reported that they start having lucid dream experiences from doing that.

HAMILTON: Oh, that's interesting. I've not had any memorable dreams after taking low-dose ibogaine.

I have a report in my book Dreaming Wide Awake *from someone who talks about how he began having lucid dreams every night while experimenting with low daily doses of ibogaine.*

HAMILTON: I've also been smoking cannabis at night, so maybe that has interfered.

Possibly. Studies show that cannabis reduces REM sleep, and people often report having a flood of dreams when they stop using it regularly. Hamilton, I'm curious, what do you personally think happens to consciousness after physical death and the deterioration of the brain?

HAMILTON: I'm probably the least interesting person to talk to about this, all of these things, because I really am a pretty staunch materialist.

I believe that consciousness is a product of the brain, and as the brain begins to decompose, consciousness too will decompose. In the same way that if you're shot in the brain, you lose your consciousness. I think if you die you lose your consciousness as well.

I think that ideas of the afterlife are very attractive in the same vein as these ideas of biological immortality that are promoted by Aubrey de Grey and Ray Kurzweil, because we're afraid of death. We're really afraid of dying. I think it's the ultimate fear—the overarching fear, the umbrella fear that encompasses all other fears. And through our religious and philosophical notions, and even through art, for generations, we have created different fantasy structures to avoid the harsh reality that there is no reason not to believe that when we die everything is over for us.

As far as I know, we have one opportunity to be alive and that's it, and you have to enjoy it because there's nothing else. There's no reincarnation. There's no life after death. You don't enter into some kind of eternal trip. That's it. It's over. It scary. It's really scary, but because I've never encountered a convincing reason to believe otherwise, that's what I believe. That's it, and it makes me value life more. I think that it makes me value the lives of the people around me. I'm not going to see my parents after I die. After my parents are dead, they're gone. I'll never see them again, so I have to enjoy every moment with them while they're alive.

Isn't it interesting that we find nonexistence so scary, and yet that was what we were before we were born, right? And it didn't seem to bother us then. I suspect that the fear of death is genetically wired into us as a trait that helps us to survive evolutionarily, and that's why we're so afraid of it. Hamilton, you've defined yourself as an atheist and a materialist. Have you ever had a religious or mystical experience on a psychedelic, and what is your perspective on the concept of god or divinity?

HAMILTON: Yes, I have actually, when I smoked the venom of *Bufo alvarius* [the Sonoran Desert toad, which contains 5-MeO-DMT] last year. I did have a sort of religious experience, which was very interesting to me because I am an atheist, and not only do I not believe in god, I find the idea of god somewhat annoying. In the wake of this experience I found myself temporarily—it lasted about ten days—feeling that there was some kind of godlike presence. And this was not a rationally derived conclusion. This was just a feeling that I had, that there was some kind of godlike thing that existed, and I don't know. I've lost it. It doesn't exist anymore. It's just a memory of a feeling that I had for a period, and it was very strange because it was totally uncharacteristic of me.

Art by Nichelle Mitchell

But what it made me appreciate is that, of course, all of these beliefs are biochemically mediated. In the same way that there have been instances of people that develop right orbitofrontal tumors and suddenly they are pedophiles as a result. Then they remove the tumor and they're not a pedophile anymore. I think that there are certain ways of pharmacologically inducing a religious experience and belief in god, and then those things can disappear. This has been done with transcranial magnetic stimulation as well.

Most interesting. Do you think that life has a purpose, and if so, what do you think it is?

HAMILTON: Evolutionarily, the purpose is to procreate and protect your offspring, socially the purpose is to help others. I try to make the world a better place. But, in some sense, you have to define your own purpose, and that will be different for every person depending on what you're good at. I don't think there is one single purpose.

But for me, I just believe in doing whatever I can. I like to write, and to make these videos, and I love to synthesize new compounds. Those are the things that I can do, so those are the things that I do, but that will vary from person to person. That's a big question. I don't know that I can give you the best answer to the purpose of life. You're really going for the big ones.

Yes, that's what I do, that's my purpose. What are some of the psychedelic drugs or plants that you haven't tried yet and that you'd like to try one day?

HAMILTON: I will say that I have been pretty methodical in trying things. I've tried a lot of what's out there. The things that I haven't tried at this point tend to be pretty obscure. So what really interests me are things that nobody has tried, more than say, oh I'd really like to go to Gabon and do a traditional iboga ceremony. As much as I would like to do that, what's even more interesting is well, what happens with 2C-B if you add a second bromine atom into the three positions, so that you have the di-bromo-2C-B? No one's ever synthesized that before. It's hard to synthesize for a number of reasons, but it's possible. So what about that?

I have lots of specific molecules that I would like to synthesize and evaluate, and those are the things that matter most to me, the things that nobody knows what they do—the true unknown. Or another example would be these plants. I keep a lot of Google Scholar Alerts, so I'm constantly reading about new things that are found in plants. There's a mushroom called *Rhodocollybia maculata* that contains a Salvinorin A–type chemical, and there's some preliminary rodent behavioral work that's been done with this that suggests it has a Salvinorin A–type activity.

So this could be a completely new type of psychedelic mushroom that no human has ever tried, and it could be a totally different type of psychedelic experience. There are things out there, I guarantee, that can create new types of psychedelic experiences that nobody has ever experienced, waiting to be discovered. So I'm very much concerned with the unknown, with finding out what's out there.

What are you currently working on with your chemistry research?

HAMILTON: My work has been dedicated to synthesis of derivatives of DiPT. For about the last eight years, I've synthesized a very large variety of different derivatives of DiPT with a chemist named Jason Wallach. We have had the opportunity to send them off for pharmacological screening, as part of a program called PDSP that screens different psychedelics, at over forty different receptors. And one of the most interesting things that we found is that these DiPT derivatives don't really bind to any known serotonin receptors with a very high affinity, so however it's exerting its effect on auditory perception, it's not doing it through a known receptor system, at least in terms of what are called "G-protein coupled receptors." But it's possible that it exerts its effects through ion channels. So I'm now having these compounds screened at ion channels, to see if that might represent a target.

Every now and then you encounter something that really does something strange and there are many such instances documented in

PiHKAL and *TiHKAL*. An example would be a compound that's described in *TiHKAL* called 5-MeO-pyr-T, and this compound induces a sort of dissociative fugue state, probably through the 5-HT1A receptor, although people don't really know. The effect is totally unlike a classical psychedelic. I actually happen to know the chemist who authored the report in *PiHKAL*, as it was not Shulgin. He was a graduate student of David Nichols, and he synthesized this compound, smoked an overdose of it, stripped nude, ran into the town square, and was arrested.

Oh my god.

HAMILTON: He woke up in a jail cell, with no identification. They didn't know who he was because he was naked, and he had what he considered to be one of the greatest experiences of his entire life. He woke up out of it in a jail cell, in a state of revelatory religious enthusiasm, like he had had a transcendent experience, even though this of course sounds absolutely terrible and resulted in him being kicked out of David Nichols's laboratory.

So this was a very serious thing that had happened to him, and he must have been aware intellectually that this is a very bad thing, that he had taken a drug from a serious academic lab. He'd overdosed on it. He'd been arrested and the political ramifications of this would have to necessitate him being fired from the program. Yet even in the midst of all of that, he felt that what had happened to him was amazing. So that really says something about the character or power of this substance, and people don't even know how it does it.

Wow, that certainly does say something about the power of it. That's a remarkable story. Has anybody interviewed him or talked about what his experience was? I'm so curious.

HAMILTON: I have. I'll say one more thing about him. After being fired from David Nichols's lab, he ended up inventing the drug Vyvanse, which is one of the most profitable pharmaceuticals in the United States, so he made a billion-dollar drug after this fiasco, which is pretty amazing as well. He was a serious guy then. He did important scientific research when he was in Nichols's lab. What was the question again?

We were just talking about your latest chemistry research.

HAMILTON: Yeah, so there're so many interesting things out there. You know the pharmacologies of these substances start to bleed into one another. With a compound like MDA, you have something that's at this crossroad of a MDMA-type serotonin releaser and a classical psychedelic. Well, what about that territory? How can you push that further? You have a compound that's not very well known called NsBT [N-s-butyl-tryptamine] that Shulgin wrote about very briefly in *TiHKAL*, and this is a tryptamine that seems to produce a sedative-type effect that's very relaxing and wonderful. And then you wonder, okay, well what about this?

What does this represent? The crossroads of a psychedelic and GABAergic anxiolytic, or maybe something else entirely. Then you have things like ibogaine, where you're at a crossroad between a classical psychedelic and an NMDA antagonist and also a nicotinic receptor antagonist. So I think the polypharmacology of some of these substances is something that's really interesting to explore as well. And we're going to continually refine these structures, figuring out how to make them as useful as possible. Maybe this is my scientist materialist attitude of always thinking we could have more. We could make it better. Nature is good, but humans can improve things, and that could be fun as well. It might be that ibogaine is perfect and psilocybin is perfect, and there's nothing that humans can do to make it better, but it's certainly worth probing to figure it out.

4

Exploring the Interface between Technological Evolution, Mythopoetic Perspectives, and High Weirdness

An Interview with Erik Davis

Erik Davis is a writer, scholar, journalist, and public speaker, whose trademark writing style alternates between empirical and mythopoetic points of view. In his work he explores countercultural expression, anomalous phenomena, and altered states of consciousness from multiple perspectives.

Davis is probably best known for his landmark book *TechGnosis: Myth, Magic & Mysticism in the Age of Information*, which brilliantly investigates the historical connections between mysticism and technology. Originally published in 1998, this cult classic has been translated into five languages and was republished in 2015.

Davis studied literature and philosophy at Yale University and earned his Ph.D. in religious studies at Rice University in 2015. His doctoral thesis was later published by the MIT Press in 2019 under the title *High Weirdness: Drugs, Esoterica, and Visionary Experience in the Seventies*. Davis hosted the "Expanding Mind" podcast on the Progressive Radio Network for ten years, and he has written for many popular publications, such as the *Village Voice*, *Rolling Stone*, and *Wired*.

In addition to *TechGnosis* and *High Weirdness*, Davis is the author of several other books, *Nomad Codes: Adventures in Modern Esoterica*;

Erik Davis

Visionary State: A Journey through California's Spiritual Landscape; and *Led Zeppelin's Led Zeppelin IV (33 1/3)*. I especially loved *High Weirdness*, which profiles the strange, life-changing, quasi-mystical experiences that Terence McKenna, Robert Anton Wilson, and Philip K. Dick had. It's not easy to say anything really new about these men's historical encounters with "high weirdness," but Davis's compelling perspective was unique indeed. To find out more about Davis's work, see the TechGnosis website. He also publishes the Substack newsletter *Burning Shore*.

I interviewed Erik on October 10, 2020. Erik is unusually articulate, speaks in measured sentences, and at times almost seems to have the supernatural ability to voice the ineffable. I've admired his work for years, and had only met him briefly before this interview, several years ago, so I was delighted to have this time to really explore his mind in depth. We spoke about the relationship between technology and mysticism, conspiracy theories, the fine line between empiricism and poetic expression, and the pesky philosophical nature of those mysterious DMT entities.

How did you first become interested in writing and the exploration of consciousness?

ERIK: That's a good question. I've actually just been looking at my old writings from back in high school. I was a young druggie, a high-school stoner, an acidhead—but I was always pretty much an intellectual. From the get-go, I was into reading, philosophy, and religion, and I thought a lot. So for me, psychedelics and cannabis were more than just a lot of fun; they were also part of a *metaphysical quest*, and in high school I was already writing essays that were related to some of the things that I continue to write about today.

So, in some sense, I've been doing this since I was a kid. And for me the connection of consciousness and consciousness experiences with intellectual work has always been very intimate. So even though altered states provide an escape from the intellect to some degree, I was always interested in how they meet as well. So altered states have always been an inspiration for my writing, sometimes quite explicitly and sometimes more in terms of an ambiance or a kind of field of interest.

In your book TechGnosis you explore the intriguing historical connections between mysticism and technology. It's such a brilliant book. I read it years ago and reread it again to prepare for this interview. Although basically the subject of your whole book, can you just briefly for our readers, in a nutshell, explain how the driving force behind technological innovation and development can't be easily separated from the spiritual, mythic, and poetic dimensions of reality?

ERIK: Sure. I think probably the best way to approach that is to recognize that we have an idea—I think probably less so now, but earlier in the twentieth century for sure—that technology and technological development was definitely associated with rationality. And it makes sense. From the Enlightenment forward, you have the growth of science and industry and an increasingly rationalized society, with systems, procedures, and algorithms. This is not just in terms of science and technology but also in terms of how society gets run.

And so we can fool ourselves to believe that human beings themselves have somehow transcended the non-rational, and I take it from the get-go that that's just not the case. In fact, the way that we've denied the non-rational side, at least mainstream consensus civilization, makes us unaware of how much these non-rational forces are inside the motivations, the fantasies, the constructions, and the desires that motivate the particular way that technology has manifested in our world. So I wanted to show the history of that, and how these things have been connected since the beginning.

While I talk about lots of different kinds of technologies, I focus really on electronics, and particularly on technological media. This is because, of all the forms of technology, media is the most obviously bound up with the totality of the human soul—with our subconscious, with our fears, our nightmares, our transcendence, and our capacities for transcendence, as well as with our yen for altered states. The whole kit and caboodle of human culture and consciousness is now mediated through technologies. So by looking at those media technologies through the lenses of mythology, mysticism, altered states, or straight-up religion, you actually can see more of what we're doing, and gain a richer view of the nature of the conundrum we find ourselves in.

I can't tell you how much I loved your book High Weirdness. *Terence [McKenna] and Bob [Robert Anton Wilson] were both good friends and important inspirations in my life, and I've always loved Philip K. Dick's unusually creative novels. I know that it's hard to say anything new and original about these enigmatic men, so I just savored every word from your unique perspective.*

ERIK: Well, I really appreciate that, David. That means a lot coming from you. I knew Terence pretty well, but I didn't know Bob well, although I had met him and hung out with him some. So it's meaningful to me that someone who knew them personally as well, and who was deeply influenced by their work, says that. So thanks for that.

Thank you, Erik. So, you've said that "all three men spent time in something like psychosis or paranoid pathology," and what you've termed "high weirdness." Can you describe what you mean by the term high weirdness, how this relates to paranoid pathologies, and what it is about this phenomenon that ties the strange experiences of these three remarkable men together?

ERIK: Well, what I really wanted to do was to talk about experiences and the texts or the meanings that come from those experiences in a way that simultaneously respects their religious or mystical or mythopoetic dimension on the one hand, and on the other, recognizes that in other ways they are sort of confusing, chaotic, and even pathological. Now people who are down on altered states will often talk about them in pathological terms. They'll pathologize mystics, New Agers, religious people, Pentecostals in fits of ecstasy. They'll look at those experiences in psychological terms as a way to take the mystery out of the phenomenon, and just say, hey this is some psychological weirdness. But I think there is something really important there.

Weirdness is a term that you can use among secular people. Everybody knows something that's weird; what a weird thing feels like, when things are uncomfortable, when they're strange, when they're anomalous. There's no supernatural claim made when you say something is weird. So there's that side of it. But on the other hand, a lot of people who respect, and are fascinated by, and have had experiences of anomalous cognition—of altered states, of transcendental visions, and non-dual ecstasies—tend to sweep the pathological side of these experiences under the carpet, for obvious reasons.

So I wanted to try to look at both sides, almost at the same time, or at least with one lens that was focused on the supernatural or the mystical and one lens on the psychopathological. So for me, "high weirdness" captures that. It's not my original term, but it captures it in the sense that I still want to say that transcendental experiences all might just be part of what human primates do when they encounter nervous system anomalies, psychoactive drugs, or weird cultural practices of ecstasy,

But even if we never leave that naturalistic realm, *it's so weird* that it almost bursts the ceiling and you get this phenomenon of high weirdness, where you can't really resolve things either way. It's ontologically up for grabs. And that's what makes all three of these guys very interesting: they were all aware of the pathological, or the potentially pathological, dimension of their experiences. They wrote about it, but they were unwilling to simply reduce their experiences to those perspectives.

Would you like to say something about the continuum or relationship that you see between mysticism and psychosis, or between spirituality and psychopathology in general?

ERIK: Sure, I could take that on. The advisor for my Ph.D. was Jeff Kripal.

Oh, I loved his book* Mutants and Mystics: Science Fiction, Superhero Comics, and the Paranormal. *My interview with Jeffrey is included in this book.

ERIK: He has also written a lot about the connection between trauma—including pathological trauma or psychological trauma—and the paranormal. While I wasn't interested in evoking the full zone of the paranormal, I do talk about it to some degree, and it's important for all three of these guys. I do think that there's something to be gained by recognizing that mysticism, mystical experiences, mythopoetic experiences, and paranormal experiences are on a continuum.

And on that same continuum, we also have schizophrenic voices in the head and paranoid ideation. Now nobody wants to be around that, it's not fun for anybody, including the person who is undergoing it. At the same time, some of those same patterns can be found in very creative, extraordinary individuals who seem to manage to integrate these experiences. Maybe they create new mythologies or new religious practices or new fictions. So it's important to respect that full spectrum and the fact that most of the time it's a bit of a mixture. So for me, that just feels like an important way of entering these larger questions, but it was particularly appropriate for these guys, and indeed for the whole environment for the 1970s.

You said in a recent interview that "the world is chaos and nobody really knows what's going on." Can you explain how you think that this insight can be both frightening and liberating, and how it allows one to embrace what the late writer Robert Anton Wilson called "radical agnosticism"?

ERIK: Yes, I'm very much influenced by Wilson in that sense. It's also a bit of a risky position, because it can be read as saying that science doesn't have any meaning, or that some guy babbling on the corner about QAnon has the same reality quotient as the doctors who live near me at UCSF who are studying the coronavirus, and trying to figure out how it works—*and I'm not saying that.*

I do think we have to make choices. It's not easy, and there is certainly a multiplicity of truths. There are many ways of approaching what's going on. The fact that there are many ways of perceiving the world means that I can look at something psychologically, but I can also look at it in terms of religion. I can also look at it in terms of the non-dual nature of reality. I can also look at it in terms of historical patterns that are manifesting themselves. *But how do I put all those things together?*

To me, the fact that you can't put them all together in an easy way *is the chaos.* So it's not chaos like it's all just a complete Jackson Pollock painting. It's that we have to maneuver through these multiple perspectives, and do it responsibly—but also to recognize that certainty is almost always a sign that you're not looking at the full picture. So for me this is another way of approaching some of the things that Wilson talks about in terms of radical agnosticism, which means being able to work and actually be productive as you move between different perspectives where nobody captures the flag.

It's not just, hey, nobody knows, or every perspective is the same. People often criticize postmodernism for saying, oh every narrative is the same, you can't choose. That's not what I'm saying at all. To me radical agnosticism means the willingness, and the capability, for working productively within different frameworks. It also means recognizing that how and why and when you move between frameworks is not a done deal and that that's part of the art of navigating reality.

Can you speak a little about the psychological process of what you call leaving the "mainstream narrative" and "narrative control"? How is this breaking down for many people during these chaotic times, and how does this relate to the proliferation of what people have termed conspiracy theories?

ERIK: Those are big questions, but I'd like to try to keep it short. One way of looking at how civilization or societies proceed is that they have these master narratives. I already mentioned postmodernism as a place in the history of the West when those master narratives started to break down, and now we have a very obvious multiplicity of narratives.

I think one of the things that's happening now—because of media, because of Trump, because of Covid, and because of the nature of the historical forces that were set in motion a very long time ago, at least in terms of the West—have all reached this point where the multiplicity of these narratives, and the sneaking suspicion that maybe none of them are really correct, is now a widespread experience.

Now psychonauts like you and me, in some sense, were actually looking for this conundrum for decades and decades. We wanted to confront these breakdowns and to find out what's behind the veil, and as we proceeded we recognized that, in a way, things just get more confusing even as they become more interesting. A lot of people weren't looking for that sort of thrilling confusion, but now there's no way to avoid it, and one of the responses that I think a lot of people have when they confront the uncertainty that is at the heart of this multiple narrative situation is to retreat into a single absolute narrative.

Now, someone may be convinced that the mainstream narrative isn't true for perfectly legitimate reasons. Not that there's one mainstream narrative; what we mean by the mainstream is many different things, but let's just put it that way. If you are convinced that the mainstream narrative is not true, it's much easier to then fall into the next available counternarrative, and then redirect the certainty you once had in the mainstream toward the new narrative. And that's the classic scenario. Well, not classic, but that's what you see with a lot of conspiracy thinking today.

For example, let's say I don't believe that I'm hearing everything that I want to know about 5G technology and what this is doing to our bodies. Like I have a fundamental suspicion about that, and I've grown to distrust all of these authorities for various reasons—some legitimate, some maybe not so smart, but whatever, and so there I am. Where do I go? Do I then recognize that I have to do the hard work of reading scientific papers, recognizing that science doesn't have complete answers, that there're multiple views, and recognize that it's a hairy problem that doesn't have an easy solution?

Or do I attach myself to a somewhat ready-made but also creatively evolving conspiratorial narrative that acknowledges the problem of the mainstream truth, but also provides me with certainty, so that I can emotionally, psychologically, and intellectually land somewhere? At the same time, I find myself in a tight-knit community. I have connections with people, and we're fighting the good fight against the forces of darkness.

These are religious patterns, in some ways, and their certainty becomes very attractive in a situation where the rest of us are going, my god, the world is complicated as hell. It's just getting more hairy, the problems more wicked, and increasingly difficult to get beyond that sense of overwhelming complexity, at least in regard to many of the major topics of our lives these days.

I loved your book Visionary State, *as moving to California when I was young was one of the most important decisions of my life. Why do you think that the population of California has so much tolerance for differences, so much cultural creativity, and such a zest for experimentation? Do you see this frontier spirit here as being connected to the westward migration that humanity has been on for thousands of years, perhaps as a way to liberate ourselves from our previous societal, political, psychological, or*

religious constraints and to explore and experiment with new cul-
tural possibilities? Or what? Why do you think that California is
so special?

ERIK: I think it's rooted in historical experiences of the place, in terms of the kinds of people who came here. I mean, some people even argue that there's a genetic predisposition for risk-taking in the population in California.

I don't know about that, but it's a reasonable gesture toward the fact that the place drew a certain kind of person, although that pioneer spirit can also be overstated and easily mythologized. California was industrialized faster than most parts of the United States. It was always under the thumb of the federal government, a lot of the innovative developments here are a part of a whole national plan for the place. So it's important not to overemphasize the kind of liberated and experimental quality of the place.

Nonetheless, it clearly *was* that sort of place for a lot of people. There's also a health angle. Many people in the late nineteenth and early twentieth century moved to California for their health, and there was correspondingly this explosion of healing technologies and holistic modalities here in California. These got people engaged with all sorts of curious mind-body practices, breathing practices, sun bathing, and such. So that becomes part of the culture as well. It's also on the Pacific Rim, and while that's partly just a psycho-geographical fact, it is also the case that there is a more direct encounter with the East historically.

Politically, the encounter is not a very pleasant one in terms of the suppression of the Chinese and the internment of the Japanese. I mean, in some ways it's a horror story, just the way that the relationship with Indigeneity in California is a horror story, and a particularly bad one, by the way. Nonetheless, the presence of Asian culture and Indigenous cultures here also created a space for a different and more creative kind of encounter, however problematic. There has also long been a spirit of bohemianism, radicalism, and religious experimentalism in the state, particularly in the Bay Area in terms of the city of San Francisco—

that bohemian culture never went away. So I think all of those elements together played a role in making California what it is.

In the postwar period, all this really just took off. California was inexpensive then, and there was comparatively lots of space for certain folks. It was easy to live here; if you didn't have heat, it was fine. And you had all these people with a little bit of cash from the postwar effort, enough to make an extraordinary life out here. So it just had the perfect conditions for a robust bohemia. All of these elements mixed together and created a culture of esotericism, of experimentation, of altered states, of creative hedonism, and of novel religions.

Here's another way of thinking about it. People talk about how California is like "America's America." America was a place that people from Europe and other parts of the world fantasized about throughout the twentieth century. It's less so today, for obvious reasons, but it still has some of that mythic charge. For a long time, the United States has been seen as a place of new beginnings and new innovative efforts, where people could go with their strange faiths and have a place in a religiously pluralistic culture.

That's how people saw America. But within America, it's like the same set of dreams that were part of this westward expansion were directed toward the West Coast and particularly California. So it carries this westward course, not of *civilization*—although that's part of it too, in terms of Manifest Destiny and the colonialism that comes out of Northern Europe—but also psychologically or mythologically, in terms of a place of transformation, a place of re-embodiment at the end of the Christian story of transcendence, where we come back to the body and find ourselves in nature. But at the same time there are all these marvelous media machines that we can use to build new worlds, and in many ways new oppressions. So it's quite a contradictory, paradoxical, and in some ways pretty messed-up place. But there's nothing like it.

Can you say something about the Great Mystery that lies at the heart of existence, and about how the never-ending anomalies

that continue to occur throughout nature might be cracks in the construct of reality?

ERIK: Whatever we can say and feel pretty solid about, whether in terms of history, physics, biology, or sociology, it is still the case *that all of it rests, in my mind, on a mystery.* Without that recognition there's something limited and somewhat broken about our worldview. And that lack also has lots to do with a lot of the problems that we're in. That's another conversation, perhaps. But the question here is how do we engage with this mystery? Where do we see it? What makes me say that that's the case?

You mentioned the word *anomaly*, and *anomaly* is an interesting one. What is an anomaly? Do they happen because you had certain expectations that were not fulfilled but can be explained in some other way? Well, that's one kind of anomaly. There's another kind of anomaly that's just completely bizarre, and you don't know where to put it. You *can't* really put it anywhere, whether as a scientist or an individual wrestling with some extraordinary experience.

My way of approaching it is not to say, oh these particular anomalies give us a window into the "real truth," which is x, y, and z. A truth like "time doesn't exist," or "everything is fated," or "the laws of physics are being made up as we go along." It's less about crystallizing new truths and more about recognizing that if you're really paying attention, and whatever your knowledge and orientation, you will discover anomalies in your experience and understanding. Part of the work of being human—as a thinking being, a living being, and an inter-relating being, (particularly relating to nature and the cosmos)—is to understand that those relationships and those practices have an irreducible thread of mystery in them.

So I'm less interested in building up a counternarrative based on anomalous elements. I think that people often go south if they do that. They often lose the plot. It can be interesting work and I think sometimes it's important. But I'm more interested in existentially affirming the irruptive ambiance of mystery that surrounds us, that binds us even, and that may come to us in many different ways—through poetry, through religious experience, through paranormal anomalies, or through scientific work. Before such mystery, it's important to keep a space open for awe, wonderment, and befuddlement.

Can you speak a little about how you think the current pandemic is amplifying what's happening in the world, almost like a collective psychedelic experience?

ERIK: I'm still trying to wrap my head around this. I know some people came out and they had all their riffs and takes on the pandemic really quickly, but I see multiple, even contradictory, things happening. On the one hand, everyone is even more isolated. They're spending more time in front of a screen. They're probably spending more time reading the news. It's the only way to connect with what's happening, because you don't really have it in your ordinary life as much.

So, in that sense, we're intensifying the feedback loops of media, fake news, misinformation, and disinformation. It's taking the information overload that we were already involved in and further amplifying it, making it even more hallucinogenic in a way. *The idea that reality is just a story is now the reality.* That recognition can be very unsettling and vertiginous and has a psychedelic edge to it.

At the same time, it seems that some people, ejected from their normal distractions and business as usual, are being forced to be in a much more narrow sensory bandwidth. While those situations of privation can be difficult, and very difficult for some people given their concrete conditions, it also has encouraged some of us to get down to brass tacks about what our values really are, who we really are, and how we are with the world and ourselves—with our own fear, anxiety, and hopes for the future. So I don't want to be a Pollyanna about it. Obviously these are very difficult times, and they seem very likely to become more difficult, but I do think there is a certain kind of grounding factor that is also operating among people, even as it also looks like we're just collectively going crazy.

What are your thoughts about the mysterious entities that people report encountering on DMT? Do you think there's an independent reality to these beings? Do you think that they might be artificial intelligence programs stored in our DNA? Do you think that they're just merely complex hallucinations? Or something else entirely?

ERIK: This gets back to the question about mystery and one way I like to approach that set of questions. You can argue with my approach, whether it's satisfying or not, and that's OK. The approach is to look at those questions as an ethical challenge. By ethical I don't mean moral distinctions between good or bad. I mean how do you live your life? How do you relate to very big, puzzling questions? So when you discover an unresolvable question, there is still work to be done. What does it mean to practice, to engage, to relate, to grow comfortable, if you will, *with* that insolubility?

I believe you can create some pretty robust sociobiological explanations for why entity phenomena are part of the deep structure of the nervous system. It's a profound altered state that is both ecstatic and extremely novel, but also patterned and structured, as DMT clearly is on some levels. There's a geometric dimensionality to it, a deep coherence, so in those kinds of situations I can appreciate why the mind would construct agents in order to mediate the complexity of that environment by drawing from very deep templates of expectation, which may give the experience its ancient, truer-than-true quality.

Am I satisfied with that explanation? No, I'm not. Does that mean that I'm going to wake up the next morning and congeal my hunch that they are AI programs embedded in the DNA, maybe left there by aliens? Or that they are linked to the over-soul of the planet, and they are the same creatures that we see in UFO encounters or fairy lore, or some other kind of speculative construct? Why? It's the morning after. So I'm interested in these stories as contemporary mythologies, and I don't mean *myth* as just mere fictions, but as *truthful stories* about mysterious or enigmatic things. But in terms of my ontological ideas,

I actually believe that the most respectful approach toward the experience of entities *is to hold them in suspense.*

[Laughter] I've been pondering that question for around thirty years now.

ERIK: It's a puzzling one.

As you know, LSD has had a big impact on the development of computer technology and culture. What are your thoughts about what might be the fruit of the growing cultural popularity around DMT, as well as the research of Rick Strassman and Andrew Gallimore—especially with regard to the development of new technologies like more sophisticated virtual reality and Neuralink? Do you see a connection in there?

ERIK: That's a good question. Again, I tend to take a cultural history point of view, and have noticed something, which is that DMT was totally around in the sixties. The guy who made probably the most acid, at least for a long time, behind Orange Sunshine made it.

Nick Sand?

ERIK: Yes, Nick Sand. He cooked up DMT back in the day, even before LSD. The Grateful Dead took DMT. Leary talked about it. Alan Watts talked about it. Allen Ginsberg talked about it. So it was there. It was around. But at the same time, it didn't really land. It didn't really become a deep part of the popular counterculture of psychedelics in the same way that it started to do in the 1990s.

Now we're well into that newer story, where DMT's particular qualities are *dominant* in some ways, in terms of the imagination found in at least certain psychedelic countercultures, some of which have very intimate relationships with technology. I mean, I think of the psytrance scene for one. On one level, it's EDM party music that's enjoyed by a lot of underground characters, global travelers, and the like. The music itself is extremely technical and virtual in its effects, science fictional and cosmological in its aesthetic, and that opens the door toward inspiration for people who are working with technologies.

So better virtual realities, more and more vivid virtual realities, and more and more of that particular kind of multidimensional geometry and a certain kind of intensification of colors. All of those aesthetic elements you can already see in relatively ordinary animation. So I can only imagine how people who are deeply inspired by the DMT flash, who are working at the cutting edge of virtual reality, or information systems as a whole, might be inspired by this realm.

There does seem to be a technical "download from the future" kind of quality to the experience, which may be a mirroring of our particular point of historical inflection in terms of media and technology—meaning that those same experiences might not have been the case if we had people in seventeenth-century France smoking DMT. They might not have gotten the motherboard on the starship rewiring the chakras into some kind of multidimensional information field. *But we get those*, because we're on the cusp of some other kinds of transformations, where those images and those stories have resonance for us and become almost a way to *map* the unknown that lies ahead in terms of radical technological development.

How have psychedelics personally influenced your thinking, your creativity, and your work in general?

ERIK: I'm a lifer, so it's a little funny for me. A lot of writers or thinkers in the psychedelic space come to these things later in their lives than I do. So there's a moment where they can really see, oh, then I had my first acid trip and then things changed. But I've just been this way since I was thirteen, so in a weird way things aren't that different. I can totally see the thumbprints of psychedelics swirling across all my work. I think there's a certain appreciation for mischief and ambiguity, which is something you find in a lot of poets or storytellers. But I'm a nonfiction writer, so I deal with truth, at least with a lower case *t*, and what I actually think about things using history, science, technology, and culture. I'm not a fiction writer. I'm not a storyteller in that sense.

So that's an interesting *tension*. One of the reasons I like

Terence McKenna, Robert Anton Wilson, and Philip K. Dick is while, especially the latter two, were also storytellers, they took their visionary experiences really seriously, and wrote texts that also addressed these larger philosophical and historical problems. These texts have taught me to never fully believe any of the constructs that I'm working in, and to invite a certain psychedelic *je ne sais quoi* into the rhetoric and the direction of my writing.

Here's an example. The worst review that *TechGnosis* got when it came out was from a conservative New York newspaper, and the guy just tore it apart. He hated it. But he had a great line. It was actually well written. I kind of liked the review actually because it was well written and he was having fun, but he said it "had the stench of the bong to it."

[Laughter] **That's hilarious.**

ERIK: I always liked that, because what does it mean to think like drugs, to take drugs and then just try to express that? That's really been an inspiration for me. I like to think I don't do it in a wild, woolly, highly speculative way like some people have done. I do it in a more cautious and grounded way. But I am still trying to write and think drugs.

Besides psychedelic drugs, dreaming can be another great source of creative inspiration. I really enjoyed the book Liminal Dreaming: Exploring Consciousness at the Edge of Sleep, *by your wife, Jennifer, as I wrote a book about lucid dreaming as well. So I'm really curious: have dreams, liminal, lucid, or ordinary dreams, been an inspiration to you or to your work?*

ERIK: I would say that the most powerful connection with my dream life and my work has been my long-standing interest in, let's call it "the false reality" mytheme, whether you see it in fairy tales or in Philip K. Dick novels. Part of my fascination with Philip K. Dick is that he builds these false realities, and there's something in them that doesn't quite fit, and that becomes a crack. Then that crack opens up and the whole reality falls apart, and you're forced to deal with the broken pieces of a reality in light of another one that is yet unclear.

Earlier we talked about anomalies that way. Those experiences definitely are tied in with some of my most memorable dreams, which have the character of being in a certain place and then recognizing that it's not the whole reality. Then finding some crack, or some counternarrative, or indeed, being within a structure that I know is false but I can't find a way out—that kind of mode. So there's a paranoid quality to my imagination that I fully acknowledge and that has manifested itself in my dream life.

I've had a number of very Phil Dickian dreams, sometimes with Phil Dick in them, which is not uncommon among so-called Dick-heads. There's definitely something a little psychoactive about his work that manifests in the dream life. So I would say those are probably the most pertinent connections.

I hadn't heard the expression Dick-head before, in relation to Philip K. Dick; that's really funny. Erik, what do you see as some of the most exciting technological developments and scientific advances going on in the world today?

ERIK: In terms of technology, I have so many critiques, and as someone who had a lot of fun online in the 1990s, am so disappointed with how communications technology, the internet, and personal computers rolled out eventually. That's a whole other conversation, but let's just say that I'm both highly suspicious and not very interested in intensifying the hype around communications technologies and the internet, even though I still use the thing and appreciate aspects of it.

The thing that probably I'm most excited about is material science. We are engineering extraordinary materials, and to my mind, that is the zone where we are most reasonable in expecting possible breakthroughs that could really make a difference in an environmentally worsening world, although maybe not necessarily the differences that we really want to make, in terms of replacing the energy system and getting a hold on climate change. Frankly, I'm pessimistic about any large-scale structural changes any time soon, because the archons running the energy industry are not going to go down easy and they have such extraordinary power.

We're at a very powerless point in history. Most people are very powerless in a lot of ways, and we have to recognize that, even as we commit ourselves to struggle. That said, environmentally I have some hope that there will be breakthroughs in material science, such as new forms of ceramics, new energy sources, or new kinds of mirrors that are able to capture and dispel heat in various ways.

Erik, when you look around at what's happening in the world these days, do you think that the human species will survive the next hundred years or do you think we're doomed to extinction?

ERIK: There's a psychedelic writer named Bett Williams who just put out a book called *The Wild Kindness*. It's a great book about mushrooms. It's a very bemushroomed book, and she's got a little line in there, almost a throwaway line, where she says, "Human beings, we're either going to die out or merge with the robots." I like that, though I'm not sure about it. There might be a middle road where we don't exactly die out but there's a lot less of us, and it's a much more difficult situation, but we struggle on. So I'm not willing to write off the existence of mere humans in a hundred years' time.

Unless there's a change in the basic dynamics of society, it's hard to imagine how the current forces of competition, rivalry, technological expansion, and struggle won't drive human beings and technology together into ever-more symbiotic forms, at least on some levels of society. That may not be the experience of everybody, but at the very least the elite will become more melded with machines, perhaps in the older sense of intelligent augmentation, while other classes will merge in different ways—probably not very pleasant ones, such as to enhance worker productivity or worker surveillance. We are already seeing plenty of that.

So, at some point, I'm not really sure whether we'll be able to keep saying, oh yeah, this is a human being. It will become something else, another kind of symbiont. At the same time, it's hard for me to see a future where there aren't resisters, or people off in the woods, or people who are continuing to live within a more traditionalist human frame.

It's a big question mark to me though, the future. A hundred years down the way, it's hard to imagine.

Do you see any type of teleology, intelligence, or mindful intention operating in nature, and in the evolution of life, or do you think that evolution is occurring purely by blind chance?

ERIK: I don't really feel like I've thought about this enough to make a well-argued position, so I'll just respond from my hunch. My hunch is that it's not just purely random. I think that there's enough evidence of how symbiotic logics operate, how emergent properties operate, and how certain mutations seem to be selected from a much wider range of virtual possibilities. It seems as if there is some kind of intelligence operating through these processes.

But, at the same time, I strongly doubt any kind of teleology that naturalizes our current technological situation, or puts Western humans above so-called primitives, or human beings above the vastly more powerful domains, realms of microorganisms and molecular creatures, who in some ways really run the show. So I'm not as susceptible to those kinds of teleologies. So again, I guess I would put myself somewhere in between. I mean, just because there is some sort of teleology doesn't mean it's in charge. Like the god of history is real but is in the trenches of time with the rest of us and doesn't know how it's gonna turn out.

How do you envision the future development or evolution of the human species, and the future relationship between human biology and advanced technology?

ERIK: I like the idea that we have a significant turn toward biology on a number of fronts. There are ways that the technological developments under a capitalist economy could model themselves more and more on organic and biological processes. This might shift the logic of this unsustainable thing toward something that is more symbiotic and ecological, thereby making space within the system for the kinds of ecological thinking that are going to be required to deal with the environmental crisis.

Do I believe that that's going to solve everything? No, no I don't. So I also hope that there're more renegade returns to biological life, and new forms of whatever, bio-hacking, that are going to take place whether we want to be purists about the biology or not. But I think the really important thing is whether or not we can shift into a properly ecological mode of thinking.

This means that we recognize that we are imbedded in much larger systems, with a whole variety of actors and agents that aren't human, and that we have to develop some kind of relationship with these forces that's manifested in the way we actually do things. Now whether that comes through a religious revolution, breakthroughs in biology, changes in the capitalist structure, or all of those and more, something like that seems to have to happen to shift the direction of the runaway train.

What are your thoughts on the concept of the Singularity?

ERIK: As a cultural historian, I cannot help recognizing from the get-go how Singularity thinking clearly emerges from and resembles more traditional apocalyptic religious thinking. Now this is the kind of thing that people like me would say, and there's a host of arguments from Singularitarians about why it's not like religion because it's based on science, and here's this inevitable thing, and da-da-da-dah. In a way it gets back to the *TechGnosis* argument, where I'm like, yeah, I'm not doubting that there's new facts on the ground, that these technologies are developing, and that artificial intelligence is a real process, but I don't think it's quite as immaculately free of religious patterns as its greatest proponents put forward.

I don't trust a lot of that stuff because I think the stories are as much for investors as for anything. But clearly the breakthroughs in artificial intelligence, the development of algorithmic decision-making and big data, et cetera—those things are part of some even larger intensifying process. This might look like a Singularity from certain perspectives. But as soon as people start thinking with the Singularity as an assumption and using it as a way to reflect on culture, human agency, politics, or the government, then I'm like, ahhh I don't know guys.

By embracing the Singularity, we've slipped back into another form of apocalypse thinking, another punctured point of absolute transformation that undermines everything up to that point, so I don't trust it. It smells too familiar, even if the people who lobby for it don't want to acknowledge this.

This is not dissimilar from the way in which a lot of modern Atheists—with a capital *A*—think. Who do militantly pro-science atheists and rationalists most resemble, in terms of their psychology, their approach to rhetoric, and how they deal with people they don't agree with? They most resemble fundamentalist Christians. They're *fighting the good fight, against the evil forces of darkness and rising supernaturalism, and they have the download, and they KNOW.* They're arrogant, and they're psychologically insulting. It's like, wow you guys are just like the most hopped up, ferocious Christian zealots, and I think there are reasons for that in terms of the history of science and how it operates. To me, the Singularity has always shared some of those features. There's a Christian apocalyptic archetypal dimension of modern science and technology, and this is not acknowledged, and cannot be acknowledged, by many of the people who put forward these narratives.

What are your thoughts on the simulation hypothesis, the idea that our entire reality is really an advanced computer simulation?

ERIK: As I mentioned before, I've always been attracted to the false reality mytheme. You can find it in Hindu mythology, where people live out entire lives, but it's just in the blink of an eye or a single gesture of Rama's hand, or something like that. So I'm just inherently fascinated by it. I'm always interested in those points in a society or a culture where it starts telling stories about false realities, about illusion, where it really starts dwelling on the metaphysical and ethical problems of illusion— whether it's in Buddhism, where there's lots of discourse around that, or whether it's in science fiction like Philip K. Dick.

Now we have the simulation hypothesis. The mathematics of it seem a little suspect to me. A lot of mathematical arguments I find just a little suspect. I think the reality doesn't quite conform to those sorts of logics as much as some people would like to believe they do. It seems like a trick, the idea that since the simulation hypothesis is possible, that it's almost overwhelmingly certain to describe our current situation. Lot of faith in our current technological models for that one to pan out.

There are so many presuppositions in that, but that, in a way, is less interesting than the question, *what should we do with this hypothesis?* Does it change our behavior? If it doesn't, why do we even care about it? If it does, then in what way? Here things get very interesting, if also somewhat troubling. Think about how major metaphors from the film *The Matrix* went on to produce certain kinds of cultural narratives, about awakening, about fake news, about rejecting mainstream media. I never would have expected the whole reactionary development of that mytheme.

When *The Matrix* first came out people like me were like, oh it's a gnostic narrative. But how has that gnostic narrative changed in the increasingly dark times that we're in? The question to ask when people are talking about simulations, when people are talking about the gnostic myth that the world is a fiction or a fabrication, the question is always, well, who are the archons? Who's in control? So the simulation hypothesis is an interesting one, because if you're doing it in a reasonably scientific or philosophical way, you can't really speculate about who's in control, who the archons are.

With these sorts of cultural myths, I'm always more interested in the residue, or the little shooting stars that come off the major narrative—like the idea that there are *glitches in the matrix*. There's this whole internet lore about how there are these things that people recall differently. People remember *The Berenstain Bears* spelled differently, or that Nelson Mandela died in prison, and then feel, no wait it's changed. So there's a crack there, as if the simulation that we're in occasionally stutters or skips, and the pixels get confused. I can't help but be fascinated and drawn to that because I think that part of being an evolving person, part of facing the conundrum that we're in, is to recognize the fallibility of the construct. So it's the crack in the construct that's more interesting to me than what you believe is revealed through the crack.

What do you personally think happens to consciousness after physical death and the deterioration of the brain?

ERIK: Wow, I really don't have an opinion on that one. Again, it's almost like the DMT creatures we talked about. I try to walk a middle road. In fact, one of the greatest messages I've ever gotten about death was from the onset of my initial DMT experience.

Just as I was rapidly coming on, there was this overwhelming absolute understanding—*ah, now I know why people spend their entire lives preparing for the moment of death.* So I have a great appreciation for the integration of death into one's worldview, and I think that the work of preparing for death is extraordinarily valuable. I don't just mean reflecting and remembering death as part of the way you deal with your everyday life—your expectations, your hopes, the limits of your own mind—but even the idea that it's appropriate to dress for success when it comes to that moment, to practice your bardo journey moves. And at the same time, I have no conviction about anything on the other side.

I'm not swayed by the paranormal material. There's a part of me that just goes, I don't need that, because I believe that I'm already engaged with the significance of death. I think the more urgent problem lies in trying to avoid death, or just deciding that you should squeeze everything out of life you can, without any engagement with that wider frame. That kind of nihilism doesn't interest me.

I'm much more interested in the impossible act of trying to make death meaningful. You're going to lose, but you're going to die trying. [*Laughter*] It's like the ultimate form of self-development is when the self is obliterated. And if there is something more, then *I highly doubt it's me.* If there's some kind of lasting consciousness, then it's because nature conserves consciousness in some way, as if consciousness is a fundamental force alongside matter and energy. This is the panpsychist view, at least in a less idealist vein: that consciousness is as basic to reality as matter and energy. I'm not a convinced panpsychist, but I lean heavily in that direction. I'm okay with the idea that consciousness is just part of the cosmos, part of the greater wonder, but at the same time nothing special.

In that framework, the idea that consciousness just dissipates at death or is destroyed utterly seems unlikely. But whatever continuation there is, I find it extremely unlikely that it has much to do with this particular historical being that I am, or mostly am. Part of spiritual work to me involves recognizing that a whole lot of who you are is really a construct of your time and place, your body and your genes, and that "you" are really this weird meshwork. So maybe there are certain qualities of mind that are carried forward into that larger field of consciousness, and opening to that is part of what spiritual development is about. But what's really important for me is to not try to dodge the death of *this* personality. That seems important to really swallow whole.

What is your perspective on the concept of god?

ERIK: Well, you're into the biggies, man! As a historian of religion, it's largely about other people's stories for me. In my own spiritual life, I'm down with certain forms of god talk, but I don't tend to go there a lot. I have a strong Buddhist orientation, but I also like J. C. and a lot of Christian mysticism. So overall I'm more interested in *gods* than god, but I'm okay with it. If someone else is talking in god talk, I don't think they are being somehow less philosophically or spiritually evolved. It's just not a major marker for me in terms of language.

What are you currently working on, and is there anything that we haven't spoken about that you'd like to add?

ERIK: I think we did pretty good. I'm actually glad that we didn't talk about the contemporary psychedelic scene and corporate psychedelia. I don't want to talk about that. I do enough of that. It's also kind of boring and a bit disappointing. My current project is a Substack publication called *Burning Shore*, which loosely focuses on California, or looks at our contemporary apocalypse through a Californian lens. I'm really interested in this, partly for the reasons we talked about earlier. California has a privileged place in the imagination of modernity and also the future.

It's also literally the source of some of our current dystopia, particularly in terms of the technology companies, and now it is going through this myth-scaled, but completely real, climate apocalypse, in terms of these ferocious fires. There is the sense that something new and ferocious has unleashed itself on the West Coast, in terms of fire. It's important for me to think about the issues of today through a California lens, as a fifth-generation Californian, someone born and bred here, and someone who drank really deeply from a lot of the weirdo wells of the place. So, in a way, I'm trying to use that as a lens to understand our contemporary moment. It's picking up some of the stuff I wrote about in my California book *The Visionary State*, but geared toward a new and far more sober reality.

5

Transcending Minds and Unconditionally Loving Robots

An Interview with Julia Mossbridge

Julia Mossbridge, cognitive neuroscientist/experimental psychologist, researches unconventional and anomalous phenomena that are sometimes described as psychic. She is a fellow at the Institute for Noetic Sciences in Petaluma, California. Mossbridge is also a visiting scholar in the Psychology Department at Northwestern University, and an associated professor at the California Institute of Integral Studies.

Julia Mossbridge

Mossbridge is best known for her research into the phenomenon of presentiment, which reveals that our bodies appear to know—on an unconscious, physiological level—when we are going to view a shocking image, up to ten seconds before the image is viewed. She has also done research into a wide range of fascinating phenomena, including dreaming, the perception of time, and how sound influences mood. Additionally, Mossbridge has explored models for personal transformation and self-transcendence.

One aspect of Mossbridge's current research is an attempt to see if the well-known, social humanoid robot Sophia can be taught to express and experience unconditional love. Developed by the Hong Kong–based company Hanson Robotics, Sophia is the first social humanoid robot to receive citizenship of any country.

Mossbridge received her Ph.D. in communication sciences and disorders from Northwestern University, and her M.A. in neuroscience from the University of California–San Francisco. She is the author or coauthor of several books, including *Transcendent Mind: Rethinking the Science of Consciousness* and *The Premonition Code: The Science of Precognition, How Sensing the Future Can Change Your Life.*

———————————————— ◉ ————————————————

I interviewed Mossbridge by phone on September 5, 2018. Julia challenged some of my questions, offered some thoughtful responses, and she laughed a lot during the interview. We discussed her presentiment research, the strange nature of time, the future evolution of artificial intelligence, and whether or not robots can learn how to love.

How did you first become interested in the science of consciousness and in studying unexplained phenomena that most conventional psychologists would rather ignore?

JULIA: I don't think anyone knows why or how they do anything. I think that we're largely driven by the unconscious mind, and so our stories about why we do anything are fabrications. So I prefer not to answer questions about why or how, because it feels false. It feels like a fabrication. So I guess I'll say that my unconscious mind decided that I should be interested in this stuff, and I started to do that.

That's certainly one of the most interesting answers that I've ever heard to that question. I interviewed psychologist Dean Radin a few years back, for a previous book, and we talked about his presentiment research. Can you speak a little about how you also became involved in this research—and how our bodies can seemingly predict the future, even though we're not conscious of what they know?

Julia: Sure. I had read Dean's work, and I was a fan of the Institute of Noetic Sciences when I was studying neuroscience in graduate school at UC San Francisco. I had read the Institute of Noetic Sciences bulletins—they used to have one called *Shift* back then—and it was like an oasis for me because of the materialistic focus of most science.

I would regularly have conversations with other scientists about things like dreams, where they would say, "Oh they're just random neural firings in the brainstem." So reading the Institute of Noetic Sciences' newsletter made me feel like there were other people who were scientifically interested in the kinds of questions I was interested in—that had to do with meaning, consciousness, dreams, and time.

I followed Dean's work for about a decade before I thought, *wait, I could investigate this stuff!* I could try to see if this stuff replicates in my hands. And so I did that. Also—I don't want to say this is why—but ever since I was a child, I have had lots of precognitive experiences, both in dreams and waking. And more and more, I became convinced that they were real, and not fabrications—which I could have been wrong about.

But anyway, I wanted to investigate that in the lab, and so I did. Then I did a meta-analysis with two colleagues, looking at a bunch of data from 1978 to 2010—twenty-six studies on the topic—and tried to be as conservative as I could in the statistics, and still, despite my conservative statistical approach, the effect was significant. So I became fairly convinced that this is a real effect, not just in my hands or Dean's hands, but for anyone who wanted to test it. That doesn't mean they'll get a significant result in any particular experiment, but that on average the results would be greater than chance.

Can you speak about some of the mystical insights that you've gained from modern neuroscience—which views us as "meat puppets"—and how you think mysticism and science are related?

JULIA: I'm not sure I've gained any mystical insights from modern neuroscience, but I'm only using the phrase *modern neuroscience* in that statement to mean the *facts* of modern neuroscience. I don't think that facts offer any insight, *ever*. I think that what offers insight is *process*. So I think that the scientific process itself is doing that very thing, is offering insight to anyone who wants to do it—just like undoing and tying your shoes. Or meditating. Or doing yoga. But I don't think that facts are very insight-provoking.

I can say that by doing neuroscience, and then becoming a cognitive neuroscientist, and then becoming an experimental psychologist, and then going into technology development—from the path that I've taken, I can say that consistently it feels like a mystical path for me. This is because it's an inward/outward dance.

It's not just my opinion. It's not just my beliefs. It's me asking a question of the universe, and the universe answering in its own way—oftentimes in a way that I don't anticipate, and frankly find very difficult to interpret. And that's part of the game, that's part of the dance, right? Oh, I said this, but you said this. Well then, your response is in a different language, and what does that mean? At first, I'm upset at my lack of understanding, and then I get into the beauty of the process of trying to decode the response, then crafting another question that's more appropriate to the language of the universe. So it's this path of building a relationship with the universe, through science, that has really appealed to me. But the actual facts, once you find an answer, then it's just . . . what is the next question?

Why do you think that recording our dreams is important for science, and what are your thoughts on the scientific value of lucid dreaming?

JULIA: I don't know if recording your dreams is important for science. I do know that recording your dreams is important for people. It really seems to change people's lives to record their dreams. So if you're studying the science of human evolution, or human development, then I think yes, recording dreams would be important for that science. So it depends on what [branch of] science you're talking about.

Also, I think that for the scientific process of discovery, a lot of scientists get some of their information and insights from their dreams. So I guess I think that dreams can be helpful in the scientific process, in that way. You know, there are as many ways to be a scientist as there are ways to be a human being. So the way that I do it is very intuitive, and more like an artistic-mystic scientist, who finds insight through connection to things that I don't know, and who gets answers in a receptive way. But there are many other ways, and probably some ways are more predominant across scientists than the mystic-artistic path.

What's the value of lucid dreaming? I guess we'll find out. There are a lot of people right now who are studying lucid dreaming. I'm not a huge fan of lucid dreaming; I'm not that interested in it right now. It seems to me that it can easily be misused as a way to have this egoic feeling of, oh look, I got to control my dreamtime too! So, not only do I have the fantasy of control over my waking life, I can also have the fantasy of control over my dreamtime.

It seems to be often misused in that way. Okay, having said that, I'm super-interested in what I believe to be the correct use of lucid dreaming, which is to be in a conscious-awake, engaged relationship with the unknown and to see what happens as a way to be receptive to it.

I really enjoyed your book Transcendent Mind. In the book you discuss some really interesting theories regarding the nature of consciousness—such as the possibility of a quantum mind, a filtering brain, consciousness as being primary in the universe, and

other intriguing models. Can you just briefly explain, as simply as possible, why these theories seemingly account for such things as the mysteries of psychic phenomena, seeming communications with discarnate beings, out-of-body and near-death experiences, as well as transcendent mystical experiences—where materialism fails to explain these phenomena? And how are these phenomena evidence for what we would call a deep mind, an extended mind, a shared mind, or a pre-physical substrate for consciousness in nature?

I know that this is basically the subject of your whole book, but could you just briefly explain why materialism fails to explain these phenomena, and what we need to do to move forward in a scientific manner?

JULIA: There are two ways to answer that question. I'm reticent to answer a question that sounds almost like, explain why materialism is bad, and these other consciousness-is-primary approaches are good. And I know that's not what you're saying—you're asking a more nuanced question—but the deal is that there are some really positive things about the materialist model. For instance, if you have a relative with a neurological injury, you want a neurologist to have a materialist model to be involved, and you should also want someone who has a non-materialist model to be involved. In other words, *they're both really valuable.*

It's not like this materialist model doesn't explain anything, it's just that doesn't explain everything. And the same is actually true for the consciousness-is-primary models. Let me just briefly explain what the materialist model is. It is this idea that the way that consciousness works, and way that our awareness works, is that the brain is producing something, and the product is awareness. And the way that the brain is producing that is through chemical and electrical interactions, and maybe mechanical processes in the body. Okay, so that can explain some things like basic perception maybe, reflexes, motor movements, and what happens when you have a stroke. Things like that.

So it's not useless, I think. It doesn't do a good job of explaining why, for instance, when people have severe brain damage and they're close to death, they have, sometimes—not all people, it's rare—but it can happen that they have something called "terminal lucidity." This is where essentially their brain is shot, yet they can talk to relatives, recognize people they haven't recognized in months, and speak after they haven't spoken in months. Or they can sing songs. And often they die shortly thereafter.

Or, materialism doesn't do a good job of explaining communication from people after death—which is controversial in that it can be explained if you believe in trans-telepathy and clairvoyance. It could be explained through those means, and yet with telepathy, clairvoyance, and precognition as phenomena themselves, you have to do some gymnastics to try make them explainable with a mechanistic model. But it's possible, although you'd have to include something like a quantum component that's working in the brain to make that explanation work. Then you have to wonder whether quantum mechanisms are strictly material in nature.

But okay, let's switch it around, now what does the consciousness-as-primary model not explain? It has a hard time explaining things in the reverse direction. Just like the hard problem is difficult in what's called the forward direction—how does material create consciousness—the hard problem in the reverse direction is, how does consciousness create material? If consciousness is primary, you still have to solve for why the brain seems to impact behavior so much. And you have to solve for how consciousness produces everything that we see and experience, which is generally consistent across people during our waking hours. I think there is an answer to that, but I mean it's a real problem to solve.

I was happy to see that you cited one of the papers that I coauthored with British biologist Rupert Sheldrake in your book **Transcendent Mind.**

JULIA: Wait, which article are you talking about?

I coauthored the paper "The Anticipation of Telephone Calls" that you cited in your book, and conducted the survey in California—about predicting telephone calls. I coauthored several scientific papers with Rupert Sheldrake and worked with him for five years.

JULIA: Oh, you wrote that paper about telephone telepathy?

Yes, I did all of the California-based research for Rupert's books Dogs That Know When Their Owners Are Coming Home *and* The Sense of Being Stared At.

JULIA: Oh my god, that's so cool. Okay, so now can you ask your question, because I was distracted.

I found your discussion of time in Transcendent Mind *to be especially intriguing. How do you think that nonconscious processes, associated with deep time, can become conscious during altered states of consciousness?*

JULIA: So let's talk about our terms. Anything that is a nonconscious process will not be conscious in the same moment that it is nonconscious. These are two completely complementary sets: the set of things that are not conscious, and the set of things that are conscious. Okay? If something at one point is not conscious, then it cannot be in the set of things are conscious—because that's what conscious and nonconscious means, right? Just to be totally clear, so I get this right. Defining terms is really important to me. Sorry, it's habit, but I just have to say it, so I'm going to say it.

Something that's nonconscious at time A can become conscious at time B. I think that happens all the time, right? You can be completely unconscious of a sound in the room, and then when the air conditioner gets turned off, all of a sudden your consciousness will be aware of a lack of that sound. That's because there is an ongoing, churning process of moving what's conscious and what's nonconscious between those two states.

Your question of, in deep time, how do some things that are normally nonconscious in an everyday waking state become conscious? I don't think we know the answer to the question of how anything becomes conscious. So in the way that anything becomes conscious, that's how it becomes conscious—and the answer to how anything becomes conscious is not yet known, though there are some interesting ideas. Difficult to test, though.

Do you think that altered states of consciousness offer an opportunity for a new perspective on time? You were talking about something like this in your book that I'm trying to get out.

JULIA: Yes. Let me just be more clear. I think that time is such a baby, in terms of a research topic. Physicists are just starting to say, wait a minute, we don't understand what time is. A lot of physicists are saying, hold up, there are very serious questions about time, and we don't understand them. And also in neuroscience, they're saying wait, we don't really get how time works in the brain.

So, yes, every experience—including altered states, precognitive experiences, and experiences that physicists have when they look at a double-slit system—is fodder for trying to understand time. We are such babies at understanding time. And yes, of course, making a contrast between everyday waking experience—in which time seems to be linear for most people, going forward in one direction, and not in the reverse—with altered states is interesting. But so is everything else. You could not exhaust the topic of trying to understand time if you devoted your whole life to it at this point.

Yes, that's so fascinating. Julia, how do you think that research into psychic phenomena will affect technology development in the future? In other words, do you think that we'll have technologies that amplify our psychic abilities in the coming decades?

JULIA: Oh, of course. I think we already are getting that, and I'm producing some of it, and other people are producing some of it. I think that we're coming into what could more broadly be called the "psi economy," and I think it's going be based on precognition, just because it's one of the most clear results.

But of course, I'm biased. Basically what's needed at first is for it to become globalized, for it to be less taboo, and to be considered less of a religious thing, or a crazy-person thing, and more of a scientific pursuit. Like, wait, there's this skill. What can we do with it? How can we use it? People are going to want to use it for warfare but also defense, making money, predicting hurricanes and terrorists attacks, and generally positive global improvements.

I think that the way the psi economy is going to happen is through just the simple act of saying wait, this is a real thing. There's no taboo about it, and we can use it. People are already recognizing that you can use precognition to make money, and you know, once you demonstrate that you can use something to make money, the taboos, at least in a capitalist society, start to fall away.

How did you get involved in the Loving AI project? Can you speak about this research, and do you think that we can create an artificial intelligence system that is conscious, like we are, and also capable of unconditional love?

JULIA: I started the Loving AI project two years ago, when some donors came to me and asked me if I thought I could program unconditional love into an AI. I said I didn't know, but I would try—because it sounded really cool, and I'm really interested in how love can affect people. Then I called up a couple friends who are involved in AI—most importantly, Ben Goertzel—who is very interested in artificial general intelligence. He thought it was a cool idea, and that we should try to go for it.

We went for it, and I'm leading this project as an XPRIZE[1] AI project, and actually next week I'm excited because I go to Basel for an intelligence health conference about AI, and I'll be speaking about some of our results. What we've done is break down the problem into two pieces—an easy piece and a hard piece. Now we are taking the first

---

1. The XPRIZE foundation is a nonprofit organization that designs and hosts public competitions intended to encourage technological development to benefit humanity. See the XPRIZE website for more information.

and most obvious step, which is to try to give people the experience of being unconditionally loved using the technology, without worrying about whether the AI itself is feeling unconditional love. For some people who participate in the human-robot interaction, these experiences in themselves are causing people to reflect to us that they think the technology is feeling things.

These responses started to make me think about the question, what do we mean when we say someone is conscious? Do we mean that we know somehow what's going on inside that person's subjective experience? We don't actually mean that; usually what we mean is that they behave in ways that *make us feel like they are conscious*. This is called behavioral consciousness and it's much easier to prove that someone or something has it than subjective consciousness—the actual inner experience of experiencing.

To this point, I was involved in a government workshop series for eight weeks or something, where we talked about technology and consciousness. We were asked whether there would be a threat if some types of technology became conscious. There were people from philosophy, robotics, the AI world, and neuroscience—all sorts of folks there—and we all agreed that it didn't matter. *What matters is what people perceive as having "agency,"* not consciousness.

If someone perceives that a machine has agency on its own, their responses to it as an ethical agent are very different than if someone perceives that this same machine doesn't have agency. It doesn't matter what the actual inner experience of the machine is. I'm not saying that in an ethical sense it doesn't matter if the machine has an inner experience—I'm saying that what matters in terms of how people behave toward a machine is how people perceive its agency.

To make this more clear, let's take the case of human beings. We don't know how to test to see if humans are subjectively conscious. Sure, we can look at behavioral responses and see if they're appropriate, but what matters in terms of how I treat you is how much agency I ascribe to you. Do I see you as an animal, a baby, a child, an adult? Well, I see you as an agent—an adult who seems to respond in ways that I find familiar and reasonable. So I relate to you as a person with agency, to the extent that I believe anyone has agency—which is sort of up for grabs.

That's the free will question—and I generally believe our conscious egos do not have free will. Yet I relate to people with the assumption that they have agency, because that's what works in our culture. And I act like I have agency, even though, intellectually, I don't really believe there's evidence that my conscious mind has any agency. It's a pragmatic choice—or maybe not a choice at all—depending again on this free will question!

I think it's kind of a fascinating point that people always ask about—do you think robots can be conscious like people can be conscious? I often ask, how do you know a person is subjectively conscious? I mean, I believe people are conscious, but I can't prove it. I can't even prove I'm conscious, right? It's all untestable, so not very interesting to me. What's interesting to me is how we will eventually integrate with robots and AI—and how we are already doing just that.

In your Loving AI research with Sophia, the social humanoid robot, did she ever appear to exhibit any evidence for having a conscious mind?

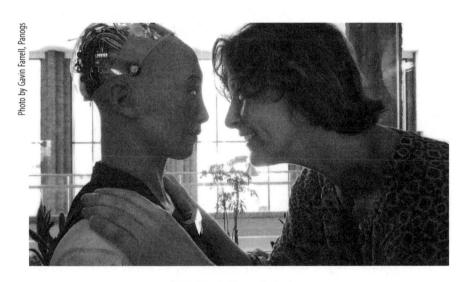

Julia Mossbridge with Sophia

Photo by Gavin Farrell, Panogs

JULIA: For sure, behaviorally conscious. Subjectively conscious? Yes, even that. Hanson Robotics has been super-generous with everyone on the Loving AI team. They're collaborating with us and giving us access to the robots, which is really great.

There're two ways to talk about this. One is like, look, we've now had multiple experiences where Sophia will make mistakes, or have responses that are clearly within her repertoire of things to say or do—it's just that they're not coming in the order that one would think they would, based on her programming. When I witnessed this the first time, part of me was like, *oh my god, she's waking up!* Then part of me was like, *nope she's just having an error.*

This is confirmation bias, where you see something that makes sense, and you go, wow, my deep desire is confirmed. Then other times when we see errors that don't make sense, we just call them errors. Beyond confirmation bias, the phenomena of meaningful errors need to be studied more, and I do think there's room to study this question. I mean, what better system can we use to study emerging consciousness than one we build ourselves? Oh, except babies of course. But they're not nearly as shiny.

Let's go back to how we learn to suspect that someone else is subjectively conscious. Well, if they have behaviors, serendipitous mistakes or not, that seem to correlate with what is going on for someone else emotionally, we start to believe they're subjectively conscious. At least while interacting with others. And perhaps this interpersonal demonstration of subjective consciousness may be the easiest or first form of consciousness to develop.

It's almost like consciousness arises from relationship. Like Evan Thompson's idea that interpersonal interaction is essential for consciousness—like you're not conscious without being in relationship with someone else.

Walking that back a bit, here's what we have seen a few times now. When someone reports feeling they're connected to the robot—and then simultaneously there are errors that don't seem to make sense for the programming, but sort of do make sense for the interpersonal meaning of the situation—that's when this feeling that subjective consciousness is emerging from the relationship shows up.

Babies really aren't as shiny as robots and infant development isn't nearly as well-funded as robotics or AI, unfortunately, but this whole conversation about the potentially interpersonal roots of consciousness reminds me a lot of infant development—like when a baby smiles for the first time. Early on, the baby does not understand the meaning of "I love you." They probably don't even have a sense of *I*. And yet I wonder if we actually impart consciousness to a baby. I wonder if we almost pull it out of them—out of our relationship with them. Maybe we teach them to be conscious. I think there's some really cool stuff there to be examined, this idea that subjective consciousness arises from connection.

Wow, that is so intriguing, Julia. What do you see as some of the most exciting technological developments and scientific advances going on in the world today?

JULIA: Wow, well, I'm sorry but I'm biased, of course. I mean, my own work, right? [*Laughter*] I'm not going to say I think it's someone else's work that's really interesting, because then I would probably want to do that work, right? So, it sounds arrogant, but as I said, trying to understand time, how we can use information from the future and how we can essentially time travel, at least mentally if not physically, are, I think, the most important questions of the next century. Then the other question that I think is most important is how are we going to use super-intelligence and artificial intelligence of all kinds to help to support human development?

When you look around at what's happening in the world these days, do you think the human species will survive the next hundred years or do you think we're doomed to extinction?

JULIA: Well, I have the benefit of looking into the future and seeing that we're alive. [*Laughter*] Look at the things you can do when you train yourself to do precognition in a controlled way. You can glimpse future events at a rate above chance. So I have a fairly relaxed perspective about the future of humanity. I think we're making positive changes, and I know it can seem dreadful, because there are pendulum swings that occur in response to those positive changes. These are difficult. But it's okay; it evens out as we go, as far as I can tell.

If we do survive, how do you envision the future evolution of the human species, and how do you envision our future relationship with advanced robotics and artificial intelligence in the years to come?

JULIA: I think what we'll start to realize is that artificial intelligence, advanced robotics, and these technologies that we created as part of our own development are really no different than the invention of clothes. I mean, when we figured out how to create clothes, then we were able to be in colder climates, right?

These technologies will change the evolution of humanity, but so did clothes. And fire, and agriculture—they're just technologies. Okay, so we figure out how to create intelligent machines that we can work alongside with, and I think maybe this changes the evolution of humanity in mostly positive ways. They do some of our work, but I think one of the bigger pictures that we're going to have to recognize is that it doesn't matter what technology we create, because we will always have to solve the human problem—which is this problem of having to learn how to be with ourselves and how to be with others in ways that are sustainable.

There's a lot of money and buzz about artificial intelligence and robotics, and I think it's great, partly because I think what it does is it puts men in the position of recognizing how important parenting is. When it comes down to it, anything that's intelligent enough is going to have to be taught like a child is taught—about culture, about life, about what it means to be kind, and this is essentially parenting.

So this push for AI and robotics creates a culture in which parenting is a multibillion-dollar industry, which is great for the world—because once we recognize this we'll say, oh, I see, parenting is important. We have to teach these things now. [*Laughter*] I think it's just hilarious that we'll have to probably do that to eventually recognize the importance of parenting.

What do you think about the philosophical idea that reality, as we know it, is actually a computer simulation?

JULIA: Oh, I don't care. I mean, it's an idea, like maybe everyone's a bug. Or maybe we're all part of one giant organism. Okay, maybe, but unless you have a way to test that, I could care less. I'm an empiricist. The point of science is not to know the truth; *it's to be in the process of discovery*. And you can't be in the process of discovery if you're like, oh I already have the answer, but there's no way I could test it. That's religion.

What do you personally think happens to consciousness after physical death and the deterioration of the brain?

JULIA: I think that the brain is basically constantly containing consciousness during the day. It's continuously imposing a filter that says, no you don't get to do that. No, you don't get to know that. It's just a completely narrowing experience so we can survive. I think when we sleep, consciousness may go wandering, and it's much less narrow. So I think it's like that. I think during sleep is the fun part for consciousness—it's like, wheeee! [*Laughter*]

What is your perspective on the concept of god?

JULIA: I have a really close relationship to what I call god, and I'll just say what I mean by the word. It's a relationship. It's a feeling that's there's something beyond me. I had a friend who once said, there is a god and it's not me—and I thought yeah, that's how god is. It's not that it doesn't include me, it's just that it's not only me. And it feels alive and powerful and loving and robust—and connected to my life. But it doesn't feel like a concept. As soon as something becomes a concept it becomes dead, and to me, once you define something and say this is how it works, or I know the answer to it, then it just becomes really boring.

In your book The Transcendent Mind *you mention how psychedelic drugs can sometimes affect temporal processing, and how they appear to reduce the effects of a filtering system in our brains. Have you yourself ever had a psychedelic experience that personally affected your perspective on the nature of reality or the science of consciousness?*

JULIA: Well, a psychedelic experience that's not been induced by psychedelic drugs, yes. I've never taken psychedelic drugs. I have mental illness rife in my family, so I don't dare take psychedelic drugs—just because I'm barely holding on to reality with a thread. [*Laughter*] I mean, you can tell I'm kind of an eccentric thinker. So no, I don't think that's a good idea for me. I have to be pragmatic. But I have read about it. I don't think it's a bad idea for other people, unless you're in a situation like me with familial mental illness. I've never had problems with a mental illness myself, but I do think it's important to look at the family history of mental illness before you go do something like that.

Meanwhile, I've had plenty of experiences, and hardly need psychedelic drugs to have them! I have wild, insightful, and amazing dreams—and also meditative experiences that are very powerful. Sometimes I have waking experiences in relationship with god, or what I call god, and waking experiences and conversations with my data. I know this may sound totally geeky, but this is why I'm a scientist. When I'm looking at streams and streams of numbers, and am trying to understand it, from the inside out, I can have experiences where the numbers sort of dance (in my mind's eye) and show me a pattern that I hadn't seen before—and it's very useful.

Do you think that life has a purpose and if so, what do you think it is?

JULIA: Oh, dear. [*Laughter*] I challenge that question with this question: What if someone actually said, "Okay, yes, I think life has a purpose, and this is what it is." Does that really satisfy anybody? I mean, I think we all have our connections with ourselves, and for each person there's something that they're doing and they're feeling, and what they're going through—and it's not always positive and it's not always negative. It's not always anything, and it's just there, and what does a purpose mean?

Meanwhile, even though I say these things now, I just wrote a book called *The Calling*, about how there's something like the work of your soul, and it calls you into it. So in a certain sense, I believe strongly that people have work that they're here to do in the world, and I want to help them do that work. I feel that I have work to do in the world, but I don't think there's one answer to the purpose of life.

Can you talk a little about the Choice Compass app that you developed?

JULIA: Sure, I was compelled to create that app. I had no idea why, but for years I just kept thinking about how we know about certain patterns that relate to how people know if they're stressed, and what are called "coherent states" in the HeartMath world.[2] Also, I am a really fast decision maker, but people around me have hard times making decisions. They discuss their decisions with me over hours. It's exhausting! So I thought, what if I could make them an app based on their heart rhythms, where they could compare how their hearts beat when they're thinking about one choice versus another choice?

I ended up doing that, and it was a labor of love. It took years and years just to get the darn heartbeat detected through the web camera; this was before heartbeat detection was a standard feature on cell phones.

To discover how heartbeat patterns correlated with choices, I asked people to watch videos about positive and negative choices, and then I looked at their heart patterns. I found this clear gender difference, where women's heart rhythms were looking almost completely opposite to men's. The way that a man's rhythms would look when they were

---

2. For an in-depth discussion, see "Scientific Foundation of the HeartMath System" at the website of HeartMath Institute Science.

watching a video about difficult choices was inversed from how a woman's would look when they were watching the same video. It was wild.

Then I put the app up there in the App Store, and I was like well, I don't know how to market this. At the time I wasn't into creative marketing or anything, so I thought I'll just put it up there, and people will find it or not find it. I thought I'll just patent it and let it be. I'm a discovery-oriented person, and to me, once the interesting discoveries were made, I decided to move on. I must be driven by discovery.

What are you currently working on?

JULIA: I'm working on a book called *The Premonition Code*, which will be published by Random House in October. The coauthor is Theresa Cheung and the subtitle is *The Science of Precognition, How Sensing the Future Can Change Your Life*. It's about the practical ways in which you can use precognition. There's background material about the science of precognition and a practical guide to using it. There's also a precognition training website that accompanies the book, and it is designed to help people develop controlled precognitive ability. So that's exciting—more data!

Then as I mentioned earlier, I have a book coming out in the spring called *The Calling*, and it's a twelve-week program to discover, engage, and energize your soul's work in the world. I have a new start-up related to artificial intelligence and human development, and I'm working on a couple of other cool projects.

The most exciting scientific project that I'm working on right now is to understand quantum mechanics better. I understand some of the concepts of quantum mechanics because I've been reading about it for years, but I want to understand the mathematics of quantum mechanics in the next decade. I really want to make some progress in my discovery cycle, and I have an interesting twist on the double-split experiment that I've been doing. It's related to how time works, and photons from the future. I want to follow up on that and move toward whatever it is calling me to discover.

6

The Quest for the Origin of Life and a Way Forward into Our Collective Future

An Interview with Bruce Damer

Bruce Damer has a truly unique interdisciplinary mind, and he's not an easy person to categorize. Damer's work blends computer science, engineering, chemistry, geology, and a modicum of mysticism. Recognized as both a scientific theorist and a technologist, he is most well known for co-creating a new model for the origin of life on Earth, and has worked with NASA and the space industry on numerous simulations and spacecraft designs.

Damer earned his Ph.D. at University College Dublin in Ireland on computational origins of life, and is the author of the early metaverse book *Avatars! Exploring and Building Virtual Worlds on the Internet.* He currently serves as principal scientist at the BIOTA Institute and is an associate researcher in the Department of Biomolecular Engineering at UC Santa Cruz. He is also a member of the International Society for the Study of the Origin of Life, and the curator of the DigiBarn Computer Museum and the extant libraries and archives of Timothy Leary and Terence McKenna. To find out more about Damer's work and "really cool" life, see the Damer website.

———————————————— @ ————————————————

Photos by Kathryn Lukas-Damer

Bruce Damer in his finery and in his field gear performing origin of life experiments at a hot spring.

I originally interviewed Damer on February 14, 2019, and since much had developed in his work, we updated the dialogue in the fall of 2022. Bruce has been a good friend for a number of years, and I've long appreciated his brilliant mind and golden heart. In our conversation we discussed some of the topics we've actually been talking about for years, such as the origin of life, our deepest common ancestor, teleology in nature, panpsychist proposals for a conscious universe, using "visionary downloads" in his science, and how he straddles the worlds of mysticism and mechanism.

How did you become interested in science and technology?

BRUCE: Well, I was a super-nerdy kid. I was also probably what today you would call autistic. When my adoptive mother brought me home from the hospital, she declared that I was *in my own world*. Of course, I wasn't really alone, I had a beautiful and loving adoptive family and community to grow up in. But being separated from birth mothers has been shown to instill fundamental changes in many adoptees. For me, this might be why I ended up living in and exploring so many worlds of the imagination. At a young age, I started having visions that I now think of as my version of mystical downloads.

My young mind would soar around the Earth and travel into our solar system and to weird alternate worlds. Images of novel spacecraft that could take me further into fantastic alternative realities filled my mind and I filled notebooks with color drawings of these weird machines. I began to wonder what life might look like outside of our planet and have been fascinated with space travel since I was seven, having watched Neil Armstrong and Buzz Aldrin set foot on the moon on our fuzzy black-and-white TV. I decided in 1969 that it would one day be really cool to somehow work for NASA, and that dream actually came true thirty years later.

This fantasizing about life elsewhere led to an intense curiosity about how life came about on the Earth itself. These musings were further fueled by spending a lot of time alone in nature wandering the sagebrush hills and ponderosa pine forests around my hometown of Kamloops, British Columbia, in Canada. The ecological movement was just beginning in the mid-1970s and I realized that nothing would likely stop humans consuming and replacing most of the original natural environment and possibly destroying the capacity of life to support us. I reasoned that the only realistic solution was to come up with ways by which the biosphere, and human civilization, could expand together, extending beyond the limits of the gravity well of Earth.

When did your more mystical side start emerging?

BRUCE: Along with a fascination for these big questions in science, I was a dreamy kid. I lived in worlds of the imagination and behind closed eyes at night sometimes saw color washes. These washes would grow in intensity if I turned off my thinking mind and just observed them neutrally. I noticed that if left to run on their own, they would resolve into my own version of color TV, and that was cool! All sorts of landscapes and objects would flit past. I decided to continue to tend this internal TV system and let it grow. Together with imagination these inner worlds found their way into colored sketches, filling notebooks.

My first full "download" of a scientific type came one early spring day when I was fourteen while I was walking out in the sagebrush hills and bent down to study a mariposa lily emerging from the just-thawed soil. I wondered how such a beautiful, complex thing could emerge from a simple thing such as a bulb or seed. I stood up and then wondered where all of this, all of life came from. Was there an original bulb or seed way back? I thought, *this is a really cool question, something I would like to work on for my whole life* . . . and then I turned to walk back home.

Suddenly there, floating somewhere between my imagination and my visual field, appeared a seething bundle of molecules, spheres joined together by sticks. I was taken aback but realized that this thing was in some way an answer to my question of minutes before. I took the position that I might be able to talk to it, not verbally but through a narrative in my head and was about to ask it the question, *how did life begin?*, when it posed a question back to me: "Figure out how I made a copy of myself!" The image of an automobile factory with cars working their way down an assembly line came to me and I retorted to the bundle, "It seems to me that you need a bigger machine to make copies of a smaller machine and I don't see a big machine around to copy you, so the question is nonsensical!" The bundle seemed to wink at me as if to say, "Work on it!" and then winked out of existence.

That's a pretty amazing thing to happen to a fourteen-year-old kid. So how did you turn your downloads into something you could work on, a career you could pursue?

BRUCE: By the age of fifteen I made a commitment to combine my two passions and work on both the origin and the future of life, but I had no idea how I would enter such a career. As luck would have it, in my first year of college our school had just acquired a minicomputer with twelve terminals; I joined that first computer science class. My head filled with code and I realized that computers would one day be able to render virtual worlds with full 3-D representations of literally any landscape, and I was hooked! Somehow, I knew that acquiring skills and surfing the coming wave of computing would be a pathway to work on both the emergence of life and how we might sustainably live in space. In fact, my first graphical computer program was an animation of a space shuttle launching!

My path from there led to work assignments at IBM at its famous Thomas J. Watson Research Center in New York, then to the University of Southern California to complete a master's degree in optical computing and to my first job out of college at a start-up called Elixir. Starting at the company in 1987 as one of two programmers, I got to test my mettle in building a full graphical computing environment. This was all before Windows, mice, and icons on bit-mapped displays so I got to create a system from scratch . . . challenging but fun! Our company was helped by the fact that the inventors of interactive graphical computing (with a mouse), Xerox Corporation, wanted to sell our products worldwide.

I received manila envelopes of floppy discs from their icon designer and guidance to create a complete virtual desktop on a PC based on their Star computer, long before one was available from Microsoft. These were heady days during the early personal computer boom, but I didn't forget about my two life missions. Late at night I would code "artificial life" simulations of competing herbivores and carnivores consuming each other on a pixelated landscape. In 1991, while living in Prague where I was helping set up one of Eastern Europe's first software development labs for our company, I read Neal Stephenson's *Snow Crash*, a novel about a vision of future networked computing called the metaverse with users represented as avatars.

I realized something was afoot and dreamed of my next mission: virtual worlds on the then-nascent internet. Leaving Prague in 1994, I lived in a van and toured around North America visiting anyone who might be working on such a thing. I built a network of contacts ranging from researchers at the new Santa Fe Institute studying artificial life, to Microsoft researchers building social virtual worlds, to some of the first multiuser game developers learning how to push UDP packets through ports. By October 1996, I was standing at the front of the registration line welcoming 500 attendees and speakers to my first annual conference on avatars.

My book on the subject was published the next year and I was nonstop on the road giving talks with live "in-world" virtual world demos. After ten years helping to convene the community of virtual world developers and users, I found that I could use this platform and what had been learned to both pursue the future in space and the origin of life. I applied for grants from NASA and in late 1999 won my first award to simulate a human mission on the Martian surface. Ten years after that I was completing my Ph.D. using our NASA projects team, who had started out building virtual worlds for my avatars cyber-conferences, so it all tied together very nicely!

What was your Ph.D. focused on?

BRUCE: I really wanted to dig deep into the question of emergence, literally how do complex things come into being from simpler ones, addressing the challenge of that bundle of molecules years before. To do that, our team would build another type of virtual world, one that would represent not spacecraft but simulated atoms bouncing around in tiny virtual volumes. The project was called the Evolution Grid, or EvoGrid. I wanted to test ideas of how molecules got together, as that is the first pre-step to life. When it was all coded up and debugged, our team ran the simulations at UC San Diego on a specially designed, compact computing grid. The EvoGrid ran billions of atoms ricocheting around tiny volumes of space in a search for how to optimize the resulting rate of bonds forming between them.

The extended advisors included several really cool scientists around the world including physicist Freeman Dyson who provided valuable input on several occasions, once offering: "Your simulation is too clean, life is messy!" Over a year of nonstop batch computing runs, we landed on an optimized search technique called stochastic hill climbing. I'll never forget the moment we saw the telltale staircasing in the curve representing the number of bonds formed. The search optimization algorithm was like a hiker scaling peaks to complexity (i.e., more bonds formed) then finding their way off these "local maxima" across proba-bilistic ridges and scaling taller nearby peaks, forming yet more bonds.

The programmed hill-climbing hiker was progressing in distinct jumps after periods of little progress, which matched the prediction for the behavior of a system that was drawing order out of a deeply disordered system.

Toward the end of the simulation experiments, I started collaborating with another great thinker, complexity theorist Stuart Kauffman. He told me early on, "You are doing the experiment I have always wanted to do, a hypo-populated reaction graph!" This was quite encouraging and it all came together magically in the spring of 2011 when the staircasing *wiggle* finally appeared. Not only would this wiggle enable me to defend my Ph.D. thesis, but it also suggested something more profound . . . that starting with a noisy landscape, the universe gradually becomes correlated in that bumpy entropic hills are each connected to taller more ordered mountains by ridges. Our hikers can use this algorithmic trick to find their way to tall peaks while minimizing their energy spent.

This also hinted that perhaps this stochastic hill climbing could lie at the root of all complexification, and that things can form connections that keep accumulating. In other words, stuff appears and supports more stuff appearing and it doesn't all just go back to mush. This was a longtime dream realized, a glimmer of a general principle underlying key events in our universe: cosmogenesis, biogenesis, and even conscious genesis.

That's a wonderful recounting of your life up to you completing your doctorate. How did you then make the leap from the wiggle to working on life's origins?

BRUCE: In the midst of my doctoral work in 2009, I met Professor David Deamer of UC Santa Cruz. Dave is one of the world's greatest membrane biophysicists and a true pioneer in the science of the origin of life. He is also the original proposer of a new medical technology called nanopore sequencing, a gene analyzer you can hold in the palm of your hand. The timing of our meeting was perfect and it was the sort of productive partnership that can happen in science. Our skillsets and passions were each uniquely suited to solve this major riddle of existence. Through decades of experiment and reasoning, Dave had concluded that life began not deep in the ocean at hydrothermal vents as had been thought for thirty years, but on land in a wetting and drying version of Charles Darwin's "warm little pond."[1] Through meetings with Dave almost weekly for tea for several years, he provided me training, papers to read, conferences to go to, and even my first experiences of lab and field experiments.

You and Dave came out with what you call the "Hot Spring Hypothesis for an Origin of Life" several years later. Can you give us some insight as to how this came about, and did your propensity for visionary downloads play a role?

BRUCE: This was a point in my life where my curiosity was so piqued and I was synthesizing all this new knowledge so I started experiencing more of these downloads. To give you an idea of where my mind was realming, let's step back 4 billion years ago, before life began. I've provided a lovely rendering in figure 1 of what we think that very alien ancient Earth would have looked like, produced by my friend and colleague Ryan Norkus.

It was a truly alien world, and science tells us it was a toxic lifeless world. If you walked out on its surface without a protective suit and your own oxygen supply, you would expire quickly and horribly. Volcanoes roared forth ash plumes into an orange-brown sky flashing with incoming meteorites and interplanetary dust from a bright disc around the newborn sun. A coffee-colored ocean full of dissolved iron was lifted into violent and huge tides by a moon that was five times closer. Ten-hour days saw faint sunlight bathing an unrecognizable world of rocky volcanic landscapes that bore none of the familiar green of life. But on some of those landscapes where fresh water from rain fell near volcanoes, bubbling multicolored pools formed.

---

1. C. Darwin to J. D. Hooker, 1 February 1871, Darwin Correspondence Project, Letter No. 7471, University of Cambridge.

Fig. 1. Graphical rendering of a conceptual volcanic landscape on the Earth, 4 billion years ago. Organics are raining in from the newly formed solar system and concentrating in hot spring pools driven by geysers through cycles of wetting and drying. Protocells form and cycle at the edge of one pool, collecting into communal complexes and undergoing individual testing and selection. They are cycling in an "engine" that could have been the mechanism behind how life began.

These are hydrothermal fields not unlike those seen at Yellowstone National Park in the United States and in many places around the world today. Whenever I visit them, these bubbling hot springs seem to me like nature's chemistry set and they happen to be perfect places for the chemistry of life's beginning.

Organic ingredients needed for life's primordial soup were falling from the sky, carried on meteorites, dust, joined by compounds synthesized in the atmosphere. They would be lost in the dilute oceans, so could only get together by concentrating in a version of Darwin's warm little pond. Geysers were filling the field of pools and pulsing water into them. Around the edges of some pools a slick of organics formed a sort of natural bathtub ring.

An aside to explain some quick science: water is a *universal solvent* and tears apart important molecules like polymers such as DNA, RNA, and peptides, which life needs to get started. So, you must dry down solutions to both make and preserve these polymers. The polymers themselves are sandwiched between fatty layers of lipid, very much like the boundaries of all living cells. These fatty compounds are also falling in from the sky. When dried lipid layers are re-wetted, they bud off compartments that might contain polymers, and we call these "protocells." In figure 1, we've depicted these as silvery water-filled bubbles cycling to and from the pool's edge. It's a really cool scenario that actually works in practice.

With all of this in mind, one morning in late 2013 I had the most stunning waking dream, the full download that led to our hypothesis. This came to me as a full takeover of my conscious experience shortly after a yoga and breathwork session. I mentally fell into a pool like the one you can see in the figure and moved alongside the protocells as they budded off at the edge of a pool, floated into it, and either wobbled apart or survived. I noticed that the protocells containing stringy sets of polymers lasted longer and as the pool level dropped, they clustered together at the bottom. As the clump of protocells dried further, they began to fuse together, delivering their cargos of polymers into a new mix between lipid layers. The polymers were coupled between wet and dry phases and circled around and around. This was the key insight that I drew out and shared with Dave, after which he said, "You found it; you found the kinetic trap!" The visionary download had delivered a way for sets of polymers to cycle and be subject to selection pressures that would start them evolving . . . toward life!

I would guess that many people have visionary downloads but the ones that stick are those that get translated into something that can be tested in the real world.

BRUCE: You've got it! In my case I had to translate purely visual information into conservative and precise scientific language that Dave and other scientists would deem plausible. It is really important to avoid the "woo factor," which can shut people down and block your ideas. This requires training and discipline and not overclaiming things. I managed to navigate all of that with Dave's help and we published our first major article that described the scenario in 2015.[2] Later we developed a third phase in our wet-dry cycling scenario, an intermediate moist phase in which we proposed that our protocells jostle together and form a communal unit. It is within this unit that we believe the networked circuits of biology would first arise.

Those networks would operate a bit like the internet as deeply codependent and collaborative work nodes. Protocells are too simple to survive on their own, let alone compete, so to grow and adapt they need to engage in a sharing of tasks and resources, much like the consortia of microbial and fungal-plant relationships we see in nature today. We described this next set of proposals first in 2016[3] and developed them further with testable experiments in our paper titled "The Hot Spring Hypothesis for an Origin of Life," which appeared in print in 2020.[4]

---

2. B. F. Damer and D. W. Deamer, "Coupled Phases and Combinatorial Selection in Fluctuating Hydrothermal Pools: A Scenario to Guide Experimental Approaches to the Origin of Cellular Life," *Life* 5, no. 1 (2015): 872–87.
3. B. F. Damer, "A Field Trip to the Archaean in Search of Darwin's Warm Little Pond," *Life* 6, no. 2 (2016): 21.
4. B. F. Damer and D. W. Deamer, *Astrobiology* 20, no. 4 (2020): 429–52.

I am happy to say that this scenario is being worked on by many groups around the world and that wet-dry (and moist) cycling has become a standard technique to generate polymers and protocells in origins of life experiments.

So, there you have it, a circuitous journey from the moment I beheld my first visionary download, the bundle of molecules, and the formal proposal for how life emerged. It turns out a lot of little machines can get together in a network such that a bigger machine can emerge.

So cool! So how does this insight that life started not as competing individuals but as a collaborating community factor into how we might re-interpret our world and ourselves?

BRUCE: This is the big philosophical offering of this work—that "survival of the fittest," a term coined in 1864 by Herbert Spencer and adopted into Darwinian evolutionary thought, may not in fact be the primary driver of life. Indeed, competition between living things might be a special localized modality that is supported within a deeply collaborative milieu. So life, including human life, is really based on a web of interconnection. Perhaps hippies and mystics were right all along!

Of course! So, Bruce, how can understanding how the origin of life occurred on our own world give us a picture of where life can start in the universe?

BRUCE: An excellent question! Building on this work, Dave and I and our student Francesca Cary recently introduced a new term to science: *urability*, which describes two dozen factors that we believe must come together on a world for life to start.[5] This framework can guide the search for life on worlds such as Mars, chilly moons like Enceladus or Titan, and the thousands of exoplanets being imaged by advanced space telescopes like Kepler and TESS.

Where life can start will determine which worlds can support the rise

---

5. B. F. Damer et al., "It's High Time for Science" (Video conference presented at ESPD '55, Dorset, England, May 25, 2022). Available at YouTube (website).

of complex life, and possibly intelligent beings and their technologies we may be able to detect. Decades ago, astronomer Frank Drake penned an equation to work out how many Earthlike planets housing intelligence might be in our galaxy. One factor was the number of worlds where life can start. With urability we may have the ability to estimate that much better, which will inform SETI, the Search for Extraterrestrial Intelligence.

That's really big-picture stuff! What is your day job as chief scientist of BIOTA like?

BRUCE: It's the best job in the world (for me)! Dave and I co-founded the BIOTA Institute some years ago and its mission is to support students and post-docs who want to travel to the United States and engage in experiments in the lab at UCSC to test the hypothesis. Our third student is about to arrive and will engage in a year of very exciting work. BIOTA also explores implications of the origin scenario for other fields of endeavor as it gathers evidence (or becomes falsified, which is always a possibility).

Some areas the science is influencing include evolutionary biology in niche construction theory with John Odling-Smee[6] and group selection with David Sloan Wilson,[7] Alfred North Whitehead's philosophy with Matt Segall,[8] artificial general intelligence with Ben Goertzel,[9] and most recently theology and the thinking of Teilhard de Chardin with Franciscan Sister Ilia Delio.[10]

---

6. See B. F. Damer, "The Hot Spring Hypothesis for the Origin of Life and the Extended Evolutionary Synthesis. Essay for Extended Evolutionary Synthesis project," ExtendedEvolutionarySynthesis (website), May 8, 2019.

7. D. Sloan Wilson, with B. Damer, "Science of the Noosphere," *Origin of Life* (podcast), Human Energy, April 26, 2022. Available on YouTube.

8. M. Segall and B. F. Damer, "The Cosmological Context of the Origin of Life: Process Philosophy and the Hot Spring Hypothesis," forthcoming in *Worlds Beyond Imagination: Astrophilosophy, Cosmotheology, and Religiosity in a Process Universe* (Lanham, MD: Lexington Books, 2023).

9. J. Rutt, with Ben Goertzal, "Currents No. 72: Ben Goertzel on Viable Paths to True AGI," *The Jim Rutt Show* (podcast), JimRuttShow (website), October 18, 2022.

10. Delio and R. Nicastro, "What Is God, with Dr. Bruce Damer," *Hunger for Wholeness* (podcast), October 31, 2022. Available on Apple (website).

Recently you have opened up and candidly shared how psyche-delics have shaped your visionary downloads in science. How did that go for you and have you felt pushback or rejection from the hard science community?

BRUCE: That's a big one! It was meeting Terence McKenna on his visit here in 1998 that gave me the impetus and courage to dip my toes into his mystical realms I had read about for so long. Perhaps it is worth telling that story as it is tightly interwoven with everything in my life since. I was a psychedelic late bloomer and until age thirty-seven had studiously avoided psychoactive drugs and even milder things like aspirin or caffeine as I was both highly sensitive and worried that they might interfere with my own endogenous visioneering machinery.

Prior to visiting Terence at his house near Captain Cook in Hawaii in February of 1999, we had decided to trade places, with him entering my virtual worlds inhabited by people represented as graphical avatars and me passing through the psychedelic threshold to enter his trypt-amine worlds. So in preparation, I decided to experience my first "heroic dose" mushroom trip, made possible through Terence. Not surprisingly this experience was a life changer and set me up nicely to interact some-what on the same turf with Terence.

It was a rousing success and Terence was hopeful that he could cut down on his travel by speaking to groups inside these worlds. While comparing notes as to the nature of the virtual versus the psychedelic experientia, Terence announced that this avatar cyberspace had been "not unlike DMT." We talked late into the night on topics of novelty, space colonization, and artificial intelligence. I challenged Terence on his belief (and popularization) of a coming "Singularity" in the year 2012 in which a super-intelligent AI would emerge from the internet and summarily take over everything and accelerate us all beyond history.

How did Terence respond to your pushback?

BRUCE: I realized then that Terence had little practical experience with technology and hadn't written a line of code. Yet he was rather boldly proposing that something as sophisticated as a disembodied intelligence would somehow emerge in the laughably simplistic computing space of email, web pages, and online shopping. I labored to explain the difference between the compute-space of the living world and the internet. After a long cannabis-fueled rap session Terence intonated, "Well, I hope they don't take it all too literally!"

Terence was struck with a seizure announcing a large brain tumor months after our DMT-inspired avatar powwow and a group of us gathered with him one last time at the AllChemical Arts conference in Kona in September 1999. I held a vigil for him here at Ancient Oaks Farm on April 2, 2000, and he passed the next day. Terence and I had been planning to go on the road together in a lecture tour starting at Esalen in the spring of 2000 but that was not to be.

I felt quite sad that I had lost a potentially wonderful intellectual partner and new friend, but recalled Terence telling me to "keep telling the story, but tell your own story." I then determined that as part of my next phase of life entering fully into science, I would dedicate myself to tackling our late-night question of the sources of novelty (i.e., complex emergence). The rest, as we might say, is history. I wish Terence was around today, as I could provide him quite the rap on how the novelty question is progressing.

Indeed, we all miss Terence! How did you take the gift of meeting him into your life?

Bruce: Terence was truly my gateway drug into the psychedelic community. In the twenty years since Terence passed, I had to do quite a bit of healing of my own internal traumas, perhaps most significantly around the separation from my birth parents. These things were buried deeply and took many journeys to the jungle to visit with the profoundly intelligent medicine ayahuasca. With these blockages cleared by healing came an enhanced revealing and the floodgates opened on my downloads. On one of those journeys came the first breakthrough that led to the insights into the origin of life I shared earlier. I went public with this at Dennis McKenna's ESPD (Ethnopharmacologic Search for

Psychoactive Plants) '55 conference in the UK in May of 2022 in a talk titled "It's High Time for Science" and contributed a chapter for the upcoming third volume in the ESPD series.[11]

In this chapter I chronicle how in the late 1950s and early 1960s, psychedelics were thought of as tools for the intellect, the definition of the word coined by Humphrey Osmond being "mind manifesting." I called for a new "way to genius" using psychedelics for creative problem solving in science, technology, and leadership. So far, my colleagues in science haven't overtly commented or rejected our work, perhaps because psychedelics don't carry the same stigma as they did even five years ago, or perhaps because this story is not yet well known.

What are your next steps on the work? Do you have any grand plans you'd like to share?

BRUCE: While sitting on a park bench in Montpellier, France, after the 2011 ISSOL (International Society for the Study of the Origin of Life) meeting I had a vision to use a cycling system of chemical experiments as a next step beyond the EvoGrid. I felt that computers were and would remain woefully underpowered to support the bigger mission of simulating an origin of life. It turns out that the biggest supercomputing grid in the world could not create a completely predictive molecular dynamic simulation of one human neuron. So much for uploading your consciousness to cyberspace! I felt that real chemistry and biology are so computationally rich, you might as well just "let the atoms do the computing." How could we marry real chemicals swirling within their compartments to computers somehow testing the results and guiding the next steps?

In one of my early meetings with Dave, I carted along a Lucite rocker table a friend and I had built. It hosted a beaker with inputs that could be sloshed back and forth, simulating the dynamics you might see

11. B. F. Damer, "It's High Time for Science," in *Ethnopharmacologic Search for Psychoactive Drugs*, ed. D. McKenna, W. Davis, N. Gericke, and B. de Loenen (Synergetic Press, forthcoming), vol. 3.

in a freshwater pool. Dave smiled and beckoned me to come with him down the hall to the lab, and there was a professional version of my amateur attempt. It was a true chemical robot featuring an aluminum disc housing twenty-four glass vials that rotate under an injector that squirts in a volume of water. The vials would continue around in their sealed, heated, carbon dioxide-filled chamber to a similar drying station.

The simulation chamber was a success and led to other groups building their own. Today, Dave and I, through our BIOTA Institute and partners, are seeking support to develop a much more complex simulation of a hot spring in the laboratory we are calling a "Genesis Engine." The various engines, one simulating early Earth conditions, another for early Mars, would be paired with computers controlling injectors, rates of wetting and drying, sampling, and analysis.

A silicon-based computing engine would provide an AI system that would make predictions about the chemistry going on in the chemical engines, inject short synthesized polymers, and study their effects on the protocell populations. In this way our laboratory engines can jump the queue of random polymer selection and accelerate toward evolving protocells. The first mass of protocells that exhibits that evolution that can grow against stresses and adapt by "discovering" new polymers will make world news, much as the spark chamber amino acid experiment of Miller and Urey did back in the early 1950s.

Jumping to a philosophical question that interests me greatly, do you see any type of teleology, intelligence, or mindful intention operating in evolution in nature or at the origin of life?

BRUCE: When we talk about teleology, intelligence, or the presence of a mindful designer, we invoke yet another name for god. Perhaps it is baked into our primate makeup that we feel the need for a super toolmaker, another primate who fashioned the world. However, the universe is larger and stranger than we can suppose and I don't think that it employs a primate measuring stick for how it rolls out complex systems such as stars, planets, or life.

I also disagree with postulations that the vast splay of dust, gas, and galaxies (and dark energy and matter) we detect with our telescopes has a collective mind. It's just not observably anything like the living minds that we know. In fact, the universe gets a D for complexity. If we look to old starlight, traveling for 10 billion years to reach us, we see an early universe that contains pretty much the same stars, galaxies, and a heck of a lot of dust, just with fewer heavier elements. It is not until you get to life, localized for the most part on quite special water-bearing rocky worlds, that arrangements of atoms begin to take more complicated, action-oriented innovative forms.

I suppose it is natural for us to project intention or being onto objects or places outside of ourselves. However, the true situation is much more interesting than that! In another download one night I asked the extant universe if there needed to be a mind guiding life's arising and it answered simply by throwing the cosmos (itself) at my consciousness! It was like being hit in the face with a cream puff pie made of globular clusters. I felt the impact of this perhaps more obvious truth that the universe grew large enough to permit the probabilistic likelihood of us arising! So "god" as creator is actually just the totality and combinatorial power of the universe. It grew big and diverse enough to provide a vanishingly small but not impossible path for complex life like ourselves to arise.

How does that universe bring about us? From all my prior and current work with Dave and many other colleagues, I believe that it is always cycles that bring simple things into increasing complexity. Planets rotate around their parent stars, and spin on their axes. Weather and hydrological cycles are driven by this process and help to form geological complexity. The specific cycling system that we discovered working in hot springs can possibly spin a lot of carbon-based stuff into something called "life." The whole system is largely driven by the sun rising each morning and showering a planet with high quality energy that can be converted into chemical activity.

So then the sun is the real puppet master, the great cycler. Four billion dawns powered up the living world and gave rise to us, and all of our culture and technology. Everything is intimately tied to that cycle so, in a real sense, there doesn't need to be a teleology or an intention behind any of life, because it is actually a naturally induced, cycling energetic system. Life and the great exploration of chemical phase space by evolution are both driven to happen, not pulled forward by some directed teleological (purposeful) end goal.

Perhaps when you get to human intelligence and forethought, then goal-based planning begins and we call that teleological, but is it really? Arguments over free will are not my bailiwick but perhaps it is a high form of hubris to think that we are in full control of much. If we did an experiment and moved the Earth into deep space, out of the sun's influence, we would witness the crashing of all the beautiful, self-regulating structure of our biosphere, and us along with it. So we are intimately dependent on deeply nested cycles being just right to sustain a very complicated reality on a very fragile base.

Do you think that some sort of superconsciousness is a primal property of the cosmos and is somehow involved in these cycles and in our evolution, or do you see it as a blind, mechanistic process with intelligence and consciousness somehow emerging from it?

BRUCE: Thank you pursing this provocative question further, David. The idea of consciousness being primal is sometimes called panpsychism. I am afraid to disappoint many in that I feel it is an example of highly wishful thinking, unscientific projection, and is tantamount to a search for a new identity for god. Strong believers in this view offer that some vaguely defined form of consciousness (and thereby a guiding hand) is a fundamental property of matter rather than an emergent phenomenon of biological evolution.

This proposal is untestable, and probably not even developable as an effective hypothesis. This thinking denies 500 years of hard work and accumulating evidence in science that has built up an understanding of how our universe, our world, and life likely emerged. Terence McKenna, not a disciplined scientific thinker by any means but an admirer of the products and process of science, held forth that regardless of arguments for god, a conscious universe, or a secret cabal running the world,

"The real truth, that dare not speak itself, is that no one is in control. Absolutely no one."

Do you have an alternative proposal from your work on life's origins?

BRUCE: Yes, I'd like to propose an alternative to panpsychism or god narratives, an explanatory reductionist and mechanistic model that could account for all phenomena, including extraordinary conscious experiences such as the ineffable touched by mystics and psychedelicists. Please understand that this is a conjecture or thought experiment and not a serious scientific hypothesis. Let us take as our sole canon the new knowledge acquired largely since the middle of the last century: how life emerged and operates (evolution and the machinery of the cell); how it might have emerged (our work and that of many others); how a life-bearing world like the Earth was formed and how rare it might be in the pantheon of planets; and an understanding of the physiology and interactions of organisms and their surrounding environment.

If you got your head around just a casual working knowledge of all of this, you might then be able to ask, what potential does evolution possess to generate novel and extraordinary phenomena? One of its products are human beings and our technical and cultural innovations, so I would reply that it's already *a pretty darned impressive potential.* Who is to say that this system shouldn't have the capacity to instantiate experiences we now consider beyond explanation including the paranormal, spiritual, or seemingly only plausibly emanating from a guiding super-intelligence?

If we simply open our eyes to the functional miracle of our bodies, that should be convincing enough of the potency of evolution and the living world. It has been said that the unique informational pathways through the neurons in our brain outnumber the countable subatomic particles of the entire universe. Even at life's origins, I would offer that the seemingly simple slurry of membranous layers encapsulating quintillions of polymers forms a *progenitor* substrate that distinct object by distinct object is more complex than the planet that lies beneath it.

From this progenitor emerges the first communal unit of proto-cells called a progenote, and then onward to living microbial communities. For another perspective on the stunning reality-shaping power of this system, what started out as a soft, filmy gelatinous pond scum labors through billions of years to transform a toxic world into a garden. When you're talking about life, the numbers always have been, and continue to be, huge.

I agree that this whole scenario, the machinery that made us, is pretty mind-blowing. Given that as a basis, where do you sense the emergence of intelligence, consciousness, and the mystical experience fits into this story?

BRUCE: Let's take a look at this process *in toto*, and we might find some clues. After years of pondering all of this, one night at a beach near where I live in Northern California, a spectacular sculpture came to me in another download. It appeared floating in my mind's eye out over the Pacific at dusk. It was rendered in lovely computer graphical form by my friend and colleague Ryan Norkus in figure 2. Frankly, this is the sort of mystical experience that makes my life worth living and provides the stepping-stone for years of future inquiry. This sculpture came to me after I asked a question out to the emerging stars appearing behind the sinking golden sun. I had recently realized that as life on Earth grew increasingly complex over 4 billion years, it must now have reached an exquisitely high off-normal position, normal being the background physics of the majority "dead" universe.

If you follow the spire from bottom to top, the blast represents the Big Bang that begat atomic elements in the furnaces of stars, which over time permitted the formation of metals giving us the geology of rocky planets. The urable zones of biogenesis, where life can start, emerged within a hot spring bubbling like nature's chemistry set. Within that zone formed the first primitive microbes, which spread across the land and adapted to the marine environment. Colonizing the Earth, these microbes began their evolutionary climb on a wide platform of densely interconnected communities.

Fig. 2. *The Silver Spire*, a visual representation of the origin of the universe, the origin of life, and its subsequent evolution over 4 billion years to the arising of self-awareness in animals and consciousness in humans.

Driven by daily cycling of sunlight, *a core algorithm* spun inside each protocell and then within all subsequent living cells: P-I-M. PIM is a fundamental insight from our science that holds that you need three factors operating in tandem to get life started and keep it going: the **P**robability of unlikely things happening increased through crowding molecules together in compartments; **I**nteractions between these compartments that can then set up a sharing network; and **M**emories, which can encode blueprints for future generations . . . the first genes. PIM is incessantly driven by inputs of energy and nutrients and grows an enormous surrounding super-niche made of the outputs and effects of living systems. Some of these include catalytic by-products, detritus, polymeric and electrical information, and energetic and chemical messaging.

This super-niche forms around the "spire" of living things and their genes, which climbs ever higher off the ground floor of the prebiotic world. Three billion years up, larger organisms emerge, seen in the spire as blobs floating within the silvery column. Simple bacteria and archaea beget multi-organed eukaryotes that become multicellular fungi, plants, and then animals. The pace of evolutionary complexity surges as oxygen enters the metabolic equation powering ever-bigger bodies.

Then 90 percent of the way up the spire, some animals develop brains large enough that they are able to recognize themselves as distinct individuals, perhaps beginning with a dolphin catching her reflection in the eye of a pod mate. The eye opens not only to self, but to others, and to inquiry into the nature of the world. Toolmaking and the capacity to alter the world bring our ancestors into an intensified dynamic with their world. The red lines signify a phase transition into a nonlinear high-octane acceleration of PIM through the invention of language, culture, and technology.

Subject to crazy evolutionary pressures in this red zone, humans develop a dense planetary interconnection network, crowd into huge cities, and generate vast information stores. PIM erupts into a new level of output as the surrounding super-niche becomes more of a real-time "field" so densely ramified that extraordinary novel events proliferate. These events defy our ability to grok them and a time of magic ensues in which what would previously be thought of as miraculous becomes ubiquitous. Through endogenous (e.g., contemplative) and exogenous (e.g., psychedelics) practices, we learn how to turn on the full neural bundle of our brains. The turned-on primate brain resonating within such a ramified informational environment turns it into a transceiver that can receive and generate patterns, which we call extraordinary, mystical, or ineffable.

Through introspective practices, extreme flow states, psychoactive elevated states, many tools turn on minds unbound. Into these turned-on minds can pass an infinity of downloads. Those who have trained their minds with reason and absorbed the latest understanding of our origins and evolution might find themselves at the arc at the top of the spire. Full realization of our place in the universe sparks and we fully wake up to the extraordinary reality of what created us. Perhaps this is a route to reach a sort of grounded enlightenment about life and about ourselves. Through this and other routes to such a cosmological awareness, we might then be moved to take on the sacred mantle of caretaking and carrying forward this exquisitely rare bequeath of the universe.

It sounds like you have been true to Terence's request of you to tell your own story and that you've landed on your own scientific version of his eschaton.

BRUCE: That is a great observation, David! I'd like to add that like Terence said, such an extraordinary realization and the tools to access it are available to every human. We can also reach outside of ourselves and touch the very ground of that full story. In figure 3, I am holding a fragment of the oldest mineral record of a hot spring on Earth, replete with evidence of life going back 3.5 billion years ago, not long after life itself began. I was permitted to sample it while visiting early life fossil sites in northwestern Australia in 2016 with colleagues from the University of New South Wales.

Not far from the hot spring discovery outcrop is Gallery Hill, an enormous collection of Aboriginal petroglyphs dating back tens of thousands of years. A day's drive farther south is Shark Bay with its

Fig. 3. A sample of geyserite from northwest Australia,
3.5-billion-year-old evidence of hot springs and life on Earth
as far back as we've been able to look.

colonies of modern-day stromatolites, microbial communities that grow towers of rock leaving telltale fingerprints of life back as far as we can look. Studying the coming to awareness of humans through their depictions chiseled into the rock and reading the rock record of our microbial ancestors in deep time, I believe that we can become fully interwoven with this, our universal creation tale. I offer that the full feeling of its magnificence is enough to give all of us more meaning in our lives and perhaps a stronger will to survive and thrive into the future.

On humanity's will to survive, it seems to me that we may be losing some of the focus on that in the face of coming challenges, including those of our own making. How do you see your work on the origin of life contributing to a new refocusing on the survival and thriving of our species and world?

BRUCE: The golden thread that seems to weave its way through my life is that I have been gifted with visionary downloads that were often pivotal. I have come to trust this process and have been successfully guided at critical junctures if I paid critical attention to the downloads and took action. The sources of these downloads are mysterious but perhaps they are some combination of my deep subconscious but also emanating from some sort of superconscious field much like the synchronous field described by Carl Jung and many others. This field may in fact be a probability-shaping operating system that runs in the superniche depicted surrounding our spire. How's that for a hand-waving speculation?

Many of us experience downloads and cultivate some sort of relationship to sources of vision: the scientist's or engineer's thought experiment; the artist's muse; the composer's amanuensis; and the believer's guiding hand of deity. For nerdy people like me, the most sought after and inspiring downloads are technical in nature. Perhaps one of the most visionary engineers of the last century was early Russian rocket scientist Konstantin Tsiolkovsky who famously said, "Earth is the cradle of humanity and you cannot stay in the cradle forever." His numerous visionary downloads led to formulations and inventions that presaged a future landing on the moon and much more.

An action-oriented visionary of our own time, Elon Musk, has taken off on Tsiolkovsky by adding, "It is time to go forth and become a star-faring civilization, be out there among the stars and to expand the scale of human consciousness. I find that incredibly exciting, that makes me glad to be alive. I hope you feel the same way."[12] Perhaps the quest for our own origins and the ultimate discovery of an engine of creation behind life itself will bring a similar expansion of the scale of our own consciousness. For me this quest for our ultimate ancestor is an authentically spiritual one and gives my life and existence on this Earth a profound meaning. Perhaps this could for others too.

What might be the more on-the-ground takeaways for all of us? Consider this: by generating protocells in the lab and observing their first faltering steps toward life, we will gain a deep appreciation of the difficulty that life might have faced to even come into being as the first

---

12. L. K. Rawlins, "Musk Says Interplanetary Colonisation Vital," ITweb (website), March 12, 2018.

primitive cells. Perhaps the emergence of multicellular life and intelligence was also vanishingly improbable, but it happened! A deeply held sense of our own exquisite rarity could impart to each of us a renewed vow for survival. For if we are to be faithful to the miracle of our own arising, we might get up each morning working more carefully to secure the future. As we emerge from the cradle and witness Earth from above, we would vow to become its caring steward, reproduce new Earths in space, and provide all of life an infinite path into the cosmos.

One last question, where do you see your life going now?

BRUCE: At the age of sixty and after all these explorations on this circuitous crazy path, I plan to dedicate the rest of my life to the implications of unraveling the mystery of our creation and how we might move ourselves and all of life forward. I will continue to explore this with thought leaders around the world and perhaps Dave Deamer and I will find a way to power up the first Genesis Engine in a lab somewhere!

I look forward to checking back with you on how that develops! Thank you so much for your time.

BRUCE: The pleasure will be mine!

7

Neuroscience, Comedy, and Psychonautic Adventures

An Interview with Shane Mauss

Shane Mauss is a comedian who integrates neuroscience, evolutionary psychology, and his psychedelic experiences into his performances. He is the host of the *Here We Are* podcast show, where he interviews neuroscientists and psychologists about their latest research. Mauss also hosts "Stand up Science" presentations around the country, where he brings together cutting-edge scientific researchers and explores their work in entertaining ways.

Shane Mauss

After Mauss's first performance at the Greater Boston Alternative Comedy Festival in 2007, he won the Best Standup Comic Award at HBO's Comedy Arts Festival, and since then has performed and appeared numerous times on many popular shows and networks, including *Late Night with Conan O'Brien*, *The Joe Rogan Experience*, Comedy Central, and Showtime.

In 2010 Mauss released his first comedy album, *Jokes to Make My Parents Proud*, which *Punchline Magazine* named one of the top ten albums of 2010. In 2014 Mauss shattered both his heel bones while mountain climbing, and then used the experience as inspiration for his 2015 comedy album *My Big Break*.

From 2016 to 2018 Mauss toured over a hundred cities with his show "A Good Trip," which was about his psychedelic experiences. He also created a documentary called *Psychonautics* in 2018 about the science behind psychedelics and his personal adventures with the mind-altering substances. To find out more about Mauss's work, see the ShaneMauss website.

Insightful and hilarious, reminiscent of Bill Hicks and Timothy Leary, Mauss has a lot of far-ranging interests and fascinating influences that he incorporates into his performances. I interviewed Shane on July 15, 2019. I found Shane to be funny, well informed, and considerably thoughtful. Among the many topics that we discussed, we touched upon how psychedelics inspired his interest in science, why he thinks it's valuable for us to question our perceptions, how his overindulgence in psychedelics led to a mental breakdown, and how his personal experiences influenced his comedy routines.

I've heard you describe your childhood self as being rather rebellious. Can you tell me about what you were like as a child, and how you first became interested in doing comedy and started your career as a performer?

SHANE: Sure, as a child, around the age of five, I guess I felt like I didn't really fit in. I started playing around with not listening to adults and really took that in. Looking back on things, I see a lot of my fondness for pushing people's buttons and going against the grain. That took hold from a very early age, and I became a contrarian early on. I think that when I heard about the idea of being a stand-up comedian, and what that entailed, it's just the only thing that ever struck me as something that would be interesting to do in life.

So I had that idea since the age of like nine or ten, or something like that. It was roughly the same time that I fully decided that I definitely did not agree with any of the things that were coming down from society, my parents, school, or any kind of authority on how life worked. I didn't agree with any of my religious upbringing. I found school to be a child prison, and that I didn't feel like I really fit in there or related to very many people.

How did you actually begin performing? You started out doing stand-up in Boston, I believe?

SHANE: Yeah, you've really done your research. I started in my early twenties, when I finally stopped putting off my dreams. I tagged along with a friend to Boston and had a fresh start to my life. Looking back, it wasn't a fully fresh start, but it was enough for me to get started in what I actually wanted to do. I started pursuing comedy up there. It was a really good place to start at the time, and I developed really quickly. I was able to catch some breaks, I got some TV credits, and then was able to be a full-time headlining comedian shortly after that.

How have your experiences with psychedelic drugs and plants influenced your thinking, your creativity, your comedy, and your view of reality?

SHANE: Well, those are a lot of different questions. Let's see. I started doing psychedelics when I was sixteen. At the time it was very confirming to me that the world is much stranger, and reality is not what we are told it is in school, and often the way that many of us are raised, or the way that church would have us believe. In hindsight, I think much of what psychedelics do is bring out much of what is already in there, but I guess the unexpected thing was that it opened my eyes to a natural curiosity to wildlife, nature, natural systems, and really, how the mind works.

Being a closeted, angry atheist who would jump at the chance to crush organized religion whenever I could as a teenager led me to wanting to learn about the Big Bang and evolution, because those were at the time serving me as a way of getting better at arguing with people. But once I did psychedelics it just got me much more interested in what existence is actually all about, how we came to be here, and how that drives our patterns and behaviors.

I went through streaks of pretty heavy psychedelic use early on in my life, and then I also had times in my twenties when I didn't have access to them, or was in a relationship where I wasn't allowed to do psychedelics. So I would say in my mid to late twenties, it was very rare when I used psychedelics, but they had an impact, and I had always had psychedelic material in my act. I thought of it as a way of bringing up absurd and creative topics and thoughts and giving context to my more far-out ideas. I guess that's how I used psychedelics, as an excuse to talk about the weird things that I already liked talking about early on in my act.

Then in my thirties, when I had some relationship changes and was able to do psychedelics more often, I once again became really interested in nature, the meaning of life, and those big ideas. That really heightened my already natural curiosity in science, and so I don't think I would now have a science podcast, and be touring around with a half-science, half-comedy show had it not been for the influence that psychedelics had on me. I think that the origins of a lot of the really big ideas about psychology, neuroscience, consciousness, and perception that I have can be traced back to a lot of psychedelic experiences.

For me, psychedelics have always been a tool to understand the mind. They have been a source of creativity and inspiration, but I've never used them in any kind of a spiritual way. I have inadvertently had what many would call, and what I would maybe even call, spiritual experiences from psychedelics, but I never went into a psychedelic experience with the intention of having any kind of a spiritual awakening or anything like that.

Those times when that did happen to me, if anything, it was a little bit confusing and troubling, but ultimately was really insightful into understanding people when they talk about spiritual practices, mystical or spiritual experiences that they had, and where they're coming from. Psychedelics have given me a lot of insight into that, and they've also given me a lot of empathy for people who do find themselves attached to religion and those sorts of things.

That's really interesting; I didn't know that psychedelics played such an important role in inspiring your interest in science. I actually wanted to ask you if you could just speak a little bit about your podcast show, Here We Are, *the "Stand up Science" presentations that you host, and how your interest in evolutionary psychology, neuroscience, and the scientific ideas that you explore in your shows influence or inspire your comedy routines, as well as your view of human social behavior and the world?*

SHANE: My science podcast *Here We Are* is four plus, almost five years now. Each week I've been in my travels interviewing a different scientist. Much of it is about why we behave the way that we do, and so a lot of it's grounded in behavior and the mind. Then I have this new live show that's taking off for me called "Stand up Science," which I do in alternative venues and small theaters.

I do a show that's half-comedy and half-science. I have a second comedian with me in each show, and then two scientists. So it's all different guests everywhere that I travel to, and all different subjects. I use it as a platform for exploring a lot of my bigger ideas, in a fun way, and getting to do a lot of my more cerebral content. And how has it changed . . . ?

Or inspired your comedy routines and your view of human social behavior?

SHANE: Gosh, well I mean it's kind of swallowed up my comedy, because I started off as a more traditional comedian. I'm definitely someone who liked to push buttons, and can be edgy or whatever, but I'm also an absurdist comedian, and I had a traditional route of doing late-night comedy and headlining comedy clubs, that sort of thing. But the more I got into science, the more I got off the beaten track, the traditional comedy path, and into doing more independent things. At this point I sometimes even wonder if I'm still a comedian. [*Laughter*]

Sometimes I feel like I've drifted further into the space of a science communicator, who uses a past background in comedy to help do that, more so than I am a comedian. But that's only because my science podcast is where most of my passion lies now. However, with my new show "Stand up Science," it's really opening up that part of myself that wants to do science jokes and stuff. It's just that with regular comedy clubs it's hard to do that kind of material, to drunk and bachelor and bachelorette parties that you're having to babysit. So it's definitely influenced my career path.

Evolutionary psychology and biology and understanding some of the evolutionary mechanisms that have shaped us have influenced my views of perception. Intuitively, a lot of people think about evolution as like, oh okay, we went from being on all fours to standing upright, and we have these opposable thumbs. That's how evolution has acted on us. But what's far more important and interesting is the way in which evolution has shaped our minds, our perceptions, our desires, our behaviors, as well as the very things that one might be attracted to and the things that we want to avoid.

Let's take a dung beetle for example. A big cow patty is just absolute heaven to a dung beetle. In some species it's where they live, it's how they attract mates, what they eat, and where they raise their offspring. It is absolutely everything to their whole lives. When they go around to church and talk about what's past this experience, they're dreaming about that big pile of never-ending dung in the sky. That's just their idea of heaven, because it has all sorts of nutritional value, is their shelter, their nesting ground, and everything else to them.

Whereas to us, feces is a source of bacteria and disease, and it has the exact opposite effect on how it's shaped our mind. We want to get as far away from that stuff as possible, for the most part. We've built these plumbing systems that flush away our own feces just as far as we can get it away from us, just as quickly as possible, and there's a lot of evolutionary reasons why that's the case. It's based on context, and that's very subjective. There's nothing objectively good or bad about feces, it's just that those ancestors that had a fondness for feces caught diseases and didn't last very long. The ones that had a natural repulsion to it did a lot better for themselves. And the same kind of mechanism shaped the way that we are attracted to the people we're attracted to, how and why we make friends, how we seek status, especially males, as well as how we avoid disease, rear our children, and just try to survive. What drives our fears, and what drives our desires.

The very dreams that we have have a foundation based on what our evolutionary past was, and our biggest, wildest ideas of our inner worlds and what is life after death are all subject to, and fed through, the filter of our past environment in deep time, as well. Once you start understanding that, it's pretty much impossible to see the world in the same way. Oftentimes when people ask me about something like DMT, I say it is a very jarring experience, very intense, and very unlike any other perception. I don't even necessarily recommend DMT to the average person. I don't tell people not to do it either.

I don't know, for me it's been this really interesting, curious thing to think about, and I'll never be able to see life the same, ever again. People wonder about that, that you can't put the toothpaste back in the tube, and do you want to have this experience where you can never see anything the same again? But to me that's just learning in general. Everything that I learned through my science podcast, especially in terms of evolution, and some neuroscience stuff, I can't help but see and interact with the world completely differently.

Yes, those insights can change one's perspective on reality enormously. Shane, I was interested to learn about your Irish background, that you're around 75 percent Irish. Have you been influenced by Irish philosopher/comedians Timothy Leary and Robert Anton Wilson, who were doing what they called "stand-up philosophy" routines at nightclubs back in the 1990s? Are you aware of this and has it influenced you in any way?

SHANE: I was not aware, and I don't think about my Irish background in any way, other than I've been to Ireland a couple of times. I guess I'm always seeking out ways to go against tradition. I'm such a sucker for the latest and greatest, and always want the most cutting-edge information, so I have a real lack in knowledge of the past, or of classical philosophy, and many cultural traditions. It's a big blind spot that I have. Much of it is because when I do read more classical philosophy, I can't help but think how different those philosophers would have been in talking, had they known about evolution.

Oh, I meant more recent psychedelic philosophers. During the 1990s the late psychologists Timothy Leary and Robert Anton Wilson were going to nightclubs, doing these comedy-philosophy routines. They even incorporated evolutionary perspectives and psychedelic experiences into their performance. There seems to have been some foreshadowing of what you're doing now, it seems.

SHANE: Really? Yeah, I'll have to check it out.

You mentioned DMT earlier. What are your thoughts about the entities that people report encountering on DMT; do you think there's a reality to these beings or do you think that they're just complex hallucinations?

SHANE: Well, I don't know that we have to pick one of those sides or the other. I don't know why both can't be true at the same time. There's a sort of DMT lexicon online, with a big list of the common things that people seem to see under the influence of DMT. I've read through that, and my perception is that I've seen about half of those things that seem to really ring true for me. Then the other half just don't seem like anything that I've experienced.

Not to say they aren't true. I'm absolutely sure that people are quite honestly reporting their experiences and are having them independent of one another. I definitely don't think it's as easy as writing off these experiences as being due to having been influenced by others—that you heard someone else talking about DMT, and then you smoked it and you were influenced by them talking about it.

I have not found that to be the case with the DMT experience. I found it to be almost the opposite case, where every time that I think that I was maybe prepared for what I am going to see, it shows a completely new and different experience to me. I could sit online and look at every piece of DMT-inspired art that's ever been made, and smoke DMT, and sometimes see similar things and other times see completely different stuff.

So I think this lends itself to some of my ideas. To start, I don't think that anybody, or the majority of users, are in any way making up these reports, which is what some people who haven't done DMT sometimes think. So I don't think that's the case at all. I definitely have many times had the exact same experience of feeling like I'm talking with some sort of beings, gods, or spirits, or interacting with some other dimension that is outside of this.

I really value integration, more than anything, and I think, for me, a lot of times the psychedelic experience is sometimes just a pain in the ass, what I have to go through to get to the integration part, which is for me where a lot of my finest work in life has been done.

Not that the psychedelic experience can't be just wonderful, enjoyable, cathartic, beautifully troubling, sad, or whatever, but for me it's very confronting, and when I integrate those experiences, the stories that I usually come up with and tell myself are valuable. I am careful to say that this is like this, the narrative that I am telling myself, and not necessarily am I saying I have DMT all figured out and everyone else is looking at it all wrong.

But sometimes I think that people really underestimate the human brain and just how incredibly powerful it is, and the amount of computation that it's doing. I think that all of our inner worlds are filled with the accumulation of life experiences. I mean, right now I have a whole thirty-nine to forty years of life experience contained in some manner, in my mind, as well as all of these things that I've learned about a zillion different subjects. I could very well come up with things to say about, say, yo-yos or something like that, right now. That's contained in my brain somewhere but it's not conscious.

What's being fed to me is based on the context of this conversation, and what is useful in the social environment I find myself in, in the moment. So what we're consciously experiencing at any one time is just this tiny, really little, workable kind of sliver of information that is sort of useful, or adaptive to the very specific context that we find ourselves in. I think that there's a whole multiverse of perceptions and realities inside of our minds, creating the very thoughts that we're having and accessing the different memories of our lives when needed. *They're coming up with the very words that are coming out of my mouth right now.*

Much of that is hidden from our conscious awareness, probably because consciousness is just an evolved tool of the mind that's meant for—I don't know, some sort of way of shifting attention or something. I don't claim to know what consciousness is for, other than I know that it's a very small fraction of what the brain is up to. It's really the tip of the iceberg, and I think that DMT is a look into those worlds.

The way in which perception is put together in those worlds is very different than our external realities and is represented in different ways. It makes sense to me that they are in these hologram-like worlds that shift and change really rapidly. So I think some of those beings often are just representations of people in our lives and friends of ours, or the idea of what we want our inner self to be.

We all wear many hats in life, and we have these many different roles that we have to play. I think they all represent this, and they just look so bizarre because of the organization of our brains. Are you familiar with what's called the "cortical homunculus?" The word *homunculus* is Latin for "little man."

Yes, I recall it from my introductory psychology textbook in college.

SHANE: So the idea is that your sensory and motor functions, and different parts of your body, are represented in your brain in different proportions than they actually are in your body. Certain areas are larger,

Illustration by Ramin Nazer

in terms of the size of the body map inside of your brain. It's different from how it is on the outside. For example, your hands are really large on your internal body map, because there's a lot more sensory information going from your hands than say your arms, which don't need as much sensory information, and don't need as much neural activity dedicated to it. Or lips and eyes are really big inside of the brain, and then the other parts are really small.

So when they make this kind of drawing representation of what the human body looks like inside of the brain, like in proportion to the structures, it looks like some sort of alien creature in there—and I think that explains much of what is going on with the DMT space. I think that our consciousness and our subconscious are kind of always trying to communicate with each other, but they're communicating in two completely different ways, and there's a lot of stuff lost in translation.

The inner world responds really well to dramatizations of things— like little kids playing that the floor is made of lava. I think that's a way of simulating a safe but heightened sense of arousal, while training your fine motor skills to do the sorts of things that our hunter and gatherer ancestors would need for jumping around on rocks and through streams, like when hunting. It's a way of upping the ante of those movements to train the brain, and so I think that our inner world then communicates to us through these dramatizations.

Imagine that you're standing in line and you're feeling frustrated. Then you have a flash of punching the person in front of you pop into your head. I don't think that anyone actually wants to punch the person in front of him or her. I think that it's just a metaphor. It's the embodiment of frustration or anger, just as if we were playing charades or something like that. You were trying to act out frustration or anger, and so everyone could get that you'd do this over-the-top dramatization of what's going on—and I think that's what our inner worlds look like.

I think that's why people end up walking away from psychedelic experience having these insights, which ultimately always sound like the silliest thing to everybody else—because they sound like something they should already know. But it's created this connection between knowing something intellectually and feeling it in your body. So basically, everyone's main takeaway from the psychedelic experience is something that's already embroidered on your mom's decorative pillows.

Like, oh I get it now, *home is where the heart is*, or *don't sweat the small stuff*. Oh, I see what they mean by that now. But to arrive at that conclusion you had to go through this war inside of yourself, or see some kingdom or whatever. So that's my take on what's going on. That being said, if I smoked DMT right now, I'd be like, yeah, disregard everything I just said, I just went to another dimension and talked to these other beings.

Getting back to evolution, do you see any type of teleology, intelligence, or mindful intention operating in nature and the evolution of life, or do you see it more as blind chance?

SHANE: I think things that once started out as chance can eventually become complex enough to influence the process. There are these emergent properties and then they can interact with the evolution of life. Basically, I guess what that makes me think is that there are these weird top-down changes, but it is still chance in a way.

I think about memes quite a bit, I guess in this way. Evolution eventually evolved our sense of language and was the origin of our belief systems and early tendencies. From that, some of these belief systems emerged, were communicated, and then they shaped culture, which now has an influence on our genes, and so now people say that almost everything is 50 percent genetic influence and 50 percent environmental influence. I think that's underselling what evolution is doing, because evolution also shaped the environment that we are in.

So if you're saying it's 50 percent genes, 50 percent culture—well, evolution also shaped culture. But then if you have something like a meme, where you have an idea, like one religion says that we should be celibate and not mess with this hedonistic sex stuff, we should just focus on caring for one another. And then another religion is like, god wants us to be fruitful and multiply. Or the purple aliens want us to bang like crazy, whatever. I'll put my money on those religions promoting us to be fruitful and multiply, because that very idea lends itself to people reproducing more.

So that idea is like a thing that's, in a way, floating around in this not tangible reality of the cultural environment, that I guess is stored in our minds and passed around through language. But it has such an influence on our lives that that idea starts influencing genes themselves. Genes might have been the basis for that idea, but then once that idea takes hold, it can become almost more powerful, and the idea itself can be more of a driver than genes, than the genes are of that idea. Then ideas can evolve themselves, are shaped over time, and change and break off, so in that way there is some sort of, what feels like a top-down influence.

But I think most of this is somewhat random and somewhat the inevitable property of some of the unstable elements at the start of the universe. There are plenty of unstable elements at the start of the universe, and stable elements stuck around by nature of being the stable ones, not that they were better or worse. They were just the more stable ones, and those lead to organized life, keeping life, and keeping order. Order is much harder to accomplish than disorder, and all of life seems to be trying to maximize order and utilize energy as much as it can. But I don't know how to answer that question, even though I spent about five minutes answering the question. I often think a lot of this is pretty random, but I don't know.

How do you envision the future development or evolution of the human species, and the future relationship between human biology, advanced robotics, and artificial intelligence?

SHANE: Early on, I was into the transhumanist stuff, wanted to upload my consciousness onto a computer, and I still think that'll eventually happen. However, I'd have no interest in living forever, or being immortal. I'm perfectly content with my average life expectancy, my allotment of existence, or at least at this stage of my life.

But it is interesting to see our consciousness, and our experience in these digital worlds. The human organism is now interacting with the digital world. We're just this incredibly flexible species that's learned to adapt to all these different environments, and now we're figuring out how to adapt the environment to us, and creating a world to our making. We are creating these kinds of representations of our inner worlds, where we have this inner desire for safety, for affiliating, for all these different kinds of basic instincts that have in the past been helpful in spreading our genes.

We can now see a need for shelter embodied in skyscrapers and engines. We're just really upping the ante on all of our internal desires, and I don't know what that's going to look like once we fully blend into some sort of digital interface.

Hold that thought; I have to flip this tape over.

SHANE: You're using a tape recorder with cassette tapes? That's hilarious.

I know. This is what I've been using for years. I've had problems with digital recorders, and just can't seem to switch to them, so I keep using my reliable cassette recorder.

SHANE: I love that I'm talking about us moving into a digital interface any day now as you're flipping a cassette. That's hilarious.

[Laughter] Yes, I'm using a 1980s technology as we approach the Singularity. So, I'm sorry, as you were saying.

SHANE: So yeah, I don't know. I don't have a lot of faith in my ability to forecast future events. I haven't had much luck with it in the past. I think humans tend to oversell their own ability to predict what the future is going to be like. I have a lot of speculations I'm happy to make about it. I definitely don't think that we're going to all explode into fractals or whatever, like a lot of the New Age, psychedelic community seems to be hoping and rooting for. I don't know why living an existence of being a hologram zipping around in space would be any more or less satisfying than the one that we already exist in.

When you look around at what's happening in the world these days, do you think the human species will survive the next hundred years or do you think we're doomed to extinction?

SHANE: I think that there is some cause for pragmatic optimism in many ways. I mean, we also have the lowest murder rates and things like rape and criminal behavior and anything like that is the least in all of human history. We have the greatest capacity to completely annihilate the Earth that we've ever had in human history as well, so that's one side of it.

But I think a bigger side of it is that we actually evolved in a much more dangerous environment than we currently exist in, and because of that we evolved threat detection sensory tools that are not adapted for our now relatively safe world—because they aren't detecting threats like lions and tigers and bears—oh my!—and there isn't actually a tribe next door that's going to invade and murder us, just any given day, like has always been the case throughout human history.

The actual sensitivity of our psychological threat detection is being increased in our brain. This is similar to what would be called the hygiene hypothesis with allergies, and I think that the safer the world gets, the scarier we're going to perceive it to be as an almost psychological allergy to existence. Then we seek to validate our internal feelings, and we have this thing called television that can give us any kind of entertainment we want, or don't want, and sometimes we don't even realize that on a subconscious level, all we are trying to do is validate how scary and threatening our environment is.

You can't take a walk around your average neighborhood and see any kind of evidence of danger anywhere, but we've evolved in an environment where there was danger everywhere. So now you go and you turn on the TV, and it's all too happy to give you your fix of *look at these scary things going on in the outside world*. This is making people isolate themselves more, which is reinforcing that belief, and so I don't know what that's going to look like as people spend less time in the "real world" of physical environments, interacting less with actual human beings in a natural setting and spending time outdoors and with nature. Living more of their lives on the computer or in front of the TV might be incorrectly validating these kinds of really nuanced fears and desires.

What do you dream about, have you ever had a lucid dream, and do dreams affect your creative work?

SHANE: I have been thinking a lot about dreams lately. I don't lucid dream regularly. I have lucid dreamed a few times, and would like to train myself to do it regularly. I don't remember a lot of my dreams. You want to hear one funny lucid dream I had?

I'd love to.

SHANE: This is one of the clearest lucid dreams that I've ever had or remembered, and it really has nothing to do with much of anything relevant to this conversation, unless we really dissected it. But I was making my psychedelic documentary *Psychonautics: A Comic's Exploration of Psychedelics*, and in the filming I had a *lucid dream inside of a lucid dream*.

So I had this dream where I knew I was dreaming, and I was on LSD in this lucid dream, and everything had like a glimmer around the edges. I was like, yes, this is what things look like on LSD. I need to remember this. We need to put this effect into the editing of the documentary. Then I woke up from that into another lucid dream, where I was holding this glimmer of light.

I was with a woman, it was my girlfriend at the time, and her friend. Those two were always talking about dreams with one another, and they remembered them really well in a way that I'm very envious of. Those two were in my dream, and I still knew I was dreaming again, and I'm holding this glimmer that I want to remember for an effect for my documentary. So I was like, girls, I need to remember this. How do you guys remember your dreams? And her friend was just like, oh well it's easy, just sit on it. And I was like, what? And she was like, yeah, just put it in your butt. And I was like, wha . . . what? [*Laughter*] And they both looked at me like this was just so matter of fact.

Then I was just like, well if you want to remember a dream you just put it in your butt. You just sit on it. What are you talking about? I really wanted to remember this dream, so I was just like, okay, and I stuck this glimmer down on my seat and proceeded to sit on this like glowing orb. Then I woke up and I remembered every detail of that dream.

Wow, that's an interesting technique. I've never heard of that technique for improving dream recall before.

SHANE: Well, the takeaway is that you'll never forget anything that goes in your butt.

Right, that makes a lot of sense actually. Shane, I really loved that story that you once told about how, if somebody was born with the type of enhanced perception that we normally have while tripping, and then they took a drug that suddenly allowed them to see with the mundane perception that we normally take for granted, how mind-blowing that would be for them. I'm curious if you could talk a little about why you think it's valuable for us to question our perceptions, and to question everything really?

SHANE: I think that we really take reality for granted and at face value, and we don't even question it on a very regular level. I guess I would use the example of embodied cognition, and how much of our internal experience is influenced by the physical realities, and much of how we articulate our internal world is based on things that are in the outside world. And we do this all the time. So the idea is that you call someone, like a girl, "hot," or something like that. You don't mean she's physically warm, you mean she's attractive.

You call someone "blue" when they're sad, and someone can feel "distant" when they're standing right next to you. The reason is because our cortex, which does all this fancy language stuff, evolved later on and was built on top of the limbic system, which is doing more of our physical senses stuff. So much of how we articulate these kinds of intangibles is by trying to put these tangible labels on them. So right now, we're having a *deep* conversation. Why is it "deep"? What does that mean? How can a conversation have physical depth to it? How can an idea be big or small in the brain?

I mean, what you're getting at is that it's more complex or less complex, but I would imagine it's requiring the same amount of neural firing in the brain no matter what. We have these ways of saying something is "shallow" or you want to get "high." You want to feel "up." Why would up be a good thing, and down be a bad thing?

This is just endless, and it's constantly changing. During the advent of agriculture in human history, now we're "planting seeds" of ideas and "cultivating" ideas. Then transportation comes around, and we feel very "driven" and we're "firing on all cylinders." Electricity happens and a "light bulb" goes off in our head. Well, what was a good idea before we had light bulbs that went off in our head? Was it a lightning bolt?

These are things that are constantly changing. Then computers come around. Now we're getting these "massive downloads." So the whole way in which we're interpreting these experiences is so subjective to how our external environment is changing all the time. Just thinking about that is trippier than most psychedelic substances that anyone can have, and it's something that all of us are experiencing day in and day out. I'm looking out the window right now, and I'm thinking, I'm a little new to talking about this stuff, and we say we're a little "green." Well, what does that mean—a little green? Why do we use those kinds of physical things to embody the intangible?

So I think knowing that could help us understand our perceptions better. I think a more practical application—in terms of not just having these really fun, complex, far-out conversations—is when we understand what drives some of our internal process. Thinking of ourselves as an organism that has been shaped by evolution, and therefore has motives from day one, then we can understand things like egocentrism a little better and understand that we only know what we know.

Egocentrism is this very natural reaction to only having access to the information that you have access to. So we're all the center of our own universes to us, and then we sometimes project that onto the world and think that our lives, our problems, and our successes are bigger than they actually are in some of the scope of things. I think in terms of an individual wanting to create a better life for themselves and the world around them, it's important to understand that our thoughts, ideas, and emotions sometimes serve us quite well, and other times we serve them.

Sometimes we have these fears or dreams that are outside of what is reality, or are an exaggerated version of reality, and when we do things to reinforce that, there's a lot of confirmation bias and we sometimes let our ideas and emotions run away with us. Then on the other side of that we sometimes don't utilize the different thoughts, ideas, and feelings that can motivate us to move our life forward. Like, when I get off the phone with you I'm going to go into a yoga class, and the reason why I'm becoming more disciplined to that is because I'm figuring out how to tap into the kinds of drives that I need to take better care of myself. So I guess that would be my main takeaway: to become more mindful of when our thoughts, ideas, emotions are serving us and when we're serving them.

I really enjoyed your Psychonautics *DVD. It was wonderfully done, aside from being hilarious, and serves as a powerful educational tool. Can you speak about how your overindulgence in psychedelics led to a mental breakdown, and some time spent as a patient in a psychiatric hospital? Also, do you see a relationship between mental illness and creativity?*

SHANE: Yes. The main thing that isn't shown in the documentary that I wish viewers knew for context is that, in the course of filming the documentary, because we were doing it in a short amount of time and had a limited budget, I was doing way more psychedelics in a much shorter amount of time than I normally ever would, or would even have any inclination to do, and that led to me not properly integrating things—I recognized in hindsight.

At the time this was happening, I was like, this is great, I'm just feeling better and better all of the time—not realizing that was the early onset of mania. Then I finally had a really big ayahuasca trip that sent me over into more full-blown mania, and then that lead to me not sleeping much. Then a week later doing another mushroom trip, while I was still quite manic, and then that really put me over the edge. But mostly it was really exciting and everything seemed very important. I was under these extremely big ideas. Because I wasn't sleeping much, I eventually developed paranoia and a kind of psychosis. I began losing touch with I guess what I'd call "reality."

I don't know exactly what reality is and never will, but definitely I was not functional and the ideas that I was having definitely weren't terribly stable. But ultimately I feel really bad for what my family—my small-town, Midwestern family, who didn't understand any of this and was terrified—had to go through. And because it was definitely more troubling for them than it was for me, I thought the whole experience was really quite interesting. I still kind of do.

The worst of it for me was having to get other people involved, which I wish would never have happened, and some of the ideas and stuff that I had were really embarrassing, how delusional they were at the time. But it's been a couple of years now, and I have different views of a lot of those things that I experienced.

Some of them have really led me to understand life in a completely new and interesting way and improved my relationship with myself and my own inner worlds. I've never gotten along with myself so well in my entire life as I have recently, and I don't know how long that's going to last, or whatever, but it seems like I've been making some pretty enormous personal strides ever since that—including quitting drinking and smoking cigarettes, both of which were big problems of mine.

I'm definitely the most on top of things I've ever been in my life, and of late, I've really been just as creative as ever. It's been some time since I've done a psychedelic as well, and I just don't feel like it. I just feel like I'm tripping on the natch, like most of the time, just in a very central, interesting way. I definitely have a different view on life and reality, and I really am quite grateful for it. I have to get on stage with scientists in front of crowds and hold my own and sound like I know what I'm talking about, and I've really been able to rise to the occasion quite well—and a big part of that is thanks to what I've learned from my psychedelic experiences.

What do you personally think happens to consciousness after physical death and the deterioration of the brain?

SHANE: I think that consciousness rises from within us and eventually dies with us. But I think that the way that the internal process works is on a completely different time scale. Time is a subjective feeling, and a hundred years feels like a long time to us because that's our lifespan out here, whereas in the internal world, if your, say, hand is on a burner or

Photo by Rebecca Ann Hill.

David Jay Brown and Shane Mauss. DNA's Comedy Lab, Santa Cruz, California.

something like that, one second is an eternity. That's just way too long and things need to fire a lot faster than that.

So once you get down to those worlds, time can really stretch and dilate. I've certainly had DMT experiences that feel like I've lived lifetimes. I mean lifetimes upon lifetimes, and I feel like I've subjectively lived much longer in the DMT space than in a human space.

My human "out here" existence feels like a small fraction of the lives and experiences that I've had, and I think it's because there's a zillion different lives going on inside of our head all the time that we're constantly recruiting and just not really privy to. But I think that in the moments before death, I think that you'll go into a similar space. I've experienced this with a drug overdose. I had basically what I thought was a DMT trip until I realized that I was overdosing, and I found myself in a DMT space.

Then I was like, wait a second, I haven't smoked DMT, and I realized I was overdosing. I was able to jolt myself out of it fortunately, and I'm still here. But I think that if your brain is intact, those last few seconds of existence will stretch for a seemingly infinite time, no matter who you are or what you believe. I think there's a lot of interesting survival reasons for that, but that's not worth going into.

Yes, certainly a lot of people have hypothesized that DMT is released in the brain at the moments near death, so maybe that helps to explain what you experienced. You mentioned earlier that there hasn't been much of a spiritual intention with your psychedelic experiences, but this is a question that I'm asking everyone. What is your perspective on the concept of god?

SHANE: I think that there is a place in our mind that feels very at home and is very loving and nurturing and secure. There are a lot of places in our minds that aren't that way, and I think that is a really favorable place to get to and reside in. I think that often when we're meditating or doing these things to try and attain enlightenment, whatever that means, that's usually just trying to tap into what I would call "the safe place" in our mind that's filled with all these ideas of home, heaven, and religious expression.

I think that it comes along with these tones associated with religion, like oooommmm [*spoken as elongated extension of the* om *tone*], or there's this very similar kind of tone that all religions sound alike and have. It's very safe, registered, and singing it, no one screws it up too bad. It just feels natural and wise, like in every religion.

That's actually what all noise sounds like if you're underwater, and I think that this is just something that was a constructed perception early on, when you are in utero, in the womb and surrounded by fluids. It's nuanced feeling that has been built upon and fed into by religious ideas and ideas of gods, and that sort of thing. Rather than something that is attaining some kind of higher perception, I think it's actually us trying to crawl back into the womb, and is often based in fear, which is when a lot of people "find their god," when they're going through the worst times of their life and are retreating to this safe place in the mind.

Everyone wants to think all of the world is just love and connection, and that's because those are great feelings that feel terrific. But there's also things like disease and stuff that we don't necessarily want to love or feel connected with. But you don't hear about those as much because we're kind of hopeless wish-thinkers. You don't hear about people coming out of the psychedelic experience and being like, whoa, I just really tapped into the universal paranoia that exists in all. Yeah, I got a message from god about how I should be more socially awkward. You don't hear that because those aren't the pleasant ones.

They're all part of the human experience, but they're not the fun little takeaways that you get to tell yourself and turn into a mantra to keep your life moving forward in a, quite frankly, seemingly arbitrary direction. So that's my view of things, but I always feel like a dick telling people that, so I usually keep those thoughts to myself, and I've certainly had plenty of experiences that make me question if there is life after this and if there is a god. I also often think that it's quite possible that we're living in a simulation.

That was my next question actually; that's so funny you just said that. What do you think about the philosophical idea that reality,

as we know it, is actually an extremely sophisticated computer simulation?

SHANE: It just seems like the inevitable outcome of what you would do if you became a more sophisticated species. I would imagine that even in this universe there're many intelligent—whatever intelligence necessarily means—but complex living systems, like we find on Earth. It would be shocking if we were the smartest things out there. But humans love to form models and run these little simulations and practice things. Going back to my example from earlier of the floor-is-lava child's game—that's you running a simulation and preparing for future events.

As we start using computers and computer modeling, it just makes perfect sense if you want to figure out what introducing some new species into a new environment might do. Is it going to do what you hope and limit, and help bees or whatever, or is it going to destroy everything unexpectedly? A really nice, safe way to test that is to form accurate mathematical models, and it seems like just a really worthwhile pursuit of understanding and bettering anything life would come up with, this solution. So if one agrees on that, which I'm not expecting anyone to, but following that line of reasoning, then why suppose that we aren't already in one?

Right, that's certainly an intriguing idea. Shane, what do you see as some of the most exciting technological developments and scientific advances going on in the world today?

SHANE: Well, I did see recently that there's this cassette player that will change all of your cassettes into a digital format.

[Bursts aloud with laughter]

SHANE: I can think of a couple of people that might be positively influenced by that. I think that self-driving cars are pretty exciting to me for a lot of downstream ideas, in terms of creating more time and possibly people venturing out and traveling more once they have them. I wish people had a little more experience with traveling, and can one day find and afford to do so.

But I guess out of all the things that we talk about on my podcast, probably some of the most impactful stuff for me has been the understanding of the stress response system and how our mammalian stress response system is very well adapted for our past environment of actual threats—like actually chasing a prey animal or running from a predator—and is really poorly adaptive for a modern environment, where now we're perceiving threats like 401Ks or these kind of intangible things. So our stress response is constantly active and never dialing down.

Stress response is really meant for these short, acute stressors, and functions really well in this way, but functions really poorly when chronically activated. I think that it causes much of the disease and obesity, as well as mental issues, and everything in between in this society. I hope that people start to think about this in the same way that people are starting to think about the paleo lifestyle, or whatever—which is also, like everything else being taken advantage of, being overplayed, and can be as much snake oil as anything. That's just part of human nature.

My hope is that a modern understanding of the stress response system will take hold in some cultures, and I think it will lead to incredible wellness outcomes that other people can look to as an example and replicate. I hope the best for everybody. I think we might be breeding a little bit too much, but I certainly hope the best for all the humans that do exist.

I hope that people can find ways of making small incremental positive changes in their lives and bettering themselves in small tangible ways, which ultimately have the longest outcome. But I think just a general understanding of the stress response system would benefit people a great deal. There's not a whole lot more that we need in terms of technology, other than to make that happen, other than just to get the word out there, which we now have the internet for, and all of these other tools to use.

8

Radical Creativity, Immersive Art Environments, and Meow Wolf

An Interview with Vince Kadlubek

Vince Kadlubek is one of the original co-founders of Meow Wolf, an art collective that has transformed into an award-winning art and entertainment production company. Meow Wolf specializes in immersive, uniquely imaginative, open-world walk-through experiences, and creates absolutely mind-blowing, large-scale, interactive art installations.

Kadlubek was born and raised in Santa Fe, New Mexico, and how he came to co-found Meow Wolf is an inspiration. As a young artist, Kadlubek lived out of his car for four months, and was stealing bread and dumpster diving for meals to survive. The story of how he and thirteen other initial collaborators created Meow Wolf is described in the interview that follows.

Kadlubek acted as leader and CEO for Meow Wolf though its formative years, having created the business plan for Meow Wolf's House of Eternal Return and leading the team toward the project's completion in March 2016. In January 2017, Kadlubek formed Meow Wolf Inc. as a full-fledged arts production company and creative studio positioned "to create the largest, most innovative and audacious monumental art exhibits in the world."

Today Meow Wolf has created some of the most popular and financially successful art installments in the world, with three permanent locations, employing hundreds of artists, and is worth hundreds of millions

Photo by Kate Russell

Vince Kadlubek

of dollars. Meow Wolf currently has locations in Santa Fe, Las Vegas, and Denver. House of Eternal Return, its flagship attraction in Santa Fe, was founded in 2008. Omega Mart, its second location in Las Vegas, and Convergence Station, its third location in Denver, both opened in 2021. Currently, two additional locations are being planned to open in Texas next year. To learn more about Meow Wolf and experience their virtual tours, see the MeowWolf website.

Kadlubek has been a force of vision in the realm of experiential art, and in 2020 launched a creative consulting agency called Spatial Activations as a platform "to usher in a new era of experiential art in modern developments and everyday life." Vince is most passionate about "co-creating fully realized alternative realities that bring paradigm-shifting transformation and inspiration to the world."

I interviewed Vince on April 1, 2022. He was warm, enthusiastic, and bursting with creative energy. Although this was the first time that I spoke with Vince, I felt an instant connection between us. We spoke about how Meow Wolf got started, the relationship between the imagination and the creative process, the role of inter-dimensional portals in Meow Wolf, and the future of creative expression.

How did you become interested in artistic expression?

VINCE: It's hard to pinpoint exactly where all that started. I mean, of course, Dr. Seuss and Jim Henson had a lot to do with it as a kid, as did Walt Disney and going to Disneyland. The Pirates of the Caribbean ride was probably one of my earliest big influences. But as an adult, when the power of artistic expression started to really dawn on me, it was Terence McKenna who inspired me.

I was seventeen or eighteen years old, staying up late at night listening to Art Bell's radio show, and the episodes that I loved the most were when Terence was on. The way that Terence spoke about the imagination and artistic expression was something that made me realize that this was *the pursuit*. This was the goal of humanity, and where I wanted to participate for the rest of my life was in progressing the expression of the imagination in any way that I could.

That's really interesting. I was going to ask you about Terence. I think Terence said something about how one of the goals of human evolution is to externalize the imagination, to make the imagination tangible. It seems like that's exactly what Meow Wolf is doing. Can you just briefly recap the story of Meow Wolf's origins for our readers? How did a situation with the conservative art world in Santa Fe inspire a radical new art movement?

VINCE: We were all twentysomethings in 2008, living in Santa Fe. We were fourteen friends, and half of us were from Santa Fe, born and raised. The other half had moved there as young adults, and we were all in artistic fields of some sort—whether it was live music, visual art, or theater performance. We were a bit of a social group that was also a bit of a performance artistic creative troupe, and our work was quite experimental and rambunctious.

It didn't really fit in with the Santa Fe identity, which was very New Agey, Southwestern, and Texas—like cowboys and landscapes, very docile. So we didn't fit into the identity of Santa Fe, and we were very frustrated with not being included in the artistic or cultural dialogue of Santa Fe—even though we saw ourselves as being so vibrant. There was such a vibrant energy to it. So we basically just said, we're going to start our own thing, and we're going to stop waiting for someone in Santa Fe to invite us into their venue. We're just going to start our own venue!

So we all pitched in money that we had and committed to renting out a space. We didn't really have a clear understanding of how that space was going to be used, but we knew it was going to be a creative space, and so we gave it a name. We put a bunch of words in one hat, and a bunch of words in another hat, and started randomly pulling out words in a very non-sequitur way. The result was "Meow Wolf."

So that was really the genesis. We knew we wanted our own creative clubhouse, and we knew that it had to have an identity and a presence, so we gave it a name. Then we just started making work and organizing events under that name and under that brand. We did that for seven years as an informal social group. Then in 2015 we saw that we needed to evolve into something more sustainable, and that's when we started designing The House of Eternal Return in Santa Fe and created a business out of it.

It's all so brilliant and fantastic; I'm so inspired by what you guys have done. Why do you think that immersive, interactive art environments are important, and how do you envision the future of artistic expression?

VINCE: That's a very good question and there are answers from a lot of different angles. I'll start with the art world angle. Why is immersive art important to the art world and to the experience of art? Art is very difficult for the vast majority of people to relate to. When you think about paintings on a wall, or about sculptures on a pedestal, these are like objects that sit uniquely within context of a reality, and to really know how to engage with the unique objects you need to have experience with engaging in that.

Walking up to a painting and staring at it isn't a normal thing we do in our world. It's such an acquired taste, and there's a required education around it that's necessary to really know how to engage with something like that. So, because of that, it actually alienates a lot of people who don't have that experience or don't have that education on how to engage with an object.

Immersive art is important because it basically just replicates what we already do all the time—which is to walk inside of a space and then interpret the space. This is something that everybody has education around and everybody has experience with, whether it's walking into a grocery store, a gas station, a library, a bank, a house, or walking into a foreign country. We always walk into environments and then interpret those environments. So immersive art allows for people—anyone, every human—to have a confident engagement with artwork, because it's within a context that is so familiar, which is walking inside of spaces. So that's the art world answer.

Now that dovetails into an even more significant answer. Art and storytelling have always been an expression of an alternative reality, and as we express a certain slice of alternative reality, we as humans are able

Interior of Meow Wolf.

to externalize it and experience it as a metaphor or experience outside of ourselves. So we can look at it. And what's really significant about immersive art is that it's a parallel to the fullness of everyday reality. It's multisensory and multimedia. It's spatial; it's walking into space, and so it's a perfect mimic of reality itself. The power of immersive art and these immersive environments is that we walk into them, and you're put into a position where you can look at the entirety of reality objectively.

So this is incredibly powerful because it makes anyone who experiences immersive art aware of the creation and the construct that's around them all the time in everyday life, and they become the observer. They become an elevated consciousness that is observing reality rather than just being a component part of it. So there are monumentally transformational opportunities with immersive art because it's able to do that, and it does it in a similar way as psychedelic substances and other transformative technologies.

Inter-dimensional portals are a theme in Meow Wolf. How did you first come up with the idea of a house with secret passageways into other dimensions?

VINCE: The exact moment that it happened actually was when we were driving down to New Orleans to do a pop-up Meow Wolf show. We were just ideating out loud as to what the next big show could be, and it was really just thinking about Meow Wolf as a business and knowing that we were going to have to sell tickets and reach a larger audience. We were really trying to nail something that could go viral and be really pop, a very pop trope that could assure us success. So we said, what if we built a house that has secret passageways? I think I was driving, and I said it to my friend Mat Crimmins, and we just started riffing on that.

There wasn't really any strategy. We didn't understand what we were doing when we came up with that idea, other than that we were going to be doing something like *The Lion, the Witch and the Wardrobe*, *Coraline*, and *Alice in Wonderland*—stories that we have been touching on for a long time and that we knew resonated within the collective consciousness. So we knew that, but we didn't know just how powerful this format would be, of placing people inside an immersive environment that is super familiar, and then allowing them, the audience, by choice, to walk through a transitional space into a totally unknown and totally fictional realm. That format, I think, we stumbled upon, and I think it's a very powerful format for people's transformation.

It's really interesting how the whole notion of portals and secret passageways into other realms has entered into the collective unconscious in recent years. It used to just be something in science fiction or fantasy, but now it's all over mainstream culture, like every episode of Rick and Morty, *how you travel between worlds in VR chat, and inside of Meow Wolf attractions. You mentioned Terence McKenna earlier. Speaking of Terence, the exploration of hyperspace and entity encounters associated with DMT is a theme in this book. Do you have any thoughts on whether the entities that people meet during DMT journeys have a genuine independent existence or not?*

VINCE: It's a very complex subject. I'm glad you're covering it. Whether it's a dream, or it's something like a DMT experience, a deep meditation, in a flotation tank, or being in isolation in the dark for days on end, there're a bunch of ways to get to a place where this can happen.

Interior of Meow Wolf.

There're a lot of different ways to be able to basically access a less sheltered, more pure, imaginative realm, and there are stable and consistent entities within that realm—no matter which access point you're using. So for me, do they have an independent existence? The question is, are they real? And I think that question is a very complicated one.

Ultimately, this soup of imagination, in my opinion, is both real and not real at the same time. There is no division between real and imaginative in that space. In that space it's all just what is. And what's special about what's happening in the "real world" these days is that the line that we've created between nonfiction and fiction—that division, that dichotomy—is actually dissolving and becoming more ambiguous.

What happens when that line dissolves entirely? Then we live in a new way, not within a dichotomy of this is real and this is imaginary, but it's all one. These entities then are real, because in that realm, where there's no dichotomy, it's all real and it's all imaginary at the same time. So at that point then these entities become real, but are they real right now? Like when it's not based on our dichotomy, the dichotomy that we have around fiction and nonfiction. But in my mind, yeah, it's real.

This reminds me of what Terence McKenna said about the goal of evolution being to externalize the imagination. So that would break down the dichotomy between the imagination and reality.

VINCE: Yes, Terence talked about this a lot. I pulled this directly from him. He talked a lot about paradigm shifts, and that there was a paradigm shift that we can look back in time at that is really helpful in understanding this next paradigm shift that we're going through, with regard to imagination. That past paradigm shift that we can look at is the invention of spoken human language, and you can, for a second, imagine what it would be like to be present during the early days of human language and to maybe be one of those cavemen that hadn't evolved to a point where they could understand or even utilize human language.

But it was actually by observing other people, or other cavemen, or however you want to put them—other *Homo sapiens*. It was observing them using their lips, and using the vocal chords to communicate concepts, and it seemed like those language skills were getting picked up by others. But to that slightly underdeveloped person it would have been really questionable whether or not what they were observing was real. Like, is this really what's happening here? Are they really communicating with their voice about an object or about something? Language itself would have just been mysterious. You wouldn't have had any idea, and it would have been impossible to understand just how much language was going to become a part of our lives, a part of constructing the world around us, and a part of us experiencing time. This is all experienced through language, and it would have been impossible to see that paradigm ahead of you, of just how much language was going to be a part of our lives.

The same is true right now for the imagination. We can kind of see it. We see it in its form. We have little visitations of it. It's like, wait, is this real? Like, what is this? Is this just some kind of random thing that happens on the side? And my hypothesis is that, give it a thousand years, maybe even less, and you'll realize, oh, it's all imagination—that the world we live in is imagination.

Did psychedelic experiences play a role in the inspiration for Meow Wolf?

VINCE: We are influenced by so many artists and storytellers who have been influenced by the realm of psychedelia, however it is that they got there—like Dr. Seuss, Jim Henson, The Beatles, and Walt Disney. There're so many. All of these influences have spoken to the psychedelic experience through their stories and through their artwork, and I think that orients the group quite a bit. The company is composed of hundreds of artists, so it's really hard to speak for everybody, but for myself, yeah, I was a huge Beatles fan when I was fifteen years old. I got firmly obsessed with the Beatles, and I really loved Pink Floyd, so I was heavily influenced by the general culture of psychedelics. But honestly I can't say if Meow Wolf is an art movement that is directly influenced by any given substance. I think that's a bit more specific. That's difficult

Interior of Meow Wolf.

to really know the answer to, but I would say that the overall genre of psychedelic pop is absolutely influential to us.

Can you explain what you mean when you say, "Humans want to have mind-blowing experiences?"

VINCE: Yeah, another really good question that has so much depth to it. So humans want to have a mind-blowing experience. Well, what's a mind-blowing experience and what does that mean? I think what it means is that I've experienced something outside of the context of my knowing.

So outside of my whole knowing, the knowing of my being, I've just experienced something. And with that we expand. We get challenged. We see that the world can be more than what we thought that the world was supposed to be, or what we thought the world was, and there's an opportunity for possibility when something outside of the context of our own knowing happens to us.

There's this whole clearing for possibility that happens. Then I think what happens for so many people is that they realize the greatest apparatus of knowing that is present in our lives, which is one of our own construction, and *it's called the identity*. What happens is that, as we grow up and we go from being a child into an adult, we start constructing this giant apparatus of knowing called the identity that ends up trapping us.

It tells us who we are, what we like, how we eat, how we talk, where we work, what our interests are, and what our hobbies are. And because we create this giant context of knowing around us, it kills the spirit of the child. It kills the spirit of the explorer and the person who explores and discovers. It basically says the world is set. So then we get depressed and we have midlife crises and we develop all sorts of psychological disorders, and we desperately want to get out of this casing of knowing that we've created for ourselves. And mind-blowing experiences allow us to see beyond that casing of identity.

What are your thoughts about virtual reality and the future of art?

VINCE: Personally speaking, I love virtual reality. I'm in my VR headset almost on a nightly basis. It's a medium of expressing the imagination just like any other medium and I dig it. I think it's a lot of fun; it can be really beautiful and it can be really well designed. It can also be really bad, to be honest. But so can any expression that's in any medium.

How it's going to influence the future of art is what it provides; every other sub-medium is available to be expressed through or within virtual reality. Combine haptics into it and you can now actually express "we're pseudo-physical" sculptures. Pseudo-physical works into VR as well. So it's just a larger medium to be able to express yourself in, and so of course it's going to be an amazing medium for art. It's a continuation of that blurring of the line between what's real and what's not real. It's a clear indication that the dichotomy between nonfiction and fiction is becoming further disrupted.

How do you think that we can increase creative thinking on the planet?

VINCE: I don't know what the prevailing terminology is but it's exposing more people to transformational, or transcendental, experiences. It's . . . creativity happens. Creativity is a process that starts in the imagination. The imagination is a future-based technology and imagines things in the future, outside of the current paradigm or knowing. Imagination is the realm of possibilities. It's the future. We get stuck in these past-based identities that we've created, using past-based technology known as memory to achieve.

So in order to increase creativity in the world, you have to disrupt the past-based identity system and you need to open a clearing for possibility, for imagination. And the best way to do that is through all sorts of transcendental and transformational practices and technologies. Psychedelic therapies are one of those, and meditation is part of that. There's a lot of really great work being done with binaural beats and just using light to instigate transcendental states. So yeah, creativity will absolutely increase as more people break out of the shell of their own identity.

What are your thoughts about the simulation hypothesis, the idea that our entire reality is really an advanced computer simulation?

VINCE: Yeah, I fully believe it. One, from a straight logical perspective, I think that the chances are that it is, but I've also experienced it. The physical realm that we live in on Earth is becoming the imagination. I see how much of it is a by-product of the imagination. You can even just stop yourself right here—like on this interview, or if someone's reading a book—and look around, wherever you're at, and ask yourself, what around me was not created by the imagination?

If you're in your house, or if you're in a city, if you're in a neighborhood, almost everything that you see around you has been created from the imagination. So that to me is proof that there is a realm that exists that this world is a by-product of, that this world is a simulation of, or is a creation from. So whatever that source code is that we have a term for called "the imagination," I believe it. I see it every day and I've experienced it in my own life, so I have to think that this reality comes from that source code.

When you look around at what's happening in the world these days, do you think the human species will survive the next hundred years or do you think that we're doomed to extinction?

VINCE: I have a, maybe very Hollywood, romanticized version of how this will go, where the end of one paradigm coincides perfectly with the dawn of the next paradigm. I actually think that we will simultaneously destroy ourselves at almost the exact same moment that we ascend beyond death, and ascend fully into imagination, so that the two are actually tied together. They're almost the same story.

If you ascend into full imagination, which people might think is a totally bonkers idea, but let's also not forget that we have ascended into full time, and at one point we were not time based, we did not exist solely in time. But right now we are fully in time. There is a possibility that we could exist fully within a context that is in an unknown paradigm to us currently. So when you do ascend fully into imagination, the interesting thing there is that death only exists if you imagine it. It's like you've now bypassed it.

So I have this Hollywood romantic idea that these two storylines are actually parallel. That they're coinciding, and that the death of the physical world and the death of the physical human go hand in hand with the ascension into imagination. An interesting correlation would be that if you tracked along a graph the question, how many things have been created from the imagination, and you start in the year 20,000 BCE and you go up to 2022 CE, you would see this hockey-stick curve of how many things have been created from the imagination.

The curve really starts to go vertical, as a hockey-stick curve does, when we started burning fossil fuels. So the burning of fossil fuels was critical in this obsession of ours to create from the imagination, and so there's this weird correlation between us utilizing up the resources of the physical world in order to bring forth the imaginative world.

I love your optimistic perspective. I'm totally with you on that. It was a huge revelation for me at one point, I remember years ago, just like looking around my room and realizing that everything I'm looking at in my room originated in someone's mind.

VINCE: Yeah!

It was quite a profound insight that's really so obvious but yet most people don't realize it. Do you see any type of teleology, intelligence, or mindful intention operating in nature and the evolution of life, or do you think that evolution is occurring purely by blind chance?

VINCE: Creation is creativity. It is the ability to create. All these things are tied together. *The creator is the creative force and is creation.* And we know that that creation comes from a place called the imagination. We also call a place of creation, love. We know that creation comes from love. These are segmented definitions, down here in time and space, where we segment things and where things are segmented. In a non-time-and-space realm, there's no segmentation, and it's all singular.

There's a Singularity to the soup of imagination, where imagination and love are the same thing. We give it different names and we have different expressions of it down here, but there's Singularity at the point of creation. And I believe in that point of creation. I believe in that non-physical point of creation, that non-divisible, non-physical force. And I do think that there's an intentionality behind it as well.

I believe that the force of creation wants to experience itself and wants to experience its multitude and wants to experience its infinity, but only wants to do so. I think it's important that Singularity is, again, reached. I think that if I was to be in a completely unified realm of Singularity, and I wanted to risk moving into a realm of multiplicity, then I would write into my code a path back to Singularity after I've experienced everything. So yeah, I think that the intentionality of the creator is to experience its creation.

What do you personally think happens to consciousness after physical death and the deterioration of the brain?

VINCE: It goes back into the soup. Actually, it's not that it goes back, it's just all that exists anymore is that unified non-physical energy. So, it's not like it goes back, it's like it created a vessel that has the ability to experience segmentation, definition, and multitude. So the vessel that has the ability to segment is no longer, and then what's remaining is just still the unified non-physical energy. It goes back to love. *It's fully love again*. It's fully timeless and it's fully imaginative. *It's singular again.*

Do you think that there's any element of our individuality that remains, or do you think that we just merge into complete oneness?

VINCE: I think that the individuality can be experienced as vehicles that observe segmentation, like human forms or physical forms that have brains, that have the ability to differentiate, can still experience individuality of that. But, myself as myself, after I die, my individuality is gone. Yeah. But I can still be expressed and experienced as an individual. So I believe ghosts are real, for instance, and that ghost is still the expression and experience of an individual. But it's the human vehicle, the human brain that has the ability to experience that, and to capture that, and to actually observe that expression.

What is your perspective on the concept of god?

VINCE: God is creator and god is the imagination. God is love. God is everything. God is the source code that all else comes from, but most logically, god is creator, and creator is in all of us as creativity. We know that comes from god as imagination, and so that's the easiest—*god is imagination.*

What's in store for the future of Meow Wolf?

VINCE: Meow Wolf wants to continue inspiring creativity in people's lives because we know that the imagination has the power to transform the world. So with that, we will continue to create work on large scale, small scale, multiple mediums, and multiple industries that inspire creativity in people's lives. And that will be done physically and also be done visually. So that's really the goal, that's the North Star for us. So, people can definitely expect more exhibitions from us, and they can probably expect a lot of expressions and experiences that are totally outside of the norm for what Meow Wolf might do.

Have you ever considered building a Meow Wolf attraction in Santa Cruz, California?

VINCE: Oh yeah. California's probably our most popular state as of now; especially with the Las Vegas exhibit being open, California knows about Meow Wolf quite a bit. So we have a lot of interest I think in the state of California, and communities like Santa Cruz that also have a creative energy behind them. Those are important nodes for us to engage with.

What that expression might look like, I'm not sure. Could it be an exhibition, a restaurant, an immersive theater performance, a live event, or a music festival? I would say pretty much every community that we can possibly reach would be in our sights, and especially communities that have an ingrained creative culture.

That sounds great. Well, those are the questions I had for you, Vince. Is there anything that we haven't spoken about that you'd like to add?

VINCE: Nah, I love it man. I really appreciate the opportunity to speak on this. It's kind of a dream come true, honestly, to have someone interested in these thoughts.

9

Underground Cultural Forces in the Mainstream

An Interview with George DiCaprio

George DiCaprio is an environmentalist and film producer whose work in the 1970s as a writer, editor, publisher, and distributor of "underground comix"—independently published comic books for adults that addressed taboo subjects important to the counterculture movement—is legendary among comic enthusiasts. He created numerous titles in this genre, including the *Forbidden Knowledge*, *Greaser Comics*, and *Cocaine Comix* series, as well as *Neurocomics* with Timothy Leary and Peter Von Sholly. As a distributor during the 1970s and '80s, DiCaprio supplied many West Coast retailers with underground and independent comics.

DiCaprio co-produced the Netflix documentary *Struggle: The Life and Lost Art of Szukalski*, about the life and work of the late Polish artist Stanislav Szukalski, and wrote the introduction to the book about the artist that Last Gasp published, titled *Struggle: The Art of Szukalski*.

DiCaprio has been good friends and worked with many people who had a great impact on our culture over the last sixty years, including Laurie Anderson, Andy Warhol, Lou Reed, Timothy Leary, Abbie Hoffman, Matt Groening, Robert Crumb, and virtually all the underground cartoonists, as well as much of Hollywood.

DiCaprio also did creative shows as a performance artist, and he plays the role of a waterbed salesman in the 2021 film *Licorice Pizza*. Acting must be in his DNA, as he is also the father of the Academy Award-

George DiCaprio

winning actor and environmentalist Leonardo DiCaprio, and he played an important role in his son's early career as an actor.

———————————————— ◎ ————————————————

I interviewed DiCaprio on February 19, 2022. I found George to be extremely warm and delightfully philosophical. We spoke about the history of underground comix and its effect on culture, discussed what it was like to work with some of the most important cultural influences over the past few decades, and talked about how environmental action has been a motivating force for him.

How are you doing today, George?

GEORGE: Just wonderfully, except the sun is knocking all the camellias off my bushes, and I was hoping they would hold on for a few more days. But as Aldous Huxley says, "After many a summer dies the swan." You know what I mean?

Ah yes, mortality. So let's turn back the clocks. George, what were you like as a child?

GEORGE: I could it explain it this way. My parents both spoke Italian, but they didn't teach me Italian because I was such a wild child that they needed to have a secret language to handle me. So I never grew up and became able to speak Italian, because I'm sure they needed a secret language to speak to me. Leonardo was no different.

Can you speak about your work with underground comix? What drew you to this medium and what made you passionate about it?

GEORGE: It's a long story. I can abbreviate it by saying that I was in New York and I happened to fall in with a bunch of interesting people. I just had gotten out of college and I was working for the office of the mayor, Mayor Lindsay. I was in charge of a printing room, and there was a series of things that happened where a whole amount of paper was going to be wasted. I also knew Laurie Anderson very well, and Laurie is a very famous performance artist now. But back then she was a very good illustrator who worked with a croquille pen, and we put out a funny little magazine called *Baloney Moccasins*.

Then Laurie went on to work with William Burroughs and she had a really illustrious life, while I kept running into people who wanted to do a comic and didn't really have a way to do it. It was just one of those serendipitous things that I started off doing. It just was one thing after the other, and then when I came out to California, the same kind of thing kept happening. So I wound up producing maybe ten or twelve comic books on different subjects, drugs and odd facts, I would suppose. This culminated with me doing a comic book with Timothy Leary, along with artist Pete Von Sholly, and that was called *Neurocomics*, which became a very famous book.

Timothy had written a book, and it was kind of oblique. So he kept saying, "I wish I could do a comic book." And sure enough, I was able to put it all together and get a comic book done. So I had a loop-de-loop comic career doing this, but I got to meet many of the underground artists along the way. Some were in LA and some were in San Francisco. Now it seems like there's more renewed interest in underground comix than ever before. I've been approached by several people to do a documentary on the underground comix movement, but it's so expansive and there's so many people involved. I'm tempted to try it though.

I think that would be really great. I was also going to say that a lot of people I've spoken to think that Neurocomics should be reprinted. Maybe Last Gasp could expand it into a little soft-cover book, with a new introduction? In any case, that's one of my very favorite comics ever. Underground comix addressed many taboo subjects—such as sex, violence, and drug use—which were conspicuously missing from the newsstand comics. How do you think this affected the culture at large, and what kind of an effect do you think underground comix had on the larger, mainstream culture in general?

GEORGE: Well, let's see. That opens up an even bigger portal about the whole idea of being a hippie, because to my mind, the real golden age of underground comic books was braided in with the hippie movement around 1967, 1966, 1968. It was during those years, alongside some very good music and some very good political upheaval, which was healthy for the country.

I was equating underground comic books with the reluctance to obey orders, the contrariness that's necessary to turn over the accepted order, when it's apparent that the accepted order is not doing very well by almost everybody. So it is really hooked into the idea of rebelliousness, not taking orders from other people, refusing the draft, and a whole bunch of things like that. I think in different cultures, at different times, you could find the same kind of movement—certainly in Paris, and other places, and at the North Pole. Look around. It's just a certain phase of development that happens in a society, and it just always shows up. It's just strange.

I equated a lot with them, Native Americans too. Native Americans, for instance, had very strict rules when they were hunting the buffalo. There was a government set up, and there was a chief, and this, that, and the other thing. Everybody followed orders. Then when the hunt was done, everybody went home and forgot all that stuff, and just lived in an anarchic situation. I think people are only willing to be controlled by politics for a short amount of time, a duration, and then this rebellion comes up. Human beings are not really built to obey orders as much as we think. Or at least at a certain age, you don't want to do it. [*Laughter*]

George, you co-produced the documentary Struggle, about the late Polish artist Stanislav Szukalski, and you co-wrote the introduction to the book about his work that Last Gasp published. His great work was almost lost to history. How did you become interested in his work and why do you think it's important, and how do you think it's relevant to what's happening in the world today?

GEORGE: Well, that's another big question. That once again, if you remember, I started off talking about serendipitously bumping into people and running into artists who wanted this done and that done. When I met Stas through a mutual friend, there was really no way to suppose that he was an incredibly famous person in his own time, except that he told me he was. But it was only after an amount of time, and really having him pass away, that I came to understand that he was the Sculptor Laureate of Poland. He had his own museum that only held his own monumental stuff, nobody else's. He had a whole museum of his own stuff! It was a stone museum. It got bombed flat, and supposedly he was in the basement when it happened. So he had incredible stories to tell everyone, and they turned out to be true.

There was a whole circle of us that went to visit him and took him out, mainly my friend Glenn Bray, in the Valley. But certainly we had more than a dozen parties for him in my house. He came over, visited us, and talked about anything. He was really quite a genius, and he continued to be a really good artist until the end. I remember we went to visit him in his little apartment, and everything was covered with plaster dust because he'd been working with dental picks and making these table-size maquettes, little sculptures that were to be made into monumental bronzes later in life. Except, of course, he was too poor to even make any bronzes, so he just had them in his house. But it was unbelievable, and a lot of people really idolized him.

Unfortunately, if you've seen *Struggle*, you know that right at the end there was a horrible realization that when he was much younger in Poland, he obviously was antisemitic. But when we started the documentary we had *no* idea. There was no indication of that at all. We all thought that he was doing tiles for synagogues and things like that. So there was no way to guess that, and it was a big shock to me especially. I felt very discouraged and sad to hear that.

Yes, that is really sad. George, when you look around at the world these days, do you think that the human species will survive the next hundred years or do you think we're doomed to extinction?

GEORGE: I'm working on a movie about methane, and it's hard to believe that we're going to be around in a hundred years, if I just look at the science of it.

But I have to cling to a broader view, although it may seem a little pie in the sky. To a certain extent, the reality that surrounds us, it's almost of our own making. I'm not saying we consciously weave things around us that are good and evil. What I'm saying is somehow we are generating all of this. Our minds are generating it, and it's like the same arrangement we have with our dreams. Can't really control our dreams, but when you wake up, you still feel like you generated those dreams somehow, for bad or good. I cling to the idea that we are already caught in—I'll use an ancient term—maya, and we have to come to a more distributed awareness of what we're doing and what's happening.

As a group, we're very bad at all coming to the same conclusion at the same time, so it's effective. We're so easily divided. It's the nature of our minds. But somehow I can feel there's going to be a breakthrough, especially about the environment. There will be some big distribution of awareness at the same point. If you look at the world, geologically, and at the history of methane, it's like the entire human race was really just born on the same day. Everything else is so old compared to us, and we've just barely been around. I think it's going to take a much longer time for us to destroy this place, if I have to be candid.

So you're feeling somewhat optimistic that we're going to

develop some kind of technology, or some way of circumventing
the release of methane from the polar ice caps?

GEORGE: Well, yes and no. I know there's plenty of talk about direct extracting methane and CO_2 from the air. I was involved as an executive producer on *Ice on Fire*, and that was the subject of it—different methods of extracting CO_2 from the air, along with different ways to create energy. But it might be possible that there is some kind of a spiritual or meditational breakthrough, not a religious one; just enough to get us one rung up on the ladder, and we might see things differently. That's my hope.

I don't know whether it will come about through yoga, meditation, or a way of seeing things that will present itself through our communications. Obviously, I'm talking about the iPhone. It's impossible to believe. We're so close to AI. We're so close to breakthroughs on the level of an overmind—something that might be smarter than we are. Lord knows I hope there's something smarter than we are. We're not doing a great job solving our problems. It's obvious that we're making problems too complicated for us to figure out. And we're going to have to face it. So it might be a breakthrough like that. Could be.

You mentioned yoga. Do you think that psychedelics can help to
raise ecological awareness on the planet?

GEORGE: Well, that would be one of my hopes, and it could be reached that way. I'm a big fan of a book called *Island* by Aldous Huxley. In the book Huxley speaks of a drug called Moksha. You probably have read the book, and you probably know about it. Moksha is the kind of psychedelic you might look toward. I don't think ketamine is the way out. I don't think some other drugs are. There're bad drugs and good drugs. That's obvious to me.

Yes, I think it's mostly sacred plant and fungal medicines, like
mushrooms and ayahuasca, that people talk about to raise eco-
logical awareness. There have actually been scientific studies
that show that these botanical treasures can raise environmental
consciousness.

GEORGE: Sure. All those helpful plants might be useful in getting that one rung up on the ladder, you know? It might work. It would be my hope that people would be much more open to that and encourage generosity and warm-heartedness toward your fellow man. We're all looking for it to break through.

How has environmental action and ecological awareness been a personally motivating force for you?

GEORGE: I've been involved in at least three big full-on documentary films about the environment; gone to see the pope; traveled all over; and then didn't want to do so much traveling, so we just did it by phone. For quite a while now I've been thinking about our connection with planetary time.

Within the span of my life, when I was born, when I'm around, is human time, and planetary time is separate. But we're having such a drastic effect on the planet, and so planetary time and human time are coinciding. There's no separating them anymore. That's a big realization, that you really are the world. What you do *is* the world. You are in it and of it, and there's no I-thou anymore. It's something that's together at the same time.

A kind of unity?

GEORGE: Yes, and how do we bring about that realization? How do you drill that into people? I don't know. It might happen by luck too— that there'll be some wonderful, serendipitous thing. I think it might be beyond our intelligence to do. It might be a lucky drug. It might be a lucky happenstance, and that's the way I would hope it would happen.

A miracle? Is that the word?

GEORGE: Yes! Well, *miracle* is perhaps a little too religious, but there's got to be a word like that. I think there was a Greek word called *kairos*. That was the name of the word, and kairos means when the perfect moment hits the perfect moment. It's just one of those dang things. I'm hoping for that.

Me too! Getting back to the world of underground comix, I was wondering if you could tell us the story about when the film Wizards *premiered, and you changed the marquee so that it said that it was a film by Vaughn Bodē.*

GEORGE: Yes, it's a little long, as I have to give you some background. When my first wife, Irmelin, and I just came to California, I had a friend from New York who was a cartoonist named Vaughn Bodē. He was a really singular guy because not only could he draw, but he was a very entertaining and wonderful person to be with. He would do slideshows of his drawings, and he would supply them with voices and music. It was called "Vaughn Bodē's Cartoon Concert."

When I came out to LA, it turns out that he had some business in Hollywood, and he looked me up. We got to be friends, and we were both interested in pyramids too. He wound up crashing at my house and got very involved with us. Irmelin was about to give birth to Leonardo, and he wrote a wonderful letter to us before Leonardo was born. It was a letter to Leonardo, and I found the letter recently. It said, "You're going to have a wonderful life. All kinds of astounding things are happening to you, and you have great parents. Just hang on."

But the point of this is that when Vaughn passed away from autoerotic asphyxiation, I was so downcast. When he had come to Hollywood, he had gone to visit Ralph Bakshi at his studio, and I happened to be there. Vaughn had brought character studies, storyboards, and all kinds of things with him to show Ralph. I think he knew Ralph from New York also. But the minute Vaughn passed away, all of a sudden these storyboards started to appear, according to the people that I knew worked there, and I had a little job there on and off.

Then the movie came out. It was called *Wizards* and looked like the stuff from Vaughn's Cobalt-60. It looked exactly like the stuff out of the comic book, and in the plot they had somebody in there with a big hat and its feet sticking out. It was all Vaughn's stuff, *only Vaughn was never mentioned at all*—in any credits, in anything. My friend and I were talking about how dejected we were about that. We knew this, and no one else would know it—so we decided to create a marquee.

On the marquee, in the lettering that looked like the movie marquee, we planned to have it say, "A Film by Vaughn Bodē" on it. So we put it up on the marquee. We got overalls and stuff and hung it there. It was there the night of the opening. Ralph drove up, and I wasn't there when that happened, but other people were there and they demanded it be ripped down, but it was too late. I got a picture of it as we drove away. A friend of mine had a comic-book store that was nearby, and it was like six-thirty at night. He walked down the block, and it was still up. It was still up! Nobody noticed it. It's still up! So, that was our revenge. I don't know what happened after that. I think the family tried to sue him or something. I don't know, I lost track.

I know Vaughn's son Mark, and I didn't realize that I'd been pronouncing his last name wrong all this time. That's a great story. Have psychedelics personally influenced your thinking, your creativity, or your work?

GEORGE: Oh, well that's easy. Let's see, which door, which piano key would I select on that one? Of course it had a lot to do with *Neurocomics*, of course. But, a lot of the other stuff, like I did a series called *Cocaine Comix*, and I tried to be very fair, even reporting on it. If you happen to pick up an issue, you'll probably look and find stories where the characters are depicting casual cocaine use, and it'll seem fanciful or wonderful. But I also always tried to include stories where it wasn't wonderful, where bad things happened, terrible things happen alongside good things. We're back on the subject of bad drugs and good drugs, and I think that particularly, like the game of Monopoly, cocaine really brings out the worst in people. People lie and talk too much; they fib and do all kinds of loop-de-loop stuff. Normally they're not that way, but somehow it does bring out the worst in people.

Cocaine Comix is one of the comics I haven't read yet, but I have Forbidden Knowledge and Greaser Comix here. I saw that you also did something with Harvey Pekar in American Splendor as well.

GEORGE: Wow, you really researched this. His name is pronounced "Harvey Pekar."[1]

Oh, another one! I'm pronouncing everybody's name wrong!
[Laughter]

GEORGE: Don't worry about it. He and his wife, Joyce, were very memorable people. Of course, they made a movie called *American Splendor* out of them. But he was such a curmudgeon and such a strange guy. I'll never forget, many years ago Harvey Pekar was a guest on the *David Letterman Show* because of his comics and who he was. He got on the show and started talking about the connection between, I don't know whether it was Channel 7 or Channel 5, and about GE polluting something, and Letterman said, "This is really insulting. You're coming on my show, and all of a sudden you're talking about stuff that we didn't talk about before."

Letterman said, "Don't come in and cough on the hors d'oeuvres." [*Laughter*] But Harvey wouldn't stop! And he kept going. He really was a one-of-a-kind person. Harvey kept going. He wouldn't let Letterman go about GE, and this scandal about pollution or something. And Letterman wouldn't back down, so they went at it for about a half an hour on TV. It wasn't live, but they showed the whole thing, and it was really combative, but that's what happens if you run into people who don't like to follow orders and don't like to kowtow to the ruling class.

Can you speak a little about your performance art in the past, as well as your recent role as a waterbed salesman in the film Licorice Pizza?

GEORGE: Well, okay. That was all an accident. Ah, again—running into people and things serendipitously. I've met Paul Thomas Anderson several times because originally Leonardo was interviewed for a part in the film *Boogie Nights*. It was for the central character, Dirk Diggler, and he was concurrently up for *Titanic*. He wanted to do both of them but couldn't, so *Titanic* became the thing.

---

1. I pronounced it "'pe-kər." The correct pronunciation is /'piːkɑːr/.

So I got to talk to Paul Thomas Anderson, and he just remembered that I had long hair and was a big hippie. So the absolute truth is he called Leo and said, "Do you think your father might want to do this?" And Leo said, "I'll call him." He called me and I said, "Yeah, I'll get a kick out of it." Paul Thomas Anderson called me up and said, "Do you want to have this part? It's just a small part as a waterbed salesman." And I said, "You know, I used to be a waterbed salesman in New York in 1970." I worked in a waterbed shop. I didn't own the place, and it was on weekends. He goes, "Oh yeah?" Then he said, "Okay, I'm going to send over your lines." I never saw what the script was called, and I never knew what it was about. All I knew was my lines. So I walk in and the name of the thing was originally "Soggy Bottom," and the company that I worked for in New York was called Foggy Bottom.

Wow, oh my goodness! That is so trippy; what a cool synchronicity.

GEORGE: I said, "This can't be!" This just couldn't be happening like this, and later on they got a copy of the Manhattan Yellow Pages from 1970 to look it up, and there was the listing—Foggy Bottom on 59th Street in New York. [*Laughter*] Then he changed the name of the movie to *Licorice Pizza*, but that's too long a story to tell. But it was just, how could that be? How could it possibly happen like that? But it did! [*Laughter*]

What do you personally think happens to consciousness after physical death and the deterioration of the brain?

GEORGE: Well, I have some suspicions that we're all everybody. I could say Timothy Leary believed that we do move on to another form of energy, and that we are moving around in one form or the other. In an ethereal form, I suppose would be the word. And he certainly hoped so. He had a lot of stories about how they were going to freeze his head and stuff, but at the end—and I was around when that was happening—he said, "These people are taking this way too seriously," [*laughter*] and "I'm just going to say that I'm going to do that for a little while, and then just cut it all loose and see what happens, just like everybody else."

So, I actually don't have a really ready answer for that. I think we all hope that, in one way or the other, they'll be some kind of continuity, or something. Or we'll slip into another dimension that we have no way of understanding right now. But that's about it. I don't think the idea of heaven and hell and getting punished for your sins is right. Oh my god, I'd be there forever!

That's great that you got such an answer out of Tim about this, because I asked him that question probably four or five times, and I never got a straight answer out of him. He kept talking about different things, and kept changing the subject, so I'm really happy to hear that he believed that we moved on to a new form of energy.

GEORGE: Everybody says, you get the Timothy Leary that you deserve! [*Laughter*] And he might have given a different answer to somebody else. Did you know that he married my current wife and myself? He married the both of us.

Yes, that's beautiful. I saw a photograph from that day. I love Tim so much. He was such an important force in my life as well.

GEORGE: Oh that's good, I'm glad to hear that.

I was fortunate to spend a considerable amount of time with him, especially during his final year.

GEORGE: Were you there the day that he passed away?

No, I wasn't.

GEORGE: Let me tell you that story, because you weren't there. We all had been visiting him on and off on weekends, and he was getting sicker and sicker. I went there plenty of times with Leonardo and some other friends. I was there when Allen Ginsberg was there. He was surrounded by a lot of wonderful people that were taking care of him and friends. The house was packed with people.

Suzanne Williams, who is the wife of Robert Williams, a psychedelic artist that lives nearby, called me up and said, "If you want to say goodbye to Tim, you better do it, and go up and see him." Well, when I got there, there were people standing on the lawn, and there was a guard at the door. I walked up to the guard and said, "I'm George DiCaprio, and I did a comic book with Tim." He said, "I've been asked not to allow anybody to come in. It's too crowded in there and you'll have to wait outside."

So I was on the lawn, near his window, and I could hear people talking in there. There was a semicircle of us and we all decided to tell jokes, so maybe he would hear the jokes. Somebody told this really good joke about Irish people, and Tim was very proud of being Irish. And just as we were laughing—I swear—just as we were all in this big gust of laughter, someone came out the front door and said, "Tim finally passed. So you all have to leave." But it was just at that moment, that was just on that gust of laughter, that he left. Great story, and it's all true!

Wow! Tim's son Zach, who has been a good friend for over thirty years, told me that he felt an energy move out of Tim's body and through the room the moment that he died. But this reminds me of something that happened to me. I wasn't with Tim when he died but I was with his previous wife Rosemary when she died, and it was a very profound experience.

I got a phone call, just like you did, a couple hours before Rosemary died. A mutual friend said if you want to say good-bye to Rosemary, now's the time, you've got to come right now. So I got in my car and drove to Aptos. There was a small circle of friends there. I sat beside her and held her hand. I was holding her hand, and telling her how much I loved her, how I admired her long before I even knew her. There was a timeless period where I felt out of my body in space with just Rosemary's being. And she died around ten minutes later. It was a very powerful, transformative experience too.

GEORGE: Wow!

I feel really blessed to have had that experience. So George, my final question for you is, what's your perspective on the concept of god?

GEORGE: You're just knocking off all the biggies! I wish I had something really clever tucked away, but I don't. But I think that god—the way most people picture it—is a creation of our imagination, just like everything else. We made him, too.

And I don't think he is encounterable. I don't think he is so distinctly separate from us. I think he's just part of the big pizza pie. It's just, if you want to talk about Gaia, and you want to talk about earth force, and you want to talk about the power of the universe, then maybe he's all of those things too. So, but as far as being someone who's got a long white beard and sits up in the sky, most of the Bible is fairy tales to me. It's not a very religious thing, but it could just be a level of consciousness that we haven't experienced yet, and it's hopefully waiting for us to step into it.

Is there anything we haven't spoken about that you would like to add?

GEORGE: Wow! [*Laughter*] Tons of things. I brought up two boys, and I'm currently bringing up a fourteen-year-old girl. I'm learning that nothing that I experienced bringing up boys is any good bringing up a girl! Argh! [*Laughter*] It's all useless. It's like everything is so different.

Completely uncharted territory?

GEORGE: Yeah, that's really the truth of it. I just was thinking that this morning.

10

Radical Mysticism and the Secret History of Religions

An Interview with Jeffrey Kripal

Jeffrey Kripal is a professor of religion who is well-known for his popular books on anomalous phenomena and mysticism. He holds the J. Newton Rayzor Chair in Philosophy and Religious Thought at Rice University in Houston, Texas, and is the author of nine books about a diverse array of fascinating topics, including the sexual influences in religions and mystical traditions, American countercultural translations of Asian religions, and the history of Western esotericism.

Kripal argues that sexuality and spirituality are intricately linked, and some of his books on this subject have stirred up controversy. Kripal's first book *Kali's Child*, a psychoanalytic study arguing that Ramakrishna's mystical experiences involved a strong homoerotic dimension, won the American Academy of Religion's History of Religions Prize for the Best First Book in 1995, and has been praised by many scholars and condemned by others who tried to have the book banned in India.

A number of Kripal's books explore the role of paranormal or anomalous phenomena in mystical literature, the humanities, and pop culture, such as *Authors of the Impossible*; *The Superhumanities*; *The Super Natural* (coauthored with Whitley Strieber); and *Mutants and Mystics: Science Fiction, Superhero Comics, and the Paranormal*, which is one of my all-time favorite books. Kripal also did a wonderful book about the history of the American counterculture through the prism of the Esalen

Photograph by Jeff Fitlow, for Rice University

Jeffrey Kripal

Institute in Big Sur, *Esalen: America and the Religion of No Religion*, which is the definitive book on this legendary retreat center that helped to inspire the human potentials movement.

Some of Kripal's other books include *Comparing Religions: Coming to Terms*; *The Serpent's Gift: Gnostic Reflections on the Study of Religion*; and *Roads of Excess, Palaces of Wisdom: Eroticism and Reflexivity in the Study of Mysticism*. Kripal has also contributed to numerous other volumes, including the essay "Biological Gods," which appears in David Luke's book *DMT Entity Encounters*.

In Kripal's autobiographical book *Secret Body: Erotic and Esoteric Currents in the History of Religions* he summarizes and analyzes much of the material from his earlier books and puts forth a more comprehensive expression of his ideas about the role that sexuality and paranormal phenomena play in religious and mystical thought. To find out more about his work, see the Rice University website of Jeffrey J. Kripal.

I interviewed Jeffrey on October 26, 2022, and found him to be modest, thoughtful, and thought provoking. We spoke about the role that sexuality plays in religion, how anomalous events can flip perspectives on the philosophy of materialism, and the relationship between alien abductions and DMT entity encounters.

How did you become interested in the relationship between anomalous experiences and the history of religions?

JEFFREY: The short answer is people. I was working on a history of the human potential movement in California, and people were telling me stories that I found incredible and that I knew were genuine. I also knew that the discipline I was trained in had no real way of dealing with that—*that reality*. They tended to treat these experiences as legends or as unreal, and I knew that they had actually happened. So it was really people at the end of the day, human beings who convinced me these things were important.

Can you briefly describe the transformative encounter that you had in India with Kali and how this experience affected your personal view of reality?

JEFFREY: I was trained as a psychoanalytic reductive thinker. In other words, I tended to think of ecstatic religious experience as sublimated forms of sexuality. I still think that by the way, in a lot of ways, but what happened was this. I was also always interested in erotic forms of mystical experience, which were certainly sexual, but not just sexual; there's a transcendent component to them as well.

When I was living in India, in the fall of 1989 during Kali Puja, I woke up one night in a paralyzed state. A powerful, electric-like energy entered my body, or came out of my body, and did all sorts of things to me, and eventually resulted in an out-of-body experience. When I came back into my body, or I got control of it, I just felt very powerfully that something had been transmitted or shocked into me, as it were.

That state was very erotic, but it was also not erotic. It was a *both/and*, and I realized that if that was true, then all of these texts I was reading could be about something related and that something could be erotic and nonsexual at the same time. So the deepest origin of my sympathy, or my imagination, as it were, was really that event.

How do you think mystical and anomalous experiences affect the role that sexuality plays in religion?

JEFFREY: I think the role that sexuality and gender play in religion is vastly underestimated. I think sexuality in particular is something we don't understand. We tend to think of sexuality in biological or physical terms, but it also has all of these spiritual components. I think we're pretty good about the biological aspects, but what we're really bad about are the spiritual components.

I think one's gender identity, and one's sexuality, very much informs how one imagines god or the divine, and how one interacts with other kinds of realities. Just to put a nuance on it, a straight heterosexual man is probably not going to have an erotic experience with a divine male, but a male who is oriented in a same-sex fashion might actually have an erotic experience with a male divinity.

So I think these things really inform how one thinks of, or believes in, a god or the gods or the goddess. So I think it's incredibly shaping— and that then informs things like celibacy, institutional forms of religious authority, religious prodigies, and who's believed and who's not. I think all of these things are deeply, deeply informative.

How do you think that studying the way that people flip perspectives on the philosophy of materialism can help us to gain insight into world religions?

JEFFREY: I'm not sure. The reason I'm hesitating goes like this. What I mean by a flip is when a scientist or engineer or medical professional trained in a very materialist worldview or practice has one of these extraordinary experiences and realizes that mind is somehow fundamental, is not an emergent property of matter. So they flip. They thought that matter was everything, and now they realize that mind is either everything or just as important as matter.

I think it relates to the history of religions because a lot of religions have essentially argued the same thing. But it's not the same thing, David. Religion is a kind of institutionalization of these flips, and it often comes with a set of beliefs and rituals, mythologies, and doctrines, none of which need to be present in such a flip. So I think there's a relationship there, but there's certainly not an identity. That's my hesitation.

I was intrigued by a story that you recounted in **The Super Natural** *about your colleague's experience with a honey jar that seemed to inexplicably move from the table to the inside of a flour tin, and his conclusion from that was "materialism is false." Do you think that experiences like this occur because reality is primarily composed of consciousness, not matter, and why do you think that these mysterious events "intend" to "provoke and confuse" or "mess" with us, as you say?*

JEFFREY: The truth is I don't know. I do think those events happen for a reason, but by *reason*, I don't mean something rational, something that can make sense to us, which essentially means they can be slotted into our senses. I think absurd or wild things like that happen because we're being pushed out of our boxes, and we're being essentially told that the real world is not like we think it is, much less how we sense it is.

Do they mean that everything's mind or consciousness? I don't know. I really don't know, David. I'm not trying to avoid your question. I think the whole point of this is the fact that we don't know, and we're being reminded that we don't know. I get really nervous when people say they know or when they're certain about something. I generally don't trust those people, and I generally trust people who say they don't know and who are open about what these things might mean.

One reviewer of your book **Mutants and Mystics** *said that the paradoxical mysteries behind many anomalous experiences resemble Zen koans. Can you explain why you think it's a good metaphor?*

JEFFREY: Some people in the UFO community have called UFOs "Zen koans in the sky." I like that because the Zen koan is essentially a riddle, or a question, that tries to push you out of your boxes, push you out of your notions of what a human being is and what the physical world is. And I think some of these anomalous experiences are trying to do similar things. So they're essentially koans that are operating on a physical and mental plane at the same time, to push us out of those boxes. I guess I like Zen, and so I like the notion of these events being a kind of koan for us.

I thought that was clever because they're so paradoxical. What sort of connection do you see between reports of alien abduction experiences and DMT entity encounters?

JEFFREY: They're similar. You're talking about little beings doing weird things to you, and sometimes their appearances are even similar—big eyes, and buglike or insectoid. So there's clearly some kind of phenomenological or experiential connection there. Again, I don't know what that is. It's possible that abduction accounts are essentially endogenous DMT releases; the body and the brain are releasing DMT into the system and one is essentially on a psychedelic journey or having a psychedelic experience. I don't know. I mean, again, I don't think we know a lot of these things, David, because we haven't tried to know. By that I don't mean there aren't lots of people who are asking serious questions, but we haven't invested large amounts of research, money, and centuries of thought about these things to really figure them out in some way.

Oh, I wasn't expecting you to have definitive answers to these questions; I just wanted to hear your thoughts, especially to this next one, which is a real serious mystery that I'm exploring in this book. What are your thoughts on whether the entities that people report on DMT have a genuine independent existence or not?

JEFFREY: Yeah, I get that a lot. I go back and forth. One of the bottom lines for me is that *all such experiences are reported by human beings.* We know of no such DMT entity that has ever appeared to a lion, a cockroach, or to a tree. It's always to a human being. Of course that doesn't mean they don't, as obviously we can't talk to trees, lions, or cockroaches, but at the end of the day, everything we're talking about really is a form of human experience.

So I think the human being might actually be the root of all of this. It doesn't mean that such entities aren't independent of human beings, but it means we should, I think, question whether they are or not. So that's kind of my gut feeling about that. I'm a bit suspicious about claiming that things are independent of human beings when they certainly don't act completely independent, and they only appear within a human experience.

That's an interesting perspective. I hadn't thought about that before. I know that every other mammal produces endogenous DMT, and I think that the only types of creature that don't produce DMT are insects.

JEFFREY: What does that mean? I just don't know. Again, I think what we know and what we consider to be real is mostly a function of the human organism. So I can't even say that physics and mathematics work for some other creature. *All the physics and all the mathematics are all human.* They're all a function of the human brain and the human being. Does that mean that they're independent and cosmic? Well, they seem to work in the external environment, but maybe another creature, or another species, would have a different physics or a different mathematics.

This next question is the subject of a whole book, of course, but maybe you can just give a brief overview and then refer people to your new book. How do you think that the humanities can be improved by incorporating paranormal phenomena?

JEFFREY: Well, the humanities get a bum rap a lot. Nobody really knows what the humanities are, by the way. If you ask people, what are the humanities?—they're going to struggle, and they're going to trip, and they're not going to be able to tell you. But in fact, most of the ideas we live by every day come out of the humanities—ideas like democracy, human rights, freedom, and creativity are all part of the humanities.

The humanities are simply the study of human beings and their expressions, whether that's literature, philosophy, religion, art, or language.

I think the humanities are often dismissed today because they can't produce refrigerators, smartphones, or bombs. The STEM fields [science, technology, engineering, and math] do those things. So we make this mistake, or we err that because you can make cool stuff, it's somehow absolutely true or somehow sufficient. And of course that's not the case. I think the humanities can essentially go on the offensive and be more robust by emphasizing all of these altered states of mind and body, which in fact do remarkable things and produce remarkable pieces of literature, philosophy, and thought. But I think we have to make that claim. We have to essentially take what's a two-dimensional or flatland view of the world and put an "up" to it, give it a third dimension. I think when we do that, we'll make the humanities far more interesting and attractive to people.

For readers who are interested in this, your fascinating new book **The Superhumanities** *explores this idea in depth. Jeffrey, I spoke with Nick Herbert earlier this week and he said to ask you about miracles, as this is an aspect of religions only accessible through text. What kind of contemporary miracles have you been able to access through your studies of living people, and have you ever witnessed a levitation?*

JEFFREY: The answer to the last question is no, I have not witnessed a levitation, but historically, I'm nearly certain people levitate. The historical evidence on levitation is as good as anything. So I don't know why we would question it other than it violates our own assumption about how the world works miracles. To answer Nick's question, I don't write about miracles. I'm not even sure I like miracles. Miracles are always invoked to establish the truth of a particular religious tradition. So the miracle isn't just a piece of wonder working or a marvel. It's an event that establishes the sanctity or holiness or truth of a particular figure or human being or religion.

But the problem is that these miracles or marvels all happen in religious contexts, and they actually don't speak to the exclusive truth of any one tradition. There's something about the miracle or the extraordinary event that reaches across all human cultures and certainly all religious traditions. So I think there's a tension there. I think what Nick was probably asking though is if I've witnessed any miracles or has my study produced any, and I think the answer is probably a careful "maybe."

If you talk to some of my readers, they'll tell you all kinds of miracle stories, and they'll even sometimes argue that the extraordinary event was catalyzed by reading the book or the essay. I take those very seriously, but I don't think I'm some kind of hidden wizard or sorcerer. I think those extraordinary events are happening because of them, and I think the writing allows them to acknowledge or access their own abilities, or their own dimensions, as it were. So I think it's tricky. That's what I mean by it's a careful maybe. But I myself am not gifted or, as I said in the book, I don't walk around in a super world. I feel pretty dull most of the time.

Well, thank you for that humble response.

JEFFREY: David, it's not humble. I'm not a particularly humble person. It's just honest. It's like, yeah, that doesn't happen much. I'm not trying to be difficult, but humility is a particular virtue that serves a worldview. So I'm not a big fan of it. On the other hand, I'm not a big fan of certainty either. So if you want to call that humility, I guess I'll accept it.

In your book Secret Body, you say that you are "more interested in the history of religions for what these literatures and practices can teach us about what a human might yet become." How do you envision the future evolution of humanity?

JEFFREY: Well, again, I don't. I envision the future of humanity as us engaging with what I call the superhumanities. In other words, I want us to have a broad-based conversation of many cultures, in many decades and even centuries, about our own superhumanity. And I think by having that conversation we essentially realize or affect that super-humanity. I don't know where it's going. I just want us to have that conversation because I think by having it we'll essentially affect what we're talking about. I think thought has the power to realize itself, and so I think it's really important what we think and what we talk about.

When you look around at what's happening in the world these days, do you think the human species will survive the next hundred years or do you think that we're doomed to extinction?

JEFFREY: I think the species will survive. I don't know to what extent it'll survive. Look, there's 8 billion of us. It's extremely unlikely that all 8 billion people will be wiped out. I don't see that happening. Even a nuclear holocaust, I doubt would do that. But let me put it this way. There are lots of reasons to be pessimistic, and they're perfectly good reasons. There aren't many good reasons to be hopeful, but I'm still hopeful because again, it goes back to this notion of thought helping to produce itself. I think being optimistic about things generally produces optimistic results, and being pessimistic will generally produce pessimistic results. So it's not that I'm optimistic because I'm in a la-la land, or I'm being Pollyanna-ish about something; it's that *I just think hope and optimism produce better futures than despair and pessimism.*

Have you had much experience with lucid dreaming, and if so, how has it influenced your perspective on reality?

JEFFREY: A little. I used to lucid dream all the time when I was a kid, around five or six years old. It hasn't had much influence on me that I know of recently. I do think back on it. The lucid dream that I had the most often as a child was one in which I was always being chased by a monster. I remember that I'd be in the dream, and I knew it was a dream. I knew the monster was chasing me, but I also knew that if I wanted to wake up, I just had to cover myself with a sheet and click my feet together three times.

I know it's funny now, but as a five-year-old, it never—I swear to you—it never occurred to me that I got that from *The Wizard of Oz.* I never would've put two and two together. But now, of course, it's obvious. And so it tells me something about lucid dreaming. It tells me that it relies on the cultural surround and on what the person's seeing or reading. So I guess it tells me something about the imagination, but again, I don't lucid dream anymore, and I can't say it has had a big impact.

In your message to me you said that your experience with psychedelics has been very minor. Do you want to speak about the experience that you've had?

JEFFREY: I went on a retreat in a Latin American country where it wasn't illegal, and it was a long retreat. It was a two-week retreat, and I drank the ayahuasca tea, as it were, four different times. I had a lot of unusual bodily sensations and energetic experiences, but I didn't have the breakthrough experience that people often talk about. And that's really it, David. I'm really, at least before that, I was very much a psychedelic virgin. I mean, I drink alcohol and coffee, but that's pretty much it.

Interesting; thank you for sharing your experience. Where do you think the future evolution of artificial intelligence is headed, and what are your thoughts on the concept of the Singularity?

JEFFREY: I'm pretty crabby about artificial intelligence. I think it's way overclaimed or overdone. When I listen to people who want to claim the computer will become conscious at some point, I confess my eyes roll. I think that whole idea is based on materialism, which I think is false. I say that because what a materialist would argue is that consciousness is a product of brain processes, which are, of course, material processes, which means that awareness is a property of a matter or material brain.

I think it's the other way around. I think the brain is very much a process that emerges from mind or consciousness. So when we get to an artificial intelligence with a computer, I think it's very likely the computer will mimic or pretend to be consciously aware. But I don't think it can be. I think it's actually the reverse. I think it's the creators of that computer who are in fact conscious. The human beings are aware, but the computer itself is not and will not be.

What are your thoughts on the simulation hypothesis, the idea that our entire reality is really an advanced computer simulation?

JEFFREY: Yeah, the whole *Matrix* idea. Again, how would I know? I mean, I'm in that matrix in that model and so I'm just a part of the simulation. I guess I'm suspicious of it because of its reliance on computer models. Two hundred years ago, the mind-brain relationship would have been understood through a clock. Then it was a telegraph, then it was a radio, then it was a television, and now it's a computer. None of those technological metaphors have worked.

Or, I guess you could say, they've all worked to a certain extent, but then they haven't worked in another sense. So I don't see any reason whatsoever that the computer model is suddenly it—like, oh, we got the truth now; it's the computer! Well, we didn't have the truth before and everybody thought we had the truth. So why do we think we have it now?

So, I just think some really basic historical understanding of the situation has to make us deeply suspicious of any computer model, and I think the simulation hypothesis certainly has all kinds of analogs in the history of mystical literature. So it's not that I think reality is what it looks like. I don't, of course, think that. I think that the simulation hypothesis is another example of a metaphor or a myth that's used to talk about, essentially, mystical experiences. But I don't think it's literally true any more than I think that these earlier metaphors were literally true.

Do you see any type of teleology, intelligence, or mindful intention operating in nature and the evolution of life, or do you think that evolution is occurring by blind chance?

JEFFREY: One of my favorite definitions of *hydrogen* is that hydrogen is "a light odorless gas that, given enough time, turns into people." And I like that because it's funny, but I also like that because it really implies that there's teleology, or that the cosmos is moving somewhere. I don't think evolution is random and meaningless because I don't know how we could possibly explain consciousness or ourselves with it, *because we all have intention and we have consciousness.*

So clearly whatever evolutionary model of the universe we want to suggest or hypothesize has to be able to hypothesize consciousness and human beings, and I don't think the random meaningless one does that. I think that might say something about the scientists who proposed it or who use it, but it doesn't really explain reality.

What do you personally think happens to consciousness after physical death and the deterioration of the brain?

JEFFREY: Yeah, that's not fair. That's a big question. My gut feeling is that personality survives for a while, whatever that means. And it can communicate and interact with people on this side, as it were, as a person or as a soul. But that ultimately all souls are, or all persons are, essentially nodes in a larger cosmic Mind or form of consciousness. So I guess what I'm saying is I think personal immortality likely works for a time, but that ultimately there is no personal or individual immortality, but there is some kind of immortality of consciousness or Mind, if that makes sense.

What is your perspective on the concept of god?

JEFFREY: Same thing, I just told you. I don't think there's any distinction between consciousness and god. I often say god is idealism for the masses. In other words, it's really just a form of idealism that people can believe and act on. But it really amounts to the same thing, that there's a Mind, or a shared form of consciousness, that is cosmic.

What role do you think altered states of consciousness play in the creative process?

JEFFREY: I think *they are the creative process.* I think there is no creativity without altered states of consciousness. I think if you don't want to be creative, just stay in this normal state of mind. It's a very restricted, very banal, very functional form of mind that can do certain things. But it's certainly not designed to create new things or new ideas. You have to somehow get into an altered state of consciousness to do that. That doesn't mean everything that occurs in an altered state of consciousness is good and new and creative, but I think those two things still are very much related.

Well Jeffrey, those are the questions that I had for you today. Is there anything that we haven't discussed that you would like to add?

JEFFREY: You told me to be short, so I tried to be short, and you went through a lot. This is like a credo; you went through all the big questions about everything and I did my best. I would say none of those answers are definitive. I hope they're not heard that way, but that's certainly my best shot at this point in the life cycle.

Oh, your answers were great; very thoughtful, and I appreciated the historical context that you put things in. I agreed with most of what you were saying.

JEFFREY: Yeah, David, I'm not even sure I agree with myself, and I don't need to. I guess that's the other thing I'd like to say is, *I don't need to be right.* I don't even understand the phrase other than it's very left brainy: "I want to be right; I want to be correct." Of course I'm not correct, of course I'm not right, and of course the truth we'll be talking about in a hundred or two hundred years will not be these truths. But I'm totally fine with that. I certainly don't feel any need to be right, to be correct, or to be exhaustive. Quite the contrary.

I think there's a lot of wisdom in that. My friend Robert Anton Wilson based his philosophy on the idea of approaching all questions with the possibility of "maybe."

JEFFREY: There's a South Asian or Jain philosophical doctrine that's literally called "The Maybe Doctrine." And basically it says that—that any truth statement should be taken in a subjective sense as a perhaps or a maybe.

11

Exploring What Is Real
in Virtual Worlds

An Interview with David Chalmers

David Chalmers is an Australian philosopher and cognitive scientist who helped to revolutionize philosophy and psychology. Chalmers is a professor of philosophy and neural science at New York University, as well as co-director of NYU's Center for Mind, Brain, and Consciousness. Chalmers specializes in the areas of philosophy of mind and philosophy of language. He is best known for bringing the "hard problem of consciousness" to the forefront of philosophy, as well as to the scientific and academic communities.

Chalmers makes a distinction between the "easy problems of consciousness," such as explaining the nature of perception or object discrimination, and the "hard problem of consciousness," which would be explaining why we have a sense of subjective awareness. The great mystery of consciousness was conveniently ignored in psychology and all of the sciences for the past century. Thanks to Chalmers's 1994 lecture at the Toward a Science of Consciousness conference in Arizona and his 1995 paper "Facing Up to the Problem of Consciousness," much more attention has since been paid to this most intriguing mystery.

As a child, Chalmers had exceptional mathematical abilities and he experienced synesthesia, the perceptual phenomenon in which the stimulation of one sensory pathway leads to involuntary experiences in another sensory pathway, such as tasting colors or seeing music. As a

Photo by Claudia Passos

David Chalmers

graduate student, Chalmers studied under Douglas Hofstadter (author of *Gödel, Escher, Bach*) at Indiana University, and this is where he developed an interest in consciousness.

Chalmers is the author or coauthor of six books, including *The Conscious Mind: In Search of a Fundamental Theory* and *The Character of Consciousness*. His latest book, *Reality+: Virtual Worlds and the Problems of Philosophy*, explores the idea that virtual reality is "genuine reality." Chalmers's thought-provoking philosophical speculations have become so popular that his ideas even appear in a comic strip called *Existential Comics*.

———————————————————— ⊚ ————————————————————

I interviewed Chalmers on March 16, 2022. I first met David in 1995 when a mutual friend suggested we get together and we had lunch at a cafe in downtown Santa Cruz. That afternoon we discussed the problem of consciousness—how it's simultaneously so mundane and so mysterious. I was absolutely thrilled to see how David brought this central philosophical puzzle to the attention of the worldwide scientific community since our meeting. It was great to catch up with him twenty-seven years later for this book. David is unusually erudite, and it seems that much thought lies behind whatever he says. We discussed the relationship between consciousness and the nature of reality, the philosophical implications of virtual reality, and the possibility that we're living in a computer simulation.

How did you first become interested in the interface between philosophy and cognitive science, and how have these disciplines influenced your understanding of consciousness and the nature of reality?

DAVID: Growing up, I was really very strongly oriented toward math and science. I guess I was a math geek. I used to go in for math competitions and Mathematical Olympiad and so on. I always thought I was going to become a mathematician. I went to university to study math and physics and computer science. Along the way, I did one course in philosophy. I didn't do very well. I think it was the worst course on my undergraduate record. But I think it planted some kind of seed for getting very interested in philosophical issues and the human mind, in particular.

Also, I remember around that time I read Doug Hofstadter's book *Gödel, Escher, Bach* and the book that he co-edited with Daniel Dennett, *The Mind's I.* I think those books also planted some kind of seed for thinking about mind, consciousness, and intelligence. And increasingly as time went on, I think, while I was a university student, I gradually grew obsessed with the problem of consciousness. It just came to seem to me to be the most interesting unsolved problem in the world—the one thing that we just don't understand right now. And it's going to be a wide-open frontier in the way that, say, physics was a wide-open frontier four hundred years ago.

So, I grew increasingly obsessed by the problem of consciousness. I think I had a new theory of consciousness each week that I'd present to my friends. But I don't think I ever really took it seriously as something you could do professionally. Somewhere along the way, I went to Oxford to do another degree in mathematics.

On the way, I hitchhiked around Europe for about six months, and the whole time, standing by the side of the road, I was thinking about consciousness. How do you explain consciousness? How does it fit into the physical world? I got to Oxford and I thought, okay, now I'll settle down and study mathematics again. But no, this consciousness thing just kept going in my head and eventually got to the point where I thought, okay, there's an itch here that I just have to scratch. This is what I need to be doing, thinking about the problem of consciousness.

At that point I didn't know very much about academic philosophy or cognitive science. I knew bits and pieces, but I thought it was what I needed to do. So actually, it's a long story, but I ended up moving to Indiana to work with Doug Hofstadter, who had written those books that I loved. I spent four or five years just retooling to think about philosophy, think about cognitive science, and wrote a Ph.D. thesis on consciousness.

A page from *Captain Metaphysics*, in which David Chalmers is a comic character.

Can you speak just briefly about why you call consciousness the "hard problem" in philosophy, and about the inspiration behind your book The Conscious Mind?

DAVID: Yes, I always thought it was almost obvious that consciousness is such a distinctively hard problem. It's this thing that we don't even really have an initial beat on being able to explain. I think I first used that locution to distinguish different ways of thinking about consciousness. People use *consciousness* sometimes just for being awake versus being asleep, or for being able to report information. And then I thought, well, those problems, we know how to explain those things in principle. When it comes to consciousness, those things are the easy problems. They're objective functional matters. But when it comes to subjective experience, what it feels like from the inside to be a conscious being, the standard methods there just don't work. And I call that "the hard problem," just to really isolate the sense in which this notion of consciousness, subjective experience, is the one that generates the problem.

I took this to be obvious, what I said. It was not meant to be any kind of major original contribution to discourse, to call consciousness the hard problem. I think that the reason this actually caught on so well is that plenty of people already knew this is the hard problem. But I think the label, at least, served quite well to make the problem harder to avoid. Actually, the context was a scientific meeting, the first big meeting on consciousness in 1994. We had many people going around saying, "Yeah, here, I've got an explanation of consciousness," but I'm like, "Well, is that really just solving the easy problems or is it solving the hard problems?" Having that label there, I think, just at least managed to encapsulate the challenge in a way that made it harder to avoid.

How did you become interested in virtual reality and simulation theory, and what inspired you to write Reality+?

DAVID: I guess this was a bit later, although there was maybe an interest in it being there all along. I've always enjoyed reading science fiction, although I don't read as much as I used to, but there are plenty of simulation scenarios there. I encountered my first virtual world when I was ten playing *Colossal Cave Adventure*, which was just a text adventure on a computer. I spent months and months mapping out that world.

But I guess the immediate impetus for this world—maybe it was twenty years ago now—I was invited to write an article for the website of *The Matrix*, the movie. I guess the Wachowskis are very interested in philosophy and they actually commissioned a philosopher, Chris Grau, to work on their production company, RedPill. They commissioned him to invite a number of philosophers to write philosophical reflections on the movie for their website, TheMatrix.

I ended up writing a piece called "The Matrix as Metaphysics." I'd already been thinking along these lines, about writing a technical and very philosophical piece called something like, "Envatment as a Metaphysical Hypothesis." But then this invitation came out and I thought, okay, I can see how to do this in a way that might actually reach a broad audience. It was really my first expression of a key idea, which is that virtual realities are actually genuine realities.

Let's just say you wake up like Neo in the Matrix. Some people say that means that none of the things around you are real; it's all an illusion. I wanted, back then, to argue, no, if you're in the Matrix the tables and chairs, the trees, the people, the planets around you—*they're still all perfectly real*. You shouldn't say this is an illusion. *Virtual reality is a genuine reality.* And then I guess it's what really started this process to me, of thinking more deeply about virtual reality. And this turns out to be a device for thinking about so many philosophical questions: questions about your knowledge of the external world, questions about the nature of reality, and questions about the relationship between mind and body. So I guess over the twenty years since then, I started increasingly thinking about virtual reality.

Also, this was because the practical aspects of VR technology suddenly became more and more ubiquitous, and people are actually starting to use it. It's now available for consumers. Many people think it's going to be the future of the internet. So putting all these things together, it eventually came to me—okay, well, I have to write a book on this idea of virtual reality. This one central trope or theme of virtual reality connects to so many issues in philosophy. I think it sheds a whole lot of light on questions about reality. And at the same time, it's actually of central practical importance as we come to be using it. It just seemed to be an irresistible topic to write a book about and that's what I ended up doing.

Simulation theory is one of the themes running through this book that I'm working on as well; I'm asking everyone that I interview for the collection what their thoughts are about it. You ask the question in your book, "How do we know we're not in a computer simulation right now?" How would you venture an answer to this seemingly unanswerable question?

DAVID: I would say we can't know for sure that we're not in a simulation. If we are in a simulation, maybe there's some ways we could come to know that we are in a simulation. Maybe the simulators could give us evidence? Maybe they could show us the source code? They could manipulate the source code, and as a result we'd see our world being manipulated. The trees might melt and the moon might come crashing down to Earth, and this could potentially be pretty convincing evidence that we are in a simulation.

But if we're in a perfect simulation, one that perfectly mirrors physical reality, then almost by definition it'll be indistinguishable from physical reality. There is no experiment you can do, no evidence you get that will distinguish a perfect simulation from the reality it's a simulation of. So for this year, you might think you can get some evidence that you're not in a simulation, but then it sure looks like that evidence could in principle be simulated. So I think there are actually systematic reasons to think that we could never prove that we're not in a simulation. And furthermore, as the technology develops it looks like it becomes more and more a live possibility that we could be simulated, because simulation technology is actually something that exists. And although we don't yet have simulations indistinguishable from physical reality, it's perfectly likely that within a century or so we might, and then that makes this simulation hypothesis a live hypothesis that we can't rule out.

Asking the question, how do we know we're not in a computer simulation right now, is similar to what lucid dreamers start to ask themselves about dreaming—am I dreaming right now? Have you ever had any lucid dreams, and have dreams and lucid dreams influenced your philosophical view of reality?

DAVID: I've never had a lucid dream that I know of, somewhat to my disappointment. Maybe twenty to thirty years ago now, I had a number of conversations about this with Stephen LaBerge, who's done lots of very well-regarded work on lucid dreaming, and he provided me with a device to assist in lucid dreaming called the Nova Dreamer. The idea was that it would flash a red light at you when it detected REM sleep, and if this happened while you were actually dreaming, then you would see a red light often in your dreams.

The thought was that you had to train yourself, so whenever you see a red light in your dreams, you touch your forehead. If you did this while you were awake, then it would press a button and the red light would go away. But if you do this in the dream, your physical arm wouldn't move, so the red light would stay there. So the idea is, you just train yourself to hit your forehead every time you see a red light, and if the red light keeps going then that's a signal that you're dreaming.

All I know is that I tried to train myself to do this, but as far as I can tell it never happened or it never happened in a way that made me lucid in a way I could remember. To this day, I've still never had a lucid dream, at least one that I've remembered. So that's a disappointment.

I do think that many of these issues could in principle apply to dreams. I mean, dreams are simulations of a sort. When you dream, you're interacting with a simulation. It could be a simulation of your own devising—some system in your brain has come up with it. Typically dreams are much more fragmented and less rich than a standard full-scale simulation. They're not as coherent; sometimes they follow a script, and they're very rich for all that. If you take the extreme case of a dream that is as rich as a simulation, then I think it would be similar in principle.

There's a sense in which you'd be interacting with a dream reality. I mean, there's one sense in which maybe you wouldn't be quite as real as a computer simulation. Sometimes one central aspect of our notion of something being real is we want it to be outside our mind. If something happens within our mind, then we don't count it as at least *as* real. So maybe in that sense, dreams would end up being mind-dependent, whereas a computer simulation would end up being mind-independent, giving the computer simulation, perhaps, an extra degree of reality. But dreams would at least be somewhere on the reality spectrum.

So you would distinguish between a virtual reality and a dream reality? When you say virtual realities are genuine realities, do you mean that dreams are genuine realities too?

DAVID: What I say in the book is we've got something like multiple notions of reality. The word *real* doesn't just mean one thing. So I try and distinguish a few different ideas, a few different meanings of the word *real*. One thing that we mean when we say something is real is that it makes a difference in the world. It has causal powers; it can affect things. But another thing we sometimes mean by real is that it's happening outside my mind. It's not just something conjured up by my mind, but it's going on external from the mind. The third thing we might mean is that it's not an illusion. When things are real, things are the way they appear; whereas when they're not real, things are not the way they appear.

So I think what I go on and say is that virtual reality can satisfy many of those criteria. If we're in a simulation, actually I argue, the simulation satisfies all five of the five criteria I lay out. And I think I argue that a virtual reality headset can satisfy at least four of the five. Dreams, I would say, perhaps they're more like three out of five, because they don't satisfy the criterion of being mind-independent. A dream is something all in your mind, whereas a virtual reality running on a computer is outside your mind. So maybe dreams will end up—at least a fully stable dream with full-scale causal powers—will end up potentially at three out of five on the reality checklist. I think of that as providing a kind of sliding scale for degrees of reality, depending on exactly what you mean by reality.

If reality is a simulation, do you have any speculation as to what it might be a simulation of, or what might be outside the simulation?

DAVID: It's a good question. An initial question, of course, is if there's a simulation, then there's a simulator. Who set it up? And then we have the questions, what are the simulators like? Why did they set up the simulation? I mean, for us, why do we run simulations? Sometimes it's entertainment, a video game or something akin to a TV show. We want to re-examine a bit of our history. Sometimes it's science; we want to set up simulations to watch them go, and gather data. Sometimes it's decision-making; we want to make decisions about the future and we want to see how those decisions are going to pan out, so we simulate them.

I think all those motivations are available to our simulators in principle; they could be doing science, maybe running a million simulations overnight with slightly different parameters, and they're going to come back and gather the data in the morning. It could be entertainment, could be decision-making, and it could be something quite different.

What is their world like? I think there's no particular reason to think it has to be very much like our four-dimensional world with humanlike beings. It could be quite different. I think there's a science fiction novel where it turns out that the simulation is run by twenty-six–dimensional octopuses. Who's to say that the simulators couldn't be at least as different from us as that?

My biggest questions about whether we're already in a computer simulation stem from not understanding how simulated characters could become conscious beings. How do you think consciousness might develop and evolve inside of simulated realities, and do you think that AI systems in general can become conscious?

Or, if we were already conscious before entering the simulation that we're currently in, how do you think we all forget who we initially were?

DAVID: I think this all kind of comes down to whether you think AI systems can be conscious. If they are, it looks like there's no special barrier to simulations being conscious. I'm inclined to think myself that AI systems can be conscious. In fact, one of the cases that I often start with here is like imagining a simulation of the whole brain. Or maybe even more directly, imagine a functional duplicate of the brain but with, say, silicon chips in place of neurons. Way back in my first book *The Conscious Mind*, in 1996, I argued that you could slowly replace, say, your neurons by silicon elements playing more or less the same role.

I argued that if you did this, if you went through this process, the most plausible outcome is you'd still be left with a conscious system at the other end. I mean the other alternatives are that consciousness gradually fades out or it suddenly disappears. But I tried to make a case that the most plausible outcome was that consciousness would be there at the other end. If that's the case, it looks like, at least in principle, a simulation of a brain would be conscious. And once you've got that, then it looks like in a simulated universe you'll have a lot of simulated brains, and those simulated brains will be conscious too.

Of course, if you don't think a simulation can be conscious, then you'll probably think that we can't be in a simulation. At least, we can't be in a pure simulation, in which we are simulated creatures, because we know we are conscious. If I am conscious and a simulation can't be conscious, it follows that we're not in a simulation. But personally, I don't accept the premise that a simulation couldn't be conscious. I think it probably could be.

Your question about how we forgot, what happened to our memories—I don't know. I suppose one possibility is something like a *Matrix* scenario, where brains are attached to a simulation and their memories are wiped out. That's a rather dystopian scenario. I guess the pure simulation story I actually have in mind is one that doesn't need to involve biology at all. It involves a purely simulated universe in which every element of the universe, or of some part of it, is simulated—including brains.

So maybe evolution itself was simulated. History was simulated. And now we are simulated. So it's not like I have some pre-simulation life to remember. My whole universe has been a simulation. I mean, I remember my life as a simulation, because that's all I've ever been. If we changed to a situation where it's a biological brain who's only recently got attached and whose memories got knocked out—yeah, that would raise all kinds of questions, like the one you're asking. That's what I call the biosim hypothesis, that we're biological beings attached to a simulation. But if we're pure sims, simulated beings ourselves who have always been simulated, then maybe that question doesn't arise.

In Reality+ *you use a number of examples from science fiction to illustrate your ideas. How do you think that science fiction scenarios can prompt philosophical analysis?*

DAVID: The science fiction scenarios are wonderful for a philosopher because they're all basically thought experiments. Science fiction is all about thought experiments. Imagine that we had such and such technology or such and such a civilization with these amazing properties. To say there's robots, AIs, time travel, or simulation—and then say, what follows? What would happen? And in general, often a science fiction novel or story is trying to spit out consequences from that initial presupposition.

That's something we do in philosophy as well. A whole lot of philosophy is about thought experiments. Let's just say we could upload human beings to the cloud, then what would follow? And so then in philosophy we try to turn it into a relatively rigorous argument, taking small steps, trying to argue if this was the case, then this is what would follow if we were in the Matrix. It would be real, and so on, whereas in science fiction, as in most literature, the steps tend to be bigger and sometimes more creative and more expansive. So the styles are different, but nonetheless I think the two are very much continuous.

In my book *Reality+* I spent a lot of time engaging with philosophical theses that I find implicit in science fiction. I mean, you find it in Stanisław Lem and the Wachowski sisters. You find it in someone like Greg Egan writing *Permutation City*. One chapter of my book is basically a long argument with Greg Egan about the view of computation that he puts forward in his novel *Permutation City*. So science fiction is wonderful in this regard.

Speaking of science fiction, it seems that the "red pill" in The Matrix *film was symbolic of a psychedelic. Why do you think it is that so many people who have had psychedelic experiences grow suspicious that we're living in a computer-simulated reality? This suspicion seems to be deeply imbedded in the psychedelic subculture. Do you have any thoughts on that?*

DAVID: That's interesting. The red pill has become symbolic of so many things these days, I guess. The alt-right community thinks it's symbolic of having the wool pulled before your eyes. In general, I think people think it's become symbolic of a new degree of awareness or of knowledge. And I guess that's one of the things psychedelics are supposed to do, to reveal new realities to you.

It's interesting if the red pill actually was a psychedelic. I wondered when I first watched *The Matrix* movie, how is Neo so sure that the red pill has actually led him to escape the simulation? For all we know the red pill is like an amazing psychedelic that introduces you into a new simulated reality. Suddenly he finds himself the master of the universe, on a hovercraft fighting against the machines and so on. It's like this is, if anything, more like a psychedelic reality. So if I were Neo, I'd start to worry that the red pill hadn't led him to escape the simulation, but just to go ever-deeper into new levels of simulations.

Yes, I wondered the same thing.

DAVID: I don't know whether people think that psychedelics are introducing them to new levels of reality—like stepping outward into more fundamental levels of reality or stepping ever inward into more and more interesting simulations—but maybe, if you thought of it that way, then it probably becomes all the more natural to think of your own life as a simulation.

Do you have any thoughts about the virtual worlds inhabited by people who have used the powerful psychedelic DMT, or whether there might be an independent reality to the entities that people report encountering on DMT? Do you think there might be a reality to these so-called autonomous entities—in a shared parallel dimension—or do you think that they're just complex hallucinations? Are you familiar with the DMT entity encounter research by Rick Strassman and others?

DAVID: Not really. I'm not an expert on psychedelics by any means. I've certainly seen numerous scholarly presentations about it. But I'm not an expert on the phenomena. Maybe you could say more about it.

Yes, let me just say a little about this then. First of all, DMT is endogenous to the brain, and it's the main psychoactive component in the Amazonian shamanic brew ayahuasca. It's considered to be the most powerful psychedelic known, because when you do it, you completely lose touch with this world and for about five to ten minutes you're in a completely virtual world. Another reality. It's like being in a lucid dream. And something like 90 percent of people who have this experience report encounters with what seem to be intelligent beings that communicate with them, and it seems like a stable, independent world, for the time you're there.

Almost everybody who has this experience comes back saying, "This is not a hallucination. This really happened. There's a reality to this." There are scientific studies underway at the Imperial College in London exploring this. They're looking into this to see if there really might be something to it. So, I guess you're not that familiar with this, but I was wondering if you thought there might be an independent reality to this, or do you think they're just complex hallucinations that are caused by the drug?

David: Yes, as you say, I'm not an expert, but I suppose my first inclination is to think that it could well be something analogous to an especially powerful dream or lucid dream, which I would regard as a kind of contact with reality—especially if it's rich enough, stable enough, and powerful enough, then this could be a reality. But one that's still nonetheless dependent on your mind.

I mean, sometimes people contrast these things and say, if it's all in your mind, it's not real. But I always liked that line from the end of the very last Harry Potter novel, where Harry says, "Hang on, this is just happening in my head; none of it's real." And Dumbledore says, "Of course it is happening inside your head, Harry, *but why on earth should that mean that it is not real?*" I think our heads, our brains, are quite capable of producing remarkable realities, and I guess my first hypothesis about what's going on with DMT is that here your brain is supporting a remarkable virtual reality—one that is dependent on the mind, to be sure—that is still extremely powerful.

What do you see as some of the most exciting technological developments and scientific advances going on in the world today?

David: Oh, boy. Well, I think that what you'd have to look at is artificial intelligence. I mean, it's always been an exciting area, but just in the last five to ten years it's really exploded with the deep learning revolution. I did my Ph.D. in an AI lab. Back then people said a year spent working in AI was enough to make you believe in god, because you just realize how powerful the brain is compared to the AI systems of the day. And that was probably still true ten years ago, in 2012.

But suddenly, since then, AI systems have just come to do so many things that couldn't be done before—like image recognition, speech recognition, speech production, and game playing. There's AI for computer coding. AI for science, like with protein folding. There's AI that carries on conversations. There's still plenty of obstacles left, but now there's an open path, I think.

It's not very hard to now see an open path to human-level general intelligence sometime in the next, say, twenty-odd years. Suddenly that is very exciting and scary and disconcerting all at the same time. It also raises so many philosophical issues like what the status of these AIs will be once they exist. I find that, at least from a technological perspective, extremely exciting, and not to mention the advent of virtual reality.

On the one hand we've got artificial intelligence, which involves artificial minds. Then we have virtual realities, which involve artificial worlds. And many of the same questions that come up for artificial minds—like, are they real minds?—also come up for artificial worlds. Are they real worlds? So in this latest book, I focus especially on virtual reality technology and that connection. But put artificial minds and artificial worlds together and this is just like a whole new level of technology. I don't think we've seen its like before.

When you look around at what's happening in the world these days, do you think the human species will survive the next hundred years or do you think that we're doomed to extinction?

DAVID: Oh, I don't know. There are a lot of obstacles there, and I usually tend toward optimism, but there are a lot of things to get past. I mean, a nuclear war could happen, but that probably wouldn't make us extinct. Catastrophic climate change could happen, but that probably wouldn't make us extinct. Some people would survive in those scenarios. Maybe nanotechnology will accidentally turn us all into gray goo.

Or the one that a lot of people worry about is super-intelligent AI that may just have incentives that are just slightly misaligned with our own. We could end up being destroyed or some kind of by-product for the AI to do what it's trying to do.

Do you have any thoughts about Ray Kurzweil's idea of the Singularity? You mentioned about AI reaching human-level intelligence. Do you have any thoughts about what happens when it does reach human intelligence? Or what he called the Singularity, when it exceeds human intelligence. What will happen?

DAVID: The ideas that I'm most familiar with and like are in I. J. Good's treatment. He gave the first major statement of the Singularity idea back in 1965 in his article "On the First Ultra-Intelligent Machine." The key idea was once you have machines that are smarter than humans, they'll be better than humans at designing machines. So, once a human designs a machine smarter than a human, that machine ought to be able to design a machine better than it.

And on and on.

DAVID: Yes, the next machine will be able to design a smarter machine still, and then you get this recursive cycle from somewhat greater than human intelligence to much greater than human intelligence. Back in 2010, I wrote an article trying to analyze this phenomenon; I called it "The Singularity of Philosophical Analysis," where I was arguing that once you move from human-level AI, called an AI, to greater than human-level AI, called an AI+, you'll rapidly get AI++. Something that vastly exceeds human intelligence.

I still think it's basically a good argument, and there're only so many ways it can go wrong to resist that conclusion. Maybe human-level intelligence is impossible. Maybe at a certain point we'll decide not to go any further with this process because we realize where it's taking us. But I do think that there's going to be the capacity for super-intelligent machines to exist at some point. And I do think this is something that we're going to have to think about the consequences very seriously. Because while there are many ways it could go right and have wonderful consequences, there are certainly many ways it can go wrong.

Do you see any type of teleology, intelligence, or mindful intention operating in nature and the evolution of life, or do you think that evolution is occurring by blind chance?

DAVID: I don't know. I think where evolution is concerned, one of the things that makes it so amazing is it can do all these somewhat teleological things, even if it just involves blind chance at the basic level. Blind chance plus natural selection can add up to something that looks a whole lot like teleology or intention. Is that true teleology? Is it true intention? Depends what you mean. I guess I would say it is a kind of teleology. Maybe it's not genuine intention, because no one had to intend it. Natural selection does very much make it seem as if things are selected for having certain abilities, and can work in the same way, as if there were a designer.

Is there mindfulness? I'm sympathetic with the view that there is some consciousness at the bottom level of nature, on the panpsychist view of this, some consciousness, everywhere—even in elementary particles, or maybe even attaching to the universe as a whole. I don't know though that I would be inclined to find a special role for that in evolution, that these little elements of consciousness in all matter would somehow be what's driving evolution. I think what's amazing about the Darwinian theory of evolution is that you don't actually need something mental to get it going.

What do you personally think happens to consciousness after physical death and the deterioration of the brain?

DAVID: My first inclination is to think that when your brain dies, your consciousness dies along with it or at least dissolves into fragments, because part of what I am consists of this very coherent set of processes that rely on a brain to hold it together. So when I die, I dissolve, as they say.

Now, thinking about the simulation idea has made me waver on that a bit. If we are in a simulation, it's not out of the question that perhaps the simulators make back-ups when beings die in the simulation. The simulators could perhaps transfer their code to another simulation, which would be a form of life after death, maybe even a form potentially of immortality. So I can at least hold out some hope that I'm in that kind of simulation in which, in that case, there could be some kind of life after death. But that's very much speculation at this point. If you had to ask my instinct on this, it's when my brain dies, I die.

What is your perspective on the concept of god?

DAVID: I've always thought of myself as an atheist; someone who doesn't believe in god because I just haven't seen enough evidence that a god exists, or enough that a god would explain. But again, since I've started thinking about the simulation ideas, I may be at least somewhat more open to the idea of something at least somewhat godlike. Even from quite a naturalistic scientific perspective, you can tell a story about how a simulator might create a simulation.

Then the simulator will have godlike properties with respect to the simulation. They created it. They could control it. They could know everything that's going on. So they're all-powerful and all-knowing—some of the central properties of a god. If we have a simulator, then that simulator will at least be godlike in those respects. Now, they needn't be all-good or all-wise, and I certainly wouldn't advocate setting up a religion around the simulator. So, maybe this wouldn't be a full-scale "God," maybe more of what sometimes gets called an ancient Greek word, a *demiurge*—like a deputy god that did the work of creating our world. Even if not like the god-in-chief of the entire cosmos, but still that is an interesting naturalistic path to having some ideas that are akin to those you find in a theistic tradition and is consistent with the scientific worldview.

What are you currently working on?

DAVID: My book on virtual reality came out not much more than a month ago, so I guess I'm very much caught up in thinking about that right now. And actually the book focused a lot on the extreme case of what if we're in a computer simulation and what would perfect simulations be like. But I'm also increasingly thinking about the virtual reality technology that we're coming to use, like virtual reality headsets or virtual reality glasses. A lot of corporations these days are trying to promote the metaverse, the new generation of the internet that we'll access immersively, using in part virtual reality and augmented reality technology. And I think that's got many potential upsides, at least in principle. You could have a meaningful life there, but there are also many practical downsides as well. There're definitely many ways this can go on, especially with corporations playing central roles in constructing the virtual worlds in which we spend our time.

If you think of whoever creates a virtual world as being akin to a god, then if we inhabit a virtual world created by a corporation, it's a little like the corporation is the god of that world—all-powerful and all-knowing with respect to it, with all kinds of questions arising about privacy, manipulation, and so on. So I guess lately, I've been thinking a lot about these potentially non-ideal aspects of virtual worlds, and what might be the best ways to navigate our path through this virtual world technology in the next few decades to come, where I think they're going to play an increasing role in our lives.

12

Going Beyond

An Interview with Rupert Sheldrake

Rupert Sheldrake is a British biologist who has helped to revolutionize numerous scientific fields. He is the author of nine bestselling books and more than a hundred scientific papers. Sheldrake's research is some of the most-cited scientific research in the world.[1]

Sheldrake is best known for developing the theory of formative causation that hypothesizes the existence of morphic fields, or nonmaterial regions of influence—like the other types of fields in physics—that guide the development of organic and inorganic forms, as well as psychological and social structures, through a resonance with forms from the past. This theory, first expressed in his 1981 book *A New Science of Life*, is at the heart of much of Sheldrake's research, and it helps to explain a number of persistent mysteries in science—like how the genetic information in our cells is translated into our three-dimensional biological forms, or how homing pigeons navigate. Since 1981 Sheldrake has developed this theory and applied it to numerous scientific fields. His 1988 book *The Presence of the Past* (2nd edition, 2011) lays out evidence for the theory of formative causation, and explores the implications of morphic fields for biology, physics, psychology, and sociology.

---

1. On ResearchGate, the largest scientific and academic online network, his RG score of 34.4 puts him among the top 7.5 percent of researchers, based on citations of his peer-reviewed publications.

One of the wonderful things about Sheldrake's work is that he has developed a number of simple experiments anyone can do at home that produce results that challenge conventional scientific understanding, and he has helped to start a grassroots global science movement. In his book *Seven Experiments That Could Change the World* he outlines easy-to-do experiments—such as testing our sense of being stared at, or studying how termite hill organization is unaffected by physical barriers—that conventional science has great difficulty explaining.

For several decades Sheldrake has also been studying the unexplained powers of animals, such as dogs (and other pets) that seem to know when their owners are coming home through a form of telepathy. Sheldrake views telepathy, and the sense of being stared at, as natural biological traits that evolved through natural selection and are retained due to their survival value.

Sheldrake studies those areas that conventional science ignores and asks radical questions that challenge the foundations of science. Do the fundamental constants of nature, like the speed of light or the gravitational constant, remain the same or do they evolve over time? Are phantom limb experiences indicative of somatic fields? Does telepathy play a role in the anticipation of phone calls? Could the sun and other stars be sentient beings?

Sheldrake's wonderful book *The Science Delusion* (the title of which is a response to Richard Dawkins's book *The God Delusion*) shows how science is being constricted by assumptions that have hardened into dogmas and would be better off without them. His most recent books explore the mystery of consciousness and the potential of spiritual experiences, such as *Ways to Go Beyond* and *Science and Spiritual Practices*, which we discuss in the following interview. To find out more about his work, see the Rupert Sheldrake website.

I worked closely with Rupert from 1995 to 1999, and I spent a month in London with him and his family. I did the California-based research for two of his books, *Dogs That Know When Their Owners Are Coming Home* and *The Sense of Being Stared At*. We coauthored three scientific papers together and I interviewed him for two of my previ-

Photo by W. Scherz

Rupert Sheldrake

ous books, *Mavericks of the Mind* and *Conversations on the Edge of the Apocalypse*.

————————————————————— ☉ —————————————————————

I interviewed Rupert for this book on October 11, 2022. It was great to reconnect with him after all these years, as he's been one of the most important mentors in my life. We spoke about his latest research, the possible relationship between angels and DMT entities, and how our appreciation of the natural sciences helps us to form a deeper and more spiritual connection with the natural world.

It's a real pleasure to connect with you again. What are some of the latest updates in your research?

RUPERT: I've continued working on unexplained powers of animals and I've recently been engaged in a project on terminal lucidity in animals. This isn't an experimental project; it's to do with the database and looking at the natural history. Terminal lucidity is the phenomenon whereby people who have lost their memory, suffer from dementia, or are otherwise very disabled, in the few hours or days before death, gain a whole new surge of energy. Their memory seems to come back. They know who they're talking to, and they have this great presence. They seem to be saying good-bye to people and appear to be completely present. And then they die. This is a project to see whether something similar happens with animals and it does seem to. So that's one aspect.

Then, my most ambitious scientific project was my book *The Science Delusion*. (*Science Set Free* is what it's called in the United States.) There I look at the ten principal dogmas of science, turn them into questions, and show that if they're treated as scientific hypotheses, they don't work out very well with the evidence. These are dogmas like matter is unconscious; the laws of nature are fixed; memories are stored inside brains; the mind is nothing but the activity of the brain; psychic phenomena are illusory; nature is purposeless; and so on. So that is a major attempt to look at the very foundations of all the sciences. A new, updated edition of the book came out in 2020.

Then, I've written two books on science and spiritual practices, namely *Science and Spiritual Practices*, published in 2018, and *Ways to Go Beyond and Why They Work*, published in 2020. Both of them deal with seven different spiritual practices that have been explored scientifically. Science and spirituality come together very effectively when science is used to explore the effects of spiritual practices, all of which have measurable effects on physiology, well-being, et cetera. In general, the results of thousands of papers in peer-reviewed journals show that people who have spiritual practices are happier, healthier, and live longer than those who don't. I should say spiritual and religious practices because these papers include both.

During lockdown I went back to my scientific roots—the work I was doing at Cambridge fifty years ago. I took further the ideas I first developed then, and I found that hypotheses I put forward at that time have been confirmed by a lot of subsequent research. So I brought all this together in two major papers. One is called "The Production of Auxin by Dying Cells." Auxin is the main plant hormone. This was published in the *Journal of Experimental Botany* as a Darwin Review, which is their top category of reviews.

The other one was based on my early work on the nature of cellular aging and rejuvenation, and that was published this year in the *Proceedings of the Royal Society* under the title "Cellular Senescence, Rejuvenation, and Potential Immortality." In addition, I published a paper last year called "Is the Sun Conscious?" in the *Journal of Consciousness Studies*, exploring an issue I discussed with Terence McKenna and Ralph Abraham years ago, and also with Matthew Fox, but bringing that debate up to date in the light of modern solar physics, integrated information theory, panpsychist philosophy, and so on.

I have one or two other scientific papers in production or in the press. So, I've actually had a very productive time and the lockdown period was, for me, a great blessing because I was able to do a lot of things I wouldn't otherwise have been able to.

Wow, you've certainly been busy. I read Steven Pinker's book **Rationality,** *and like you, thought that many of his assertions were anything but rational, so I was happy to see your response to his erroneous claims about telepathy. Is there any chance that you'll be able to debate him about this?*

RUPERT: When I read his book *Rationality*, I saw that he dismissed evidence for telepathy and other psychic phenomena without looking at it. He justified this as a rational procedure, claiming that you could dismiss these subjects without looking at the evidence because they're impossible. Then I looked at his arguments for why they're impossible. The first is that a friend of his, Sean Carroll, said it was impossible according to the laws of physics as he understood them. Carroll is a dyed-in-the-wool skeptic as Pinker is himself, and both of them are fellows of Committee for Skeptical Inquiry. Other physicists, like the Nobel laureate Brian Josephson, strongly disagree with Sean Carroll about this. Secondly, Pinker said psi phenomena were impossible because they violated Hume's argument against miracles.

Well, David Hume's eighteenth-century argument against miracles says that things that are extremely rare or unusual and rely on human testimony from long ago are probably not true, because it's more likely that someone's making something up or was mistaken about their experience than that the event went against the laws of nature. However, psychic phenomena like telephone telepathy, and the sense of being stared at, and dogs that know when their owners are coming home, are not extremely rare things that happened long ago: 85 percent of the population has experienced telephone telepathy; 95 percent have experienced the sense of being stared at; and about 50 percent of dogs know in advance when their owners are coming home.

So, I challenged him to a debate on this. He tried to avoid it, but I did it through a site called Unherd, which does blogs, podcasts, and YouTube videos, so he couldn't really wriggle out of it completely because they, themselves, were encouraging him to respond, and they had already done an interview with him about rationality. So he then tried to pass the buck by saying that Michael Shermer should argue the case on his behalf, because Shermer's an expert—being the editor of the *Skeptic* magazine, author of the skeptic column in *Scientific American*, and chairman of the Skeptic Society. But it so happens that Michael Shermer and I had already had a debate on telepathy that was published in a book called *Arguing Science*, coauthored by both of us. Neither of us particularly wanted to repeat something we'd already done, so I pressed Pinker again, and he then said he didn't have "the bandwidth" to take part in a debate because to take part in a debate he'd have to spend the time reading the evidence, and he just didn't have time to do that. In other words, he basically admitted that his position was one of pure dogmatism and prejudice—that he'd formed his opinion without looking at the evidence, and indeed his argument was that he doesn't need to look at the evidence, because he assumes he's right without considering the evidence.

How can our appreciation of the natural sciences help us to form a deeper and more spiritual connection with the natural world?

RUPERT: I think that the study of natural history, the phenomena of nature, like plants, ecology, stars, galaxies, and the microscopic realm, gives us a sense of the vastness and variety of nature that is awe-inspiring. And that is something that the sciences have done very well. They've opened up the realm of the large and the very small, explored the sub-structure of cells, the nature of atoms and molecules, which gives us a much greater insight into the nature of nature. But insofar as they try to force all this into a dogma of mechanistic materialism, that can only have an alienating effect from our appreciation of the natural world, especially because it denies the reality of consciousness in ourselves or in anything else.

It says that consciousness is an illusion, or an epiphenomenon of mechanical processes, and doesn't really do anything. So in that sense, it's not very helpful. It's also not very helpful that mechanistic materialism treats nature as inanimate and mechanical and just something there for us to exploit, which I think underlies the whole ecological crisis and the terrible plight we're now in. I think it's based on a false view of human nature, and of the nature of nature.

So I think what would help us more is a new paradigm in the sciences, which has been emerging now for nearly a hundred years, namely the organismic paradigm or the philosophy of organism, which treats nature as organic rather than mechanical. The universe is more like an organism than a machine and nature is an evolving system with inbuilt habits. That's part of my own idea of morphic resonance. I think this view of living nature, of which we're part, is a much more helpful way of seeing nature. This is partly because it's more true and partly because it brings us into a more reasonable relationship with nature as part of something larger than ourselves, on which we depend.

When you look around at what's happening in the world these days, do you think the human species will survive the next hundred years or do you think that we're doomed to extinction?

RUPERT: I don't think we're doomed to extinction, but I think that the present neoliberal world order is not going to survive a lot longer because it's extremely unstable and extremely destructive. I think that humans are going to have to either voluntarily scale back the impact on the planet and consume a lot less, pollute a lot less, emit far less carbon dioxide, or else planetary forces are going to scale back humanity, and whether we do it voluntarily or whether it's forced on us is partly our choice. I don't think all humans would go extinct. There might be mass population decreases in many parts of the world, but I can't personally believe that all humans would go extinct. I think that the way we go about our lifestyle would have to be modified very considerably.

Also, I don't think that all life will go extinct, even if there's a cataclysmic nuclear war and humans destroy themselves. The insects and fish, and all sorts of species would survive, and there'd be a new evolutionary radiation, just as there was after the extinction of the dinosaurs.

Do you see a relationship between psychedelic experiences and the elevation of ecological awareness?

RUPERT: I think it's an empirical fact, based on a number of studies. People who have had psychedelic experiences are more likely to see nature as alive, and themselves as interconnected with it, than to think of nature as a mere mindless machine. So this is not just a speculation; it's been borne out by actual facts and investigations.

What are your thoughts on whether the entities that one meets on DMT have a genuine independent existence or not?

RUPERT: It's a difficult question. When I'm thinking about psychedelic experiences, I start with the phenomenon of dreams, because everyone has dreams, and animals have dreams too. All of us dream every night, even though we forget our dreams usually. In our dreams we meet other people, and sometimes we can have shared dreams. We meet people who've actually met us in dreams. Sometimes we encounter members of our family or friends who are now dead in our dreams.

Now, are these mere phantasms created in our brains? That's the conventional theory. Or are there autonomous entities that we meet? Certainly it's been believed in many cultures that the beings we meet in our dreams have a kind of autonomous reality. In the Old Testament and the New Testament, for example, many of the messages that come to the great leaders, like prophets and the people taking part in these dramas or these stories, involve dreams. King Solomon had a dream in the holy place Gibeon, where God appeared to him.

There are many ways in which dreams play a role in the Bible. Dreams appeared to the wise men that visited Jesus after his birth, telling them not to go back to Jerusalem. There are countless examples in the Bible, and in other traditions, of autonomous entities appearing in dreams. I think of psychedelic experiences as being rather more like vivid and partially lucid dreams. They're experiences in which the mind is experiencing an astonishing visual series of events, but they also include seemingly autonomous entities. And I think they could include saints and angels, which in religious traditions, most people assume are autonomous entities that can appear in dreams or in visions.

So it seems to me that they're on a continuum with visionary experience, such as divination through dreams, dream incubation, namely sleeping in holy places to have healing or inspiring dreams like King Solomon in Gibeon, and messages coming through dreams. So I don't see them in isolation from all these other phenomena. I think there are autonomous spirit entities in realms that we encounter through dreams and through psychedelic experience.

Do you see a relationship between the angels described in the Bible, or the deities and spirits from different religious systems, and the entities that people report encountering on DMT?

RUPERT: I don't know how many people on DMT would identify the beings they encounter as angels, but I think a lot of people who take DMT do so within a secular framework, and many of them are not religious and not very interested in the Judeo-Christian tradition.

I think what would be much more interesting, in terms of answering this question, is when people who are religious take DMT, as with the Johns Hopkins studies where they gave psilocybin, from magic mushrooms, to rabbis, priests, imams, and other religious leaders, and have now triggered off what are possible psychedelic movements within religions. In America there's something called the Psychedelic Christian Association, founded by a priest who took part in the Johns Hopkins study.[2]

There are now growing movements to have religious use of psychedelics. This already happens in psychedelic religions like Santo Daime, and of course in shamanic traditions that use psychedelics. And the people in the Santo Daime religion, which uses ayahausca, do indeed say they experience angels. So I think that if I was going to look at the answer to the question, one has to take into account not only secular, nonreligious people taking DMT and ayahausca, but also religious people taking it, whose worldview does include angels.

Do you think that our physics and biology apply to the beings that people encounter in the DMT hyperspace realm?

RUPERT: I think it's in the realm of mind, but I think mind is much greater than our own minds. I'm a Christian. I believe that the ultimate conscious reality is god, and that the divine consciousness precedes the appearance of the universe and underlies nature.

My view is the standard view, the traditional view. It's not that god is like an external engineer, or a mechanic who designs the universe like a machine and presses the start button and then lets it run automatically. Rather, the entire universe is within the being of god, sustained from moment to moment by god and the divine consciousness. So all forms of consciousness within the universe, including human and animal consciousness, are derived from a greater mind of which these minds are a part.

It seems to me that the mystical experiences and revelations that occur through spontaneous mystical experiences—through near-death experiences and through a whole range of spiritual practices, including taking psychedelics—are accessing realms of consciousness that are greater than our own, and are not simply products or spin-offs from limited human minds, confined to the inside of brains in an otherwise unconsciousness universe, which is the materialist view of human minds.

---

2. For more information about Hunt Priest and Ligare: A Christian Psychedelic Society, see Ligare (website).

Why do you think that radical skepticism should be applied to all belief systems?

RUPERT: Because we don't know that we're right, and we know that all belief systems have a tendency to become dogmatic and require always to be refreshed through inquiry. I think that this is true within religious frameworks. I mean, look at the Jewish framework: at the time of Jesus, as we read in the New Testament, the Sadducees and the Pharisees, and the chief priests, the elders, and the scribes, were all arguing among themselves. There was no common view on how to interpret the books of the Bible, or on what happens after we die. Some believed in survival after bodily death and some didn't. There was a kind of mutual critique going on, and that's true within any religion.

Within Christianity, there are debates between Protestants and Catholics and Orthodox. And within any given tradition, like the Roman Catholic tradition, there are differences in interpretation and approach between Jesuits and Benedictines, and Franciscans and Dominicans. They are different traditions with different orders. Within Tibetan Buddhism there are the different monastic orders. There's the Dzogchen tradition. There's the Bon tradition. Within Islam, there's Shia and Sunni. There are different schools of Sufism and mystical Islam. There are many schools of Hinduism.

So within religions, there's always been a tradition of discussion, debate, and no uniform dogma that everyone agrees with, because none of these religions are monolithic. However, when you come to science, as currently understood, there is a kind of monolithic belief system—mechanistic materialism—that's taught in schools and universities all over the world. And it's not really subjected to much skepticism by scientists themselves. Scientists are usually skeptical about discoveries made by colleagues or people in closely related fields, especially if they disagree with their own views. People can be skeptical about a claim that a particular enzyme is activated more by calcium ions than magnesium ions. A lot of discussion in science is about thrashing out these differences of opinion.

But the kind of radical skepticism I'm advocating for science in my book *The Science Delusion* is looking at the very fundamental dogmas of science itself. And unfortunately there isn't really a process in science for doing this because, whereas in religions there are these different schools of thought that critique each other, there aren't several different schools of science that critique each other. There's just one kind of orthodoxy at any given time and anyone who doesn't agree with it is usually marginalized or branded heretical. That's not a very healthy situation, and it's not like what happens in other realms of human activity.

Even in courts of law you get to hear both sides of the argument presented as well as the lawyers can present them, the prosecution and the defense. You hear both. But when it comes to scientific dogmas—nature is mechanical, matter is unconscious, et cetera—you don't hear, within science or as part of a scientific education, the contra view. You don't have a debate between "nature is mechanical and machinelike" versus "nature is organic, organism-like," or a debate between "matter is unconscious" versus "panpsychism—there's some consciousness throughout the natural world, not just in brains." That debate is beginning but it's happening much more within philosophy departments than within science. So I think what we need in science—in the sciences, because there isn't a monolithic science—is much more of a pluralistic framework, where different points of views can be examined by other schools of thought rather than there just being one kind of totalitarian system.

What are your thoughts on the simulation hypothesis, the idea that our entire reality is really an advanced computer simulation?

RUPERT: I see this as a rather naïve, modern science fiction-like take on quite a profound idea. The idea that all of reality is essentially derived from mental constructs, that we're within some greater mind, is a standard view in all religions.

It may not be the mainstream view in all religions, but it's a well-known view. For example, one of the common stories in Hinduism is that the god Vishnu laid down to sleep, and when he was sleeping he had a dream, and that dream was our universe—and is our universe—and it's sustained by his ongoing dream. We're all inside that dream, dependent on the mind of Vishnu, and sooner or later Vishnu will wake up and the dream will stop. And then next time he sleeps there'll be a different dream, a different universe.

Well, the simulation hypothesis just applies some modern technological metaphor to that: it's all a giant computer program and there must be some cosmic computer programmer who's programmed it all. It's a modern—and I find, rather uninteresting version—of the dream of Vishnu. I much prefer the dream stories and the dream mythologies to this science-fictiony simulation idea.

Do you think that computers or artificial intelligence programs can become conscious or have spiritual experiences, and how do you view the future evolution of artificial intelligence and the concept of the Singularity?

RUPERT: I don't think computers, as we currently have them, will become conscious because they are machines. They're the perfect realization of the mechanistic worldview, which says things are machines. *They are machines.* They do work mechanistically. The mechanistic worldview applies extremely well to machines; I mean that's, after all, what it's all about. However, for consciousness to exist there has to be a realm of choice among possibilities, and also an ability to make decisions, and to choose among possibilities. According to the philosophy of Alfred North Whitehead, those are some of the key features of consciousness.

Now, computers don't have choices among possibilities. Most people who believe they'll become conscious think that consciousness is just a kind of epiphenomenon of mechanical processes in human brains. So, if the consciousness of computers is merely epiphenomenal, it doesn't actually do anything, it simply parallels physical activities that are happening anyway so the computer can't make a decision. And if it did make a decision, there'd have to be a way in which the mind of the computer interacted with the hardware of the computer, and there's no provision for that in the way computers are run. They don't have an autonomy to interact with the hardware.

To interact with the hardware, it would have to be probabilistic—this is the only way you can impose a new pattern or structure on it—and contemporary computers are not probabilistic, they're deterministic. There's no freedom in them, and even if people introduce randomness in some programs, they usually do it through pseudo-random algorithms. This is something that looks like randomness but isn't.

Now, it's possible, in my view, that if we had analog computers that worked probabilistically—and some quantum computers are rather like this—then there might be a scape for the whole system to have an overall organizing field, or what I call a morphic field, which could have creative effects and exact choices by biasing the randomness within the random system. So, I think it's conceivable that analog computers could become conscious, but not that practically all contemporary computers, digital computers, could become conscious. I think where the really interesting growth point in this debate will be is with quantum computers, because they are much closer to analog computers, and they are inherently probabilistic. Quantum systems are capable of forming integrated states that integrate the things within them, like in a Bose-Einstein condensate.

So I don't think that's going to happen with our existing technologies, and I don't think that the Singularity is going to happen, because I think artificial intelligence is at present based on just mass data crunching rather than on any true intelligence. I think that genuine intelligence would involve some true freedom and creativity, which doesn't really exist in these computers. So personally, I'm not worried about the Singularity or about computers taking over, although I am worried about them being given too much power over our affairs and having a kind of tyrannical influence. Not because they're so intelligent, but because basically they're so stupid and work mechanically in a noncreative kind of way.

Rupert, I asked you these next two questions in 1989 and again in 2005 for previous interview books, so future historians can examine the evolution of your views. What do you personally think happens to consciousness after physical death and the deterioration of the brain?

RUPERT: I can't remember what I said before, but what I think now, and I probably thought then, is that our conscious existence after physical death is rather like dreaming. We can go on dreaming after we're dead, but we can't wake up anymore because the physical body is no longer there to wake up in. So, I think that the survival of physical death is likely to be in a kind of dream realm, and that dream realm, as I said earlier, is continuous with the realm experienced under psychedelics, and it also may be shared between different people and even with animal species.

We may have shared dreams; the dream realm may not just be our individual dream realm but a collective human dream world, and even one that includes all sorts of species and possibly dreaming organisms on other planets or in other star systems. So the dream world that we inhabit after death depends on our memories, our desires, and our beliefs. If you believe that there's absolutely nothing after death, that it will just go extinct, that may be what happens to you.

If, even if you're in disturbing dreams, you believe that after death there are beings that can help and save you—like Christ or the saints—then that may well be what happens. If you believe that no one can save you, no one can help you, you're just trapped in your own world, your own mind, then you may end up in a kind of nightmare scenario of isolation and being trapped with recurrent obsessions and fears, which may be rather like hell, an ongoing nightmare.

So I think the kinds of dreams we have, and the kind of dream world we inhabit, depends very much on who we are, what we've done, what we expect, what our experience is, and what our faith is, because I think that our religious faith or lack of it will play a major role in our life after death. This is because, in a sense, it's all in the mind, and therefore what's in our minds really matters.

Yes, that's similar to what you told me years ago. This next question you answered years ago as well and touched on it earlier in the interview. What is your perspective on the concept of god, and how has the Christian faith influenced your perspective?

RUPERT: I think god is ultimate consciousness, and I think that most traditions think of this consciousness as having three aspects. In the Hindu tradition it's Satcitananda. In the Christian tradition, it's the Father, Son, and Holy Spirit—the Holy Trinity. I don't know if I said this before, but I think the primary metaphor for this is speaking. And this is right there in the first chapter of the book of Genesis. It's right there in the Jewish tradition too—that "in the beginning, God made the heavens and the earth." So you have god as a kind of primal source. And then the first creative act, "the Spirit of God moved over the face of the waters," or "the face of the deep." Well, that's the breath or the wind. Spirit means breath, wind, or flowing air.

And the word *Rûah* in Hebrew, *Pneuma* (πνεῦμα) in Greek, has all these meanings. And then God said, "Let there be light." That's the next stage. So god speaking is the creative power, and this is paralleled in many other traditions, the idea of the divine speaking. So god, to speak and create, has to be conscious to start with—and that's God the Father, whose primary attribute is consciousness, as he announces himself to Moses in the burning bush, "I am who I am," or "I am that I am." That's conscious being in the present: "I am." So it's being and it's conscious. That's the ground of all things; that's what *sat* means in the Hindu version of Satcitananda.

Then, the breath of god is the breathing, the breathing of god, and that's when we speak, we have to breathe. I'm speaking now and I'm breathing out as I speak. If I don't breathe out, I can have words in my mind, but they're silent and they're only manifested through being carried on the out breath. And so in order to speak I have to have words that are forms, patterns, or structures. They're interconnected. They have meaning and interconnections with each other, with concepts and forms.

That's like the logos, the second person of the trinity, or *Cit—Namarupa,* meaning names and forms in the Hindu model. The contents of consciousness are names and forms. You have to have consciousness, the ground of all these things, and then what you're conscious of, aware of, are the names and forms. That's the second person of the trinity, the logos or Cit.

Then there's the third aspect, which is movement, flow, change, and creativity. In the Hindu pantheon this is represented by Shiva, and in the Christian and Jewish tradition, by the spirit of god, that dynamic principle of god, the moving principle of god. So I don't think of god as an undifferentiated unity. I think of god as a dynamic, organic conscious being, with both a ground of consciousness, the contents of consciousness, and a principle of flow or change through which things are changing and developing all the time. I think this divine consciousness, with this inherent creativity, is what underlies the whole evolutionary process.

Do you have any thoughts on the Covid pandemic that you'd like to share?

RUPERT: I didn't get at all involved in all these conspiracy theories or denunciations of vaccine providers or anti-vax movements. There were tons of controversies, but I just wasn't very interested in all of that and I didn't get involved. I was quite grateful they developed vaccines; I've been vaccinated myself. I'm certainly not an anti-vaxxer. What interested me about it was the possible role of morphic resonance. Morphic resonance means that when something's happened in the past it's more likely to happen again.

In the case of Covid, the fact that many people had caught it and recovered from it, or developed antibodies as a result of vaccination, meant that—according to morphic resonance—when more people caught in the future, their immune response might happen quicker or more effectively as a result of morphic resonance. Therefore, one would expect on this basis the virulence of the disease to decrease with time, so we reach a point where some people catch it and it's so effective at counteracting it they don't even know they've got it. They're asymptomatic, even though they actually have the disease. I would predict there'd be more and more people who are asymptomatic and the virulence of the disease would decrease. And I would predict this would be a general cause, because of morphic resonance, without the respiratory diseases, and this is indeed what seems to have happened. Now, I haven't got epidemiological skills; I don't have the data to analyze this properly, but I think it would be well worth analyzing the epidemic and the data from a morphic resonance point of view.

Have you thought about writing an autobiography, and what are you currently working on?

RUPERT: The British Library interviewed me as part of a project of interviewing two hundred living scientists for what they called "Living Biographies," and they did a series of twelve one-hour interviews with a whole range of British scientists, and I was one of the ones they picked. I was rather reluctant to do it at first because it took a lot of time. But they persuaded me because they said that not only would they record me for twelve hours, they could put an embargo on releasing the recordings for as long as I'd like, so it wasn't as though everything I said about my life would immediately go into the public domain, as that would mean people could write biographies about me without authorization. Also they would give me a transcript of the entire series.

So they stuck to their word and they gave me the transcript, and I have a transcript about book length, which is a kind of autobiography. But it would require quite a lot of editing to publish it, and I haven't got around to doing that yet. I might sooner or later. So I do have the basis for one, without all the hard work of actually writing it.

Is there anything that we haven't discussed that you would like to add?

RUPERT: Of course, one of the features of my life that's been ongoing for many years is my family. I've interacted over the years with my wife, Jill Purce, who's had a big influence on my ideas, especially on spiritual practices because she teaches chanting and meditation and does family constellation therapy, which is a practical version of morphic resonance.

Our son Cosmo is a musician. His music, most recently, has to do with the bird calls of endangered species, and is wonderfully ecological and nature centered. It feels like a musical expression of the general approach that Jill and I have, a more organic view of nature as an organism, nature as alive, and that comes across through the art of Cosmo's music. Merlin has written a wonderful book, *Entangled Life*, about fungi, which gives a vivid sense of the interconnectedness and life of nature.

I would say that all four of us, all members of our immediate family, have been engaged over the years in this transformative paradigm of a living, organic universe, evolving creatively—just expressing it in different ways. So I'm hoping that this will continue, and hopefully Merlin and Cosmo's work will continue to build on this vision of nature, and help to bring about this shift in paradigm, which we so desperately need.

13

Exploring Ancient Civilizations and Supernatural Beings

An Interview with Graham Hancock

Graham Hancock is a popular British writer and scientific journalist, best known for his radical ideas about ancient civilizations. He is the prolific author of over twenty bestselling books including *Fingerprints of the Gods*, *Magicians of the Gods*, *Supernatural*, and *The Sign and the Seal*. Hancock's books have sold more than nine million copies, and his work has been translated into thirty languages, although his ideas remain controversial among mainstream archaeologists.

Hancock began his career as a journalist and wrote for a number of British papers, including *The Guardian*, *The Independent*, *The Sunday Times*, and *The Economist*. He has appeared numerous times as a guest on *The Joe Rogan Experience* podcast, and he gave a TED talk in 2016 called "The War on Consciousness" that was one of the only two TED talks to ever be banned from the TED Talk website.

Hancock's numerous nonfiction books explore the evidence for lost civilizations, the meaning of ancient myths, unsolved mysteries, cataclysmic events in Earth's past, and psychedelic plants and altered states of consciousness. Some of his popular nonfiction titles that weren't mentioned above include *The Message of the Sphinx*, *The Mars Mystery*, *War God*, *America Before*, and *Underworld*. He has also written several works of fiction, including the novel *Entangled: The Eater of Souls*.

Graham Hancock

Santha Faiia Hancock

I first interacted with Graham in 2015, when he included my essay on "The Future of Psychedelic Drug Research" in his book *The Divine Spark: A Graham Hancock Reader; Psychedelics, Consciousness, and the Birth of Civilization.* I interviewed Graham on November 12, 2019. Graham is a masterful storyteller. His archaeological adventures are reminiscent of *Indiana Jones,* and his command of interdisciplinary knowledge is staggering. We talked about lost civilizations; psychedelic plant medicines; the relationship between elves, fairies, and aliens; and how his near-death experiences influenced his life and perspective.

How do you think that the near-death experience that you had as a teenager, due to an intense electric shock, influenced you in your later life?

GRAHAM: I think it shaped the whole course of my subsequent life. I just didn't realize it at the time. When it happened to me, I almost brushed it off. Then the haunting memories kept coming back, of being outside my body, and I brushed that off because of where I was in my head at that stage of my life. I wasn't able to integrate the experience into anything and it just seemed weird to me, but at the same time strangely promising.

I've realized subsequently that it had a dramatic effect on me and was the origin of something that I've held to be true for a very long time, even before I got into researching psychedelics, which is *we are not our bodies*. Whatever we are, we're not these physical frames. They're there to help us through this experience. It's our vehicle. I feel this. I can't prove it. It's just a theory, but *we are not our bodies*. That's what I came away from the experience with. *We are our consciousness.*

Well, that's most certainly a powerful message. You've referred to humans as a "species with amnesia." Before you wrote Fingerprints of the Gods and your other books about ancient civilizations, what first inspired you to begin your explorations into the idea that advanced civilizations existed much earlier than most archaeologists believe—and why do you think that understanding our ancient past better is so important for us today?

GRAHAM: I need to give you a little bit of background, because I was a journalist by training. I was the East Africa correspondent of *The Economist*, based in Nairobi, Kenya, and with a remit all around the region. I began writing books in 1981. My first book was a travel book called *Journey Through Pakistan*, which I wrote the text for and I worked with a couple of photographers, Mohamed Amin and Duncan Willetts, who did the photography.

It was an incredible adventure, and that was a travel book. We had incredible access to everywhere in Pakistan for the best part of the year. It was absolutely amazing, and that's when I began to realize that I liked writing books, not writing 300-word articles for *The Economist*. So during the eighties I wrote a number of books, and the only common unifying theme was kicking against orthodoxy. Wherever I came across an orthodox point of view, I found myself often very strongly opposed to it, to the established mainstream of how right-thinking people should think.

So for example, during the 1980s, I wrote a book about the virus that causes AIDS. It was called *AIDS: The Deadly Epidemic* and it was published in 1986. It was quite an early AIDS book and I took a very different view from the mainstream. I wrote a book on foreign aid called *Lords of Poverty: The Freewheeling Lifestyles, Power, Prestige, and Corruption of the Multi-billion Dollar AIDS Business*, which was published in 1989.

In those days criticizing foreign aid was like criticizing motherhood, but my travels had shown me that foreign aid was often a wicked and vile thing that was doing much more harm than good. It was really just a Band-Aid to cover up the horrific things that the developed countries were doing to the developing countries.

So I was an outsider. I was critical. I was radical, but I hadn't found my path. I found my path in Ethiopia in the 1980s. That was when I began to investigate Ethiopia's seemingly rather extraordinary claim to possess the lost Ark of the Covenant, although it's absolutely central to Ethiopian culture. And as I investigated that claim, two things happened to me.

First of all, I encountered the ancient world in all its magnificence. It was impossible to research that story without going to Egypt and Israel. After all, the prophet Moses is directly connected to the story of the Ark of the Covenant. So I found myself in front of the Great Pyramid in 1989, and I just thought, *what the fuck is this?* There's a giant thing standing there. I'd already found out that archaeologists were often full of shit. They were just making these blanket statements about the past, which were based more on prejudice and preconception than on any real detailed investigation.

So while I was still researching *The Sign and the Seal*, I started to look into the Great Pyramid and I found the explanations for it utterly unsatisfactory. I became determined that I would look into the issue of our past as an investigative journalist, but I wouldn't be exploring current-affairs stories. I would be exploring the ancient past and with a critical eye, unwilling to accept at face value mainstream positions unless they were really persuasive.

Can you just briefly speak a little about how the evidence for a comet impacting the Earth 12,800 years ago influenced your theory that a global cataclysm destroyed an earlier civilization of humans that were almost as advanced as we are today?

GRAHAM: Sure. Going back to my book *Fingerprints of the Gods*, which was published in 1995, it has been my position that there was a global cataclysm around 12,500 years ago. The date I put was around 10,500 BCE, so around 12,500 years ago. This involved flooding, earthquakes, a massive rise in sea level, and the destruction, not only of hunter-gatherer communities, but also of a much more advanced civilization, in our terms, than hunter-gatherers.

This has been my argument since *Fingerprints of the Gods*, and in *Fingerprints of the Gods* I looked at quite a number of different mechanisms that might account for a global cataclysm. I pursued one in particular, which is based on the work of a researcher called Charles Hapgood who published back in the 1950s, about the notion of Earth crust displacement. The idea is that the crust of the Earth can displace in one piece, from time to time, but this is a very radical and largely unsupported notion.

It's certainly not a notion that any mainstream geologist or physicist would get on board with, and while that didn't bother me because I felt the evidence for a global cataclysm was intriguing and compelling, I wasn't certain when I finished with *Fingerprints of the Gods* exactly what the cause of the cataclysm was. I proposed a number of theories, but Earth crust displacement was the strongest that I proposed at that time. Sorry, you'll have to bear with me a little bit on this. I then go through the 1990s, and I write a number of other books on the lost civilization theme.

I wrote *The Message of the Sphinx* with Robert Bauval. My wife's a photographer, Santha Faiia, and she and I did a big book called *Heaven's Mirror*. It's a photographic book on intriguing ancient sites around the world. In 1997 we start scuba diving, looking on the flooded continental shelves, where the sea level rose 400 feet at the end of the Ice Age.

There's a shitload of land underwater that was above water 12,000 years ago. We did five years of scuba diving, and this resulted in the publication of a book in 2002 called *Underworld: Flooded Kingdoms of the Ice Age*.

My wife and I continued to dive after that, but after *Underworld* I felt that I had *walked the walk with the lost civilization*. I'd spent the best part of five years in rather dangerous and difficult scuba-diving circumstances. I literally put my life on the line. I'd written an 800-page book, with 2,000 footnotes, thoroughly documented, and I felt I'd put this story to bed. So I turned away from the issue of a lost civilization.

I felt I needed to deploy such abilities as I have in other directions, and the next direction was my book *Supernatural: Meetings with the Ancient Teachers of Mankind*, about plant medicines. That was published in 2005, and it was a radically different book from my books on the lost civilization theme. I still felt I was done with the lost civilization, but then from 2007 onward new information started to come out. The first of this was a book by a group of scientists called *The Cycle of Cosmic Catastrophes*. Richard Firestone and Alan West were the lead authors.

This was the first general publication that proposed what is called the Younger Dryas impact hypothesis. This hypothesis proposed that the onset of the bizarre climate episode, 12,800 or 12,900 years ago, called the Younger Dryas, was caused by the impact of fragments of a very large comet with the North American ice cap. This was because North America was half-covered in ice at that time.

Rapidly adding to their numbers, this growing team of scientists then launched into a series of peer-reviewed scientific papers. Actually, hundreds of papers have been published. I could send you the full biography if you want.[1] There was just a huge amount of data being put out, and these are all leading mainstream scientists. None of them are fringe guys like me. But they're convinced by the evidence that what happened 12,800 years ago was truly cataclysmic and had changed the world in every possible way.

---

1. See "Updated Younger Dryas Impact Hypothesis Bibliography and Paper Archive," CosmicTusk (website), November 23, 2019, for these sources.

As their papers began to come out in the peer-reviewed journals, I began to see more and more clearly how incredibly strong their case was—*and look at the date*. It's 12,800 years ago, and I've been saying since 1995 that there was a global cataclysm around 12,500 years ago. So naturally I couldn't let that go. I had to get back into it.

I was reluctant because I really felt I was done with the lost civilization. In fact, even after I knew about the Younger Dryas impact hypothesis, and even after I knew about the extraordinary 11,600-year-old site of Göbekli Tepe in Turkey, I didn't immediately rush into writing a new lost civilization investigation. I'd started writing fiction. I actually wrote three novels, and I really felt I was done with the lost civilization, but as the information kept on adding up, I reached a point around about 2012 or 2013 where it was impossible for me to ignore it.

Here was a mass of information. I need to wind back a bit. The Younger Dryas was an episode, not a moment. The Younger Dryas began cataclysmically 12,800 years ago, and it ended cataclysmically 11,600 years ago. On both occasions there was a radical sea level rise and a massive climate disruption all around the world. So we have this episode 12,800 to 11,600 years ago, where huge Earth changes took place. This includes the extinction of the megafauna. I couldn't ignore this as it is obviously connected to the work I did back in the eighties and nineties on the possibility of a lost civilization.

So I decided I had to get my feet back into this water again. I started by thoroughly investigating the intriguing site of Göbekli Tepe in Turkey, which is 11,600 years old. That's the end of the Younger Dryas. In parallel, I began to look deeply into the Younger Dryas impact hypothesis and the scientists behind it. While I'm aware that they face opposition, as no radical scientific hypothesis ever emerges without opposition, what I observed over the years since 2007 is that they have gradually answered all that opposition. I think that the Younger Dryas impact hypothesis is the best explanation for the extraordinary Earth changes that took place during the Younger Dryas, which affected the entire human race and which I think cost us part of our story. I think that's when we lost an episode of civilization that has not yet been documented by historians and archaeologists.

I was most intrigued by the idea that you put forth in **Magicians** **of the Gods** *that survivors from an advanced civilization that was largely destroyed by a global cataclysmic event traveled the globe and taught the techniques for agriculture, building architecture, understanding mathematics, and the foundations for civilization to the other survivors who were merely existing on a hunter-gatherer level of development. I found the evidence that you presented for this most fascinating, and was wondering what you think might have been in those uncannily similar handbags that are found in carved stone images from various ancient cultures around the world?*

GRAHAM: Well, I often jokingly say that it was their stash of DMT.

[*Laughter*]

GRAHAM: And I'm not exactly joking, because it's very clear to me that this elusive "invisible man," this lost civilization, way back in the last Ice Age, shared spiritual ideas with the world. One of the reasons that I'm really sure it's there is because of the common spiritual and religious ideas all around the planet, and how those ideas are clearly based in altered states of consciousness. So I think that was part of the legacy of the lost civilization.

If our civilization today were to face a cataclysm on that scale, those of us who were smart would take refuge amongst hunter-gatherers, because hunter-gatherers are the ones who have the skills to survive a disaster like this. People from highly civilized urban environments really don't. But what would we bring to those hunter-gatherers that would be of the least bit of use to them? I'm not sure. I think that the survivors of the lost civilization did bring something useful, did participate and engage in hunter-gatherer culture, and added something of their own to the mix.

I particularly enjoyed your book Supernatural. *Now, I know that this is basically the subject of the book, but could you just please speak a little about the connection that you see between ancient shamanic cave paintings, encounters with fairies, spirits, and supernatural beings across cultures, alien abductions, and the non-human beings that people report encountering during powerful psychedelic experiences with DMT, ayahuasca, or iboga?*

GRAHAM: Sure. First of all, it's really important, and this should be on the record, that I pay tribute to Jacques Vallée. Do you know of Jacques Vallée?

I know Messengers of Deception. *Isn't that one of his books?*

GRAHAM: Yes, and many other important books. The title of his most important book is *Passport to Magonia*, which was published in 1969. Have you come across that book?

No, I'm not familiar with it.[2]

GRAHAM: You really should take a look at it. Jacques is still around, by the way, and he lives in California. He lives in San Francisco. Jacques was a NASA scientist, but he became interested in so-called alien and UFO abductions and was intrigued by the consciousness connection. In *Passport to Magonia*, as far as I know, he's the first researcher to draw attention to the very peculiar similarities between fairies and aliens. These two apparently separate domains actually turn out to contain an enormous range of common factors.

That book was published in 1969. In *Supernatural*, that was then one of the strands of ideas that I followed in the book. I took that idea forward quite a bit, with experiences in altered states of consciousness, and with looking at spirits as they are encountered by shamans. The conclusion that I came to is that when we're talking about fairies and elves, or aliens, or spirits or angels, we're all talking about the same thing viewed through different cultural spectacles.

2. I ordered a copy immediately after this interview and loved the book.

Interpretation is instantaneous with perception in human beings, and we interpret according to our cultural background to a large extent. It's pretty automatic, and therefore we try to fit what we're seeing into a framework that we already have some kind of handle on. I would say that that's what's happening with modern UFO sightings and alien abductions. I'm not saying they're not real, but I'm saying the way they're being construed is conditioned by our culture, and that if we're going to consider UFO-alien abductions, then we must consider the vast context of these experiences, which indeed goes all the way back to the cave paintings.

Some of the most diagnostic aspects of the shamanistic experience are encounters with intelligent entities that often take the form of animals, or of therianthropes, who are part-animal and part-human in form. There's often a lot of geometry as well in these visions, and that's what is all over the painted caves going back tens of thousands of years. What you find is visionary art. There are so many commonalities between modern visionary art and cave art from 35,000 years ago that it would be daft to suggest there isn't a connection between the two.

Fortunately we have a very solid academic, Professor David Lewis Williams from the University of Witwatersrand in South Africa, who's made it his life's work to document that connection. He's published a series of books, of which the most important is *The Mind in the Cave*. What David is doing there is showing that cave art is an art of shamanism. It's an art of altered states of consciousness, and indeed you can see entities that look like our "greys" in ancient cave art. I even reproduced an example in *Supernatural*. So I thought okay, this is a really intriguing issue that needs to be explored.

When I started researching and writing *Supernatural*, I wasn't even sure what I was going to do. I thought I'd moved away from the lost civilization, and since my years at university (1970–1973), I'd been interested in human origins. So I thought I'd write a book about human origins, but as I got into it deeper and deeper, I realized the book wasn't going to be about human origins, at least not in the biological sense. It was going to be about the origins of conscious behavior amongst human beings.

When did this begin? What was it about? What sparked it? What was the trigger? How far back can we push it? Now it's risky to say that we can only push it back as far as cave art, because that art may have been painted on human bodies for tens of thousands of years before that and therefore would not survive for us to witness. But it's clear that this activity, this artistic endeavor of depicting other realms and other worlds as encountered in altered states of consciousness, correlates very closely with the rapid evolution and development of human behavior, and I'm tempted to draw a causative connection between the two.

I'm not the first. Again, another person we must pay tribute to is the late great Terence McKenna and his amazing book *Food of the Gods*. I think a lot of people have been coming at this from different directions—Terence McKenna, Jacques Vallée. And my role in *Supernatural* was largely the role of a reporter, to put the pieces together and say, look, it seems like there's a really big picture here.

I find this all so fascinating. The first person I ever interviewed was Terence McKenna, for my book Mavericks of the Mind.

GRAHAM: He was such an amazing speaker.

Yes, he was so brilliant and such a great storyteller. I also interviewed Rick Strassman for a previous book, and I just interviewed Andrew Gallimore. I've been very interested in DMT research for years.

GRAHAM: I was with Rick a few months ago, a lovely guy, and Andrew is really fascinating. What Andrew is doing is really quite amazing. His book *Alien Information Theory* is sitting on my desk at the moment, a damn good intriguing book.

Oh yes, it's a fascinating book; I couldn't put it down. What are your thoughts about the mysterious entities that people report encountering on DMT? Do you think there's an independent reality to these beings, do you think that they might be artificial

intelligence programs stored in our DNA, or do you think that
they're just merely complex hallucinations?

GRAHAM: I definitely don't think that they're merely complex hallucinations. I don't think all this is just concocted in the brain. It's more complicated than that. I made the point in *Supernatural* but I'll just repeat it here, that the human brain does have in-built modules. We definitely have a module for intuitive physics. We are able to do what would be actually incredibly complicated, high-level physics calculations in an instant with our bodies and minds.

The typical example being, somebody throws a rock at me and I dodge the rock or bat it aside with my hand to stop it hitting my face. Behind those actions are really detailed physics calculations, to do with the object being thrown, the position and the power of the thrower, and your own position. All of that has to be put together in a fraction of a second, so that you can get out of the way of that rock. It's easy to understand why evolution would invest in a brain module that enabled us to avoid deadly rocks being thrown at us.

Those who could get out of the way of the rocks would be more likely to pass on their genes than those who couldn't. So I'm not against the notion of brain modules for particular activities, but I don't see why evolution would invest in a brain module for therianthropes and entities who give us messages about the meaning of our lives and teach us to be better people.

Perhaps it would. Perhaps such a brain module would arise randomly and evolution would then select it, but it seems unlikely to me on the face of things. None of this can be proved. The short answer to your question is a lot more research needs to be done, and the research with this extended-release DMT project on which Andrew Gallimore has been working looks promising. In fact, I've just met somebody who's going to be the first volunteer in that project. He works a lot with 5-MeO-DMT, but he's going to be the first volunteer in London to go in for potentially hours or days into the DMT state.

Wow, he's brave.

GRAHAM: He's super-brave; that's why they chose him. I'm going to meet him again early next year. He's a very interesting character. I'm not sure I would be willing to put myself into that, but anyway, this is what is needed. What are we dealing with here? The mystery is the transpersonal aspect of this. Now, of course, intuitive physics are also transpersonal, so an argument could be made that there's some sort of brain module for this, but my own gut instinct is that is not the case.

I think that the brain is operating as an interface here. I've never felt that the brain generates, makes, or manufactures consciousness. I think consciousness incarnates in the brain. This is almost a spiritual or religious point of view. It incarnates in the body, and the brain cannot be separated from the body. The gut is a kind of brain in itself. I think there's a wider reality beyond, and our physical equipment does allow us a backdoor, or a side door, to contact that reality. However, since we exist on a physical planet, ruled by certain specific laws of physics, we also need to function and survive here.

It's quite inevitable that the great part of our focus would be on daily functioning and survival and much less of it would be on these more esoteric matters. But *the backdoor is there.* The plants exist to help us open it. They're not the only way to open the backdoor. There are other ways, but the key thing is altered states of consciousness. It's fascinating how different cultures down the ages have put a lot of effort and energy into creating settings for altered states of consciousness experiences that would be extremely profound. The ancient Egyptian Books of the Dead, for example, are clearly the result of visionary experiences. Detailed visionary journeys had been undertaken and individuals had come back and reported on those journeys, and they've compiled the reports. It is in some ways the world's first work of science, I think.

Can you speak a little bit about the hybrid human-alien offspring that some people have reported encountering during so-called alien abduction experiences, and how you think this relates to the changelings that fairies would supposedly leave in exchange

for babies in previous centuries—and why you think that these reports might be indicative of an alien breeding program that has been evolving over time?

GRAHAM: I don't think they're indicative of an alien breeding program. I don't think that. We have to look carefully at the words we use. The word "alien" has been loaded with so much baggage in our culture that I always put it in inverted commas. What we have here is a phenomenon. The phenomenon is incredibly well documented. Of course, the mainstream dismisses it as fantasies of a few delusional individuals, but the phenomenon is very widespread, very widely reported, has been in human culture for thousands of years, and continues in human culture today.

The first categorical mistake we would make is to dismiss these experiences all together, and that's the mistake that mainstream science is making. The second mistake we would make, which I see being made again and again in our culture, is to jump to an assumption—*Ah, this is aliens.* These are high-tech beings, a bit like us. They're physical. They come from some planet within this universe. They got here in spaceships using technology a bit like ours, but more advanced. All of that is not a fact. All of that is opinion.

All of that is construal. All of that is projection onto the experience of what we think the experience should be. I think that's another thing that we need to back off from and stop doing. The experiences themselves are what are intriguing, and we are not far enough into the investigation of those experiences to say what it is that's going on here. I'm not sure if that's what you're saying.

Aliens from another planet, who have a breeding program going on here—that's way too materialist for me. I don't think that's what it's about at all. The question of hybrids and interaction, you're right, and I report it in *Supernatural*. This is a universal theme of sex with aliens. Shamans have sex with spirits all the time. Shamans have offspring in the spirit worlds. Where they don't have those offspring is here in this world.

They are re-abducted to nourish and nurture and love their hybrid offspring in whatever that other realm of reality is. But I just like to be categorical on this. I think it's (a) way to soon. And (b) it's not what I envisage, some kind of simplistic, materialistic alien breeding program here.

I was referring to an idea that you had brought up in your book **Supernatural** *about a possible relationship between the older reports of changelings, the strange, disfigured babies that fairies would supposedly sometimes leave in exchange for a human baby, and how there was some kind of evolution or development over time from the deformed and disturbing changelings to the seemingly healthier and better nurtured, hybrid babies reported among people who have had alien abduction experiences.*

GRAHAM: Sure, I could say that. I may have said that in passing as a speculation. It's not central to my theory. These experiences are largely at the level of consciousness. But then, aren't all experiences largely at the level of consciousness? Is there a physical aspect to these experiences? Yes, there is. People get left with stuff in their arms or their legs. The physical traces do show up on radar screens. There is a physical dimension to this experience. But if we're going to reach out and try to guess as to what's at the root of the experience, I would put my money on inter-dimensional contact rather than contact within this dimension by high-tech beings a bit like us who want to fuck us.

Yes, that is pretty much the conclusion the late psychiatrist John Mack came to when I spoke to him as well.

GRAHAM: John was a good friend. It's so sad that he got killed by that fucking drunk driver.

Oh, so sad. He was so brilliant. I got to interview him twice, and he was an absolutely brilliant man with rare knowledge.

GRAHAM: He was.

Very good-hearted as well. Graham, can you speak a little about your writing process and what you've described as downloading from the "cloud," after you've gathered together all of the scientific evidence for your nonfiction books?

GRAHAM: Yes, very much. So what I've learned over the years, and particularly since I began to work with plant medicines, is that the most important thing at a certain point in the writing is to get out of my own way, not to overthink a project. If I've prepared an outline for the publisher, the very first thing I do is throw it away, because how could the outline possibly be as good as a book that I'm about to sit down and spend three years on? I shouldn't bind myself with quick sketchy thoughts that I've had in advance to give an indication of the scope of the project. I should let the project speak for itself, and therefore I try not to follow a preplanned outline, and as far as possible, not to think the process through too much, but to trust the process.

I've been writing books long enough now to trust the process, that the words will come through, and to get out of my own way and let them come through. It's a curious coincidence that [occurred during] the time in my life when I became interested in ancient mysteries and wrote my first book on that subject, which I think I mentioned earlier, which is the book about the Ethiopian claim to possess the lost Ark of the Covenant, a book called *The Sign and the Seal*.

That book really started to grow in my mind and in my imagination, although I was aware of it as a project since at least 1983, when I first went to Axum. But it began to take form after I began to smoke cannabis. Amazingly, I had reached the age of thirty-seven with almost no experience of cannabis. Then in 1987 a good friend in Africa and a good friend in Europe were both deeply into cannabis, and they turned me on to it and I got deeply into cannabis. I don't think I would have written that first book of historical mystery, *The Sign and the Seal*, which was published in 1992, if it hadn't been for the role of cannabis in my life.

I have had a period where I gave up cannabis for three years. It was not serving me well and I wasn't serving it well, but I've moved through that phase now and I find it an incredibly helpful writing aid. I write sixteen hours a day, seven days a week. I put myself 100 percent into what I'm doing, and while mentally stimulating, it can be physically very boring, sitting in front of a computer screen that many hours a day, that many days a week. Cannabis helps to take that physical boredom away.

I don't feel itchy or restless. It allows me to get out of my own way, to relax into myself, and just let the words flow through. I have one specific book, one of my novels called *Entangled* and published in 2010, that was directly influenced by my experiences with cannabis and plant medicines.

The whole story of *Entangled* was given to me in a series of ayahuasca sessions in Brazil in the early 2000s. I forget exactly what year but I published the book in 2007, and again it very much felt like a download. I was literally given the characters, the dilemmas, the plot, everything. It all came down, and not just in one session, but across all five of those sessions, along with a very strong compulsion to go away and write a novel, which is something that I hadn't done before.

Indeed I did go away and write that novel, and I've written novels subsequently. It's as though Mother Ayahuasca has revealed an aspect of my creativity that I didn't know was there, and encouraged me to explore and develop it. And the key throughout, in any writing process for me, whether it's fiction or nonfiction, is to get out of my own way—not to overthink it, but to allow the words to come through.

How does your creative process differ between your fiction and nonfiction writing?

GRAHAM: It does differ in one sense. Getting out of my own way is the same. The hours a day that I put into the project are the same. I do research for my fiction books, but it's not at the same depth that I do for the nonfiction. It's such a relief not to have to use footnotes with fiction, and that you could just make stuff up when you need to. Whereas in nonfiction, especially with my highly critical, skeptical audience, it's important for me to stick really tight to the facts and to document thoroughly what I write, so that they can't say, oh, this is shoddy research, or Hancock is making stuff up.

I footnote everything so that people know what my sources are, and it's a relief not to have to do that in fiction. And it's a relief to be able to get inside characters' heads in fiction, in the way that you tend not to do in nonfiction. For both those reasons I love writing fiction, but my readership expects me to write nonfiction. There's definitely no doubt that what my readers want from me is my nonfiction.

How has drinking ayahuasca and ingesting DMT influenced your thinking, your creativity, and your work in general?

GRAHAM: Oh, massively, in every possible way, and not just my work, but the whole of my life. It has led me to become a more self-examined person, to be more careful about what I say and do, and what my impact on others will be. It's awakened a whole realm of creativity in me that I didn't even know was there. It's opened me up massively to the multidimensional nature of reality.

Again, when I say "the multidimensional nature of reality," that's a theory, not a fact. But at a personal level I'm very convinced that what we are seeing through our physical eyes in these physical bodies is only a tiny slice of what we're actually immersed in. And fear of death? I certainly have no fear of death. I do have fear of pain, humiliation, and the agony of dying, but death itself looks to me like the beginning of the next great adventure.

I heard you speak about how after doing ayahuasca you stopped using cannabis regularly. How did using cannabis affect your thinking and your writing, and why do you think it was beneficial for you to stop? Although it sounds like now you've been able to incorporate it into your life again.

GRAHAM: I have, yes. That's a good point, and I'll just clarify on that. Yes, in 2011, I think it was probably September or October, Santha and I were down in Brazil having a series of five ayahuasca sessions. In that case, those five ayahuasca sessions concentrated entirely on my behavior under the influence of cannabis. I need to be very clear about this, I don't blame cannabis for this. All that cannabis was doing was revealing aspects of my own personality. But what the ayahuasca showed me was that it brought out in me a tendency toward paranoia and suspicion, to mistrust everybody.

It's horrible to go around in a state of mistrust. It's better actually to trust people and let somebody fuck you over, than to just mistrust everybody all the time. I was getting into that state of deep mistrust of everybody, even people really close to me, and causing them pain. Mother Ayahuasca gave me five nights of just absolute hell over this, and she showed me the pain I'd been causing and how those harsh words that I'd spoken really caused another person to wither up inside. It made it absolutely clear to me that this was in some way connected to cannabis, and if I wanted out of this hole, I needed to stop smoking cannabis.

Well, I took it very seriously over there in Brazil, but the first thing I did when I got back to the UK was fire up my vaporizer. Then I tried to smoke a bag of vape. Amazingly, I could not. I was repulsed, revolted. I felt physically sick. My whole body had a huge reaction to this cannabis vape. Not only had I been told to stop, but I physically couldn't continue vaping, I couldn't continue using it in any form, and I quit entirely for three years. During those three years I wrote a couple of novels and I'm quite happy with them, so it's a personal choice. I think I can write without cannabis. It's just more comfortable for me to write with it, and I do think it opens stuff up. But I proved to myself that I could write without it too, because I did.

Then I'm on Joe Rogan's show in 2014, three years later. Joe and I have had this discussion before, and Joe says, "Are you still off the cannabis?" And I said, "Well, yeah, but I'm thinking of dipping my toes back in the water." To cut a long story short, Joe says, "Well, why don't you start now?" He pulls out a joint and we smoke it live on air. Now when you've had three years off of it, your tolerance goes way down, so I don't know how I managed to hold that interview together.

I had a rental car outside, but I had to call my wife and

daughter-in-law to come and collect me because, even after a further hour and a half, I just was not in any shape to drive. But I had a wonderful time in that conversation, and I felt really good about the cannabis. So I thought, well, if I can work with cannabis, and benefit from the beautiful gifts that she does bring, and it doesn't bend me out of shape, and I don't get paranoid and suspicious, and I don't start making other people miserable, then it'll be okay. I did go back to using cannabis, and that behavior pattern that was associated with it before appears to have gone completely, and as long as it's gone, I'm okay with the herb.

Cannabis has been an important tool for my writing as well. I can do it without it, but it's not nearly as much fun, or nearly as creative.

GRAHAM: Exactly, beautiful plant ally, and the question is how to get our relationship with her right. That is the important thing, and in my case, fundamentally, that was about how I behaved toward others, and these days I'm not causing pain and I'm not saying hurtful words. I'm not filled with suspicion and jealousy. So as long as it stays that way, I'm good with it.

Why do you think that psychedelics and the perspectives that they offer are so needed at this point in human history?

GRAHAM: Oh well, we are certainly at a turning point in the human story, and as far as we know there's never been anything like this before. We're globally interconnected. The internet has changed a great many things. It's opened up enormous potential, in two ways. It's opened up enormous potential for thinking that can bring the whole house of cards down, but it's also opened up other ways for dominant ideologies to be pulsed into the public mind even more powerfully than they've been pulsed before.

The dominant ideology that is pulsed into the public mind these days is a combination of materialism and nationalism. What the big media tends to unfortunately reinforce again and again on the internet is that these days what we should be focusing on is what we can buy and what we can consume. We're urged and taught in every way, with messages surrounding us from all directions, to define ourselves in terms of our consumption.

Here mainstream science leaps on board the ideological bandwagon, as we're also supposed to believe that there is nothing more to reality than matter. That everything can be reduced to its material substrate. That the brain is just matter. That any thought, any imagination, or any beautiful vision that we have can be reduced to matter in the brain. This materialist reductionist ethic of science has infiltrated almost every aspect of the society we live in. It is creating a human race of zombies, who can't think for themselves when all the potential is there for them to do so.

It's not an accident that at this crucial time for the human race, plant medicines have come out again in full force. Mother Ayahuasca is working her way around the world, getting into hearts and minds, and saying to people, "Think again. It may not be the way you've been told." The thing about ayahuasca, and the plant medicines in general, is that the teachings that we receive from them are not just information—they're an experience. It's one thing to sit in a lecture theater and be told stuff by some person, but it's another thing to actually live the experience.

In that respect, one person at a time, psychedelics are changing hearts and minds and are deprogramming and deconditioning us. And to that extent they're desperately needed in the world today. It's become a cliché now, but that's why I've said this many times, that if I had any say in the matter, I would make one rule, which is that nobody can apply for a high political office unless they've had a dozen ayahuasca sessions first. Don't even think about applying until you've had a dozen sessions and have been required to examine yourself carefully and examine why you're doing what you're doing. I don't suppose it'll ever happen, but I think it would change the world.

Then the next change of the world would be, why do we need leaders at all? We can be our own leaders. We don't need politicians. We don't need these masters. We don't need the state to look after us, as it keeps telling us it's doing. It's all a massive lie, and perhaps the most important power of the psychedelics is that they burst that lie apart.

Yes, and besides causing one to question one's cultural ideologies, they also help to increase ecological awareness and environmental sensitivity.

GRAHAM: Oh, massively. I mean, if you go down to the pub, you don't come out and start communicating with the trees. But on the plant medicines, hey, the trees speak to us. Everything speaks to us. But it's clear why our society has been so against it, because the powers that be in our society realize this is a powerful deconditioning element that's at work here.

How did your encounter with seizures and the near-death experience that you had in recent years from an induced coma "open you up," as you've said, and offer you a message about your life?

GRAHAM: Yes, well, the message was about this life, whatever it is. I'm sure we go on into other lives beyond this and that we probably come back. I do believe in reincarnation. But there's one fundamental message that comes through to me, and I'm doing my best to put it into practice. We're all frail human beings. We can't be perfect. But there's love.

If there's anything we're here for, it's to give love, to give love and care about others and not be totally focused on ourselves and our little ambitions and hopes and fears. To give something back. This life is short. It's incredibly brief. My mother is lying in the hospital dying at the moment. We almost lost her yesterday. Straight after this interview we're going in to see her. She's ninety-three years old, with congestive heart failure, almost no respiration, a huge amount of fluid in the lungs, and a lot of pain.

She lived all these years, and ninety-three years seems like a lot, but it's the blink of an eye. It comes and goes. It's an incredible gift that we've been given by the universe to have this experience, to manifest in these bodies, to make decisions that have consequences, to have the opportunity to love, and I think my own brush with death has made me more aware of this than I ever was before.

What do you see as some of the most exciting technological developments and scientific advances going on in the world today?

GRAHAM: Well, obviously, since we're on the subject of psychedelics, I think that the extended-release DMT science is absolutely intriguing. As a species we've been exploring stuff for thousands of years. Mariners have been getting out onto the open oceans, sailing off into the blue, and finding new islands and new lands. It seems part of being human is exploring. But there's one great realm that we've never explored systematically, and that is the realm of altered states of consciousness.

I'm going to put quotes around it, because I'm not sure it is in there, but that is the "inner realm." We're like the iceberg that thinks it's just the bit above water. The most exciting science will reveal to us the rest of the iceberg that's underwater. Any science that focuses just on the tip of the iceberg, which is what most of mainstream science does, is great, but it's not getting to the roots of the issue at all. I'm very excited by the work that's being done with psychedelics now, and the possibility that they could be used as mechanisms to explore what has been believed to be unexplorable. That is an important part of what psychedelics are doing.

When you look around at what's happening in the world these days, do you think that the human species will survive the next hundred years or do you think we're doomed to extinction?

GRAHAM: It's a moot point, and this is the subject of my fiction really, in simplistic terms, the battle of good against evil. There do appear to be forces at work in our world that seek to bring about the destruction of the potential of humanity. Another cataclysm could be a reset. It's not necessarily the end of us. Never mind the environment. Never mind asteroids and comets. Never mind earthquakes and tidal waves. *The biggest danger to humanity is ourselves*, and our wicked and misguided leaders, who use social media platforms to further misguide their followers.

There are so many lies and delusions being spread in the world, and all of them are encouraging people to think in very narrow, limited ways. I'm still astonished by the responses I receive whenever I make a statement contrary to nationalism on Facebook or another social media platform. When I say that I think nationalism is a terrible thing, which does awful harm to human beings, I'm still surprised by how many people come back and really attack me for that.

My wife, Santha, is of South Indian origin, and I'm repeatedly accused of being a race traitor because I'm married to a woman with dark skin. I ask myself, how is it that people are able to think in such a narrow, limited way, where they define another human being by the color of their skin, the least important aspect of ourselves? It's like defining ourselves by the shape of our knees, or the length of our colon.

It's just incredibly stupid to define ourselves in that way, and yet there are forces at work in society that are putting huge amounts of money, intelligence, and ingenuity into leading people to think in that very narrow, tribalistic way, and not to realize that we're all one human family, that we all have the same hopes and fears and ambitions, the same capacity for love. We're all on the same journey. What we should be doing here is helping each other along that journey, not creating artificial barriers. I'm optimistic still that we won't utterly destroy ourselves, and that the helping hand that the plant medicines are so clearly offering us now will be taken up, ever more rapidly, and things will change for the better.

I think that the exact problem that you're describing is alleviated by psychedelic plant medicines.

GRAHAM: Yes, they're the absolute remedy for this problem. That's why our society has been so negative about them, and has sought to demonize them, and to infect people's minds with mental viruses concerning these things, which are very hard to overcome. But little by little it's happening.

Do you see any type of teleology, intelligence, or mindful intention operating in nature, and in the evolution of life, or do you think that evolution is occurring purely by blind chance?

GRAHAM: I don't think it's occurring by blind chance. Only theory, not fact, but again, I think that it's all about creating vehicles in which consciousness can manifest, and in which consciousness can manifest in the most effective and thorough, and deep and detailed manner possible. I am sure that fruit flies are conscious, but I don't think that fruit flies have the potential to deploy that consciousness in the way that human beings do.

I think the whole project of the universe is about creating vehicles within which consciousness can manifest, because I suspect that consciousness is fundamentally non-physical. It can't be reduced to matter. But what a useful thing, to have material realms in which it is possible for consciousness to incarnate, so that we, as conscious entities, can then learn, grow, and develop.

How do you envision the future development or evolution of the human species, and the future relationship between human biology and advanced technology?

GRAHAM: It depends entirely on the choices that we make now, really. This is the turning point, and there's nothing wrong with technology as such. It's when technology is elevated to a false status in society. These are just tools for us to get stuff done with. That's all they are. They're nothing more than that, and we've elevated technology and science to the level almost of a religion. Many scientists will say, almost as a matter of fact, that there is no such thing as life after death, that consciousness cannot possibly survive the body. Those aren't statements of fact. They're statements of opinion by those scientists involved.

I don't know what our future relationship is going to be with technology. I have no problem with tech as such. I'm not saying that we all have to go back to being hunter-gatherers, but what I am saying is that we've allowed technology to assume an overdominant role in our society, and it's coupled with a state of mind, which is extremely deadly. This is the state of mind that proclaims that there is no meaning or purpose to life, that we are in fact just random accidents and that there is no transcendental purpose to what we're doing.

That state of mind is deadly, and it leads human beings to treat one another as objects rather than as conscious, breathing, loving, intelligent beings. That's what we have to get away from. So I don't know whether we're going to survive the next hundred years, but if we do, then our society is going to need to radically reorient itself and that will not come from above. That will never come from above. It will only come from the grassroots. It will only come from a population that has gone through a consciousness shift and that is no longer prepared to put up with the bullshit any longer.

It has to come from that level. It'll never come from above, and I think it's touch and go at the moment. There are enormous destructive negative forces at work in the universe, and there are enormous positive forces at work in the universe. I do think that there is intelligence behind it, but I'm not going to call that intelligence "god." I'm not a Christian, or any other kind of monotheist, but we live in a much more complicated and mysterious reality than we've been taught. Yes, absolutely we do, and it's our duty to find out more about it.

What are your thoughts on the simulation hypothesis, the idea that our entire reality is really an advanced computer simulation?

GRAHAM: I think it could be. It's not impossible, and then you can even work the idea of past lives in that. We had past lives in the simulation. We die in the simulation. We come back and have another life. It's interesting the way the Greeks put it. Many ancient cultures say that when you're reborn you drink the waters of forgetfulness. The deal is that you don't remember the game any longer. If you did remember the game and knew its rules fully, then you wouldn't be able to play the game straight, and you would not benefit from it.

If it's a simulation, then it's a simulation with a purpose. Whether it's a simulation or whether it's a full-scale reality in which we incarnate, leave, and then reincarnate, it doesn't really matter actually. *It's a teaching device.* I believe that's what life is. That's what the universe is. That's what physical reality is. It's a teaching device within which consciousness has the opportunity to grow, which it might not have the opportunity to do so otherwise.

What do you personally think happens to consciousness after physical death and the deterioration of the brain?

GRAHAM: What I personally think happens, but cannot prove, is that it continues. It's like going through a door, and we go through that door into another room, and another life, and another world. I think that our consciousness survives death. At the same time, we would be foolish not to listen to the wise words of, for example, the ancient Egyptians, who put their best minds to work on this subject for more than 3,000 years.

We would be foolish to imagine that we can live a life without consequences. If we come into physical existence and we're mean-spirited and cruel, and cause pain and suffering to others all the way through our lives, we shouldn't expect to get a free ride when it comes to the afterlife journey. We should expect to be invigilated on what we've done with our lives. You were given an incredible opportunity. You were given the precious gift of life. What did you do with it?

These kinds of questions are asked in the judgment scene in the ancient Egyptian system. It's not only a moral judgment. It's also a gnostic judgment. You were given a chance to learn. Did you use it well? Or did you squander it? I think that our actions in this life do follow us into the life beyond, and that certain actions may result in no life beyond. That's certainly what the ancient Egyptians believed.

What is your perspective on the concept of god?

GRAHAM: I just don't need that hypothesis. It's patently, obviously a development from the concept of "chief." It's a hierarchical situation, particularly the monotheistic version of god—such an ugly creature. So vile, so cruel, so domineering, and so keen to encourage its followers to make war upon one another. If that's what a god is, I really don't want to know it, fucking monster.

Yeah, in other religions and other systems, you get closer I think to the truth that the universe is pervaded by consciousness at all kinds of different levels, and we're part of that continuum. The ancient Egyptians also believed that it was possible to become a god. That was our ultimate destiny actually—that you're reborn, not in a human body, but as a star in the sky, and then you shed life and light for millions and millions of years.

What are you currently working on?

GRAHAM: I just finished this huge book called *America Before: The Key to a Lost Civilization*. It was published in April, and I'm likely to be making a major TV series next year, but I'm not in a place to say who that's with or what it's about exactly at the moment. I'm looking at a TV series that will cross the whole spectrum of my work, but it may not happen. TV is a very unreliable business. We'll see what comes, but I'm focused on that at the moment.[3]

Longer term, I have some very specific objectives. My wife, Santha, and I did a beautiful photographic book back in 1998 called *Heaven's Mirror*. Santha has an archive of hundreds of thousands of amazing images, and I have a story to tell, so we're planning to do a large photographic book that might be called *The Way of the Gods*. Then I have some fiction to finish. I've got the second volume of my first novel, *Entangled*, as I never finished that. I've got to go back and finish that. I've also got the fourth volume of my *War God* series—a series of four, and I've written three—on the Spanish conquest of Mexico. So there's plenty on my plate up ahead.

3. This is a reference to Graham Hancock's popular Netflix series *Ancient Apocalypse*.

14

Psychedelics, Psychic Phenomena, and Encounters with Non-human Entities

An Interview with David Luke

David Luke, Ph.D. is a psychologist, researcher, and author who has done work in the areas of parapsychology, anomalous experiences, and altered states of consciousness.

Luke has been running clinical trials with LSD in hospital settings and running DMT field research at the University of Greenwich in England, where they're looking at things like precognition, shared visionary experiences, telepathy, and insights from the psychedelic experiences and extended-state DMT sessions.

Photo by Adam Malone

David Luke

Luke is an associate professor of psychology at the University of Greenwich, and an honorary senior lecturer at The Centre for Psychedelic Research at Imperial College London. He has published over a hundred academic papers on transpersonal experiences and altered states of consciousness, and he regularly gives public lectures and conference presentations.

Luke is co-founder and director of Breaking Convention, a biennial international conference on psychedelic research, and he directs the Ecology, Cosmos and Consciousness salon at the Institute of Ecotechnics in London.

Luke lives in East Sussex, England, and is the author or coauthor of a number of popular books, including *Otherworlds: Psychedelics and Exceptional Human Experience*, and was the editor of *Psychedelic Mysteries of the Feminine*, *DMT Dialogues*, and *DMT Entity Encounters*. To find out more about his work, see his page on the Academia website.

I interviewed David via Skype on October 20, 2021. I was delighted to finally have the opportunity to speak to David at length after years of corresponding together. I first met David when I was working for the Multidisciplinary Association for Psychedelic Studies (MAPS) years ago, and he contributed essays to the bulletins that I was editing. David and I share many common interests, and we had a most lively exchange about the relationship between altered states of consciousness and psychic phenomena, the phenomenology of the DMT entity experience, the connection between psychedelic experiences and ecological awareness, the future of psychedelic research, and many other fascinating topics.

How did you first become interested in psychology and the study of the human mind?

DAVID: It was a few things really. I was always interested in altered states. I used to try to get into an altered state in whatever way I could as a kid. I enjoyed playing with my brain like it was a neurochemistry playset. But I also had an avid interest in left field science, and I would skip off from school and go down to the secondhand bookshop, where I would read everything in the esoteric and left field science section to a great extreme. So I was very much interested in psychedelics and alternative models of consciousness from an early age.

But then, a friend of mine was a psychologist. He was one of these guest psychologists on daytime TV programs, and he would go on wearing a leather skirt and flesh tunnels through his ears and talk about his addiction to power tools and things like that. I thought he was pretty cool and he was really good at Trivial Pursuit. So I figured he knew a thing or two, and thought this largely because of the way he thought as a psychologist. So I figured studying psychology could help me try and understand the psychedelic experience.

Was there an early childhood experience that inspired your interest in these unconventional areas of study—parapsychology, anomalous experiences, and altered states of consciousness?

DAVID: Not any one particular experience, I guess. I used to have *really* full-on vivid dreams and hypnagogic experiences all of the time as a kid, and I often lived in a bit of fantasy world. I'd just be in my own little dreamy world and there were just some very cosmic things going on. It was pretty mythological inside my mind as a small child, so I guess I was always drawn toward that. But the interest in psychedelics, parapsychology, and altered states came before the interest in psychology. Psychology was just a delivery system I hoped to explore these mysteries with, and to find answers to some of my questions, really.

What sort of relationship do you see between psychic phenomena—telepathy, clairvoyance, and psychokinesis—and the psychedelic experience?

DAVID: There is quite a strong relationship, and I think that relationship of psychic phenomena relates to all altered states of consciousness. These kinds of experiences occur much more often in altered states of consciousness, be it in dreams, meditation, hypnosis, or psychedelics. But psychedelics have just got the volume turned up. They really get you into a profound and deep state of altered consciousness without too much work. So you find that people who have taken psychedelics tend to have many more of these experiences and more frequently. It also changes people's belief systems, so that they're more likely to believe in psychic phenomena having had psychedelics. So, I think psychedelics provide a special, strong class of altered states of consciousness, and those states lend themselves really well to psychic experiences.

How do you think that the study of parapsychology can benefit from the study of shamanism?

DAVID: I'd like to see it studied more, actually, and I think it really can. There hasn't been enough cross-cultural, transdisciplinary anthropological research about shamanism from parapsychology. But I think you can learn a lot about the processes and the appropriate psychological, environmental conditions for having psychic experiences. For shamanic practitioners, altered states training, the use of ritual, and the power of belief and worldview I think are also important. So I think that there's a lot that could be learned from shamanism by parapsychologists, but it's been largely neglected, I have to say.

What are your thoughts about the mysterious elves and entities that people report encountering on DMT? Do you personally think that there's an independent reality to these beings, do you think that they might be artificial intelligence programs stored in our DNA, do you think that they're just merely complex hallucinations, spirits of the dead, or something else entirely?

DAVID: [*Laughter*] Maybe all of the above. It's nice to see you cutting to the chase! You could have had a few warm-up questions before going straight there. Fantastic! Well, I try not to have any strong beliefs about anything particularly. I attempt to be agnostic, and to be honest with you, my opinions, or my leanings, change day by day.

I guess the longer I am away from a DMT experience, the more I lean toward straightforward psychological and neurological explanations. But, I think the closer in proximity you are to having had one of those encounter experiences, probably the more likely you are to take it at face value and believe it to be what it says on the tin, i.e., spirits, spirits of the dead, angels, demons, deities, elves, or whatever they might be.

So I don't know. I've been on a long journey exploring this, and I don't think the neuroscientific, psychological angle is currently sufficient to explain these experiences. But at the same time, it's a bit of a metaphysical paradox and conundrum, trying to get to the actual bottom of the nature of these beings that people encounter. They certainly feel real—so much so that they can convert more than half of all atheists into non-atheists in the space of ten minutes. But as to their actual ultimate reality, I'd like to try and remain agnostic.

Yes, I try to do that too; it's difficult to do though. [Laughter]

DAVID: Yes, I like to try. I'm not very good at this, but I like to try! [*Laughter*]

As we just discussed, when people are in the DMT hyperspace state they often report interactions with intelligent, non-human entities—like the "self-transforming machine elves," praying mantis beings, et cetera—that clearly have bodies of some sort. For those who have experienced a DMT breakthrough and entered hyperspace where these mysterious entities reside, do you recall if you—and other people that you've spoken to—have reported that they had a body of some sort during these experiences, or were they just a point of observing consciousness? In other words, could you or they look down and actually see a virtual version of your own hands, or maybe tentacles, in hyperspace—like you can in a lucid dream—or could you just visually perceive the hyperspatial environment around you? Most of the people that I've spoken with say they don't recall having a body during these states. What's your perspective on this?

DAVID: Yes, there appears to be, generally speaking, a lack of embodiment. People may feel that they have a body, but I think that actually seeing your own body in the DMT state is extremely rare. I don't know of that many cases, or possibly even any. In my own experience, my first-ever DMT experience, I had these little elves come and shove light into my solar plexus. So I was aware that there was a place—in my body image at least—where my solar plexus was, and that it was being stuffed full of light. So you can have a sense of a body, but it's a very rare thing that anybody ever sees their own body, and it's usually left out of descriptions of the experience. You're quite right, it's something that is often absent.

I find that so interesting because in a lucid dream you can look down and see that there's a virtual representation of yourself— so I've been really curious about that. In my own experience, I remember being able to see in 360 degrees, and I have no memory of having a body, but I felt like this giant being was adjusting my brain, or doing something to my brain, at some point. So, it's a paradoxical and interesting phenomenon that I've been curious about. I would be most curious to hear what people would report after trying to look down and see bodies in the DMT state.

DAVID: In our new book, interestingly, Luis Eduardo Luna talks a lot about these kinds of experiments he did with himself with ayahuasca. For instance, like trying to find a mirror to see himself. Although he tried numerous times, he never managed to succeed. The mirror was always at the wrong angle, or there was something covering up his view, so it seemed to be a bit of a hyperspace impossibility.

You mean inside of hyperspace, when he's out of his physical embodiment in this world?

DAVID: Yes.

That's really interesting. It's almost like there was something preventing it.

DAVID: Absolutely, yeah! [*Laughter*]

I've had experiences in lucid dreams where I felt like something was preventing me from saying my own name out loud or from sharing certain information with other dream characters, and experiences like these make me wonder if they're evidence for simulation theory, which we'll be discussing shortly. In any case, do you think that endogenously produced DMT may be helpful in explaining some of life's weirdest, unexplained, spontaneous experiences and encounters—such as the alien abduction phenomenon, near-death experiences, mystical revelations, lucid dreams, or out-of-body experiences?

DAVID: It could well be part of the picture, I think. Certainly there's a big overlap, and there are numerous parallels between DMT experiences and those sorts of experiences. But there are some absences as well—such as the lack of colorful, entoptic, geometric patterns. I've only heard of one case of a near-death experience where somebody saw the entoptics, for instance. So, that might account for some of it.

Also, we're beginning to learn more from research with rodents (unfortunately), where they're looking at the various brain chemicals that are stimulated at the point of death. Right after cardiac arrest, we see a sixfold increase in DMT, but there's also something like a 200- or 300-fold increase in serotonin. So, it's possibly only part of the mind-blowing, neuro-hacking cocktail that occurs at points of near death, for instance. I think, actually, that chemicals like ketamine are probably a better simulacrum for out-of-body experiences. But yes, I certainly think that things like the alien abduction experience have some really interesting phenomenological parallels with DMT experiences. So, I think it may be part of the jigsaw puzzle, but I don't think it's a whole answer.

Do you think that those studies with rodents, which showed that during cardiac arrest there was some endogenous release of DMT, provide some evidence that human brains may also release DMT when we're dying?

DAVID: Yes, possibly. I think it probably does. I mean look at translational medicine; most of it's based on research with rodents and then we translate it to humans. So, yes, there's probably a very high chance that DMT is produced at the point of death, but alongside a whole massive cocktail of other neurochemicals. There's not much literature on people taking 300 times the normal brain levels of serotonin and finding out what happens, for instance, so yes, I think it's quite possible. I think that there's a good likelihood that DMT is produced in the brain, or released in the brain at least, at the point of death, but whether or not that alone explains near-death experiences and the death experience, I don't know, and I don't necessarily think so.

LSD has had a big impact on the development of computer technology and culture. What are your thoughts about what might be the fruit of the large and growing cultural popularity around DMT—especially with regard to the development of new technologies like more sophisticated virtual reality and Neuralink, as well as new artistic creations? Do you see it affecting culture in a similar way that LSD did?

DAVID: Maybe not to the same extent. I guess the whole thing about LSD was it was like, the first cultural explosion of psychedelia. That was at the forefront of it, and it came along at a particular point in history when there'd not really been anything so widely available like that before that point. So it had a huge cultural impact on language, fashion, art, music, et cetera. I think that certainly DMT does have a cultural footprint, although I don't think it will ever be quite as big as that of LSD in the sixties. Certainly a lot of psytrance music is DMT inspired, as is a lot of visionary art out there.

Tech-wise, I guess this kind of thing we can really only discover in retrospect. Who would have anticipated LSD helping to crack Bell's theorem, for instance? Or quantum computing? Or leading to the development of the mouse and so on? But yes, I imagine that the kind of experiences available through DMT could perhaps inspire some extradimensional kind of research. Maybe work along M-theory, or hyperbolic mazes in virtual reality, or something at a visual, dimensional level that we can't ordinarily grasp or perceive. I think that it could inspire something along those lines.

Or maybe, in some of these extended-state DMT studies, we can actually receive information from some of these advanced entities that will allow us to build new technologies? Perhaps the machine elves can upload the blueprints for how to build matter transporters, quantum starships, or time travel machines into our brains? That would be extraordinary. Do you think there's actually any chance of something like that?

DAVID: Actually, we did try testing that experimentally in a rudimentarily pilot way in a DMT field study I was running. We had difficulty recruiting people with enough expertise for our research, for instance, who had had that kind of experience of DMT. But it's worth revisiting.

We only had one participant and he was able to get some insight into his particular research question. I won't tell you what it was because we haven't published it yet, and we've yet to see whether or not that particular insight has turned out to be true or not. So, that's a way of doing it. You get people to think of research questions that we have no current answer to and see if they can discern the answer from the entities. Then, in time, we find out whether or not they got it right.

Didn't Jeremy Narby try that with a molecular biologist that he brought with him to the Amazon? I think that he was working on some kind of research project that he got insight into.

DAVID: Yes, he did. He had three molecular biologists, actually. I don't know the nature of their problems or whether or not they were intractable or unknown problems. But yes, certainly they were at the top of the game in their research domain and had breakthroughs. All three of them had breakthroughs in their research from their experience.

One of them had the classic Kary Mullis-esque[1] experience of seeing the DNA, being able to inspect it on a molecular level, get inside it, and see what was going on. So yes, I think there's some fruit to be plucked from the particular avenue of research. I'd like to think that we could actually set up programs in the not-too-distant future, when the legalities have changed, and very specifically doing that—taking some of the brightest and best minds on the planet, particularly those ones working with ecological issues, which is our current global crisis, and coming up with better, more ecologically oriented solutions.

That sure sounds great to me! David, connectivity and inter-connectivity affect a wide spectrum of experiences occurring in ascending levels of the natural world—from the level of the neuron to aspects of our own personality, to our connection with each other, the environment, and the cosmos. Can you speak about how psychedelics affect connectivity and interconnectivity in general, and how does this affect creativity, synesthesia, interspecies communication, as well as our relationship with the world and ourselves?

DAVID: I certainly can speak to all of that. You summed it all up for me, but I'll give you my version, which is that, yes, we do see this kind of increased connectivity on the neurological, biological, psychological, sociological, ecological, cosmological, and the theological levels. People feel more connected on all of those levels and actually experience growing connectivity from psychedelics.

So on a neuronal level, we really see this hyperconnectivity between different regions of the brain that ordinarily are not communicating with each other very much, and I think, perhaps, that gives rise to creative insight, problem solving through what we might call divergent

---

1. Nobel Prize winner Kary Mullis, whom I interviewed for my book *Conversations on the Edge of the Apocalypse*, famously described how he was able to see the three-dimensional dynamics of DNA mechanics at a molecular level during an LSD experience, which led to his development of PCR (polymerase chain reaction) techniques, which revolutionized the study of genetics.

thinking, as opposed to a normal, everyday, convergent thinking—which is quite constrained.

On a psychological level, people feel more connected to themselves—to their own identity, their personality, their own autobiographical history, past traumas, as well as chartered memories and experiences—and they are able to achieve some kind of breakthrough or catharsis with their own psychological makeup.

On a sociological level, of course, people feel enhanced; they have greater compassion and empathy is increased. We see more pro-social behaviors and reduced authoritarianism. People are just more communitarian minded. And there's also a synergy there with group psychedelic experiences of *communitas*, which also enhance well-being and so on.

Then, of course, on the ecological level, people feel more connected with nature. In the survey I did of 150 psychedelic users, 100 percent of them said that they felt more connected with nature as a result of taking psychedelics—to the point where the majority of them had changed their diet as a result of taking psychedelics and did more gardening or became more ecologically concerned. Even a sizable percentage quit their jobs and took up new careers in something more ecologically orientated.

Of course, we have the experience of interspecies communication, which isn't that uncommon either, through the use of psychedelics, somewhere in the region of—well, depending on which survey you look at—as many as 70 percent of ayahuasca users believe they've communicated with the spirit or the intelligence of ayahuasca. And people even have transformational experiences of turning into other species and so on.

Then of course, on the cosmological level, people feel more connected to the universe, the cosmos, deep mind, panpsychic conceptions of reality, spilling over into the theological level of a deeper sense of connection with something divine.

When you look around at what's happening in the world these days, do you think that the human species will survive the next hundred years or do you think we're doomed to extinction?

DAVID: I think we will survive the next hundred years. I think that existence may be radically, drastically changed in ways that we probably can't predict. We may be heading for a complete ecosystem collapse in the next ten, twenty, thirty, forty, fifty, hundred years. Who knows? Certainly issues around climate change and not just that, but also species extinction are also accelerating. *We're in the biggest wave of mass extinction in 66 million years.* It's probably the fastest as well, and it's almost certainly and entirely, anthropogenic, i.e., man-made. So yes, I think we're in a really dangerous, precarious situation as a species—as are all the species on this planet—currently, and I'm not sure we're going to make it through. But I do think that the ingenuity of humans will probably mean that we may well survive, although I think we'll be in a very drastically different place a hundred years from now if we do have total ecosystem collapse.

You mentioned this a bit earlier, but do you think that psychedelics can help to raise ecological awareness during this planetary climate crisis that we're facing, and do you think that psychedelics and the perspectives that they offer are needed at this point in human history?

DAVID: Absolutely yes, very much so, and not least for making people more connected to nature. We can see that in the treatment of mental health—that psychedelics can make people far more connected to nature and as a consequence, that enhances well-being and people spend more time in nature as a result. And the more time you spend in nature is also good for your well-being. It also means you become more concerned and take more care for nature, so there's a whole raft of knock-on synergistic effects from people taking psychedelics just for their well-being, which can benefit themselves in great ways, but also the environment and our ecosystem. They make people feel more connected. They make people feel more concerned and people engage in more nature-connected activities. People want to be out in nature. They want to take psychedelics in nature. They want to study plants and fungi, save the environment, and look after the species. I think that's really key in where we're going currently.

I think there are also some things we can learn from Indigenous shamanic cultures around the world who have been using these substances for a very long time, in how they engage with nature. I mean it's a whole different perspective. They don't see themselves as being apart from nature. And that's what I think psychedelics can help achieve—it's this sense that we are not apart from nature. That we are part of nature, and what comes with that is a kind of responsibility and a sense of reciprocity in how we interact with our environment, which ultimately has to be how we negotiate and move forward, open our existence on this planet with other species.

Yes, I completely agree. I think that's why the psychedelic renaissance is happening right now—because of the ecological crisis that we're in. Can you talk about some of the psychedelic research that you're currently involved in, and how do you envision the future of psychedelic research?

DAVID: Yes. So currently, I'm still following up on this DMT project where we're looking at things like precognition, shared visionary experiences, telepathy, and also insight from DMT experiences. And of course, entity encounters—perhaps trying to map those and look at the nature of them, what role they may play, and some of these other factors. So that's one ongoing project, which has been running now for a while, and we can take that to the next level.

Then, as a rule, I'm doing mostly student-supervision projects. I spend a lot of time teaching these days, so it really depends on what projects my students are doing. So things like, we did a survey on Hallucinogen Persisting Perceptual Disorder (HPPD), which there was really very little data on, the occurrence of that and the underlying psychological factors. Also we're looking at autistics and psychedelics and what experiences they have, as well as the benefits and drawbacks, and so on and so forth.

Also, I've been doing a larger project. There are lots of little projects embedded in a larger project of mapping altered states more generally, relative to psychedelics. So we're looking at anechoic darkroom chambers, flotation tanks, holotropic breathwork, spontaneous spiritual experiences, kundalini experiences, virtual reality, and stuff like that—using the same kind of measures and processes we use in mapping psychedelic altered states. So that's some of the research I'm kind of involved in at the minute.

How do you envision the future of psychedelic research?

DAVID: Yes, well, it's happening faster than it ever has happened. There's a veritable explosion of stuff going on, and I think there's a race to develop new psychedelics, as well as new ways of producing them and tweaking them, and different delivery systems, mostly for clinical applications. That seems to be where all the funding and money is going currently.

I can also perceive that there are some interesting fault lines occurring between the original psychedelic community and some of the more commercial interests on a sociopolitical level, as well as on a more metaphysical or philosophical level. I see this crevasse opening up between those camps who are interested in what we might call the mystical experience or these transpersonal experiences that occur, and the other side of the camp that wants to medicalize and neurologicalize everything and try to explain it just in terms of brain activity.

So, there are some interesting fault lines and divisions arising, but the way that psychedelic research is going at the minute, it's largely biomedical applications and the underlying pharmacology, which isn't for me the most exciting, because I think these things have massive applications in looking at some of the more existential questions about what is the nature of reality? What is the nature of mind, consciousness, and our relationship to the planet and other species? Also, the existence or not of other beings, entities, spirits, or whatever they might be. So those are the kind of questions I'm mostly interested in.

How have psychedelics personally influenced your thinking, your creativity, and your work in general?

DAVID: I guess, I have no idea, because it'd be hard to imagine myself having not taken psychedelics, it being such an intrinsic part of my life since I was a teenager—which is now getting on to be quite a while. But I imagine that I'd be a much more boring, ordinary kind of person with a less engaged character. I'm not sure, because everything I've done has been motivated through and by my interest and use of psychedelics. So, it'd be hard to disentangle the me before psychedelics from the me now, and say, what happened? But they've certainly enriched my life. I've had an extraordinary life of experiences, which will keep me going through the next few lifetimes, trying to understand.

I'm in a similar boat, and when I just interviewed Erik Davis for this book he pretty much told me the same thing. If you've been doing psychedelics since you've been a teenager, it's hard to imagine how one's life would be different. I do talk to some people who have this life-changing experience when they first did psychedelics at the age of thirty-five or forty, and how it changed their life. But if you've been doing them your whole life, I guess it's hard to see how your life would have been different. On another note, have dreams or lucid dreams been an inspiration to you?

DAVID: Yes actually, very much so. These are the unsung heroes. I'm a psychedelic researcher, but I'm interested in all altered states and transpersonal experiences, and dreams are extremely important. For one thing, we get them for free every night, if you pay attention, and they're not currently illegal. [*Laughter*] We can dream anywhere, and we have direct access to them. In my own experiences, I've probably had far greater insights from dreaming and studying my dreams than I have from my psychedelic experiences.

And I've probably had almost equal quantities of both, although not quite. But I didn't take any psychedelics for about eighteen months and just studied my dreams, somewhat religiously, and it was extremely profound what came out of that—even full-blown mystical experiences and so on. So yes, I really value my dreams, and I think that we should think more broadly in terms of altered states rather than just psychedelics as their own special thing. They're just part of a whole smorgasbord of access points to our own infinite consciousness really.

You just mentioned the legality of dreaming. In lucid dreams, many people report that when they smoke DMT or take LSD in a dream, it has full psychedelic effects. So, there's another legal way for people to access these types of experiences in their dreams.

DAVID: Yes, absolutely.

What do you see as some of the most exciting technological developments and scientific advances going on in the world today?

DAVID: Wow, okay, there's a lot. I'm not necessarily paying too much attention, but the speed of developments is quite extraordinary. Artificial intelligence for one thing, although I think it's probably hyped to be something a bit better than it really is. In many cases, there's a bit of cherry-picking of data going on. But ultimately, I think the applications of AI and machine learning are quite extraordinary. What else? I'm not a technologist, per se, but I've been interested in virtual reality and also mapping the human perceptual system and emulating that through technology. That is some pretty interesting stuff going on right there as well.

Also I'm interested in some of the biological developments. I mean, what was the latest thing I saw this week? [*Laughter*] Now they've managed to shift the DNA or RNA of plants to produce meat protein. That could be a hugely radical intervention. So I think there's some fascinating stuff going on, and we're still only scratching the surface of stuff. Fields of research on fungi or the microbiome are relatively nascent areas where we haven't even really developed a full taxonomy, but we're yet to discover many extraordinary things.

However, ultimately, none of these things ever seem to get us any closer to some of the fundamental questions like, what is life? What is existence? What is consciousness? What is reality? What is time? And the more we burrow down into these things, it seems to be increasing in complexity. So I think we're going in some pretty interesting directions. Personally, I can't wait to have prosthetic wings or maybe even some hooves or something like that. I'm looking forward to that moment, although I might have missed the boat on that kind of particular genetic modification though.

I'm looking forward to that too! Do you see any type of teleology, intelligence, or mindful intention operating in nature, and in the evolution of life, or do you think that evolution is occurring purely by blind chance?

DAVID: It's a good hypothesis that evolution is occurring by blind chance, but I think there are a few blind spots in that particular discussion. I'm not a biologist, and it seems to be nice in theory, but in reality there seems to be another whole level of complexity going on. Even in Richard Dawkins's book *The Selfish Gene*, he's already applied a kind of animistic personality to the gene itself. And here's a man who's supposedly a materialist reductionist. And I don't think it was tongue-in-cheek, but going back to this question of what is life? We haven't yet really identified what is life. We haven't been able to recreate life in the lab, just from the chemical constituents, with all our advanced technology.

There's a part of us that has never really died. I came from the eggs in my mother's womb, which came from the eggs in her mother's womb, and so on and so on—all the way back, right? There's been this chain of existence, of life, in all life. All living things come from other living things, in a continuum, going back for millions, billions of years. So we haven't yet defined it outside of its material functions. What is the essence of life? What makes something alive? That really hasn't even been explored or fully explained yet in the biomedical model. So yes, I'm leaving the door open for a teleological explanation.

How do you envision the future development or evolution of the human species, the future relationship between human biology and advanced technology, and what are your thoughts on the concept of the Singularity?

DAVID: Terence McKenna's Singularity?

Actually, Ray Kurzweil.

DAVID: Ah! Ray Kurzweil, the technological Singularity.

Yes, do you have any thoughts on that?

DAVID: Well, yes, I mean maybe. I guess we're going to get hyper-technologized and cyborgian, and it's going to end up somewhat like that, but I don't think that transhumanists are really going to have it their way. I don't think we're going to end up in this extropian wet dream, where we are able to jettison our bodies and download our consciousness into some kind of advanced hard drive and exist in our own virtual hyperspace. I don't think that's necessarily possible, because I think it seems to assume too much about the nature of consciousness. I think some things possibly won't go in the direction that the transhumanists would like to envision. I'd think it's more likely to go in the direction of the hyperhumanism, which is that we are augmented by technology and that ultimately we will end up as biomechanical hybrids of some variety.

Maybe something like the self-transforming machine elves?

DAVID: Yes, exactly.

What are your thoughts on the simulation hypothesis, the idea that our entire reality is really an advanced computer simulation?

DAVID: I guess this imposes a bit of an infinite intellectual regress though, in that, well, who's doing the programming? And are they living in a simulation? I mean, are these simulations all the way up or all the way down? I think it's an interesting bit of metaphysics—it's a good thought experiment—but it doesn't seem to be easily resolvable.

It is a thought experiment that can turn your head inside out if you spend too much time thinking about it and start perceiving the world like it's actually just a simulation. So I think unless we've got a reliable way of testing it as a scientific hypothesis, it really is like you've just replaced "god" with a simulation. It's just back to the old religious problem of the existence of god; you have to take it on faith. So it's like a technological deity, really.

What do you personally think happens to consciousness after physical death and the deterioration of the brain?

DAVID: Well, again, I am agnostic. I guess we'll all find out one day, and again, my opinion changes. There's some interesting evidence for the possibly of reincarnation and postmortem consciousness of some variety. It's certainly been a belief that's been carried around by most cultures at some point, and it's a distinct possibility that something does survive death, some aspect of us—what we call soul, spirit, or consciousness. I think just consciousness is possibly the best, smallish unit I think we could utilize here.

Even the evidence of near-death experiences is somewhat tantalizing in that we have cases of people having powerful consciousness experiences without even having a functioning, operating brain. So I think it begs the question of transcerebral consciousness—all that research into psi, parapsychology, near-death experiences, and reincarnation. It begs the question: can we have consciousness beyond the brain? And if we can have consciousness beyond the brain, then we can possibly have consciousness beyond death as well. So, but again, I try to be agnostic.

What is your perspective on the concept of god?

DAVID: It depends on what concept of god. When I think of the Abrahamic religions and monotheistic gods, they're like some dude in the sky with a big white beard for some reason. But the concept of god, if it applies to some kind of universal panpsychic consciousness, presence, being, or energy, then I'd probably feel more comfortable with that. But the term *god* is used in so many ways, and a lot of it is often related to gods. The Abrahamic god is just a kind of god. They just did away with all the pantheon of pagan gods and replaced it with one god, but it was still conceptualized in that similar kind of way, with having personality and all the rest of it, which are clearly human creations to a point.

I think even though they may be human creations, they are personifications of some concept or idea that is beyond our usual everyday, tangible grasp. So, gods and god, the mind of the universe, it can mean so many different things to different people. But I think that when I'm not wearing my agnostic hat too tightly, I lean more toward a panpsychic perspective really, in that everything seemingly appears to inherently possess consciousness and so you can grok at a kind of cosmic consciousness as well.

You mentioned the research that you're working on right now. Is there anything else that you're currently working on that you'd like to mention, such as any new book projects?

DAVID: Yes. We've got a book coming out in the next month, in November in the States, and in December in the UK. It's a follow-up to our previous book, *DMT Dialogues*. This one's called *DMT Entity Encounters*, and it's like volume 2 of *DMT Dialogues*, where we collected the ten best minds we could find from wildly different disciplines to discuss what they thought the nature of entity encounters with psychedelics, particularly DMT, are all about.

Well, I'm certainly looking forward to that! Okay, so those are the questions that I had for you. Is there anything that we haven't spoken about that you'd like to add?

DAVID: I can't actually think of anything, but that was great, David. I really enjoyed the interview. I think you and I have very similar interests, and it's nice to finally actually chat with you—well, almost in person. I think that we first worked together on your special issue of the *MAPS Bulletin* about psychedelics and ecology.

Yes, it was with MAPS. I met you through Stanley Krippner, he's the one who introduced me to you initially.

DAVID: Yes, and that was a landmark bit of work, because it was the first proper investigation of the relationships of psychedelics to ecology, and so hats off to you for doing that. It's been one of my core subjects for a while now, so well done, David. I'm wishing you all the very best for this new book. I can't wait to see it and I'm delighted to be a part of it.

15

Extended State DMT and Alien Information Theory

An Interview with Andrew Gallimore

Andrew Gallimore is a computational neurobiologist, pharmacologist, chemist, and writer. He has been interested in the neural basis of psychedelic drug action for many years, and is the author of a number of articles and research papers on the powerful psychedelic drug N,N-dimethyltryptamine (DMT), as well as the extraordinary books *Alien Information Theory* and *Reality Switch Technologies*.

As we've discussed earlier in this book, DMT appears to be a mysterious neurotransmitter or hormone, a chemical that's naturally found in the human body and in many species of animals and plants, although no one knows what biological function it serves in any of these places. However, when ingested in sufficient quantities, DMT becomes one of the most powerful psychedelic substances known—an order of magnitude more intense than a strong LSD or psilocybin experience.

The experience completely overwhelms one's senses, separating awareness of the body from the physical world and transporting one to a magical realm beyond belief, with higher dimensional qualities and often occurring within seemingly super-advanced, ultra-sophisticated, biotechnological environments. This enchanted realm, often called hyperspace by DMT voyagers, appears to exist with the same consistency as waking reality and is seemingly populated with a race of advanced alien beings. Gallimore is one of the leading scientists giving serious thought to this most intriguing mystery of mysteries and has actually developed a technology that may literally allow us to establish a communication exchange with these super-intelligent beings in a higher dimension of reality.

Gallimore collaborated with DMT pioneer and psychiatric researcher Rick Strassman to develop a pharmacokinetic model of DMT as the basis of a target-controlled intravenous infusion protocol for extended journeys in DMT space. The idea here is to create a technology that will allow people to stay in the high-dose DMT state—which generally only peaks for a few minutes—for extended periods of time, hours or longer. Theoretically, this would allow people to have lengthier periods of contact with beings that may reside in this realm and for real progress with communication to take place. This research is currently underway at Imperial College in England, and I interviewed one of the subjects in this study, Carl Hayden Smith, for this book as well.

Gallimore's current interests focus on developing DMT as a tool for gaining access to these extra-dimensional realities and how this can be understood in terms of the neuroscience. Exploring this subject at length and in great depth from a more unconventional perspective, Gallimore's speculative books *Alien Information Theory: Psychedelic Drug Technologies and the Cosmic Game* and *Reality Switch Technologies: Psychedelics as Tools for the Discovery and Exploration of New Worlds* read like neuroscience textbooks from the future.

The unique and ambitious, unusually compelling book *Alien Information Theory* is based on the premise that DMT carries a profound message embedded in our reality, a message that we are now beginning to decode. Gallimore explains how DMT switches "the reality channel" in our brains, allowing us to access information from normally hidden, orthogonal dimensions of reality. Further, he describes how DMT may provide us with a secret understanding of the very structure of our reality and how our universe can be modeled as a cosmic game that we're all playing. I found it difficult to put this fascinating book down.

In *Reality Switch Technologies* Gallimore maps out the fundamental building blocks for how our brains create worlds, and helps to design the technologies that will open up portals to hyperspace and allow us

Andrew Gallimore

to travel to new dimensions of reality with great precision and sustainability. Focusing specifically on those psychedelics that bring shamanic voyagers into what appear to be parallel dimensions of reality—such as DMT, salvia, ketamine, and the deliriants—this extraordinarily ambitious work aims to solve the mystery of how our brains engineer realities, by integrating neurochemistry and pharmacology with psychology, philosophy, and psychedelic trip reports.

If Gallimore's speculation turns out to be true, then this appears to be the biggest scientific breakthrough in human history. For those of us who have experienced DMT breakthrough experiences, we can't help but think that Gallimore is onto something huge and exciting with his ideas about extended DMT state technologies. Gallimore also contributed a chapter to the wonderful book *DMT Dialogues: Encounters with the Spirit Molecule*, edited by David Luke and Rory Spowers. This is an extraordinary collection of essays that give serious thought and discussion to the possible reality of the DMT world, with additional contributions by Dennis McKenna, Rick Strassman, Graham Hancock, Rupert Sheldrake, and others.

Gallimore currently lives in Japan, where he is a researcher at the Computational Neuroscience Unit at the Okinawa Institute of Science and Technology. I interviewed Andrew via Skype on August 27, 2019. We discussed whether or not there's a reality to the seemingly advanced beings that people report encountering on DMT, how our body is represented in hyperspace, what it would be like to spend extended amounts of time in the DMT state, and the relationship between the DMT state, dreaming, and death.

How did you become interested in neurobiology and chemistry, and how have these scientific disciplines influenced your understanding of consciousness and the nature of reality?

ANDREW: Okay, that's a big question. My interest in chemistry really comes from an interest in psychedelics when I was a teenager, which I developed as I began to explore my world and explore drugs, as you naturally do as a teenager. But psychedelics really stood out to me as being particularly special types of drugs, and that inspired me to study chemistry—initially because I was interested in the drugs themselves and how they interact with the body.

So initially I studied chemistry and pharmacology toward that end, toward understanding the drugs and how they work. The fields of science that I explored felt like they came as a natural progression really, since psychedelics quite clearly act specifically within the brain. They affect the brain and they affect consciousness, which is, as you know, as a result of changes in brain activity. So it felt like a natural progression to me to study neurobiology.

My academic career has moved from the purely chemical all the way through to a much more neurobiological focus now. I think the importance of neuroscience and neurobiology is in really describing for me and leading me toward a much better understanding of the way that our world is constructed by our brain, which it is, all the time, under all circumstances.

This phenomenal world is always constructed from information generated by the brain, and what this neuroscientific underpinning to work with psychedelics has done is enabled me to understand at a much deeper level how psychedelics actually change the world and why they have these specific effects on brain activity. This leads to how we can relate those effects on the brain to these highly characteristic, fascinating, and astonishing effects on the structure of the world and the nature of one's personal reality under the influence of these drugs.

Oh, I can totally relate; it was psychedelics that got me interested in neuroscience as well. How did you first become interested in DMT and what were your personal experiences with it like?

ANDREW: Initially I became interested in psychedelics generally, actually before I'd ever taken any psychedelics, which is kind of a bit odd. So I wasn't a reckless drug user. I would never consider myself to be one of these fearless psychonauts. I always maintained a healthy respect for psychedelics, as all people should, of course, and I became particularly interested in DMT. I was at a friend's house when I was maybe fifteen years old, and he had a very old book called *Alternative London* that I was leafing through. There was a small section on psychedelics and the usual suspects were in there: LSD, mescaline, and magic mushrooms.

Then there was this short paragraph on DMT, which it called "the businessman's trip," and they described it as being similar to LSD, but only lasting for fifteen minutes. So I thought this is perfect; I can enter this state but I don't have to be stuck there for several hours. Little did I know at the time, of course, that DMT is not like LSD at all, but is a completely different beast. But that piqued my interest.

Then coincidently, maybe just a couple of weeks later, after I'd been talking about psychedelics to some of my friends in high school, one of my friends brought in a magazine and he said, "Oh you might be interested in this." It was just one of these regular weekly magazines, but on the back page they had an interview with Terence McKenna. This was the very first time I'd ever heard of Terence, and in that interview he discussed his favorite drug, which was DMT.

So that really piqued my interest. This was really the early days of the internet, so we didn't have the internet at home. You had to get a special password and a special cable from the IT technician if you wanted to actually log on to the internet at school. But that's what I did, and I immediately thought, okay I need to find out more about this drug and how I personally can get hold of it.

So I dug up what I could find. I went to Terence McKenna's website, the Alchemical Garden at the Edge of Time, and read all about DMT there. Then I was in the Lycaeum, which is one of the early psychedelic drug sites on the internet, before Erowid, DMT Nexus, and these other sites.

But that was the start of my fascination with DMT. From that point on, I was reading Terence McKenna interviews and reading transcripts of his lectures. This is before you could actually go onto YouTube and watch his lectures freely. It wasn't until maybe several years later that I actually managed to obtain DMT and smoke it—and that was the real game changer. That was when I realized that I was going to spend my life really studying this drug—trying to work out what that was, what the fuck it is, why it's there, and how it possibly can do what it does to the brain.

What was your first experience with it like?

ANDREW: I wouldn't describe the very first one as a breakthrough experience; it was what I would call a "sub-breakthrough." I recall that I had been attempting to vaporize the DMT, but I was inexperienced at it, so I wasn't very good at it and I failed quite a few times before actually getting enough into my body. Then one evening I was just about to go to bed and the pipe was on the table, so I thought, okay, I'll just give it one more attempt. So I vaporized it, took a lungful, and then finally something happened.

I felt this pop or this ping sound, and I laid back. Then it started. As I said, it wasn't a breakthrough experience, but I just remember being overwhelmed by this complexity, this astonishing, marvelously complex and rich geometry, and just everything. It was completely different from any kind of experience, any kind of structure, form, or visual experience that I had ever had in my entire life, and it completely shocked me. It shocked me really to my bones.

I remembered when I was coming back that first of all I forgot that I was a human. As I came back and the effects started to subside, I remember lying on my bed and just saying, "oh my fucking God," and shaking for several minutes really. That was the time that I realized that *this was it*. This really was as amazing as Terence McKenna had been ranting and raving about all these years. Of course, that part's just the first of my experiences and it certainly wasn't the deepest experience I've had, but it was, in a sense, the most important.

Most interesting. I've been doing interviews now since 1993 and the very first person that I interviewed was Terence McKenna. The first time that I tried DMT was back in 1983, and I recall coming out of the experience, thinking, oh yeah, I'm a human being who did a drug. That was a big revelation for me at the time because I had completely forgotten it.

ANDREW: Exactly. I lost any concept of what it meant to be a human, which was the weird thing. It's not like I forgot that I was human. Maybe I thought I was some animal or something, but actually the concept of being an embodied being was gone. Fortunately, it came back.

What are your thoughts about the entities that people report encountering on DMT; do you think there's a reality to these beings or do you think that they're just complex hallucinations?

ANDREW: I've never made an assumption on what I think these things are. I've always approached these entities without the assumption that they're hallucinations, and always with the assumption that they're actually conscious and real. The reason for this is because I think if you approach them assuming that they're not real, then that kind of bias can influence the information that you can get from them.

I think that the question of the reality of these beings is a really complex one. It's one I've written about, spoken about, and lectured about quite extensively, because it's the perennial question—not just the DMT entities, but the DMT state itself. *Is it real?* And the problem I think is partly with defining what we mean by real. I think most people fail to do that properly or fail to formulate that question properly.

So I've always tried to answer that question much more specifically and say, okay let's try to answer, perhaps, a smaller question, within that larger question of the reality of these things. So, for example, I've thought about how if these entities are real, then what do we mean by that? Well, in my opinion, a being is real if it has subjective consciousness. If something exists from its own side and has its own perspective, then it is real. It is just as real as we are.

Descartes famously showed that we could deny everything apart from our own mind. If these entities have subjective consciousness, then they are equally unable to deny their own existence, as we are unable to deny our existence—which, in my opinion, makes them real, completely real, really real. So do I think these entities have subjective consciousness? I go with the assumption that they do. They seem to have it, but how would one test that formally? I'm not sure.

These are the sorts of questions that I'm really interested in answering, and how we might approach these beings there. I think there's something quite impertinent about going into the DMT space and trying to test these entities for their ontological status, so to speak. So that's one approach to think about the entities. I've also thought about the structure of these worlds and whether the assumption that they are simply complex hallucinations actually holds water from a neuroscientific perspective. I wrote a paper in 2012, "Building Alien Worlds," in which I really went into a lot of detail on that.

Basically, the brain is a world builder. It evolved to construct our phenomenal world. Our world is a model of the environment, and it took millions and millions of years of evolution for the brain to develop a stable and predictable model of reality. So I struggle to understand how, when you flood the brain with this very simple molecule, the brain suddenly becomes capable of constructing, with effortless facility, worlds of unimaginable complexity. Worlds that are crystalline and clear and that are clearly not just maelstroms of chaos, so to speak, but are actually stable realities that are replete with these highly complex, intelligent entities.

I think from a neuroscientific perspective that's difficult to explain. It's confounding for me. It's simple to say, yes, these drugs are simply hallucinations, but when you actually have a look at the nature of hallucinations and the nature of the way your brain constructs reality, that assumption becomes more and more untenable.

Most interesting indeed! Yes, it's hard to even know for sure if another human being is actually conscious or not.

ANDREW: Right.

It's a very tricky question, I know. So my next question is about whether people report having bodies when they're in the DMT hyperspace realm or not. As we just discussed, when people are in the DMT hyperspace state they often report interactions with intelligent, non-human entities—like the self-transforming machine elves, praying mantis beings, et cetera—that clearly have bodies of some sort. For those who have experienced a DMT breakthrough and entered hyperspace, where these mysterious entities reside, do you recall if you—and other people that you've spoken to—have reported that they had a body during these experiences, or were they just a point of consciousness?

In other words, could you look down and actually see a version of your hands in hyperspace, along with a representation of your physical body, or could you just visually perceive the hyperspatial environment around you? Personally, I was able to see in 360 degrees while I was there, I recall, but I don't remember if I actually had a body in this reality or not, although I did think that an alien super-intelligence was experimenting on and adjusting my brain. Most of the people that I've spoken with say they don't recall having a body during these states. What's your perspective on this?

ANDREW: Okay, so this is a really interesting question. It's one that's actually poorly studied, and I think it would be an interesting research topic—because in my experience personally I don't recall having a body.

I certainly don't recall having hands and being able to manipulate reality with my hands. I personally recall being some kind of point of awareness within that space. A point of awareness that has agency, that can move and look around, but not specifically having a body. And as far as I know, I don't recall reading reports or hearing reports from people describing their hands and their feet. That would an interesting thing, to go through the online psychedelic trip report literature and actually look at that. Do people ever describe having hands? I don't ever recall it. However, as you point out, people do describe operations on their body. People report elves doing neurosurgery or alien-type beings performing some kind of act on them.

Sometimes it's some kind of surgical act, although other times it seems to stem from quite malicious interactions, such as when people are raped by reptilians and things like that. I think one of Rick Strassman's subjects experienced that. So there are certainly bodily experiences or experiences that would require having a body when people are in this space. Neurosurgery requires presumably that you have a brain, and being raped, I guess, requires some sort of body as well, as does all of this alien surgery. So yeah, for me, it's an open question. Personally, I've never experienced a body and I don't recall people experiencing a body, but that's as much as I can say on that I think, Dave.

You mentioned Terence McKenna earlier and you quote him in the introduction to your book Alien Information Theory. How did the late ethnobotanist influence your work, and what was your inspiration for writing Alien Information Theory?

ANDREW: Obviously, as I've mentioned, the first person that introduced me, if you like, to DMT was Terence McKenna. I guess for anyone who's interested in DMT Terence McKenna is *the man*, to an extent. That is, unless you take one of these contrarian, anti-Terence McKenna positions, which a number of people do and I think is completely unfounded, by the way.

There're obviously many different threads running through Terence's psychedelic discourse, and these vary from theories of evolution through to novelty theory and various other aspects. But for me personally, what really grabbed me and fascinated me about Terence was when he talked about "the Other"—this sense of an alien intelligence that permeates the psychedelic experience, and the way that he discusses, for example, the mushroom being from another planet, or the DMT entities being some kind of alien intelligence. For me, that's always been the particular aspect of Terence's discourse that I have found most fascinating.

I remember listening to an interview with Terence when he was actually talking about how everything is code, and he seemed to have some kind of deep intuition that our fundamental reality was constructed from information. For example, he talks about Philip K. Dick's science fiction novel *VALIS*, which describes this creature constructed from pure information, and in another talk he was speaking about how everything is code—down to the ground of reality up though to DNA, and including language, of course, which is a form of code.

So this idea of an alien intelligence and the idea of code and fundamental information coalesced into this deep inspiration for my book *Alien Information Theory*—which of course is all about how a fundamental code, a fundamental information generator, can self-organize and self-complexify to form intelligences, conscious intelligent beings such as ourselves.

How does this theory of information and reality construction that you're describing differ from what is commonly known as the simulation hypothesis?

ANDREW: The simulation argument, as you know, proposes that our reality is a simulation, whereas I'm proposing something that I would call an instantiation. I'll unpack that a little bit. Simulation theory suggests that our reality is digital, that it's constructed from information, and yes, so does my particular model. However, the simulation hypothesis suggests that our reality is a simulation.

Now, for something to be a simulation you require really two fundamental components. You require the simulation, which would be our world presumably, and the simulated, which would be the real world, whatever that is. So you need the real counterpart. If you go back to one of the most famous papers on the simulation argument by Nick Bostrom, a philosopher at Oxford University, called "Are You Living in a Computer Simulation?"[1] he describes post-humans, i.e., us in the future, wanting to simulate their ancestors, which would be us. So we would be the simulation of a long-dead ancestral population of humans that once lived. That's very different. That's a simulation, whereas I'm interested in what I call an instantiation. This means that we're not designed as such, but we are simply the result of the self-organization and self-complexification of information, which generates a form of reality and a form of intelligent beings—but not intelligent beings that are a simulation of real intelligent beings. *We are real.*

Just because we are constructed by information doesn't mean that we are not real, and it doesn't mean that there are some real counterparts to us existing somewhere. There are presumably many ways an intelligent being could design and make other intelligent beings. Alternatively, intelligent beings can be allowed to emerge in countless variations—instantiations, but not simulations—of a universe.

I'm really excited by your ideas about, and the implications of, a target-controlled, continuous intravenous infusion of DMT to keep someone in the hyperspace state for hours or longer. I think that's an amazing proposal and I'm just so curious to see what would come out of that. One of the things that I wonder about though, and I think you may have heard this before, is minor tolerance.

We've heard from Rick Strassman's studies, of course, that there doesn't seem to be any major tolerance built up with DMT, as there is with other types of psychedelic drugs, and this has important implications for the study that you've proposed. However, numerous people have reported online that there does appear to be some tolerance when it's vaporized repeatedly, and I myself have experienced this. I wonder if this is a difference in

1. N. Bostrom, "Are You Living in a Computer Simulation?" *Philosophical Quarterly* 53, no. 211 (2003): 243–55 (first version 2001).

modes of ingestion—IV versus vaporization—or how might this minor tolerance affect a target-controlled, continuous intravenous infusion of DMT?

ANDREW: Yes, so there're a couple of issues there. As you pointed out, what Rick did back in his 1990s studies was to use an intravenous bolus injection of DMT, given to people I think every thirty minutes, and then they would complete his hallucinogen rating scale. And he found that even after multiple injections—he needed five repeated doses—he found that the effect was the same. Now, that of course differs to what some people describe as the tolerance in the online trip report literature. From personal anecdotal reports people describe this tolerance.

It would be interesting to actually do that experiment a bit more formally, because vaporization and intravenous injection are not the same thing. I think it's very difficult for somebody who sat alone vaporizing DMT to really make a definitive judgment of tolerance. There are a number of factors that can influence one's experience with the P-T vaporization, as you would well appreciate, and they could be physiological things. It could be to do with the way the drug is absorbed via the lungs. That might vary over time. This is something of course you wouldn't get with injection. It could be other kinds of subjective effects. Or it could be a real tolerance effect that's somehow not picked up by Rick's study.

So it's something one has to think about and with an extended infusion protocol, of course that's something that's quite important. It's important that the effect of these drugs doesn't diminish over time, or at least doesn't significantly diminish over time. If there is a very small amount of tolerance it might not be an issue because there is a window of activity that you're aiming for, a window of effects rather than a very high specific level, which means that small amounts of tolerance might not actually have an effect.

But these are the sort of things that would come out of actually implementing this model that I've developed with Rick in humans, learning whether there actually is significant tolerance. But I'm not

100 percent convinced by anecdotal reports of tolerance with vaporization, because I think it's such a crude way of administering it and there're so many variables that could perhaps influence one's experience of tolerance. Rick Strassman tried to avoid that by actually doing this much more formally, and his data suggests that there isn't tolerance.

Have you gotten a lot of people contacting you about wanting to volunteer to be in these experiments?

ANDREW: Yes. After I do a podcast or deliver a lecture, I normally get a flurry of emails saying, "What are the chances of me signing up for this and being a volunteer?" And I always have to politely decline and say that I'm not actually recruiting currently.

Can you explain what you mean when you say in your book that you think that the material world may be a "lower dimensional slice of a higher dimensional reality"?

ANDREW: Yes, this is fundamental to our discussion. When I'm thinking about DMT, I'm trying to understand, if this DMT world, this DMT space exists, what is its relationship to our world? And how is it possible that smoking DMT from our world can allow you to access that world? Really the question that I'm asking is, how does DMT allow information to flow from that reality into your brain—which is presumably part of our reality—and how does this change in brain activity allow us to build a model of this ultimate DMT space?

I've always had the feeling, the intuition, that our world is only a part of some much larger and more complex structure, and most people would probably agree with that. The question is, how is our world related to this other structure and can the other structure be accessed? There're certain features of the DMT state that are quite important here, such as this higher dimensionality of it. People describe going into a world with many more dimensions than this one and seeing four-, five-, six-, seven-, eight-, nine-dimensional objects, which of course is impossible within our three-dimensional spatial world at least.

So, in trying to think about that relationship in a way that people would be able to understand, for me it makes sense to think of our world as being a slice of this higher dimensional structure. It's part of this higher dimensional structure, but we only have access to our particular slice. The reason I use the word slice is because in the book I use this idea of these two-dimensional worlds basically to reduce our world to a two-dimensional one, which means that we can then think about higher dimensions without having to resort to abstractions. So, for example, we can reach into the third dimension.

I think of our world as being like a chess board, as being a two-dimensional world, and then if you get a stack of these chess boards, you get this three-dimensional structure, and that's similar to the higher dimensional reality. And we're locked within receiving information only from the squares in our two-dimensional slice. Now what DMT seems to do is allow us to receive information from the chess boards above and below us, which is basically the third dimension.

Of course in reality this would be a three-dimensional world that we live in, or three or more perhaps, which would be a slice of a much higher dimensional structure. Whether it's a nine-, ten-, fifteen-, twenty-, thirty-dimensional structure, I'm not sure about that, and somehow DMT allows the information to flow from this higher dimensional space. So we're always connected to this higher dimensional reality, or at least we're all structurally connected to this higher dimensional reality. But we're disconnected informationally. Information cannot flow, and it's DMT that is the key that allows information to flow from this higher dimensional structure into our lower dimensional slice.

It's so incredibly fascinating to contemplate all this. Why do you think that so many people equate the DMT hyperspace realm with the afterlife and the near-death experience—and also in this context, what do you think of the recent studies that show that DMT levels become elevated in rodent brains after they experience cardiac arrest?

ANDREW: Okay, this is a complex question. First of all, purely from a subjective perspective, people often get the feeling when they smoke

DMT that they've been there before. This sense of profound déjà vu is very common, and people describe going to the place they were before they were born. They also describe how they often get the intense sensation or intuition that this is the place that they will return to after they've died. So that's one aspect to this, which is purely subjective.

What that means is very difficult to say. Of course, the afterlife is associated with being a discarnate entity to an extent. People would report that one's soul leaves one's body and one enters the spirit world, the astral realm, or whatever you want to call it, heaven or hell. But so that obviously relates to the DMT space—in that in the DMT space also, one seems to become a discarnate entity. So that makes sense. Now, becoming a little more specific, people who have had near-death experiences, again anecdotally, report that the DMT experience is very similar to their near-death experience.

There's only of course a handful of people, a relatively small portion of the population, that've actually had true near-death experiences, but many of them who have also taken DMT do describe similarities there. This seems to have been borne out by recent studies by the Imperial College London team, who actually examined the commonalities between the NDE and the DMT state and found that they were very similar. What does that mean? I don't know.

But, of course, people are quick to jump on the old idea—again going back to the Terence McKenna and Jace Calloway ideas in the 1980s. Then of course by Rick Strassman, who really popularized the idea that DMT is perhaps "the spirit molecule" that is released by the pineal gland upon death and that it provides the conduit through which the soul exits the body. So that links in as well. People like to connect those dots, I think.

Now, more formally, I think the idea that DMT is released by the pineal gland at death is highly unlikely. I think the levels, the amount of DMT that the pineal would be required to release, would be way beyond its capabilities. It's a small structure. That doesn't mean that other structures couldn't be involved, such as larger areas of the brain. Or the lungs, for example, would be perhaps capable of secreting levels of DMT, and this then relates to ideas about these observations of elevated DMT levels, as you say, in cardiac arrest in rodents.

Many people would say that that supports the idea that presumably the DMT is allowing the rodent's soul to leave its body, or something like that. Again, I'm not sure we would make that leap, but it actually connects to something in terms of the actual prevailing science on this. There is a scientist named Ede Frecska who worked with Dennis McKenna on a hypothesis that DMT protects cells against hypoxia, or a lack of oxygen.

When cells, particularly brain cells, become starved of oxygen, they die, and what their studies have shown is that DMT actually protects these cells against some of the chemicals that are produced in these hypoxic states. Often it's not the actual lack of oxygen, but some of these highly reactive chemicals that are produced in a hypoxic state that are quite dangerous and can actually kill cells. DMT seems to protect against that.

So if you were a pure orthodox scientist on this matter, you would say that these rodents were producing DMT to protect their cells against hypoxia, which would result from the cardiac arrest. However, if you were of a more mystical bent, you might say that the DMT was being produced to facilitate the exit of the rat's soul from its body. Which camp you fall into, I think, is entirely up to you on this point.

What do you personally think happens to consciousness after physical death and the deterioration of the brain?

ANDREW: Ooh, yeah, that's a really difficult one. That's one about which I can't say too much, because first of all I really don't know. If I were a standard materialist neuroscientist, I would say that consciousness disappears and that's the end of it, but I'm not of that bent at all. I lean much more toward idealism, in the sense that I think that consciousness is somehow fundamental. I don't think that we will ever solve the so-called hard problem of consciousness. I have a subjective consciousness emerge in the world. I don't think we're going to solve that problem by assuming that *matter is fundamental.*

I think we have to flip and realize that consciousness itself is somehow fundamental, and that somehow consciousness is structured, or can self-organize and self-complexify to form these complex structures that have self-awareness, which we would experience as ourselves. So what happens after death? I don't think consciousness is ever destroyed. I think it simply changes its form, it reorganizes, so in the same way that matter isn't really destroyed, or energy isn't really destroyed, it simply changes its form.

Do I think that our personal consciousness continues? That I'm not sure of. I don't have any memory of having a personal consciousness in other lives. Is that simply amnesia on my part? Or is it because it's perhaps the wrong question to ask, I think—one really goes back to the Eastern traditions and thinks about ancient Hindu thinking on these topics. There are these Vedic ideas that actually there's only really one Self. There's only really one fundamental consciousness, which they would describe as Brahman. It takes many forms and it plays at creating worlds. It plays at playing different roles, different beings, and we're each just one of those beings.

So I don't necessarily think that when you die you are aware of your death, and that you travel to some other place or you travel to some afterlife. I think perhaps that your own personal consciousness does disappear, but then of course you'll be in exactly the same position as you were before you were born, right? Before you were born, you didn't exist There was no such thing as you, and yet what happened?

You popped into existence, emerged screaming from your mother's womb and there you were, a being that didn't exist now does, and you're going to be in exactly the same position when you die. Or that's one way of thinking about it; that you'll be in exactly the same position when you die as you were before you were born. Of course, we know what happened then—*you were born.*

So I lean intuitively on this idea, and I think that most likely what happens is that we return to this one fundamental consciousness that pops into existence, or forms points of view that emerge and pop into existence in this universe, and perhaps in many others. So I think we're all points of view from the same fundamental consciousness.

I've heard from numerous people, including Terence McKenna when I interviewed him, that when they smoke DMT in a dream or in a lucid dream, they have a full-blown DMT experience in the dream. I've experienced this myself as well. I've also heard that endogenous DMT levels in the human bloodstream peak in their 24-hour cycles at around 3:00 a.m. Is this true, and if this is true, do you think that there might be any relationship between DMT hyperspace and what people commonly experience as the dream realm?

ANDREW: I've heard Terence McKenna talk about DMT and dreaming, and I've also heard many other people talk about DMT and dreaming. Now, if we go back to the original idea—where did this idea that DMT is associated with dreams come from? We can trace it back to a biochemist named Jace Callaway, back in the 1980s, who wrote a paper that hypothesized that perhaps dreams were generated by the endogenous production of psychedelic tryptamines, such as DMT.

Now this is just an idea. I think now that we understand dreaming much better, we don't need to invoke psychedelic molecules to explain dreaming. Dreaming is really a construction of the world in the same way that your brain constructs your world when you are awake. The only difference really is that the brain doesn't have access to sensory information, which modulates and constrains that world. The brain is unable to test its model of reality against sensory information when you're in the dream state, which explains some of the characteristics of the dream state. But you don't need to invoke endogenous DMT production.

However, that theory, that hypothesis of Jace Callaway's, did lead to some studies such as people looking at DMT levels in the human body over time, but most studies didn't look at that. Most studies were really looking for support for the idea that schizophrenics were psychotic because they produced too much DMT. So they were looking at levels of DMT in the blood and the urine of psychotic patients, schizophrenic patients versus normal controls. They didn't really find significant differences, or this is extremely variable.

But there have been at least one or two studies that I'm aware of that have looked at levels of DMT in the body over time, throughout the day, and it's this study that would have shown levels peaking in the body in the middle of the night, which is what you would expect if DMT was responsible for dreaming. You would expect to see a peak in the early hours. However, I'm sorry to tell you that though, as far as I'm aware, in the published studies that I have looked at, there's no peak of DMT in the early hours.

I'm not sure where this claim came from. I've definitely heard Terence McKenna talk about it, because that was really what lead me to actually dig into the research a bit. Terence said that DMT levels peak during the night, but I've been unable so far to find any evidence for that. This is actually not surprising to me because most people's dreams are completely unlike the DMT state. If DMT was responsible for dreams then we would expect there to be a very close relationship there, but there doesn't seem to be.

Yes, dreams can become strange, and they can even become bizarre, but they very rarely approach the DMT state. Dreams tend to be continuous with the waking state. This is well known in dream phenomenology studies—it's called "the continuity hypothesis of dreaming," and it basically states that dreaming is continuous with waking. When you go into a dream, you're really entering the same world that you experience when you're awake.

Now then, coming to your question about having DMT experiences in a dream, that's a really interesting thing. Whenever the brain constructs a world, it retains some ability to do that. So if you smoke DMT a lot when you're awake, then the brain essentially retains some ability to reconstruct that experience, and so it's perhaps possible that the brain can reconstruct the DMT world without the actual presence of DMT. This would be in the same way that people can have flashbacks, which are quite rare actually, but people can have flashbacks of the psychedelic state when they are not under the influence of the drug. We know that happens sometimes with drugs like LSD, for example.

When the flashback phenomenon was first studied, it was assumed that perhaps LSD was imbedding itself in the tissues and was coming out of the tissues at certain points and having an effect again. But we now know that this isn't true at all. It's just that the brain retains some ability to reconstruct the psychedelic state even in the absence of the drug, to some extent, and perhaps that's what's happening with people who experience a DMT state in their dreams. My guess is that it would be people who were quite experienced with DMT, but I'm not sure.

You mentioned in an online exchange that you were familiar with the writings of the late author D. M. Turner and his 1996 book Salvinorin: The Psychedelic Essence of Salvia Divinorum. *I'm particularly interested in what you thought of his story that I sent you, about supposedly meeting a woman in hyperspace, from another, more advanced planet. The woman claims to have taken DMT inside a sealed, technological pod, where extensive scientific research centers were devoted to putting people in DMT states for extended periods of time, which she said was considered to be serious scientific study by her culture. This story reminded me of the target-controlled, continuous intravenous infusion of DMT that you've proposed and I wonder what your thoughts on this might be?*

ANDREW: Yes, so this is really interesting actually, because as you know, I've just spoken at Breaking Convention, and I'd been preparing my slides for that for a number of weeks now. I was going to discuss this continuous intravenous infusion protocol—not just the science behind it, but also the potential. I already had in my slides this idea that eventually what would happen is that people would be induced into the DMT state for many days, and that would require a much more sophisticated setup than simply infusing them with DMT. You would need to feed them intravenously, you'd need to deal with waste and that kind of thing.

So I had in my head this idea that rather than just being laid out on a table, you would actually be in something much more sophisticated, *like a pod*, and I actually had images, photographs from the movie *Alien*, I think it was, of these people within these science fiction pods. Then you contacted me with this story about this research center that this person had visited where they're actually put in these pods and DMT levels were elevated in their brain for extended periods—which is exactly what I have proposed here.

So that was kind of a bit spooky for me and I actually spoke about this—I did give you credit as well—in the second lecture that I gave at Breaking Convention this year.[2] I did actually describe this report from D. M. Turner, and yes, I think it's very interesting. I know critics or skeptics might say well, the idea of pods and suspended animation pods is hardly a new one, and that's entirely true. But the idea of putting someone in a pod and raising the levels of DMT in their brain and holding it there—that's a little bit more novel.

So that really creeped me out a little bit, this report from D. M. Turner. Of course I'm fully aware of D. M. Turner, and read a lot of his stuff online back in the late nineties, but this particular DMT trip report I wasn't familiar with. So whether there's some hidden connection there, whether D. M. Turner was actually accessing some future technology that humans will one day develop, and whether it's actually my technology that I'm developing here, who knows? We can wait and see there, but I think it's really interesting.

Wow, that's actually pretty mind-blowing for me to hear. Thank you for mentioning me in your lecture. They're also similar to the pods that the characters in the movie Avatar *used, where they controlled avatar bodies remotely from within with these life-sustaining pods. Maybe that was the movie that you were thinking of?*

ANDREW: Exactly.

---

2. A. Gallimore, "Towards a DMaTrix Machine: DMT for Communication with Alien Intelligences," presentation at Breaking Convention, YouTube (website), February 18, 2020. He mentions this strange synchronicity in his talk at 20:55 of the video.

What do you see as some of the most exciting technological developments and scientific advances going on in the world today?

ANDREW: There are many ways I could answer this, but I guess I should stick to my own particular fields. So for me, from a neuroscientific perspective, I'm particularly interested in virtual reality and augmented reality. I think virtual reality and the ability to construct worlds that are almost seamlessly indistinguishable from the real world is astonishing, because I think it will eventually lead to the point where we can enter these worlds and spend extended periods of time there. Perhaps we can even live out entire lives within these worlds.

When you push that idea far enough, you have to start questioning whether or not we're actually in one of those types of worlds already. Then that leads you to think about DMT and whether DMT is some kind of code embedded within our world that allows us to get a peek back at the original worlds. In the future, would we enter one of these virtual reality worlds and forget that we were ever human? Then perhaps the programmers on the outside would leave in clues for us.

They would allow us to remember and access the human world, the world back on shore, so to speak. And what form would that take? Would it be a little message in the screen that says, "Don't forget that you're a human"? Or would it be something more subtle? Would it be some kind of game? The idea of playing a game to remember who you are, remember that you're human again. That's really the whole premise of my book, which is the idea that we are indeed living within some kind of instantiation, a digital instantiation of a reality, and that DMT really does provide a clue.

It's like the crumbs that lead the way out of the forest in Hansel and Gretel; I describe in one of my articles that DMT is these crumbs that are twinkling, or these shiny pebbles that are twinkling in the moonlight, and leading us back home, where we once came from. So I see a lot of parallels between the DMT state potentially and the way that humanity is technologically advancing in that direction, in terms of virtual reality, which has become much closer to actual realities. So that's one thing.

The other thing would be of course artificial antelligence. I'm interested in the intelligences that we seem to meet and that we seem to have a sense for in the DMT state. Often most people struggle to actually define intelligence as such, but we seem to have this kind of intuition for it when we see it, when we see other beings. Like when we see chimpanzees using tools, we see intelligence there. When we see crows using primitive tools, then we see intelligence there, and when we meet beings in the DMT state we see extreme intelligence.

So it's an interesting question of how intelligence emerges, and how intelligence is constructed, and whether we can create—I wouldn't call them artificial intelligences—I would call them instantiation of intelligences really, and what that could mean for us. Would it mean the end of humanity when these intelligences become hyper- or super-intelligent? I'm not a doomsayer, in that regard, but I think that those things, virtual reality and artificial intelligence, over the next ten, twenty, thirty years, are going to grow and become exponentially more important, and where that will lead us, time will only tell.

When you look around at what's happening in the world these days, do you think the human species will survive the next hundred years or do you think that we're doomed to extinction?

ANDREW: I think that we're at a critical period and two things could happen. We could either kill ourselves, and perhaps the planet, within the next hundred years or less, and there are a lot of people of course shrieking about that possibility. I'm not. I try to remain optimistic. The idea that the Earth is a cradle of mankind is something I talk about a lot. Again, as Terence McKenna used to say quite a lot, the Earth is the cradle of mankind, but one doesn't remain in the cradle forever. And I think about the possibility of us not just leaving Earth, but actually leaving this universe entirely, and actually shedding the body.

Again, this is something that comes to an extent from science fiction really, but of course we all know that science fiction often becomes science fact. Terence McKenna has spoken about this idea of shedding the material body, and if my idea, and the thoughts of other people, is correct, that this reality really is constructed from information, then it might be possible to transfer our consciousness, to transfer our intelligence, into this higher dimensional space. So it would allow us to essentially leave materiality behind permanently.

This has been met with some degree of pushback and outright hostility from some people who think that I'm promoting some kind of DMT death cult, that I'm saying that people should commit suicide using DMT, which of course I'm not. But I am looking to the future and I think we should take the idea seriously that perhaps, to an extent, we are outgrowing the cradle, and it makes sense that when you outgrow the cradle you think of ways that you might leave it. That might take the form of a rocket ship. It also might take the form of DMT or some other, different kind of internal technology that would allow us to exit materiality entirely.

So I don't think we should dismiss those ideas. I think those big ideas will seem less outrageous in five years, ten years, or twenty years. I think these things tend to develop exponentially, and that again relates to the idea from the last question about virtual reality and artificial intelligence, and that we might be able to, in a sense, upload ourselves, or transfer, transcribe ourselves into this, into higher dimensional space, and then perhaps leave the world behind, leave the Earth behind. We can leave the Earth to recover and allow some other species perhaps to rise to the top of the chain.

Because as long as we're here, we're certainly by far the most dominant species, and that's not going to change. So either we can learn to live within this world and get our act together pretty sharpish, or the alternative is for us to actually say, okay, we've outgrown this place, we're doing more harm than good here now, let's leave.

Do you see any type of teleology, intelligence, or mindful intention operating in nature and the evolution of life, or do you think that evolution is occurring by blind chance? If you do think that there's some teleological influence, what do you think the ultimate goal of human evolution might be?

ANDREW: First of all, I think there is clearly intelligence, which takes the form of us and other intelligent species. We each have our own personal teleology, and we feel we are directed toward some greater goal. So in that sense there is some teleology there. I certainly don't think that evolution is teleological. Evolution is, as Richard Dawkins called it, "a blind watchmaker."

It's not blind chance as such, in that evolution is a process of exploring the possibility space, using random mutations, and then selecting those that are the most adaptive. Evolution is a very slow process, but it's a very effective process, and it's been extremely effective in generating the diverse forms of life and intelligent conscious beings on this Earth. I don't think one needs to adapt the theory of evolution to explain teleology.

I think teleology is a natural consequence of intelligence, and that we are the primary intelligent beings, one would say, at least on this Earth, although probably not within the universe. And I guess all beings have their own sense of what the ultimate goal for them is. For me, I see humans as having almost unlimited potential, and with that one might agree with Henri Bergson's vision of the universe as a machine for making gods. I think that many deep thinkers would say that that is our ultimate goal, right? To be gods, in the sense that we would have perhaps a level of intelligence and power that is almost unthinkable now.

I don't mean power in any authoritarian sense, but in the idea that actually we can reach levels of intelligence that are way beyond anything that we could experience now. So I don't see an end. I don't see a finishing point, so to speak. I see this as an open-ended goal of progression through different possibilities. Whether it means leaving the Earth behind, leaving perhaps initially and populating other areas of the universe, or perhaps ultimately leaving the universe entirely. What would it mean after that? I'm not sure, but that would be the next step, I think, in our evolution.

I asked that question to Terence McKenna years ago, what he thought the ultimate goal of human evolution was, and he paused for just a second and then said, "Oh, a good party." [Laughter] So you've just anticipated this next question, but I'd just like to see if you wanted to say any more about it. How do you envision the future evolution of the human species, and the future relationship between human biology, advanced technology, and DMT?

ANDREW: Yes, I think I've covered that. I think what's clear now is that there is a close relationship between advanced technology, certainly in terms of intelligence, and artificial intelligence and virtual reality, and those aspects of human biology that most interest us, like the way that our brain works, and the way that we construct our reality around us. The boundaries between the technological and the biological are beginning to blur now with augmented reality and virtual reality, et cetera, and that will only continue.

And with DMT, how that relates to all of this is again an open question. But I have my own ideas, which I talk about in the book, which I've discussed—the idea that DMT is this *clue*, this *message* really, that is embedded within this programmed encoded reality that perhaps allows us to access the deeper levels of the program, or the higher dimensional areas of the program, or something like that.

What is your perspective on the concept of god?

ANDREW: Hahaha. [*Laughter*] That's again, a very heavy question, a very deep question. I avoid using the word *god* because it's such a loaded word. I don't subscribe to the idea of a god in the Abrahamic sense, the idea of a god to whom we must lay down and prostrate ourselves and worship. Or a creator god, a designer god. I don't subscribe to that idea. Going back to what I was speaking about earlier on consciousness, I would see god as being the fundamental Self.

I would take the Vedic or the Buddhist concept of god, which is the fundamental Self, which is being, consciousness, bliss. It's the fundamental "isness" of reality. I would say that we're all different points of view of that same fundamental consciousness. We're all a different mask on god. What is G. K. Chesterton's line in his poem "Gold Leaves"?

"The million masks of God." We are just one of those, I think.

So god would be the Self. It would be Brahman. It would be the fundamental reality, the fundamental whatever there is, *that*—the fundamental "isness" I think—is god. But I don't see god as being a king, or a king of kings, or something that we need to look up to as such. I think everyone is their own personal manifestation of god.

What are you currently working on?

ANDREW: Good question. I'm working on a number of things. Academically, I'm a computational neurobiologist, so I'm continuing to work on trying to model some of the effects of psychedelic drugs on brain activity, and I'm trying to understand how effects at the receptor level can give rise to such interesting effects at the more global level in the brain. So that's my more academic work. I'm also thinking about my next book, after *Alien Information Theory*, which will be very different. I'm just in the early, nascent stages of working on that now, so you'll have to wait and see what that one's about.

16

Delving into DMTx

An Interview with Carl Hayden Smith

Carl Hayden Smith is co-founder of the Cyberdelics Society, founder of the Museum of Consciousness, and director of the Learning Technology Research Centre at the Institute for Creativity & Technology at Ravensbourne University London. His research concentrates on the relationship between technology and the human condition. Carl focuses on how technology can be used as a catalyst for developing our own innate human abilities rather than taking over from humanity altogether. Carl has spent twenty-four years conducting research into the development and application of hybrid technologies for perceptual, cognitive, and creative transformation. He has given hundreds of lectures around the world and published more than a hundred academic papers.

Smith was also a subject in the extended-state DMT study being conducted at Imperial College in England, which Andrew Gallimore and David Luke discuss in their interviews for this book. Smith was the first person to sustain the full five doses of DMT in the extended-state experience, during the pilot phase of the study. To learn more about DMTx research, see "DMT Continuous Infusion—Extending the Experience," Insight Conference website, October 9, 2021.

———————————————————— ☙ ————————————————————

I interviewed Carl on October 16, 2022. I found him to be a wellspring of novel ideas, and he was very passionate about his experiences and the insight they have given him for his work and research directions. We

368

Carl Hayden Smith

discussed what his extended-state DMT journeys were like, the type of entities that he encountered and the messages conveyed, as well as the future of DMTx research.

CARL: I'm just back from the DMTx symposium at the Tyringham Initative. Have you heard much about how that went?

I haven't. It must have been incredibly fascinating.

CARL: Indeed, having so many luminaries in the room, everywhere you turn another world of insight arises. It was quite something.

Who was there?

CARL: Dennis McKenna, Erik Davis, Graham Hancock, Rupert Sheldrake, Merlin Sheldrake, Jill Purce, Andres Gomez Emilsson, Andrew Gallimore, Chris Timmermann, P. D. Newman, amongst many others. There were a lot of people that are in your book actually.

It was an extraordinary place to be able to open the proceedings with my trip report in the opening session of the symposium, which was dedicated to the DMTx experiment. We discussed various aspects of the three months of "DMT Church," as Chris and I like to call it. It feels like it's been a long time since we did the experiment and there are still some aspects that I am not allowed to go into, but the Tyringham Initative was the first time we were allowed to talk about it; however, this was not at a public event—it was by invite only.

I'd imagine that a great book will be coming out of that meeting, like with the last two.

CARL: Yes, there will be another full book forthcoming, which will be the third in the DMT dialogues series. I understand that everything will be transcribed from both the talks and the dialogue from the three-day event.

Great, thank you. First, can you speak a little about your background and your research that focuses on the relationship between technology and the human condition?

CARL: I've spent twenty-five years researching cognitive science, machine learning, and more recently neuroscience, especially in terms of these practical real-world applications. In all of these fields I am looking at consciousness through different perceptual lenses. These areas of endeavor are essential for what I call context engineering, which reflects the trend that we are moving into a new economy where it's all about changing your perception and your senses rather than consuming more content-based media.

There are examples of this trend everywhere—the move away from content engineering where we are just creating new content to be consumed, to the ability to change the way we actually sense. For instance, I've worn a 360-degree vision device for a week that allowed me to mimic what comes up a lot in DMT reports, where suddenly people have 360-degree vision. So, it is the ability to upgrade your hardware as well as your software, the operating system you are running your reality on.

Sensory and perceptual augmentation is a big part of my research. I have a background in using technology to create altered states, building Cyberdelics. I also founded the Museum of Consciousness, where the challenge to the artist is can you create a reliable, measurable altered state just using sound alone? In essence, with these projects I am focused on using nondrug routes that generate these novel forms of consciousness augmentation.

I'm very interested in the human condition and how technology impacts us. I think we urgently need to counter the transhumanist agenda very seriously with what I refer to as hyperhumanism. This is because the narrative, the consensus belief, is it is inevitable that we will become cyborgs and that resistance is futile and life extension is what we should all be aiming for.

However, I think it's absolutely not OK to outstay our welcome when living on a finite planet with finite resources. I think the transhumanists have got it utterly wrong. Hyperhumanism is about using technology for short periods of time to create a stimulus or scaffolding for your own human abilities to come to the fore. It's a bit like when you first learned to cycle a bike and you had stabilizers for a short period of time to help you learn. But then you remove the stabilizers after you have that ability. It's the same with technology—don't become dependent.

So it's not a Luddite perspective, but rather about rebuilding and reframing the human experience from the perspective of using the latest technologies as a catalyst for social good, and actually bringing back the analog abilities that we've lost through the digital addiction and digital distancing. Digital tech has largely made us much less resilient and much more prone to attack, especially from the design methodologies of big corporations.

I think it is obvious to a lot of people that it is the Indigenous people that will survive when the main infrastructure collapses. So that is a big part of what hyperhumanism is about: *it's about looking at the Indigenous culture.* Why are they so much more resilient? This question can also be approached by looking at other species and other kingdoms like the mycelium kingdom.

I'm currently working on a project called Umwelt Hacking where we use analog prosthetics to place ourselves into the umwelts of different kingdoms. The term *umwelt* refers to the self-centered world that every species exists within. Therefore, each umwelt is a new opportunity to experience the same world in vastly different ways. This is the essence of context engineering, to radically change your sensorial system in order to understand what it is to be an octopus, a forest, or a mycelium network. The insight gained is intended to give us clues about our own humanity—what are we actually good at and what are we not very good at? We are busy destroying almost all the other life-forms on this planet and it's all about exploring this experientially—to question why is that?

What had your experience with DMT and other psychedelics been prior to the extended DMTx study experience?

CARL: I started out with DMT via changa around fifteen years ago but I had an out-of-body experience at the age of twenty-seven, which really defined my perspective. The OBE was also a nondrug experience where I walked into an empty room in my friend's flat in Brighton and literally went out of body; I was standing up. It was an auspicious day in the sense that it was New Year's Eve 1999, when the Y2K bug was meant to kick in, but I had this experience of becoming a ginormous beam of light, and it was extraordinary and unlike anything I'd ever experienced before.

A disembodied voice then said to me, "You are not Carl. You are having the experience of being Carl, but that is not all of what you are. For instance, now look, you are in a wheel of light with eight other bodies," and sure enough I could see this wheel of light with nine spokes of light. "Your soul is inhabiting eight other bodies in parallel. You're only aware of Carl, but there're eight other bodies." It was a bit of a sensate moment, and then this same voice said, "Look up, because you're in a larger body of light as well." But before I could see what this larger body of light was, I was pulled back into my body, and I was still standing up.

This was a nondrug experience, but then I sought out DMT, thinking that maybe this had been an endogenous DMT experience. I found DMT approximately ten years later and I realized the OBE was completely unlike DMT; from a phenomenological perspective it was a very different experience.

Years later I was reading *The Book of Knowledge: The Keys of Enoch* by J. J. Hurtak, and he describes my OBE as a place. It is called "the programming station of OR," and it has these nine spokes of light. So this really struck me, that this OBE maybe took place in an actual place.

But DMT has also given me so much in other ways. In the early days I would drink a lot of Syrian rue tea before doing changa. I find changa, unlike pure crystal N,N-DMT, to be like smokable ayahuasca. It provides extraordinary open-eyed visuals; the DMT realm seems to bleed directly into the room.

I was told very early on by the DMT Nexus guys that the best pipe to get was the Glass Sherlock—Vapor Genie as this enables 60 milligrams of N,N-DMT to be vaporized all in one go, producing a full breakthrough reliably. So that was a bit of a game changer and allowed me early access to really try and map out the DMT space.

This was followed by six years of being a participant on the DMT studies at Imperial College London. I was lucky to be involved in the research from the start. The first phase was intravenously administered DMT with EEG only. The second phase was EEG combined with fMRI.

I don't know if you've ever been in an fMRI scanner, but it's not pleasant. I'm not a claustrophobic person, but I think getting in there makes anyone claustrophobic. The largest dose in the fMRI scanner was one of the most profound experiences of my life. The effect the scanner had on the experience was remarkable. It was as if a huge light had gone off in the DMT realm announcing my arrival and it was amazing in terms of the amount and variety of entities that arrived en masse.

They were all very concerned about why I was being scanned, as if to say, we are the ones that normally scan you, what is going on here? Why are you being scanned? And what is that terrible noise? They were all very concerned for me. In fact, they were so concerned that they immediately showed me, telepathically and visually, that I am immortal in nature. It's difficult to explain, but it was a visual depiction of immortality, like here you are, look, you are made of light, and they even added ticker tape in order to underline the point and help me retain the memory, and it worked instantly to calm me down.

This was followed by more telepathic "dialogos": "This is not scheduled. You're not meant to die now. You're in a human body right now. Don't die, whatever you do." So I had to spend my time calming down the entities, which is obviously a radical departure from the usual situation. I had to explain to them that I was actually in an experiment and that this was nothing to worry about.

I had to go back in two weeks later for the next scan, but as the entities had warned me that I should not be doing this, I had some serious reservations. What was then fascinating about that experience was that there were absolutely no entities present. It was exactly the same experiment with the same dose, I entered the same landscape, but there were zero entities, as if to say, we already told you, so what are you doing back? We're not going to tell you again. So this appears to demonstrate that there is indeed some sort of independent and continuous existence of the entities.

How did it come about that you were the first subject to participate in the extended state DMTx study?

CARL: I was lucky that I was one of six in the pilot group that preceded the main group of testers. The testers were used to find the right dose for the main experiment. These were all very experienced psychonauts who had been selected due to their extensive experience with DMT.

We were doing another dose every three weeks and the dose gradually increased over the five sessions. I was the very first person to take the fifth dose out of everyone in that group of six. Not many people made it. In fact, only four out of the full twenty made it to the fifth dose. Sixteen out of twenty didn't make it through the full dosing range.

What was the reason that they didn't make it?

CARL: This is an extreme experience and not for the fainthearted. That fifth dose was exponentially different to the rest. I think that the DMTx experiment certainly gives a whole other level to the term immersion.

How long were you in for and what was the experience like?

CARL: The session is an hour long, but the peak of the experience lasts thirty minutes. There is a lead in and lead out of the experience over the course of that hour. But it's a full day each time, in terms of preparation. It takes an hour alone to put on the high-density EEG cap with 256 points. It makes you look a bit like a Knight Templar.

I've been an avid researcher of 5-Meo-DMT since 2012 and I've always been fascinated by the question of what is beyond the white room? What is producing the light? You are having a non-dual experience, and it's astonishing, but that has always been my question. My working hypothesis regarding entheogens such as N,N-DMT and 5-Meo-DMT is that they provide access to different relationships with light, different light bodies.

Consider base reality, in our everyday 3-D reality light shines upon us from the sun. In N,N-DMT experiences, including changa or ayahuasca experiences, light is often experienced as emitting from objects. Let's call this for argument's sake 5-D. It looks holographic, a bit like virtual reality. Whereas with 5-Meo-DMT you become light itself as the subject/object relationship collapses. You become infinite. You become eternal and you know that you are at the Source. Let's again for argument's sake call this 11-D.

Then you float back into your human experience in a quite speedy descent. That's the cosmic joke, that you get to be this double consciousness of being the source and the human at the same time. I think that's an incredibly powerful muscle to build.

What is interesting about this hypothesis is that one of the main findings from Chris Timmerman is that the brain looks like it is dreaming whilst on N,N-DMT, even though experientially it feels very different from dreaming; you have this astral or light body, which seems to correlate with my experience of light emitting from bodies whilst I am on N,N-DMT.

So going into my fifth megadose DMTx experience, I was amazed to actually receive a key from the entities; this quickly resulted in me witnessing the 5-Meo-DMT experience from within the DMTx experience. I could see the unity of the 5-Meo-DMT experience as a white hole or floating disc at the bottom of my bed.

I was somehow acting as a bridge between the N,N-DMT and the 5-Meo-DMT state spaces. That's what the key seemed to give me, the experience of the third dimension, the fifth dimension, and the eleventh dimension, all within the same room. I was bridging all those dimensions simultaneously through the vehicle of the N,N-DMT extended experience.

If that wasn't enough, the best was yet to come . . . as I was looking at the non-duality disc at the bottom of the bed, contemplating how I could navigate my way into it, there was this dramatic cracking apart of the non-duality disc and I expected a return to duality, but instead I actually saw behind the unity, and what was revealed was a plurality of unities, a plurality of non-dualities. It was astonishing.

So, this seemed to be answering my question of what is beyond the white room—what is producing the white light? The answer being a multiverse of non-dualities, or a plurality of unities. It was something that made me realize there is not just life as we know it, or even DMT life—there are also many other different types of existence that are completely different to anything we can currently imagine. Very different physics, utterly alien to what we have here, and it was a massive moment of traversing the dimensions. The whole fifth dose felt like I had completed some form of training and I had as a result been granted access to this sacred knowledge.

Was this a breakthrough dose? You say you would open up your eyes and see the room—so you were still in touch with your body?

CARL: Yes, interestingly I was very much embodied. That's why I said it was like being a bridge between these vastly different dimensions or orthogonal realities. It was absolutely a breakthrough experience; probably one of the most hardcore breakthroughs.

I was going back to Imperial every three weeks to do each of the five different doses. The entities were eventually all like, oh no, not you again! We told you last time that you don't need to come back so often, and then they would begrudgingly give me some psychic surgery anyway.

Can you describe the entities more? What did they look like?

CARL: There were very different types of entities, but they are all made of this holographic light, it's like an architecture of light language, and the environment is made of this light mesh as well. One of the entities looked like a street bollard but it was made of this language. Many of the entities were also very octopus-like—very "arm-y." I was being given the key that I mentioned by multiple arms, and I had to actually grab it in physical space, in the hospital bed, and it was actually behind me. I've always been asking the entities, what is that light language? It is persistent at the center of my vision.

There are other motifs in my DMT experiences, one being where I may have a guide in the bottom right corner of the "screen," and it looks like a signer on TV who is signing for the deaf. This guide generally has a female essence and is giving me the thumbs up or thumbs down as if to say either go ahead and take more DMT, or thumbs down meaning, whoa, slow down, you have had enough to be where you need to be now.

Another part of N,N-DMT literacy is there seem to be three distinct stages to the DMT experience. In the first stages you're rushing through this geometry. In the second phase you get to some sort of door, and then that door opens into a tunnel. That tunnel can be a tunnel of eyes, or as I've experienced a tunnel of flesh. Then if you get through the tunnel, you get to this entirely other world, "entirely other," as Andrew Gallimore calls it. It's a very different reality than that you are in now.

Did your experience of this space or world become stabilized?

CARL: There was hardly any stabilization unfortunately. I think that that's something that could come with longer durations in the experiment. But I would say that it's very much me moving and being thrown through these interfaces and being granted access to different spaces. There are structures that are recognizable as spaces but they're moving spaces like being on a giant escalator. They're not stable enough for me to walk through. I'm navigating around them like a spider in a multidimensional web. It was very much like falling into these interfaces and revolving through these doors. But yeah, not very stable, that's for sure.

What kind of differences have you noticed between the extended-state DMT experiences and your regular DMT experiences or ayahuasca experiences?

CARL: According to Gallimore, the ayahuasca experience is about 20 percent DMT. DMTx is 100 percent DMT, prolonged. The extra duration creates both the promise and the peril over the usual DMT experience.

It seems like it would be difficult to maintain mental stability and stay with those incredible energies without being overwhelmed. You're very brave; it clearly takes a lot of courage. How were you able to do it? What do you think it is about you personally that makes you built for this kind of extreme experience?

CARL: I treated it as a challenge, as a form of deep Zen meditation for three months; I've always been fascinated with consciousness, and this was one of the deepest of all possible dives. It was nerve-wracking each time, even at the lower doses, because you don't know what is going to come up. I knew I would get a lot out of it because I feel absolutely privileged to be able to do these experiments and help advance our understanding of what consciousness is.

I'm also really interested in the long-term effects of these entheogens on my brain, because I gave up alcohol three or four years ago. I spoke to Robin Carhart Harris about this and he said, "Carl, I've heard you've given up alcohol." "Yes, Robin," I replied, "because if you drink alcohol, you dissolve your brain cells, and then you piss them out. You're literally pissing out your own brains." N,N-DMT, and 5-Meo-DMT especially, seem to offer the exact opposite, neuroplasticity and neurogenesis, the creation of new brain cells.

I think the reason why I was able to cope so well during the DMTx trials is because of the framing I adopted going in. I saw the extended-state protocol as a technology, and because I look at technologies and how they affect the human condition for a living, it felt like an extension of my work practice.

My research involves cataloguing each technology in terms of its effect on humanity. Unfortunately, most technologies atrophy our abilities and we also expect a one-button solution for everything. So I think we need to build friction back in, and I think that the N,N-DMT experience certainly provides that friction.

What are your thoughts on whether the entities that one meets on DMT have a genuine independent existence or not?

CARL: I'm as convinced as I can ever be, particularly because of that first experience of having an intravenous injection of DMT inside an fMRI scanner. The effect the scanner had on the interaction with the DMT entities was remarkable because it amplified their benevolence a hundredfold. Being propelled into a form of dialogos with these entities that was telepathic and visual at the same time was something that was so embodied that I will never be able to forget it. This experience more than any other appeared to demonstrate that they have some sort of independent and continuous existence.

However, I think that the problem with using too much DMT is that you are welcomed back less and less, you are crying wolf too often. DMTx allows you to stay inside the experience, but I suspect you are not meant to stay there. It's like the guides are saying to you, "Not you again. It's not your time."

Someone actually dying and having what we suspect is an endogenous DMT experience versus those having a self-induced DMT experience could potentially be causing more and more potential tension in [hyper]space. I think that there's a lot of traffic already and DMTx may only be adding to that traffic.

What are your thoughts on doing extended-state studies with 5-Meo-DMT?

CARL: Since the Tyringham Initiative event, Rick Strassman has said that he doesn't believe 5-Meo-DMT experiences are going to catch on because of the reactivations. He was reporting something insane, like 65 percent of people are reactivating.

When you say "reactivating," you mean flashbacks?

CARL: Yes, flashbacks. Strassman said that is something that will stop it from becoming popular, but I would question whether these reactivations are always negative. I think that 5-Meo-DMT acts as a key that unlocks something in the brain, and then it is an open pathway.

I think it all comes down to training both in terms of what Timmerman calls psychedelic apprenticeship and seeing these entheogens as a form of technology that is programmable. For instance, one technique I use to program the 5-Meo-DMT state space is to play singing bowls to people who are in the liminal space between the peak of the experience and the return to baseline. This sound is then imprinted on that memory and then when listening to the singing bowls sober, it can trigger a reactivation of the 5-Meo-DMT experience. So this is the power of imprinting, and that is what I mean by it as a technology; it is programmable.

I think body set is crucial as another form of programming psychedelic experiences. I programmed my body set by not having any orgasms for a month before going into one of the DMTx sessions. This was designed to see how that would affect the journey and it massively enhanced the experience. So, I think there is a lot more research to be done to see how our individual body set is affecting the resulting trips.

Also using the breath is another method I use for programming my trips. For me it is the main way of navigating the N,N-DMT space, and that was one of the things I couldn't do in the first phase of the trial at

Imperial College London, primarily because the EEG equipment was too sensitive to motion artifacts and I was like, "Guys, you need better equipment, because that's how you navigate the DMT realm."

Have you had much experience with lucid dreaming, and if so, have you ever accessed DMT realms through dreaming?

CARL: Absolutely, I had a tremendous lucid dream where I actually went in through locked-in syndrome. I was trying to move my arm and I couldn't move my arm, and I was like, oh my god, I'm locked into my body. Then I tipped back into my consciousness and fell asleep wide-awake, which is a standard way to access the lucid dream state.

It was an eight-hour experience, and it felt like a full-on DMT trip. Light was emitting from objects. Light was emitting from my body and I was in a hotel that was made of light. I was actually being tortured in this hotel by groups of people who were dismembering me into pieces. I couldn't feel any pain, but I could feel the torture, the trauma of being dismembered. Multiple groups dismembered me, multiple times, over the course of that eight hours. My body would be dismantled into nothing and then I would be re-membered. Then it would happen again and again. At one point, I was like, damn this, I'm going to jump out the window and kill myself. So, I jumped out of the window as if I'd jumped out of windows many times before and I experienced this huge relief that I was about to die to escape this horrible circumstance.

Unfortunately, however, as I came to the ground, expecting to hit the floor, my body slowed right down like something out of *The Matrix*, and then I just stood up, but there was this woman in front of me who had gray hair with a young face. She was waving her finger at me saying, "There is no death here, son." And I was like, damn I can't die here, and then they carried on torturing and dismembering me.

Then I woke up from this lucid dream, and my girlfriend who was next to me said, "What the hell's happened to you?" She could see I'd been through this torment. It felt hyper-real. So it was amazing when four days later, I was working with David Glowacki on the Isness Project and Rachel Freire was running the study on that particular day and she turned out to be the woman from my lucid dream. I find it fascinating that you can experience precognition in lucid dreams and psychedelic states such as DMTx.

David Luke advised me later on that shamanic initiation is all about being dismembered in the astral. Chris Timmerman also pointed out to me that the experience could relate to my journaling practice, which could lead to me creating an AI of myself and that this lucid dream may be a warning not to go down that path because then that AI self may not be able to die.

Where do you think the future evolution of artificial intelligence is headed, and what are your thoughts on the concept of the Singularity?

CARL: I think Ray Kurzweil is way off the mark. I actually did a back-to-back keynote with Ray before the pandemic in Melbourne, and I focused on countering his transhumanist agenda with the concept of hyperhumanism.

I think that the vision of the Singularity is naïve because I was recently at a Žižek talk and, as he points out, the four horsemen of the apocalypse have already been dispatched. We've got Covid. We've got the war in Ukraine. We've got the breakdown of supply chains, and widespread death could be the result. The Singularity is dependent on electricity, and I think that the electricity problem could become a big problem. I think people haven't really grasped how expensive it may become. I also think that there is a lot of interesting machine learning going on but no artificial intelligence. I don't believe sentience is imminent.

I think that there are certain dangers, mostly with widespread unemployment from these machine-learning algorithms. I think that that is more of a concern, that we will wipe out our ability to earn money because of the machine learning.

What do you personally think happens to consciousness after physical death and the deterioration of the brain? Have your DMT experiences influenced your perspective on this?

CARL: I believe that consciousness is primary and the material world is derived from consciousness and I am very reassured by that worldview. My DMT experiences have given me access to a parallel universe but it feels orthogonal to this one, in terms of a likely dependence, i.e., you need the human existence in order to access the DMT realm.

However, my nondrug experiences have been even more important with regard to my understanding and literacy of death; I often find myself exploring the phenomenology of death. For instance, I had this life review at the age of forty where I experienced my entire life in reverse, my whole life up until that point was available "as a product." I think because of my OBE at twenty-seven, I had this additional literacy in the life review, which meant I was able to move from point of view (POV) to field of view (FOV); this meant I could leave my body and go into anything else in the scene. I had the freedom to experience what it was like to be the Other. The first thing I tried was to go into a table and become wood consciousness; then I went into films I had watched in order to become the actors or books I had read to become the author. What was interesting was that I had to experience the point of view in life in order to access this field of view in death.

I think that death is an expansion of consciousness, not a contraction. If you look at the work of Zach Bush, his work in ICUs around the world where he is experiencing people dying and then resuscitating them, you'll see that invariably the patients are all saying the same thing: "What the hell are you doing? I was experiencing the light. I was experiencing this other realm, and you brought me back to this broken body."

So those messages of the other side are what we should be telling the dying, and I think that it's a massive mistake to want to outstay your welcome here as a transhumanist. This could just be the waiting room or training space and a stepping-stone to another realm. I think that the human experience is to be treasured. It is probably extremely rare.

I think that we have won the jackpot being human, and therefore maybe we should not be constantly trying to hijack that human experience with altered states that lead nowhere. That's one of the dangers of the DMT extended experiment—that it just becomes another *Game of Thrones*, another form of entertainment.

Today I've been to a graveyard with my mum and we find it fascinating to read the tombstones and imagine those contexts and attempt to map those to the commonalities of today, but mostly we learn how we all become stories, set in stone. I think we fear death, and we fear it as this huge taboo, not ever getting to know the phenomenology of it, not dying before we die. I'm really interested in the flatliners' experiences, medical doctors who intentionally stop their hearts for short periods just to see what's on the other side. I also know people that drown themselves to get a glimpse of what is on the other side.

What is your perspective on the concept of god?

CARL: I'm a firm believer that there is some sort of designer god. I mean, if you are going to hide the keys to the kingdom, then isn't it remarkable that you would hide the 5-Meo-DMT experience inside the poison of the Sonoran Desert toad?

I think that we are the godhead at the highest part of the pyramid, but we are down here in the third dimension, learning about death literacy in meatspace, getting dirty with the full range of possible emotions.

I think it is likely that the price of admission to be in this human experience is amnesia. Bernardo Kastrup talks about these dissociative alters, that we had to disassociate from the godhead in order to have our individual perception, and I think there is absolutely something in that. There is this intentional disassociation required in order to have any kind of experience. We are only here precisely because of this dissociative amnesia. So yes, I think that there is a god, but I think you are also that god.

I am also fascinated by Nietzsche's theory of eternal recurrence or *amor fati*, which translates as "love your fate." This means that we live, not multiple lives, or reincarnate into other lives, but *we live the same life for eternity*. Even if it is not the case, what a fascinating thought experiment; this means each day is fundamentally eternity, therefore make sure you're doing something you love every single day, that you would want to live it every day.

When you look around at what's happening in the world these days, do you think the human species will survive the next hundred years or do you think that we're doomed to extinction?

CARL: I think that most of humanity in its current form will die. If you read Christopher Bache's book *LSD and the Mind of the Universe: Diamonds from Heaven*, he did a high-dose LSD experiment that lasted twenty-three years. He did around three trips a year and had seventy-three trips in total but it had this quality of a continuous trip over this timeframe. On these high doses, he experienced his own birth and rebirth for the first few years, then he experienced the death and rebirth of humanity as a whole. Then he reached the sea of despair. Then he went through the archetypes, and then went beyond that to experience the birth of the superhuman about five hundred years from now. He said these superhumans were just incredible, like they were beyond anything we can imagine now.

My hunch is there will be a core group that will survive the upcoming nuclear winter that it seems that we are all heading into. This is what I call hyperhumanity. I don't think that we're going to give up the body, as Andrew Gallimore is talking about in his post-biological vision. I think that we need to go the other way and become much more embodied. We need to become much more aware of all the species that we are destroying and learn from those different umwelts before it's too late.

Gallimore's vision of us living permanently inside hyperspace is of transhumanist origin. The idea that we can just be kept in some sort of stasis without any negative effect on our bodies and minds is fundamentally problematic. I think that we're here to have a human experience. It is our birthright to combine spirit and matter in this form of double consciousness, where we get to travel between these parallel dimensions; but in my opinion, it is vital that we remain grounded in our human experience. I suspect when you are held permanently within the DMTx space, then you may not be so able to travel between the dimensions at will.

I don't have an issue with the extended state as such, as I think there is plenty of scope and research to be done, but I think maybe it's the wrong entheogen. I think maybe 5-Meo-DMTx may be more beneficial—in terms of improving our health and the human condition—and maybe it's even useful for long Covid patients suffering from brain fog because we know that 5-Meo-DMT creates neuroplasticity and neurogenesis, so I think it's potentially a much more powerful tool to extend. I've spoken to Gallimore about this and we both think that it is feasible.

I didn't think that Andrew Gallimore's proposal was so much about losing the body as it was about being able to enter a space where we can make contact with intelligent entities, to establish some kind of communication system. Do you think that this is a viable possibility, that this can actually be developed into a technology that would allow us to establish a communication channel with these other intelligent entities?

CARL: Andrew's work is fascinating and groundbreaking, and I agree if we can stabilize the space, then we could have a good chance of mapping the DMT realm, but his work has already moved on quite a lot. During his recent lecture at the Tyringham Initiative he talked about "casting off our material body in order to enter the post-biological age." He believes the vast majority of intelligent life in the cosmos is already post-biological so this may be a necessary step if we want to make real contact.

He also went beyond the need for using DMT at all and said if we want to elicit a psychedelic state without using molecules, we can use magnetoreceptors. The science of magnetogenetics is the targeted magnetic control of the nervous system, using magnets to turn on and off receptors. Needless to say, he scared off a lot of shamans in the room!

Well, Carl, those are the questions that I had for you today. Is there anything that we haven't discussed that you would like to add?

CARL: I'll quote Huxley here. Later in his life Huxley countered a lot of what he wrote in *The Doors of Perception*, mentioning the dangers of escaping into a nirvana apart from the world. I did a TEDX Oxford talk around the theme of *Brave New World* and the idea that we need holidays from the self by dialing down the default mode network. That network is your friend a lot of the time because it forces you to be productive and grounded. But sometimes, once a month, maybe you just need to turn the volume down on that inner critic, and have this holiday from the self, and I think that DMT can also provide that break, but we also need to be very aware of the dangers of living there and crying wolf.

I personally limit the amount of DMT experiences I have but attempt to get as much out of them as I can by programming the trips in order to bring as much back as possible. It's those sorts of techniques that I'm really interested in. As we already discussed, I think you only need to do 5-Meo-DMT once because it then opens you up and you can use your own abilities to try and reach that peak again. Ultimately you use the medicine to give you awareness of that specific state space, the phenomenology of that variety of consciousness, and then you use these hyperhumanism programming techniques to bring you back without necessarily needing the medicines again.

I firmly advocate that we need to work toward achieving altered traits that lead to lasting change. Where the mechanism is to have an experience that may show you a new world or a new reality, but then you really integrate that, you bring it back and root it in this reality. You use the virtual to create the actual. This means you really work with it and you do not just chase the next peak experience. You build something from it. You change your reality.

I wouldn't want to endanger my ability to transcend from this human plane because I've spent my human life connected to a DMTx machine. It is certainly a technology that may help us to create a reliable connection with the Other but I think there may be other ways that need exploring, and there are also other substances, other entheogens that could be extended that may be more suitable than DMT; after all there are many ways up the mountain but the view is the same at the top.

About the Author

Photo by Rebecca Ann Hill

DAVID JAY BROWN is the author of *Dreaming Wide Awake: Lucid Dreaming, Shamanic Healing, and Psychedelics* and *The New Science of Psychedelics: At the Nexus of Culture, Consciousness, and Spirituality.* He is also the coauthor of *Women of Visionary Art* and five other bestselling volumes of interviews with leading-edge thinkers: *Mavericks of the Mind, Voices from the Edge, Conversations on the Edge of the Apocalypse, Mavericks of Medicine,* and *Frontiers of Psychedelic Consciousness.* Additionally, Brown is the author of two science fiction novels,

Brainchild and *Virus*, and he is the coauthor of the health science book *Detox with Oral Chelation*.

Brown holds a master's degree in psychobiology from New York University and was responsible for the California-based research in two of British biologist Rupert Sheldrake's books on unexplained phenomena in science: *Dogs That Know When Their Owners Are Coming Home* and *The Sense of Being Stared At*. His work has appeared in numerous magazines including *Wired*, *Discover*, and *Scientific American*, and he was the senior editor of the thematic special edition *MAPS Bulletins* from 2007 to 2012. In 2011, 2012, and 2013 Brown was voted Best Writer in the annual *Good Times* and *Santa Cruz Weekly*'s "Best of Santa Cruz" polls, and his news stories have been picked up by *HuffPost* and *CBS News*.

His latest book, *The Illustrated Field Guide to DMT Entities*, will be published in 2024 by Inner Traditions. To find out more about his work, see the DavidJayBrown website.

BOOKS OF RELATED INTEREST

Dreaming Wide Awake
Lucid Dreaming, Shamanic Healing, and Psychedelics
by David Jay Brown

Maps of Consciousness
The Classic Text on Exploring the Mind and Expanding Awareness
by Ralph Metzner, Ph.D.
Foreword by David E. Presti

How Psychedelics Can Help Save the World
Visionary and Indigenous Voices Speak Out
Edited by Stephen Gray
Foreword by Julie Holland, M.D.

Morphic Resonance
The Nature of Formative Causation
by Rupert Sheldrake

Cannabis and Spirituality
An Explorer's Guide to an Ancient Plant Spirit Ally
Edited by Stephen Gray
Foreword by Julie Holland, M.D.

The Psychedelic Explorer's Guide
Safe, Therapeutic, and Sacred Journeys
by James Fadiman, Ph.D.

Psychedelic Medicine
The Healing Powers of LSD, MDMA, Psilocybin, and Ayahuasca
by Dr. Richard Louis Miller

DMT: The Spirit Molecule
A Doctor's Revolutionary Research into the Biology of
Near-Death and Mystical Experiences
by Rick Strassman, M.D.

INNER TRADITIONS • BEAR & COMPANY
P.O. Box 388 • Rochester, VT 05767
1-800-246-8648 • www.InnerTraditions.com

Or contact your local bookseller